SAMS Teach Yourself

UML

Joseph Schmuller

THIRD EDITION

SAMS   800 East 96th Street, Indianapolis, Indiana, 46240 USA

Sams Teach Yourself UML in 24 Hours, Third Edition

Copyright © 2004 by Sams Publishing

All rights reserved. No part of this book shall be reproduced, stored in a retrieval system, or transmitted by any means, electronic, mechanical, photocopying, recording, or otherwise, without written permission from the publisher. No patent liability is assumed with respect to the use of the information contained herein. Although every precaution has been taken in the preparation of this book, the publisher and author assume no responsibility for errors or omissions. Nor is any liability assumed for damages resulting from the use of the information contained herein.

International Standard Book Number: 0-672-32640-X

Library of Congress Catalog Card Number: 2003098381

Printed in the United States of America

First Printing: March 2004

07   06   05   04   4   3   2   1

Trademarks

Warning and Disclaimer

Bulk Sales

Sams Publishing offers excellent discounts on this book when ordered in quantity for bulk purchases or special sales. For more information, please contact

U.S. Corporate and Government Sales

1-800-382-3419

corpsales@pearsontechgroup.com

For sales outside of the U.S., please contact

International Sales

1-317-428-3341

international@pearsontechgroup.com

Associate Publisher
Michael Stephens

Acquisitions Editor
Todd Green

Development Editor
Songlin Qiu

Managing Editor
Charlotte Clapp

Senior Project Editor
Matthew Purcell

Copy Editor
Publication Services, Inc.

Indexer
Publication Services, Inc.

Proofreader
Publication Services, Inc.

Technical Editor
Jeffrey Pajor

Publishing Coordinator
Cindy Teeters

Multimedia Developer
Dan Scherf

Interior Designer
Gary Adair

Cover Designer
Alan Clements

Page Layout
Publication Services, Inc.

Graphics
Laura Robbins

Contents at a Glance

Introduction 1

Part I Getting Started

HOUR 1 Introducing the UML 7
2 Understanding Object-Orientation 31
3 Working with Object-Orientation 47
4 Working with Relationships 61
5 Understanding Aggregations, Composites, Interfaces, and
Realizations 79
6 Introducing Use Cases 91
7 Working with Use Case Diagrams 103
8 Working with State Diagrams 123
9 Working with Sequence Diagrams 135
10 Working with Communication Diagrams 157
11 Working with Activity Diagrams 173
12 Working with Component Diagrams 197
13 Working with Deployment Diagrams 213
14 Understanding Packages and Foundations 225
15 Fitting the UML into a Development Process 249

Part II A Case Study

HOUR 16 Introducing the Case Study 267
17 Performing a Domain Analysis 285
18 Gathering System Requirements 307
19 Developing the Use Cases 325
20 Getting into Interactions 339
21 Designing Look, Feel, and Deployment 351
22 Understanding Design Patterns 367

Part III Looking Ahead

HOUR 23 Modeling Embedded Systems 383

24 Shaping the Future of the UML 403

Part IV Appendices

A Quiz Answers 421

B Working with a UML Modeling Tool 435

C A Summary in Pictures 457

Index 467

Table of Contents

Introduction   1

    What's New in This Edition 1

    Who Should Read This Book? 2

    Organization of This Book 2

    Conventions Used Throughout This Book 3

Part I Getting Started   **5**

HOUR 1: Introducing the UML   7

    Adding a Method to the Madness 8

    How the UML Came to Be 9

    Components of the UML 10

        Class Diagram 11

        Object Diagram 12

        Use Case Diagram 13

        State Diagram 13

        Sequence Diagram 14

        Activity Diagram 16

        Communication Diagram 16

        Component Diagram 18

        Deployment Diagram 19

    Some Other Features 20

        Notes 20

        Keywords and Stereotypes 20

    New Diagrams in UML 2.0 22

        Composite Structure Diagram 22

        Interaction Overview Diagram 23

        Timing Diagram 24

        Something Old, Something New—The Package Diagram ... 25

Why So Many Diagrams? 26
But Isn't It Just a Bunch of Pictures? 26
Summary 27
Q&A 28
Workshop 29
    Quiz 29
    Exercises 29

HOUR 2: Understanding Object-Orientation   **31**
Objects, Objects Everywhere 32
Some Object-Oriented Concepts 34
    Abstraction 34
    Inheritance 35
    Polymorphism 36
    Encapsulation 37
    Message Sending 38
    Associations 40
    Aggregation 41
The Payoff 42
Summary 43
Q&A 45
Workshop 45
    Quiz 45

HOUR 3: Working with Object-Orientation   **47**
Visualizing a Class 47
Attributes 48
Operations 50
Attributes, Operations, and Visualization 51
Responsibilities and Constraints 52
Attached Notes 54
Classes—What They Do and How to Find Them 54
Summary 57

Q&A 58

Workshop 58

    Quiz 58

    Exercises 59

HOUR 4: Working with Relationships   **61**

Associations 61

    Constraints on Associations 63

    Association Classes 63

    Links 64

Multiplicity 64

Qualified Associations 65

Reflexive Associations 67

Inheritance and Generalization 67

    Discovering Inheritance 69

    Abstract Classes 70

Dependencies 70

Class Diagrams and Object Diagrams 71

Summary 73

Q&A 75

Workshop 75

    Quiz 76

    Exercises 76

HOUR 5: Understanding Aggregations, Composites, Interfaces, and Realizations   **79**

Aggregations 79

    Constraints on Aggregations 80

Composites 81

Composite Structure Diagram 81

Interfaces and Realizations 82

Interfaces and Ports 86

    Visibility 87

    Scope 87

Summary 88

Q&A 89

Workshop 89

　　Quiz 89

　　Exercises 89

HOUR 6: Introducing Use Cases   91

Use Cases: What They Are 91

Use Cases: Why They're Important 92

An Example: The Soda Machine 92

　　The "Buy Soda" Use Case 93

　　Additional Use Cases 94

Including a Use Case 96

Extending a Use Case 97

Starting a Use Case Analysis 98

Summary 98

Q&A 100

Workshop 100

　　Quiz 100

　　Exercises 101

HOUR 7: Working with Use Case Diagrams   103

Representing a Use Case Model 103

　　The Soda Machine Revisited 104

　　Tracking the Steps in the Scenarios 105

Visualizing Relationships Among Use Cases 106

　　Inclusion 106

　　Extension 107

　　Generalization 109

　　Grouping 110

Use Case Diagrams in the Analysis Process 110

Applying Use Case Models: An Example 111

　　Understanding the Domain 111

Understanding the Users 111

Understanding the Use Cases 113

Drilling Down 113

Taking Stock of Where We Are 115

Structural Elements 116

Relationships 116

Grouping 117

Annotation 117

Extension 117

. . . And More 117

The Big Picture 117

Summary 117

Q&A 120

Workshop 120

Quiz 120

Exercises 121

HOUR 8: Working with State Diagrams   **123**

What Is a State Diagram? 123

The Fundamental Symbol Set 124

Adding Details to the State Icon 124

Adding Details to the Transitions: Events and Actions 125

Adding Details to the Transitions: Guard Conditions 127

Substates 127

Sequential Substates 128

Concurrent Substates 128

History States 129

New in UML 2.0 130

Why Are State Diagrams Important? 131

Building the Big Picture 131

Summary 131

Q&A 133

Workshop 133

    Quiz 133

    Exercises 134

HOUR 9: Working with Sequence Diagrams   **135**

What Is a Sequence Diagram? 135

    Objects 136

    Messages 136

    Time 137

Cars and Car Keys 138

    A Class Diagram 138

    A Sequence Diagram 139

The Soda Machine 141

Sequence Diagrams: The Generic Sequence Diagram 144

Creating an Object in the Sequence 146

Framing a Sequence: Sequence Diagramming in UML 2.0 149

    Interaction Occurrences 149

    Combined Interaction Fragments 151

Building the Big Picture 153

Summary 153

Q&A 155

Workshop 155

    Quiz 155

    Exercises 156

HOUR 10: Working with Communication Diagrams   **157**

What Is a Communication Diagram? 158

Cars and Car Keys 159

    Changing States and Nesting Messages 160

The Soda Machine 162

Creating an Object 163

One More Point About Numbering 164

A Few More Concepts 164

    Multiple Receiving Objects in a Class 165

    Representing Returned Results 165

    Active Objects 166

    Synchronization 166

Building the Big Picture 168

Summary 168

Q&A 170

Workshop 170

    Quiz 170

    Exercises 171

HOUR 11: Working with Activity Diagrams   **173**

The Basics: What Is an Activity Diagram? 174

    Decisions, Decisions, Decisions 174

    Concurrent Paths 175

    Signals 175

Applying Activity Diagrams 177

    A Process: Creating a Document 177

Swimlanes 177

Hybrid Diagrams 180

New Concepts from UML 2.0 181

    The Objects of an Activity 181

    Taking Exception 183

    Deconstructing an Activity 184

    Marking Time and Finishing a Flow 186

    Special Effects 187

An Overview of an Interaction 188

Building the Big Picture 191

Summary 191

Q&A 193

Workshop 194
    Quiz 194
    Exercises 194

HOUR 12: Working with Component Diagrams   **197**
What Is (and What Isn't) a Component? 197
Components and Interfaces 198
    Reviewing Interfaces 198
    Replacement and Reuse 199
What Is a Component Diagram? 200
    Representing a Component in UML 1.x and UML 2.0 200
    Representing Interfaces 201
    Boxes—Black and White 202
Applying Component Diagrams 203
Component Diagrams in the Big Picture 209
Summary 209
Q&A 211
Workshop 211
    Quiz 211
    Exercises 211

HOUR 13: Working with Deployment Diagrams   **213**
What Is a Deployment Diagram? 213
Applying Deployment Diagrams 216
    A Home System 216
    A Token-Ring Network 216
    ARCnet 218
    Thin Ethernet 218
    The Ricochet Wireless Network 219
Deployment Diagrams in the Big Picture 221
Summary 221
Q&A 223

Workshop 223

    Quiz 223

    Exercises 223

HOUR 14: Understanding Packages and Foundations   **225**

Package Diagrams 226

    The Purpose of a Package 226

    Interpackage Relationships 226

    Merging Packages 228

A Hierarchy 230

    An Analogy 231

    Moving On 232

To Boldly Go 232

Packaging the Infrastructure of UML 234

    The Core 235

    Profiles 237

And Now At Last . . . the UML! 239

    The Four Layers Again 240

    Packaging the Superstructure of the UML 241

Extending the UML 243

    Stereotypes 243

    Graphic Stereotypes 244

    Constraints 245

    Tagged Values 245

Summary 246

Q&A 247

Workshop 248

    Quiz 248

    Exercise 248

HOUR 15: Fitting the UML into a Development Process   **249**

Methodologies: Old and New 250

    The Old Way 250

    A New Way 251

What a Development Process Must Do 251

GRAPPLE 253

RAD3: The Structure of GRAPPLE 254

    Requirements Gathering 255

    Analysis 257

    Design 259

    Development 260

    Deployment 261

The GRAPPLE Wrap-up 261

Summary 262

Q&A 263

Workshop 263

    Quiz 263

Part II A Case Study   **265**

HOUR 16: Introducing the Case Study   **267**

Getting Down to Business 267

GRAPPLEing with the Problem 268

Discovering Business Processes 268

    Serving a Customer 269

    Preparing the Meal 278

    Cleaning the Table 279

Lessons Learned 281

Summary 282

Q&A 283

Workshop 283

    Quiz 284

    Exercises 284

HOUR 17: Performing a Domain Analysis   285

Analyzing the Business Process Interview   286

Developing the Initial Class Diagram   287

Grouping the Classes   289

Forming Associations   290

    Associations with Customer   291

    Associations with Server   294

    Associations with Chef   295

    Associations with Busser   295

    Associations with Manager   296

    A Digression   297

Forming Aggregates and Composites   298

Filling Out the Classes   300

    Customer   300

    Employee   301

    Check   302

General Issues About Models   303

    Model Dictionary   303

    Diagram Organization   303

Lessons Learned   303

Summary   304

Q&A   305

Workshop   305

    Quiz   305

    Exercises   305

HOUR 18: Gathering System Requirements   307

Developing the Vision   308

Setting Up for Requirements Gathering   316

The Requirements JAD Session   317

The Outcome   320

Now What?   323

Summary 323

Q&A 324

Workshop 324

    Quiz 324

    Exercise 324

HOUR 19: Developing the Use Cases   **325**

The Care and Feeding of Use Cases 325

The Use Case Analysis 326

The Server Package 327

    Take an Order 328

    Transmit the Order to the Kitchen 329

    Change an Order 330

    Track Order Status 330

    Notify Chef About Party Status 331

    Total Up a Check 333

    Print a Check 333

    Summon an Assistant 334

    Remaining Use Cases 336

Components of the System 336

Summary 337

Q&A 338

Workshop 338

    Quiz 338

    Exercises 338

HOUR 20: Getting into Interactions   **339**

The Working Parts of the System 339

    The Server Package 339

    The Chef Package 340

    The Busser Package 341

    The Assistant Server Package 341

    The Assistant Chef Package 341

The Bartender Package 341

The Coat-Check Clerk Package 342

Interactions in the System 342

Take an Order 343

Change an Order 344

Track Order Status 346

Implications 347

Summary 348

Q&A 349

Workshop 350

Quiz 350

Exercises 350

HOUR 21: Designing Look, Feel, and Deployment   **351**

Some General Principles of GUI Design 351

The GUI JAD Session 353

From Use Cases to User Interfaces 354

UML Diagrams for GUI Design 357

Mapping Out System Deployment 358

The Network 358

The Nodes and the Deployment Diagram 359

Next Steps 359

And Now a Word from Our Sponsor 361

Empowering a Sales Force 361

Expanding in the Restaurant World 362

Summary 363

Q&A 365

Workshop 366

Quiz 366

Exercises 366

HOUR 22: Understanding Design Patterns   367

Parameterization 367

Design Patterns 370

Chain of Responsibility 371

    Chain of Responsibility: Restaurant Domain 372

    Chain of Responsibility: Web Browser Event Models 373

Your Own Design Patterns 374

The Advantages of Design Patterns 377

Summary 377

Q&A 379

Workshop 379

    Quiz 379

    Exercise 379

Part III Looking Ahead   **381**

HOUR 23: Modeling Embedded Systems   383

Back to the Restaurant 383

The Mother of Invention 384

Fleshing Out the GetAGrip 385

What Is an Embedded System? 387

Embedded Systems Concepts 388

    Time 388

    Threads 388

    Interrupts 389

    Operating System 390

Modeling the GetAGrip 393

    Classes 393

    Use Cases 394

    Interactions 395

    General State Changes 398

    Deployment 398

Flexing Their Muscles 399

Summary 400

Q&A 401

Workshop 401

   Quiz 401

   Exercises 401

HOUR 24: Shaping the Future of the UML   **403**

Extensions for Business 403

Lessons from the Business Extensions 405

Graphic User Interfaces 405

   Connecting to Use Cases 405

   Modeling the GUI 406

Expert Systems 408

   Components of an Expert System 408

   An Example 410

   Modeling the Knowledge Base 411

Web Applications 414

That's All, Folks 416

Summary 417

Q&A 418

Workshop 418

   Quiz 418

   Exercises 418

Part IV Appendixes   **419**

APPENDIX A Quiz Answers   **421**

Hour 1 421

Hour 2 421

Hour 3 422

Hour 4 422

Hour 5 423

Hour 6 424

Hour 7 424

Hour 8 425

Hour 9 425

Hour 10 426

Hour 11 426

Hour 12 427

Hour 13 428

Hour 14 428

Hour 15 428

Hour 16 429

Hour 17 430

Hour 18 430

Hour 19 430

Hour 20 431

Hour 21 431

Hour 22 432

Hour 23 432

Hour 24 433

APPENDIX B **Working with a UML Modeling Tool** **435**

What You Should Find in a Modeling Tool 435

Working with UML in Visio Professional Edition 436

    Getting Started 438

    The Class Diagram 438

    The Object Diagram 448

    The Sequence Diagram 451

A Few Words About a Few Tools 456

    Rational Rose 456

    Select Component Architect 456

    Visual UML 456

APPENDIX C A Summary in Pictures   457

    Activity Diagram 457

    Class Diagram 459

    Communication Diagram 460

    Component Diagram 461

    Composite Structure Diagram 461

    Deployment Diagram 462

    Object Diagram 462

    Package Diagram 463

    Parameterized Collaboration 463

    Sequence Diagram 464

    State Diagram 465

    Timing Diagram 465

    Use Case Diagram 466

Index   467

About the Author

Joseph Schmuller, a veteran of over 20 years in Information Technology, is a Technical Architect with Blue Cross–Blue Shield of Florida. From 1991 through 1997, he was Editor in Chief of *PC AI Magazine*. He has written numerous articles and reviews on advanced computing technology and is the author of *ActiveX No experience required* and *Dynamic HTML Master the Essentials*. Holder of a Ph.D. from the University of Wisconsin, he is an Adjunct Professor at the University of North Florida.

Dedication

To my wonderful mother, Sara Riba Schmuller,

Who taught me how to teach myself.

Acknowledgments

Writing a book is an arduous process, and creating a new edition is no day at the beach, either. Happily, the world-class team at Sams Publishing has made it a lot easier on every occasion. It's a pleasure once again to acknowledge their contributions.

For the first edition, Acquisitions Editor Chris Webb and Development Editor Matt Purcell helped turn my thoughts into readable prose. Technical Editors Bill Rowe and Michael Tobler made sure the content was technically sound. Senior Editor Susan Moore and the outstanding artists and Production Staff turned the manuscript and its numerous diagrams into production quality.

For the second edition, Associate Publisher Michael Stephens, Development Editor Christy Franklin, Production Editor Matt Wynalda, and Technical Editor Paul Gustavson did an exemplary job from start to finish.

In this edition, Acquisitions Editor Todd Green catalyzed the process. Todd and Development Editor Songlin Qiu kept everything running smoothly. They also showed the patience of saints, for which I'm most grateful. Project Editor Matt Purcell (back for a return engagement in a new role) did an outstanding job on the comprehensibility of the material, and Project Manager Jan Fisher was indispensable in keeping the book on track. Technical Editor Jeffrey Pajor supplied expertise that significantly tightened up the content.

As always, my sincerest thanks to my agent, David Fugate of Waterside Productions.

During the writing of all the editions of this book, my professional colleagues have provided empathy and cooperation. In particular, conversations with Keith Barrett and Rob Warner helped clarify my thinking on a number of issues. Sadly, the time of my involvement with the first edition marked the untimely passing of Tom Williamson, the director of the division in which Keith, Rob, and I worked. Tom was an advisor, mentor, colleague, and friend.

I thank my dearest friends, the Spragues of Madison, Wisconsin, for their continuing support and friendship. I thank my mother and my brother David for their love and for always being there for me, and Kathryn (LOML and GOMD) for always being everything to me.

We Want to Hear from You

As the reader of this book, *you* are our most important critic and commentator. We value your opinion and want to know what we're doing right, what we could do better, what areas you'd like to see us publish in, and any other words of wisdom you're willing to pass our way.

As an associate publisher for Sams Publishing, I welcome your comments. You can e-mail or write me directly to let me know what you did or didn't like about this book—as well as what we can do to make our books better.

Please note that I cannot help you with technical problems related to the topic of this book. We do have a User Services group, however, where I will forward specific technical questions related to the book.

When you write, please be sure to include this book's title and author as well as your name, e-mail address, and phone number. I will carefully review your comments and share them with the author and editors who worked on the book.

E-mail: feedback@samspublishing.com

Mail: Michael Stephens
          Associate Publisher
          Sams Publishing
          800 East 96th Street
          Indianapolis, IN 46240 USA

For more information about this book or another Sams Publishing title, visit our Web site at www.samspublishing.com. Type the ISBN (excluding hyphens) or the title of a book in the Search field to find the page you're looking for.

Introduction

It's all about vision. A complex system comes into being when someone has a vision of how technology can make things better. Developers have to fully understand the vision and keep it firmly in mind as they create the system that realizes the vision.

System development projects are successful to the extent they bridge the gap between visionary and developer. The Unified Modeling Language (UML) is a tool for building the bridge. It helps you capture the vision for a system and then enables you to communicate the vision to anyone who has a stake in the system. It does this via a set of symbols and diagrams. Each diagram plays a different role within the development process.

The goal of this book—for all three editions—is to give you a firm foundation in the UML in 24 hours of study. Each hour presents examples to strengthen your understanding, and most of the hours provide exercises that enable you to put your new-found knowledge to use.

What's New in This Edition

In preparing this edition, I went through the first two and tightened up the prose, adding and updating material where necessary. Some of the additions were necessary because of UML 2.0, the newly adopted version. Others were necessitated by the passage of time and the advancement of technology.

As in the first two editions, Hour 14, "Understanding Packages and Foundations," presents theoretical concepts at the foundation of the UML. In this edition, I've expanded this hour considerably in order to accommodate new concepts from UML 2.0.

I've refined some of the thinking behind the models and diagrams and added quiz questions and exercises. As part of the refinement, in this edition I precede every interaction diagram with a class diagram that shows the operations of the classes. The goal is to clarify the messages that appear in the interaction diagrams and make them more intuitive. If you know a little about the UML, you'll understand what I just said. If not . . . well, then . . . you won't. By the end of the book, however, I'm certain you will.

Who Should Read This Book?

This book is aimed at system analysts, managers, designers, and developers who have to quickly master the fundamentals of the UML. If you have to start working with the UML immediately, or if you have to know the UML enough to understand the work of others who use it, this book is for you.

Organization of This Book

The book is in three parts. Part I, "Getting Started," gives an overview of the UML and then moves into object-orientation, which forms the foundation concepts for diagramming objects and classes. I examine the *use case*—a construct for showing how a system looks to a user—and then show how to diagram use cases. I spend extra time on the concepts behind object-orientation and use cases, because these two ideas form the basis for the parts of the UML you're most likely to use most of the time. The remaining hours in Part I get you working with the rest of the UML diagrams.

Part II, "A Case Study," presents a simplified methodology for development along with a fictional case study. Thus, the hours in Part II show how the UML fits into the context of a development project. You'll see how the elements of the UML work together in a model of a system.

Part III, "Looking Ahead," shows the application of the UML to design patterns and embedded systems and then examines its application in a couple of other areas.

Numerous vendors provide software packages that enable you to create UML diagrams and coordinate them into a model. In Appendix B, "Working with a UML Modeling Tool," I give you an idea of what it's like to work with one as I walk you through the creation of three UML diagrams in Microsoft Visio Professional Edition. I also briefly address three other modeling tools.

For Parts I–III, however, all you'll need are pencil and paper to draw the diagrams, and a healthy curiosity about how to use models as a foundation for system design.

Conventions Used Throughout This Book

As you read through this book, you'll see that

▶ Each hour begins with a "What You'll Learn in This Hour" list.

▶ New Terms appear in a special font. Here's an example:

Extending downward from each object is a dashed line called the object's **lifeline**.

▶ Throughout the book, a special sidebar element presents useful information that's somewhat off the main flow:

Objects by the Hour

Hour 2, "Understanding Object-Orientation," Hour 3, "Working with Object-Orientation," and Hour 4, "Working with Relationships," deal with object-oriented concepts. These concepts play major roles throughout the book.

By the Way

Let's start modeling!

PART I

Getting Started

HOUR 1 Introducing the UML   **7**

HOUR 2 Understanding Object-Orientation   **31**

HOUR 3 Working with Object-Orientation   **47**

HOUR 4 Working with Relationships   **61**

HOUR 5 Understanding Aggregations, Composites Interfaces, and Realizations   **79**

HOUR 6 Introducing Use Cases   **91**

HOUR 7 Working with Use Case Diagrams   **103**

HOUR 8 Working wih State Diagrams   **123**

HOUR 9 Working with Sequence Diagrams   **135**

HOUR 10 Working with Communication Diagrams   **157**

HOUR 11 Working with Activity Diagrams   **173**

HOUR 12 Working with Component Diagrams   **197**

HOUR 13 Working with Deployment Diagrams   **213**

HOUR 14 Understanding Packages and Foundations   **225**

HOUR 15 Fitting the UML into a Development Process   **249**

HOUR 1

Introducing the UML

What You'll Learn in This Hour:

▶ Why the UML is necessary
▶ How the UML came to be
▶ How to represent UML components in diagrams
▶ Why it's important to use a number of different types of diagrams

The Unified Modeling Language (UML) is one of the most exciting and useful tools in the world of system development. Why? The UML is a visual modeling language that enables system builders to create blueprints that capture their visions in a standard, easy-to-understand way, and provides a mechanism to effectively share and communicate these visions with others.

Communicating the vision is of utmost importance. Before the advent of the UML, system development was often a hit-or-miss proposition. System analysts would try to assess the needs of their clients, generate a requirements analysis in some notation that the analyst understood (but not always the client), give that analysis to a programmer or team of programmers, and hope that the final product was the system the client wanted.

> **By the Way**
>
> **Some Terms**
>
> Throughout this book, consider a **system** to be a combination of software and hardware that provides a solution for a business problem. **System development** is the creation of a system for a **client**, the person who has the problem to be solved. An **analyst** documents the client's problem and relays it to **developers**, programmers who build the software that solves the problem and deploy the software on computer hardware.

Because system development involves communication among people, the potential for error lurked at every stage of the process. The analyst might have misunderstood the client. The analyst might have produced a document the client couldn't comprehend. To add to the mess, analysts often created wordy, voluminous requirements documents that were difficult for others on the project team to work with. Paradoxically, the sheer weight of these documents often allowed important requirements (and dependencies among requirements) to slip through the cracks. Thus the results of the analysis might not have been clear to the programmers, who subsequently might have created a program that was difficult to use and didn't solve the client's original problem.

Is it any wonder that many of the long-standing systems in use today are clunky, cumbersome, and hard to use?

Adding a Method to the Madness

In the early days of computing, few programmers relied on in-depth analyses of the problem at hand. If they did any analysis at all, it was typically on the back of a napkin. They often wrote programs from the ground up, creating code as they went along. Although this added an aura of romance and daring to the process, it has proved to be inappropriate in today's high-stakes business world.

Today a well-thought-out plan is crucial. A client has to understand what a development team is going to do, and must be able to indicate changes if the team hasn't fully grasped the client's needs (or if the client changes his or her mind along the way). Also, development is typically a team-oriented effort, so each member of the team has to know where his or her work fits into the big picture (and what that big picture is).

As the world becomes more complex, the computer-based systems that inhabit the world also must increase in complexity. They often involve multiple pieces of hardware and software, networked across great distances, linked to databases that contain mountains of information. If you want to create successful systems, how do you get your hands around the complexity?

The key is to organize the design process in a way that analysts, clients, programmers, and others involved in system development can understand and agree on. The UML provides the organization.

Just as you wouldn't build a complex structure like an office building without first creating a detailed blueprint, you wouldn't build a complex system to inhabit that office building without first creating a detailed design plan. The plan should be one that you could show a client just as surely as an architect shows a blueprint to the person who's paying for a building. That design plan should result from a careful analysis of the client's needs.

Short time frames for development are another feature of the contemporary system development landscape. When the deadlines fall on top of one another, a solid design is an absolute necessity.

Still another aspect of modern life necessitates solid design: corporate takeovers. When one company acquires another, the new organization might change important aspects of an in-progress development project (the implementation tool, the coding language, and more). A bulletproof project blueprint will facilitate the changeover. If the design is solid, a change in implementation can proceed smoothly.

The need for solid designs has brought about a need for a design notation that analysts, developers, and clients will accept as a standard—just as the notation in schematic diagrams of circuits serves as a standard for electronics engineers and the notation in Feynman diagrams serves as a standard for physicists. The UML is that notation.

How the UML Came to Be

The UML is the brainchild of Grady Booch, James Rumbaugh, and Ivar Jacobson. Dubbed "the Three Amigos," these gentlemen worked in separate organizations through the 1980s and early 1990s, each devising his own methodology for object-oriented analysis and design. Their methodologies achieved preeminence over those of numerous competitors. By the mid-1990s, they began to borrow ideas from each other, so they decided to evolve their work together.

By the Way

Objects by the Hour

Hour 2, "Understanding Object-Orientation," Hour 3 "Working with Object-Orientation," and Hour 4, "Working with Relationships," deal with object-oriented concepts. These concepts play major roles throughout the book.

In 1994 Rumbaugh joined Rational Software Corporation, where Booch was already working. Jacobson enlisted at Rational a year later.

The rest, as they say, is history. Draft versions of the UML began to circulate throughout the software industry, and the resulting feedback brought substantial changes. Because many corporations felt the UML would serve their strategic purposes, a UML consortium sprung up. Members included DEC, Hewlett-Packard, Intellicorp, Microsoft, Oracle, Texas Instruments, Rational, and others. In 1997 the consortium produced version 1.0 of the UML and submitted it to the Object Management Group (OMG) in response to the OMG's request for a proposal for a standard modeling language.

The consortium expanded, generated version 1.1, and submitted it to the OMG, who adopted it in late 1997. The OMG took over the maintenance of the UML and produced two more revisions in 1998. The UML has become a de facto standard in the software industry, and it continues to evolve. Versions 1.3, 1.4, and 1.5 have come into being, and OMG recently put its stamp of approval on version 2.0. The earlier versions, referred to generically as version 1.x, have been the basis of most models and most UML modeling books. Throughout this book, I'll show you differences between the old and the new.

Components of the UML

The UML consists of a number of graphical elements that combine to form diagrams. Because the UML is a language, it has rules for combining these elements. Rather than tell you about these elements and rules, let's jump right into the diagrams because they're what you'll use to do system analysis.

By the
Way

> **Jumping Right In**
>
> This approach is analogous to learning a foreign language by using it, instead of by learning its grammar and conjugating its verbs. After you've spent some time using a foreign language, it's easier to understand the grammatical rules and verb conjugations anyway.

The purpose of the diagrams is to present multiple views of a system; this set of multiple views is called a **model**. A UML model of a system is something like a scale model of a building along with an artist's rendition of the building. It's important to note that a UML model describes what a system is supposed to do. It doesn't tell how to implement the system.

The subsections that follow briefly describe the most common diagrams of the UML and the concepts they represent. Later in Part I you'll examine each one much more closely. Bear in mind that hybrids of these diagrams are possible, and that the UML provides ways for you to extend its diagrams.

By the Way

Models

The concept of a model is useful throughout the scientific and engineering fields. In the most general sense, when you create a model you're using something that you know a great deal about to help you understand something you know very little about. In some fields, a model is a set of equations. In others, a model is a computer simulation. Many types of models are possible.

For our purposes, a model is a set of UML diagrams that we can examine, assess, and modify in order to understand and develop a system.

Class Diagram

Think about the things in the world around you. (A pretty broad request, admittedly, but try it anyway!) The things that surround you have attributes (properties) and they behave in certain ways. We can think of these behaviors as a set of operations.

You'll also see that things naturally fall into categories (automobiles, furniture, washing machines. . .). We refer to these categories as classes. A **class** is a category or group of things that have the same attributes and the same behaviors. Here's an example. Anything in the class of washing machines has attributes such as brand name, model, serial number, and capacity. Behaviors for things in this class include the operations "accept clothes," "accept detergent," "turn on," and "turn off."

Figure 1.1 shows an example of the UML notation that captures these attributes and behaviors of a washing machine. A rectangle is the icon that represents the class. It's divided into three areas. The uppermost area contains the name, the middle area holds the attributes, and the lowest area holds the operations.

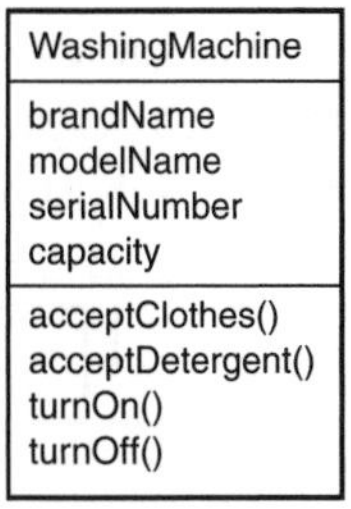

WashingMachine
brandName modelName serialNumber capacity
acceptClothes() acceptDetergent() turnOn() turnOff()

FIGURE 1.1
The UML class icon.

Notice the spacing in the names of the class, the attributes, and the operations. In UML, a multiword classname has initial capital letters for all the words and eliminates whitespace between each word (for example, WashingMachine). Attribute-names and operation-names follow the same convention, but the first letter of the first word isn't capitalized (for example, acceptClothes()). A pair of parentheses follows the name of each operation—for reasons we'll get into in Hour 3.

As you'll see in Hour 4, a class diagram consists of a number of these rectangle icons connected by lines that show how the classes relate to one another.

Why bother to think about classes of things and their attributes and behaviors? In order to interact with our complex world, most modern software simulates some aspect of the world. Decades of experience suggest that it's easiest to develop software that does this when the software represents classes of real-world things. Class diagrams provide the representations that developers work from.

Class diagrams help on the analysis side, too. They enable analysts to talk to clients in the clients' terminology and thus stimulate the clients to reveal important details about the problem they want solved.

Object Diagram

An **object** is an instance of a class—a specific thing that has specific values of the class's attributes. Your washer, for example, might have the brand name Laundatorium, the model name Washmeister, a serial number of GL57774, and a capacity of 16 pounds.

The icons in Figure 1.2 show how the UML represents an object. Note that the icon is a rectangle, just like the class icon, but the name is underlined. In the icon on the left, the name of the specific instance is on the left side of a colon, and the name of the class is on the right side of the colon. The name of the instance begins with a lowercase letter. It's also possible to have an **anonymous** object, as the icon on the right of Figure 1.2 shows. This just means that you don't supply a specific name for the object, although you do show the class it belongs to.

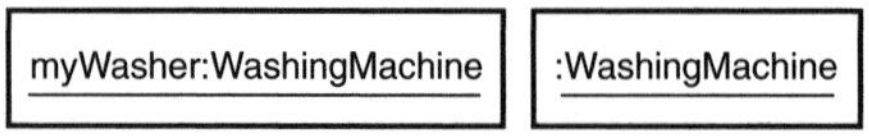

FIGURE 1.2
Two UML object icons—The icon on the left represents a named object, the icon on the right represents an anonymous object.

| myWasher:WashingMachine | :WashingMachine |

Use Case Diagram

A **use case** is a description of a system's behavior from a user's standpoint. For system developers, the use case is a valuable tool: It's a tried-and-true technique for gathering system requirements from a user's point of view. Obtaining information from the user's point of view is important if the goal is to build a system that real people (and not just computerphiles) can use.

We'll discuss use cases in greater detail in Hours 6, "Introducing Use Cases"; 7, "Working with Use Case Diagrams"; 18, "Gathering System Requirements"; and 19, "Developing the Use Cases." For now, here's a quick example. You use a washing machine, obviously, to wash your clothes. Figure 1.3 shows how you'd represent this in a UML use case diagram.

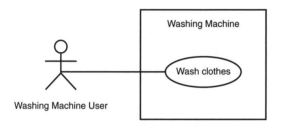

FIGURE 1.3
The UML use case diagram.

The little stick figure that corresponds to the washing machine user is called an **actor**. The ellipse represents the use case. Note that the actor—the entity that initiates the use case—can be a person or another system. Note also that the use case is inside a rectangle that represents the system, and the actor is outside the rectangle.

Pronunciation Tip

To help clarify the meaning of this concept, say the *use* in "use case" with a soft "s," as though it rhymes with *truce*. Don't say it as though it rhymes with *snooze*.

State Diagram

At any given time, an object is in a particular state. A person can be a newborn, infant, child, adolescent, teenager, or adult. An elevator is either moving or stationary. A washing machine can be either in the soaking, washing, rinsing, spinning, or off state.

The UML state diagram shown in Figure 1.4 captures this bit of reality. The figure shows that the washing machine transitions from one state to the next.

FIGURE 1.4
The UML state
diagram.

The symbol at the top of the figure represents the start state and the symbol at the bottom represents the end state.

By the
Way

Transitions
Transitions from state to state aren't always linear. Sometimes conditions dictate one path or another. We'll talk about this in Hour 8, "Working with State Diagrams."

Sequence Diagram

Class diagrams and object diagrams represent static information. In a functioning system, however, objects interact with one another, and these interactions occur over time. The UML sequence diagram shows the time-based dynamics of the interaction.

Continuing with the washing machine example, the components of the machine include a timer, a water pipe (for fresh water input), and a drum (the part that holds the clothes and the water). These, of course, are also objects. (As you'll see, an object can consist of other objects.)

What happens when you invoke the "Wash clothes" use case? Assuming you've completed the "add clothes," "add detergent," and "turn on" operations, the sequence of steps goes something like this:

1. At the beginning of "Soaking," water enters the drum via the water pipe.

2. The drum remains stationary for 5 minutes.

3. At the end of "Soaking," water stops entering the drum.

4. At the beginning of "Washing," the drum rotates back and forth and continues doing this for 15 minutes.

5. At the end of "Washing," the drum pumps out the soapy water.

6. The drum stops rotating.

7. At the beginning of "Rinsing," water entry restarts.

8. The drum rotates back and forth.

9. After 15 minutes water entry stops.

10. At the end of "Rinsing," the drum pumps out the rinse water.

11. The drum stops rotating.

12. At the beginning of "Spinning," the drum rotates clockwise and continues for 5 minutes.

13. At the end of "Spinning," the drum rotation stops.

14. The wash is done.

Imagine that the timer, the water pipe, and the drum are objects. Assume that each object has one or more operations. The objects work together by sending messages to each other. Each message is a request from the sender-object to the receiver-object. The request asks the receiver to complete one of its (the receiver's) operations.

Let's get specific about the operations. The timer can

▶ Time the soaking

▶ Time the washing

▶ Time the rinsing

▶ Time the spinning

The water pipe can

▶ Start a flow

▶ Stop a flow

The drum can

▶ Store water

▶ Rotate back and forth

▶ Rotate clockwise

▶ Stop rotating

▶ Pump water

Figure 1.5 shows how to use these operations to create a sequence diagram that captures the messages among the timer, water pipe, drum, and drain represented as anonymous objects at the top of the diagram. Each arrow represents a message that goes from one object to another. Time, in this diagram, proceeds from top to bottom. So the first message is timeSoak(), which the timer sends to itself. The second message is sendWater(), which the timer sends to the water pipe. The final message, stopRotating(), goes from the timer to the drum.

Notice that an object (in this case, the timer) can send a message to itself. Notice also that the arrowheads do not all have the same shape. You'll learn more about that in Hour 9, "Working with Sequence Diagrams."

Note: If you don't remember what an anonymous object is, go back and look at Figure 1.2.

Activity Diagram

The activities that occur within a use case or within an object's behavior typically occur in a sequence, as in the steps listed in the preceding subsection. Figure 1.6 shows how the UML activity diagram represents steps 4 through 6 of that sequence.

Transitions Again

In an earlier note I mentioned that the transitions from state to state aren't always linear, but sometimes take one path or another. It's the same for activity diagrams. You'll see that in Hour 11, "Working with Activity Diagrams."

Communication Diagram

The elements of a system work together to accomplish the system's objectives, and a modeling language must have a way of representing this. The aforementioned sequence diagram does this. The UML communication diagram shown in Figure 1.7 also does this, but in a slightly different way. Rather than show you the communication diagram that's equivalent to the sequence diagram in Figure 1.5, Figure 1.7 shows you one that captures just the first few messages among the timer, the water pipe, and the drum. Rather than represent time in the vertical dimension, this diagram shows the order of messages by attaching a number to the message label.

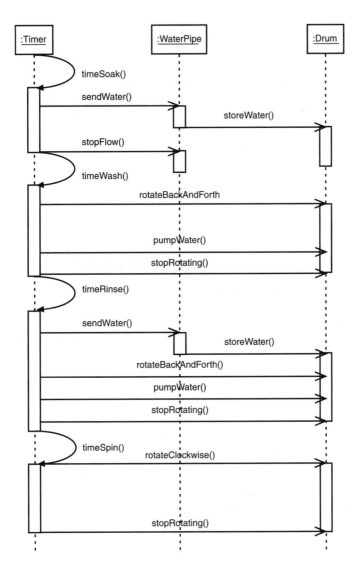

FIGURE 1.5
The UML sequence diagram.

FIGURE 1.6
The UML activity
diagram.

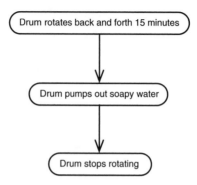

Both the sequence diagram and the communication diagram show interactions among objects. For this reason, the UML refers to them collectively as **interaction diagrams**.

FIGURE 1.7
The UML
communication
diagram.

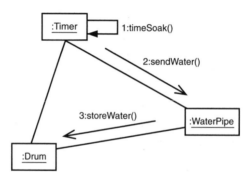

Changing Names

The name *communication diagram* is new in version 2.0. In version 1.x, this was called a *collaboration diagram*. Don't be surprised if you find the two terms used interchangeably as version 2.0 settles in.

Component Diagram

This diagram and the next one move away from the world of washing machines because the component diagram and the deployment diagram are geared expressly toward computer systems.

Modern software development proceeds via components, which is particularly important in team-based development efforts. Without elaborating too much at this point, Figure 1.8 shows how the UML version 1.x represents a software component.

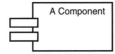

FIGURE 1.8
The software component icon in UML 1.x.

Here's where UML 2.0 makes an entrance. In response to the many modelers who felt this symbol was awkward, UML 2.0 provides a revised symbol. Figure 1.9 shows the new way to represent a software component.

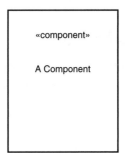

FIGURE 1.9
The software component icon in UML 2.0.

> **What's the Angle?**
>
> What are those angle brackets around the word "component" in Figure 1.9? That notation has a special status within UML. You'll read about it in the subsection entitled "Keywords and Stereotypes" a couple of pages from here.

By the Way

Deployment Diagram

The UML deployment diagram shows the physical architecture of a computer-based system. It can depict the computers, show their connections with one another, and show the software that sits on each machine. Each computer is represented as a cube, with interconnections between computers drawn as lines connecting the cubes. Figure 1.10 presents an example.

FIGURE 1.10
The UML
deployment
diagram.

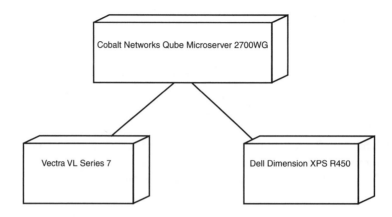

Some Other Features

Earlier I mentioned that the UML provides features that enable you to extend the diagrams. This section describes a couple of prominent ones.

Notes

It often happens that one part of a diagram doesn't present an unambiguous explanation of why it's there or how to work with it. When that's the case, the UML **note** is helpful. Think of a note as the graphic equivalent of a yellow sticky. Its icon is a rectangle with a folded corner. Inside the rectangle is explanatory text. Figure 1.11 shows an example. You attach the note to a diagram element by connecting a dashed line from the element to the note.

FIGURE 1.11
In any diagram
you can add
explanatory
comments by
attaching a note.

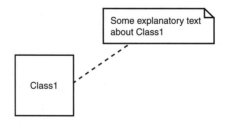

Keywords and Stereotypes

The UML provides a number of useful items, but it's not an exhaustive set. Every now and then you'll create a model that requires some new concepts and new symbols. **Stereotypes** enable you to create new UML elements by basing them on existing elements. It's sort of like buying a suit off the rack and having it altered to fit your particular measurements (as opposed to creating one out of a bolt of cloth). Think of a stereotype as just this kind of alteration. You represent it as a name enclosed in two pairs of angle brackets called **guillemets**, and then you add that name to a UML symbol. The guillemet-enclosed name is called a **keyword**.

Sometimes the UML does this for you. Rather than create an entirely new symbol for something, the UML adds a keyword to an existing element. The keyword indicates that the element is used in a somewhat different way than originally intended. The concept of an interface (which you'll read about at length in Hour 5, "Understanding Aggregations, Composites, Interfaces, and Realizations") provides a good example. An **interface** is a class that just has operations and has no attributes. It's a set of behaviors you might want to use again and again throughout your model (for reasons that become clearer in Hour 5). Instead of inventing a new element to represent an interface, UML uses a class icon with the keyword «Interface» situated just above the classname. (See Figure 1.12.)

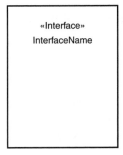

FIGURE 1.12
A stereotype is an existing UML element with the addition of a keyword in guillemets. The keyword indicates that the element is used in a some-what different way than originally intended.

The stereotype concept is particularly useful when you use a UML modeling tool. One important feature of a modeling tool is a "dictionary" that keeps track of all the elements you create in your model—classes, use cases, components, and others. ("Dictionary" is my own term. Different tools call it different names.) The dictionary can only work with existing UML elements and with stereotypes based on these elements. Thus, stereotyping allows you to create something new and store it in the dictionary. This is important because the dictionary helps you organize and manage your model and enables you to reuse the elements you create.

In Hour 14, "Understanding Packages and Foundations," I look under the hood of the UML and examine the foundations of concepts like the stereotype. For now just bear in mind that to visualize a stereotype you add a keyword to a UML icon. Also bear in mind that as you work with UML (particularly if you work with a

UML modeling tool), you'll find that UML comes with some built-in stereotypes and predefined keywords (like «component» and «Interface»).

By the Way

> **De-Evolution?**
>
> I first brought up this guillemet notation in the "Component Diagram" subsection a couple of pages ago. I mentioned that the UML 1.x software component symbol in Figure 1.8 has given way to the UML 2.0 notation in Figure 1.9. Everything I just told you about stereotypes indicates that you use a stereotype to create a symbol when you don't have one. In the case of the component icon, however, it all worked in reverse from 1.x to 2.0—a class icon with a keyword replaced an existing symbol.

New Diagrams in UML 2.0

In addition to new takes on UML 1.x diagrams (like the software component icon), UML 2.0 adds some new ideas to the mix.

Composite Structure Diagram

When you're modeling a class, you might find it useful to show something about the class's internal structure. This often happens if the class consists of component classes.

For example, let's assume that a person consists of a mind and a body. In Hour 5 you'll see the traditional way of modeling that statement. It consists of lines and symbols that join the Person class to the Mind class and to the Body class.

With UML 2.0's composite structure diagram you add a dimension. You put each component class inside the whole. This conveys the idea that you're looking inside the class into its structure. Figure 1.13 shows you what I mean.

Version 1.x allowed this kind of notation in class diagrams. Version 2.0 explicitly identifies this technique as its own kind of diagram.

FIGURE 1.13
The composite structure diagram models a class's internal structure.

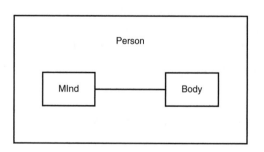

By the Way

Philosophy on the Line

As you'll see when we get deeper into object-orientation, a line that joins two classes (like Mind and Body) usually has a name. In Figure 1.13 how should we label the line that joins Mind and Body? Philosophers have been puzzling over that one for ages! They've been arguing over the name of that association, whether it even exists, whether the Mind component exists, and on and on and on. . . .

Interaction Overview Diagram

Consider once again the activity diagram (Figure 1.6). This shows you a series of steps, that is, "activities." Suppose each of those activities involves a sequence of messages among objects. If you replaced some of the activities with sequence diagrams or communication diagrams (or a combination of the two), you'd have UML 2.0's new interaction overview diagram.

Here's an example. Imagine you're at a library.

1. You find a book in the library's database.

2. You bring the book to the circulation desk to borrow the book.

3. A guard at the exit verifies that you checked out the book before you can leave the library with it.

Figure 1.14 shows a simple activity diagram that captures these three steps.

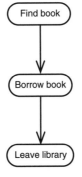

FIGURE 1.14
Three activities in visiting a library.

Now let's analyze each activity. In the first one, you ask the library database to locate the book, and the database responds by telling you to go to the book's location. In the second, you ask the librarian to check the book out to you, and after the checkout, the librarian tells you to take the book. In the third, you can leave the library only if a guard verifies that you have checked out the book.

Figure 1.15 shows how to organize all this in sequence diagrams taken in . . . well . . . sequence.

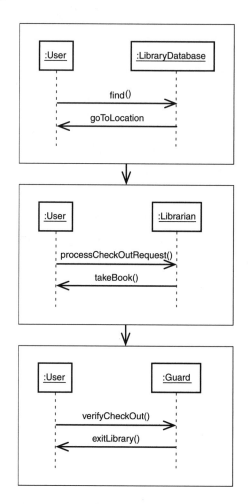

Timing Diagram

Think back to the examples involving the washing machine. I used this venerable appliance to discuss diagrams for classes, states, sequences, and communications.

In the part about sequence diagrams, I mentioned the duration of each state—5 minutes for soaking, 15 minutes for washing, 15 minutes for rinsing, and 5 minutes for spinning.

If you carefully examine the sequence diagram in Figure 1.5, you'll see that it never explicitly shows these durations. UML 2.0's timing diagram handles this. It's designed to show how long an object is in a state. Figure 1.16 shows one form of this new diagram.

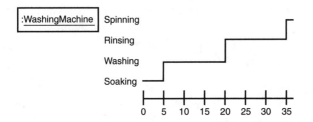

FIGURE 1.16
The UML timing diagram.

Something Old, Something New—The Package Diagram

Version 1.x includes a capability for organizing the elements of a diagram. Dubbed a **package**, its icon is a tabbed folder, as in Figure 1.17. The idea is to put elements that go together inside one of these tabbed folder icons. For example, if a number of classes or components constitute a particular subsystem, they would go into a package.

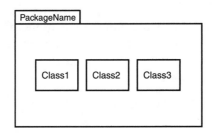

FIGURE 1.17
The UML package icon.

By specifying a package diagram, Version 2.0 gives a sort of promotion to the package. No longer considered just a way of organizing a diagram's elements, the package has attained diagram status of its own.

Why So Many Diagrams?

As you can see, the UML's diagrams make it possible to examine a system from a number of viewpoints. It's important to note that not all the diagrams must appear in every UML model. Most UML models, in fact, contain a subset of the diagrams I listed.

Why is it necessary to have numerous views of a system? Typically, a system has a number of different **stakeholders**—people who have interests in different aspects of the system. Let's return to the washing machine example. If you're designing a washing machine's motor, you have one view of the system. If you're writing the operating instructions, you have another. If you're designing the machine's overall shape, you see the system in a totally different way than if you just want to wash your clothes.

Conscientious system design involves all the possible viewpoints, and each UML diagram gives you a way of incorporating a particular view. The objective is to communicate clearly with every type of stakeholder.

But Isn't It Just a Bunch of Pictures?

Some might argue that UML modeling isn't very important. After all, isn't programming the most important part of the project? Don't developers do the "real" work while modelers just draw pictures?

To understand the importance of accurate visual modeling, consider a well-known, long-term construction project in Boston, Massachusetts. Formally known as the Central Artery/Tunnel, but more popularly known as "The Big Dig," the goal of this project is to alleviate Boston's massive traffic crush: A system of tunnels and bridges through the center of the city will ultimately eliminate an aging, undersized, elevated highway. In addition to solving the traffic problem, the Big Dig will have major economic and environmental benefits.

Those benefits better be huge, because the project has generated cost overruns in excess of a billion dollars. According to a report in the *Boston Globe*, one reason is that the drawings (that is, the visual models) that guide excavation and construction were incomplete and inaccurate.

For example, the FleetCenter (Boston's sports and entertainment facility) was missing from one drawing. That glaring omission misled contractors into thinking they had an unobstructed path for laying utility lines in a particular area of the city. Another drawing showed a manhole (intended as a connection for electrical lines) that didn't exist. Still another drawing of one of the tunnels left a 4-foot gap between tunnel sections. Workers detected this gap only after the sections were in position.

The result was a lot of costly unforeseen work to correct the mistakes, along with numerous missed deadlines.

Sound familiar?

Modeling, Learning, and Knowledge

The way I look at it, learning proceeds in three phases:

1. *You don't know what you don't know.* Perhaps a better way to say this is that you have no familiarity with a particular field.

2. *You do know what you don't know.* In other words, you get some idea of what the field is all about, and you start to see gaps in your knowledge.

3. *You fill in the gaps.*

UML (and modeling in general) is a great way to quickly get you to the second phase—realizing what you don't know and getting a start on finding out the relevant information.

By the Way

Summary

System development is a human activity. Without an easy-to-understand notation system, the development process has great potential for error.

The UML is a notation system that has become a standard in the system development world. It's the result of work done by Grady Booch, James Rumbaugh, and Ivar Jacobson. Consisting of a set of diagrams, the UML provides a standard that enables the system analyst to build a multifaceted blueprint that's comprehensible to clients, programmers, and everyone involved in the development process. It's necessary to have all these diagrams because each one speaks to a different stakeholder in the system.

A UML model tells *what* a system is supposed to do. It doesn't tell *how* the system is supposed to do it.

Q&A

Q. *I've seen the Unified Modeling Language referred to as "UML" and also as "the UML." Which is correct?*

A. The creators of the language prefer "the UML."

Q. *You mentioned that object-oriented concepts play a major role in this book. Do I have to be a Java coder or a C++ developer in order to understand these concepts and to use them?*

A. Absolutely not. Object-oriented concepts aren't just for programmers. They're extremely useful for system analysts who want to understand and model the area of knowledge their system works in.

Q. *You've made the point that the UML is a great tool for analysts. The deployment diagram, however, doesn't seem like something that would be all that useful in the analysis stage of system development. Isn't it more appropriate for a later stage?*

A. It's really never too early to start thinking about deployment (or other issues traditionally left for later in development, like system security). Although it's true that the analyst is concerned with talking to clients and users, early in the process an analyst might think about the computers and components that will make up the system hardware. Sometimes the client dictates this. Sometimes the client wants a recommendation from the development team. Certainly a system architect will find the deployment diagram useful.

Q. *You mentioned that hybrid diagrams are possible. Does UML, excuse me, the UML impose limitations on which elements you can combine with which on a diagram?*

A. No. The UML sets no limits. It's usually the case, however, that a diagram contains one kind of element. You could put class icons on a deployment diagram, but that might not be very useful.

Q. *Figure 1.3 shows a use case diagram for "wash clothes." All this says is that a washing machine user wants to wash clothes. Do we really need a set of symbols to say that? Can't we just say that in a simple sentence?*

A. If that's all you had to say, then you're right: You could probably get away with just a sentence. In a typical development project, however, use cases are like "Tribbles" in the original *Star Trek* series (Episode 42). You start with a few, and before you know it. . . .

Workshop

You've jumped into the UML. Now it's time to firm up your knowledge of this great tool by answering some questions and going through some exercises. The answers appear in Appendix A, "Quiz Answers."

Quiz

1. Why is it necessary to have a variety of diagrams in a model of a system?

2. Which diagrams give a static view of a system?

3. Which diagrams provide a dynamic view of a system (that is, show change over time)?

4. What kinds of objects are in Figure 1.5?

Exercises

1. Suppose you're building a computer-based system that plays chess with a user. Which UML diagrams would be useful in designing the system? Why?

2. For the system in the exercise you just completed, list the questions you would ask a potential user and why you would ask them.

3. Take a look at the communication diagram in Figure 1.7. How would you complete it so that it's equivalent to the sequence diagram in Figure 1.5? What problems do you run into?

4. Go back to the bulleted lists of operations for the objects in Figure 1.5. Consider each object to be an instance of a class. Draw a class diagram that includes these classes and these operations. Can you think of some additional operations for each class?

5. Take things a step further. Try to organize your classes in Exercise 4 into a composite structure diagram of a washing machine. Can you think of some additional component classes?

6. In the subsection on state diagrams, I said an elevator can be either moving or stationary. Although you don't know much about state diagrams yet, see if you can figure out how to represent the states of an elevator. In addition to the names of the states, what other information should the state diagram somehow show? (**Hint:** Account for the elevator door. When is it open? When is it closed?)

7. Look at the sequence diagram in Figure 1.5 and the sequence diagrams that make up the interaction overview diagram in Figure 1.15. Focus on the messages that go from one object to another. Try to think of what (if anything) might go inside the parentheses in each message.

HOUR 2

Understanding Object-Orientation

What You'll Learn in This Hour:

- ▶ How to understand the object-oriented mindset
- ▶ How objects communicate
- ▶ How objects associate with one another
- ▶ How objects combine

Object-orientation has taken the software world by storm, and rightfully so. As a way of creating programs, it has a number of advantages. It fosters a component-based approach to software development so that you first create a system by creating a set of classes. Then you can expand the system by adding capabilities to components you've already built or by adding new components. Finally, you can reuse the classes you created when you build a new system, cutting down substantially on system development time.

The UML plays into all this by allowing you to build easy-to-use and easy-to-understand models of objects. Programmers can create these objects in software.

Object-orientation is a mindset—a mindset that depends on a few fundamental principles. In this hour you'll learn those principles. You'll find out what makes objects tick and how to use them in analysis and design. In the next hour you'll begin to apply UML to these principles.

Objects, Objects Everywhere

Objects, concrete and otherwise, are all around us. They make up our world. As I pointed out in the previous hour, modern software typically simulates the world—or a small slice of it—so programs usually mimic the objects in the world. If you understand some essentials of objects, you'll comprehend what has to go into the software representations of them, whether the software is object-oriented or not. Object-oriented concepts can benefit legacy programmers by providing insights for modeling the domain they work in.

First and foremost, an object is an instance of a class (a category). You and I, for example, are instances of the Person class. An object has **structure**. That is, it has attributes (properties) and behavior. An object's behavior consists of the **operations** it carries out. Attributes and operations taken together are called **features**.

By the Way

> ### Notation Conventions
>
> To get you accustomed to UML notation, I'll use some of the object-oriented conventions I mentioned in Hour 1, "Introducing the UML," such as
>
> - ▶ The name of a class begins with an uppercase letter.
>
> - ▶ A multiword classname runs all the words together, and each word begins with an uppercase letter for the first one.
>
> - ▶ The name of a feature (attribute or operation) begins with a lowercase letter.
>
> - ▶ A multiword feature name runs all the words together, and each word begins with an uppercase letter except for the first one.
>
> - ▶ A pair of parentheses follows the name of an operation.

As objects in the Person class, you and I each have these attributes: height, weight, and age. (You can imagine a number of others.) Each of us is unique because of the specific values that each of us has for those attributes. We also perform these operations: eat, sleep, read, write, talk, go to work, and more. (Or in objectspeak, eat(), sleep(), read(), write(), talk(), and goToWork().) If we were to create a system that deals with information on people—say, a payroll system or a system for a human resources department—we would likely incorporate some of these attributes and some of these operations in our software.

In the world of object-orientation, a class serves another purpose in addition to categorization. A class is a template for making objects—sort of like a cookie cutter that you use to stamp out cookies. (Some might argue that this is the same as categorization, but let's avoid that debate.)

Let's go back to the washing machine example. If we specify that the `WashingMachine` class has the attributes `brandName`, `modelName`, `serialNumber`, and `capacity`—along with the operations `acceptClothes()`, `acceptDetergent()`, `turnOn()`, and `turnOff()`—you have a mechanism for turning out new instances of the `WashingMachine` class. That is, you can create new objects based on this class (see Figure 2.1).

This is particularly important in the world of object-oriented software development. Although this book won't focus on programming, it helps your understanding of object-orientation if you know that classes in object-oriented programs can create new instances.

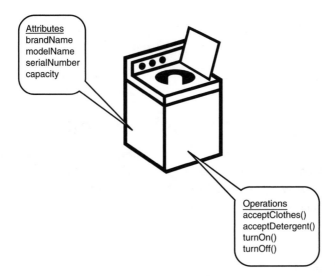

FIGURE 2.1
The `WashingMachine` class is a template for creating new instances of washing machines.

Here's something else to be aware of. Remember that the purpose of object-orientation is to develop software that reflects (that is, models) a particular slice of the world. The more attributes and behaviors you take into account, the more your model will be in tune with reality. In the washing machine example, you'll have a potentially more accurate model if you include the attributes `drumVolume`, `trap`, `motor`, and `motorSpeed`. You might also increase the accuracy of the model if you include operations like `acceptBleach()` and `controlWaterLevel()` (see Figure 2.2).

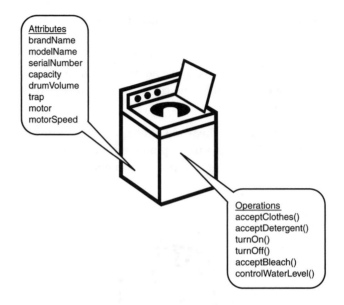

FIGURE 2.2
Adding attributes
and operations
brings the model
closer to reality.

Some Object-Oriented Concepts

Object-orientation goes beyond just modeling attributes and behavior. It considers
other aspects of objects as well. These aspects are called *abstraction, inheritance,
polymorphism,* and *encapsulation.* Three other important parts of object-orientation
are *message sending, associations,* and *aggregation.* Let's examine each of these
concepts.

Abstraction

Abstraction means, simply, to filter out an object's properties and operations
until just the ones you need are left. What does "just the ones you need" mean?

Different types of problems require different amounts of information, even if
those problems are in the same general area. In the second pass at building a
washing machine class, more attributes and operations emerged than in the first
pass. Was it worth it?

If you're part of a development team that's ultimately going to create a computer
program that simulates exactly how a washing machine does what it does, it's
definitely worth it. A computer program like that (which might be useful to
design engineers who are actually building a washing machine) has to have
enough in it to make accurate predictions about what will happen when the

washing machine is built, fully functioning, and washing clothes. For this kind of program, in fact, you can filter out the `serialNumber` attribute because it's probably not going to be very helpful.

What if, on the other hand, you're going to create software to track the transactions in a laundry that has a number of washing machines? In this program you probably won't need all the detailed attributes and operations mentioned in the preceding section. You might, however, want to include the `serialNumber` of each washing machine object.

In any case, what you're left with, after you've made your decisions about what to include and what to exclude, is an abstraction of a washing machine.

A Critical Skill

Some authorities argue that abstraction—that is, knowing what to include in a model and what to leave out—is the most critical skill for a modeler.

By the Way

Inheritance

Washing machines, refrigerators, microwave ovens, toasters, dishwashers, radios, waffle makers, blenders, and irons are all appliances. In the world of object orientation, we would say that each one is a **subclass** of the `Appliance` class. Another way to say this is that `Appliance` is a **superclass** of all those others.

`Appliance` is a class that has the attributes `onOffSwitch` and `electricWire`, and the operations `turnOn()` and `turnOff()`. Thus, if you know something is an appliance, you know immediately that it has the `Appliance` class's attributes and operations.

Object-orientation refers to this relationship as **inheritance**. Each subclass of `Appliance` (`WashingMachine`, `Refrigerator`, `Blender`, and so on) inherits the features of `Appliance`. It's important to note that each subclass adds its own attributes and operations. Figure 2.3 shows the superclass-subclass relationship.

FIGURE 2.3
Appliances inherit the attributes and operations of the `Appliance` class. Each one is a subclass of the `Appliance` class. The `Appliance` class is a superclass of each subclass.

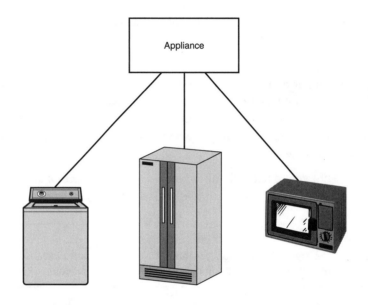

Inheritance doesn't have to stop there. `Appliance`, for example, is a subclass of the `HouseholdItem` class. `Furniture` is another subclass of `HouseholdItem`, as Figure 2.4 shows. `Furniture`, of course, has its own subclasses.

FIGURE 2.4
Superclasses can also be subclasses and inherit from other superclasses.

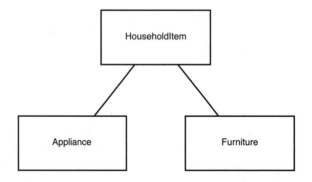

Polymorphism

Sometimes an operation has the same name in different classes. For example, you can open a door, you can open a window, and you can open a newspaper, a present, a bank account, or a conversation. In each case you're performing a different operation. In object-orientation each class "knows" how that operation is supposed to take place. This is called **polymorphism** (see Figure 2.5).

FIGURE 2.5
In polymorphism an operation can have the same name in different classes, and proceed differently in each class.

At first look it would seem that this concept is more important to software developers than to modelers. After all, software developers have to create the software that implements these methods in computer programs, and they have to be aware of important differences among operations that might have the same name. And they can build software classes that "know" what they're supposed to do.

But polymorphism is important to modelers, too. It allows the modeler to speak to the client (who's familiar with the slice of the world to be modeled) in the client's own words and terminology. Sometimes that terminology naturally leads to operation words (like "open") that can have more than one meaning. Polymorphism enables the modeler to maintain that terminology without having to make up artificial words to maintain an unnecessary (and unnatural) uniqueness of terms.

Encapsulation

In a TV commercial that aired a few years ago, two people discuss all the money they'll save if they dial a particular seven-digit prefix before dialing a long-distance phone call.

One of them asks, incredulously, "How does that work?"

The other replies: "How does popcorn pop? Who cares?"

That's the essence of **encapsulation**: When an object carries out its operations, those operations are hidden (see Figure 2.6). When most people watch a television show, they usually don't know or care about the complex electronics components that sit in back of the TV screen and all the many operations that have to occur in order to paint the image on the screen. The TV does what it does and hides the process from us. Most other appliances work that way, too. (Thankfully!)

FIGURE 2.6
Objects encapsu-
late what they do.
That is, they hide
the inner workings
of their operations
from the outside
world and from
other objects.

The TV hides its operations from the person watching it.

Why is this important? In the software world, encapsulation helps cut down on the potential for bad things to happen. In a system that consists of objects, the objects depend on each other in various ways. If one of them happens to mal-function and software engineers have to change it in some way, hiding its opera-tions from other objects means that it probably won't be necessary to change those other objects.

Turning from software to reality, you see the importance of encapsulation in the objects you work with, too. Your computer monitor, in a sense, hides its opera-tions from your computer's CPU. When something goes wrong with your monitor, you either fix the monitor or replace it. You probably won't have to fix or replace the CPU along with it.

While we're on the subject, here's a related concept. Because *encapsulation* means that an object hides what it does from other objects and from the outside world, encapsulation is also called **information hiding**. But an object does have to pre-sent a "face" to the outside world so you can initiate those operations. The TV, for example, has a set of buttons either on the TV itself or on a remote. A washing machine has a set of dials that enable you to set temperature and water level. The TV's buttons and the washing machine's dials are called **interfaces**.

Message Sending

I've mentioned that in a system, objects work together. They do this by sending messages to one another. One object sends another a message—a request to per-form an operation, and the receiving object performs that operation.

A TV and a remote present a nice intuitive example. When you want to watch a TV show, you hunt around for the remote, settle into your favorite chair, and push the On button. What happens? The remote-object sends a message (literally!) to the TV-object to turn itself on. The TV-object receives this message, knows how to perform the turn-on operation, and turns itself on. When you want to watch a different channel, you click the appropriate button on the remote, and the remote-object sends a different message—"change the channel"—to the TV-object. The remote can also communicate with the TV via other messages for changing the volume, muting the volume, and setting up closed captioning.

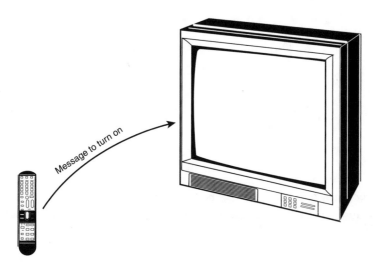

Message to turn on

FIGURE 2.7
An example of message sending from one object to another. The remote-object sends a message to the TV-object to turn itself on. The TV-object receives the message through its interface, an infrared receiver.

Let's go back to interfaces for a moment. Most of the things you do from the remote you can also do by getting out of the chair, going to the TV, and clicking buttons on the TV. (You might actually try that sometime!) The interface the TV presents to you (the set of buttons) is obviously not the same interface it presents to the remote (an infrared receiver). Figure 2.7 illustrates this.

Back in Hour 1 . . .
You've already seen message-sending in action. In the sequence diagram in Hour 1 (Figure 1.5), the arrows represent messages that go from one object to another.

By the Way

Associations

Another common occurrence is that objects are typically related to one another in some fashion. For example, when you turn on your TV, in object-oriented terms, you're in an **association** with your TV.

The "turn-on" association is unidirectional (one-way), as in Figure 2.8. That is, you turn your TV on. Unless you watch way too much television, however, it doesn't return the favor. Other associations, like "is married to," are bidirectional.

FIGURE 2.8
Objects are often associated with each other in some way. When you turn on your TV, you're in a unidirectional association with it.

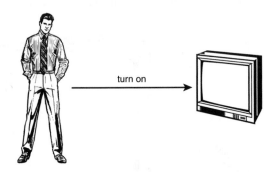

turn on

Sometimes an object might be associated with another in more than one way. If you and your coworker are friends, that's an example. You're in an "is the friend of" association, as well as an "is the coworker of" association, as Figure 2.9 shows.

FIGURE 2.9
Objects are sometimes associated with each other in more than one way.

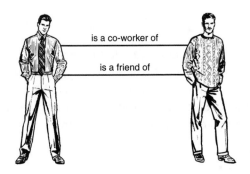

is a co-worker of

is a friend of

A class can associate with more than one other class. A person can ride in a car, and a person can also ride in a bus (see Figure 2.10).

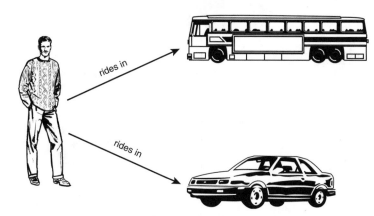

FIGURE 2.10
A class can associate with more than one other class.

Multiplicity is an important aspect of associations among objects. It tells the number of objects in one class that relate to a single object of the associated class. For example, in a typical college course, the course is taught by a single instructor. The course and the instructor are in a one-to-one association. In a proseminar, however, several instructors might teach the course throughout the semester. In that case, the course and the instructor are in a one-to-many association.

You can find all kinds of multiplicities if you look hard enough. A bicycle rides on two tires (a one-to-two multiplicity), a tricycle rides on three, and an 18-wheeler on 18.

Aggregation

Think about your computer system. It consists of a CPU box, a keyboard, a mouse, a monitor, a CD-ROM drive, one or more hard drives, a modem, a disk drive, a printer, and possibly some speakers. Inside the CPU box, along with the aforementioned drives, you have a CPU, a graphics card, a sound card, and some other elements you would undoubtedly find it hard to live without.

Your computer is an **aggregation**, another kind of association among objects. Like many other things worth having, the computer is made from a number of different types of components (see Figure 2.11). You can probably come up with numerous examples of aggregations.

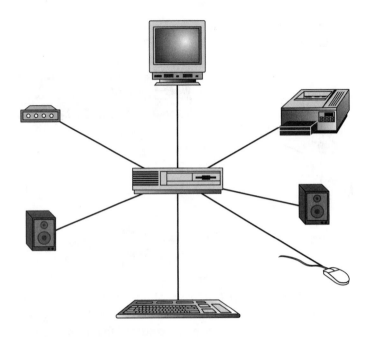

One form of aggregation involves a strong relationship between an aggregate object and its component objects. This is called **composition**. The key to composition is that the component exists as a component only within the composite object. For example, a shirt is a composite of a body, a collar, sleeves, buttons, buttonholes, and cuffs. Do away with the shirt and the collar becomes useless.

Sometimes a component in a composite doesn't last as long as the composite itself. The leaves on a tree can die out before the tree does. If you destroy the tree, the leaves also die (see Figure 2.12).

Aggregation and composition are important because they reflect extremely common occurrences, and thus help you create models that closely resemble reality.

The Payoff

Objects and their associations form the backbone of functioning systems. In order to model those systems, you have to understand what those associations are. If you're aware of the possible types of associations, you'll have a well-stocked bag of tricks when you talk to clients about their needs, gather their requirements, and create models of the systems that help them meet their business challenges.

FIGURE 2.12
In a composition, a component can sometimes die out before the composite does. If you destroy the composite, you destroy the component as well.

The important thing is to use the concepts of object-orientation to help you understand the client's area of knowledge (his or her **domain**), and to illustrate your understanding to the client in terms that he or she understands.

That's where the UML comes in. In the next three hours, you'll learn how to apply the UML to visualize the concepts you learned in this hour.

If You're Interested in This Sort of Thing . . .

One of object-orientation's appeals is that it seems to be right in line with human nature. Perhaps we categorize the objects around us because it's easier for our brains to deal with a few categories rather than with many instances.

Recent research points to brain areas involved in object categorization. Psychologists Isabel Gauthier and Michael Tarr used novel objects expressly designed for this research in conjunction with imaging techniques that show the brain in action. They found that as people learned to categorize these objects (according to rules defined by the experimenters), a specific area in the cerebral cortex became increasingly active. (It's called the *fusiform gyrus*, if you must know.)

By the Way

Summary

Object-orientation is a mindset that depends on a few fundamental principles. An object is an instance of a class. A class is a general category of objects that have the same attributes and operations. When you create an object, the problem area you're working in determines how many of the attributes and operations to consider.

Inheritance is an important aspect of object-orientation: An object inherits the attributes and operations of its class. A class can also inherit attributes and operations from another class.

Polymorphism is another important aspect. It specifies that an operation can have the same name in different classes, and each class will perform the operation in a different way.

Objects hide the performance of their operations from other objects and from the outside world. Each object presents an interface so that other objects (and people) can get it to perform its operations.

Objects work together by sending messages to one another. The messages are requests to perform operations.

Objects are typically associated with one another. The association can take a variety of forms. An object in one class may associate with any number of objects in another.

Aggregation is a type of association. An aggregate object consists of a set of component objects. A composition is a special kind of aggregation. In a composite object the components exist only as part of the composite.

Q&A

Q. *You said that object-orientation has taken the software world by storm. Aren't there some important applications that are not object-oriented?*

A. Yes. The ones that aren't object-oriented are often called "legacy" systems—programs written long ago that in many cases are starting to show their age. Object-orientation offers numerous advantages, such as reusability and fast development time. For these reasons, you're likely to see new applications (and rewritten versions of many legacy applications) written the object-oriented way.

Q. *How and when did this whole object-oriented thing get started?*

A. Object-orientation emerged in Norway in the mid-1960s when Ole-Johan Dahl and Kristen Nygaard developed the SIMULA 1 programming language as a way of simulating complex systems. Although SIMULA 1 never came into wide use, it introduced classes, objects, and inheritance, among other important object-oriented concepts.

For more on the object-oriented paradigm, read Matt Weisfeld's *The Object-Oriented Thought Process, Second Edition,* ISBN: 0-672-32611-6 (SAMS Publishing, 2003).

Workshop

To review what you've learned about object-orientation, try your hand at these quiz questions. You'll find the quiz answers in Appendix A, "Quiz Answers." This is a theoretical hour, so I haven't included any exercises. You'll see quite a few in the hours to come, however!

Quiz

1. What is an object?
2. How do objects work together?
3. What does multiplicity indicate?
4. Can two objects associate with one another in more than one way?
5. What is inheritance?
6. What is encapsulation?

HOUR 3

Working with Object-Orientation

What You'll Learn in This Hour:

- ▶ How to model a class
- ▶ How to show a class's features, responsibilities, and constraints
- ▶ How to discover classes

Now it's time to put the UML together with the object-oriented concepts you learned in the last hour. In this hour, you'll firm up your knowledge of object-orientation as you learn more about the UML.

Visualizing a Class

As I pointed out in the first hour, a rectangle is the icon that represents a class in the UML. From Hours 1, "Introducing the UML," and 2, "Understanding Object-Orientation," recall that the name of the class is, by convention, a word with an initial uppercase letter. It appears near the top of the rectangle. If your class has a two-word name, join the two words together and capitalize the first letter of the second word (as in WashingMachine in Figure 3.1).

Another UML construct, the package, can play a role in the name of a class. As I pointed out in Hour 1, a package is the UML's way of organizing a diagram's elements. As you might recall, the UML represents a package as a tabbed folder. The package's name is a text string (see Figure 3.2).

FIGURE 3.1
The UML class
icon.

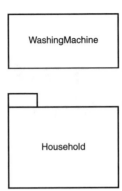

FIGURE 3.2
A UML package.

If the `WashingMachine` class is part of a package called `Household`, you can give it the name `Household::WashingMachine`. The double colons separate the package name on the left from the classname on the right. This type of classname is called a **pathname** (see Figure 3.3).

FIGURE 3.3
A class with a
pathname.

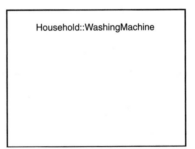

Attributes

An **attribute** is a property of a class. It describes a range of values that the property may hold in objects (that is, in *instances*) of that class. A class may have zero or more attributes. By convention, a one-word attribute name is written in lowercase letters. If the name consists of more than one word, the words are joined and each word other than the first word begins with an uppercase letter. The list of attribute names begins below a line separating them from the classname, as Figure 3.4 shows.

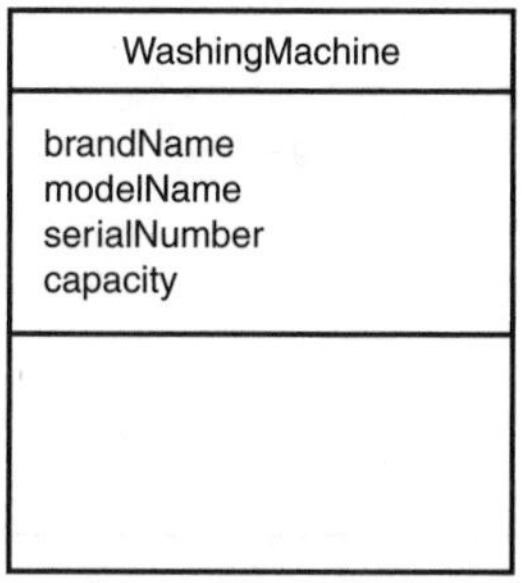

FIGURE 3.4
A class and its attributes.

Every object of the class has a specific value for every attribute. Figure 3.5 presents an example. Note that an object's name begins with a lowercase letter, precedes a colon that precedes the classname, and the whole name is underlined.

Naming Objects . . . or Not

The name <u>myWasher:WashingMachine</u> is a **named instance**. It's also possible to have an **anonymous instance** like <u>:WashingMachine</u>.

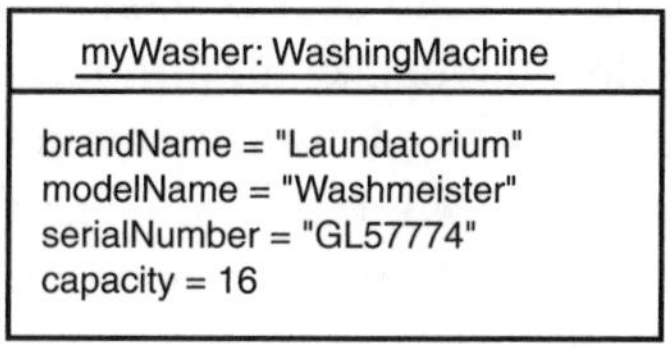

By the
Way

FIGURE 3.5
An object has a specific value for every one of its class's attributes.

The UML gives you the option of indicating additional information for attributes. In the icon for the class, you can specify a type for each attribute's value. Possible types include string, floating-point number, integer, and Boolean (and other enumerated types). To indicate a type, use a colon to separate the attribute name from the type. You can also indicate a default value for an attribute. Figure 3.6 shows these ways of specifying attributes.

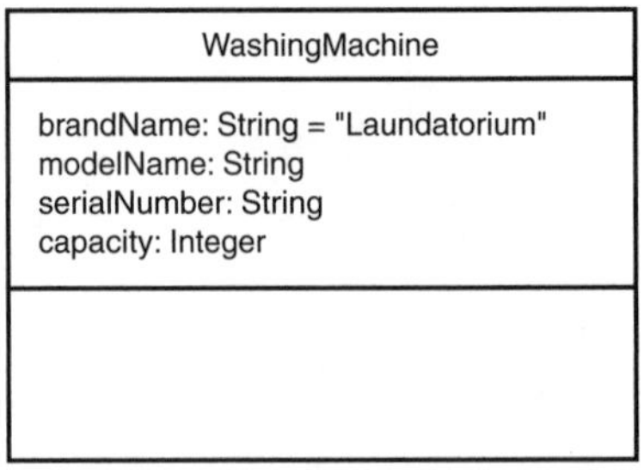

FIGURE 3.6
An attribute can
show its type as
well as a default
value.

WashingMachine
brandName: String = "Laundatorium" modelName: String serialNumber: String capacity: Integer

By the Way

Naming Values
An **enumerated type** is a data type defined by a list of named values. Boolean, for instance, is an enumerated type because it consists of the values "true" and "false." You can define your own enumerated types like State, which consists of the values "solid," "liquid," and "gas."

Operations

An **operation** is something a class can do, and hence it is something that you (or another class) can ask the class to do. Like an attribute name, an operation's name is all in lowercase if it's one word. If the name consists of more than one word, join the words and begin all words after the first with an uppercase letter. The list of operations begins below a line that separates the operations from the attributes, as in Figure 3.7.

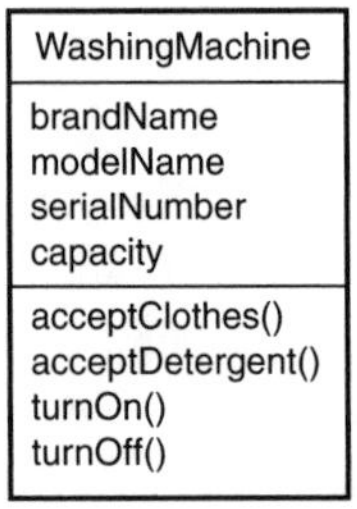

FIGURE 3.7
The list of a class's
operations appears
below a line that
separates them
from the class's
attributes.

WashingMachine
brandName modelName serialNumber capacity
acceptClothes() acceptDetergent() turnOn() turnOff()

Just as you can indicate additional information for attributes, you can indicate additional information for operations. In the parentheses that follow an operation name, you can show the parameter that the operation works on, along with that parameter's type. One kind of operation, the **function**, returns a value after it finishes doing its work. For a function, you can show the value it returns and that value's type.

These pieces of information about an operation are called the operation's **signature**. Figure 3.8 shows a couple of ways to represent the signature. The first two operations show the type of the parameter. The third and fourth show the type of the return value.

```
WashingMachine
--------------------------------
brandName
modelName
serialNumber
capacity
--------------------------------
acceptClothes(c:String)
acceptDetergent(d:Integer)
turnOn():Boolean
turnOff():Boolean
```

FIGURE 3.8
Signatures for operations.

Attributes, Operations, and Visualization

We've been dealing with classes in isolation thus far and showing all the attributes and operations of a class. In practice, however, you'll show more than one class at a time. When you do that, it's typically not useful to always display all the attributes and operations. To do so might make the diagram way too busy. Instead, you can just show the classname and leave either the attribute area or the operation area empty (or leave them both empty), as Figure 3.9 shows.

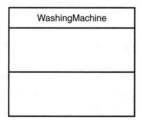

FIGURE 3.9
In practice, you don't always show all of a class's attributes and operations.

Sometimes it might be helpful to show some (but not all) of the attributes or operations. To indicate that you've only shown some of them, you follow the list of the ones you've shown with three dots "...". This is called an **ellipsis**, and omitting some or all of the attributes or operations is called **eliding** a class. Figure 3.10 shows the use of an ellipsis.

FIGURE 3.10
An ellipsis indicates that the displayed attributes or operations aren't the whole set.

If you have a long list of attributes or operations, you can use a keyword to organize in ways that will make the list comprehensible. As I mentioned in Hour 1, a keyword is enclosed inside two pairs of small angle brackets called *guillemets*. For an attribute list, you can use a keyword as a heading for a subset of the attributes, as in Figure 3.11.

FIGURE 3.11
You can use a keyword to organize a list of attributes or operations.

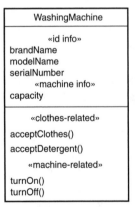

Responsibilities and Constraints

The class icon enables you to specify still another type of information about a class. In an area below the operations list, you can show the class's responsibility. The **responsibility** is a description of what the class has to do—that is, what its attributes and operations are trying to accomplish. A washing machine, for example, has the responsibility of taking dirty clothes as input and producing clean clothes as output.

In the icon, you indicate responsibilities in an area below the area that contains the operations (see Figure 3.12).

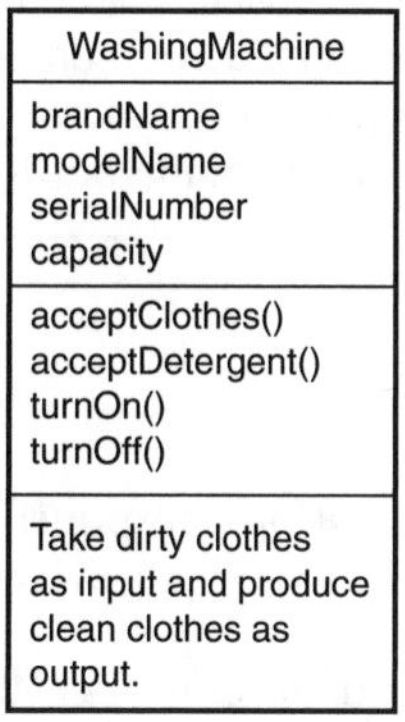

WashingMachine
brandName modelName serialNumber capacity
acceptClothes() acceptDetergent() turnOn() turnOff()
Take dirty clothes as input and produce clean clothes as output.

FIGURE 3.12
In a class icon, you can write the class's responsibilities in an area below the operations list area.

The idea here is to include enough information to describe a class in an unambiguous way. Indicating the class's responsibilities is an informal way to eliminate ambiguity.

A slightly more formal way is to add a **constraint**, a free-form text enclosed in curly brackets. The bracketed text specifies one or more rules the class follows. For example, suppose in the WashingMachine class you wanted to specify that the capacity of a washer can be only 16, 18, or 20 pounds (and thus "constrain" the WashingMachine class's capacity attribute). You would write {capacity = 16 or 18 or 20 lbs} near the WashingMachine class icon. Figure 3.13 shows how to do it.

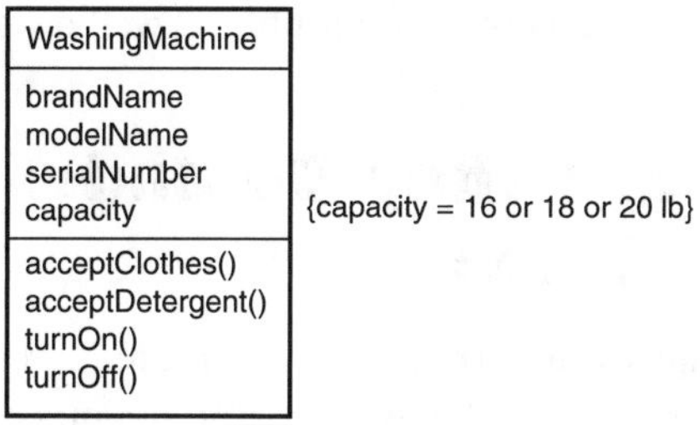

WashingMachine
brandName modelName serialNumber capacity
acceptClothes() acceptDetergent() turnOn() turnOff()

{capacity = 16 or 18 or 20 lb}

FIGURE 3.13
The rule in curly brackets constrains the capacity attribute to be one of three possible values.

By the
Way

More on Constraints

The UML works with still another—and much more formal—way of adding constraints that make definitions more explicit. It's an entire language called **Object Constraint Language** (OCL). An advanced and sometimes useful tool, OCL has its own set of rules, terms, and operators. The Web site of the Object Management Group (www.omg.org) provides documentation on OCL.

Attached Notes

Above and beyond attributes, operations, responsibilities, and constraints, you can add still more information to a class in the form of notes attached to the class.

You'll usually add a note to an attribute or operation. Figure 3.14 shows a note referring to a government standard that tells where to find out how serial numbers are generated for objects in the WashingMachine class.

FIGURE 3.14
An attached note provides further information about the class.

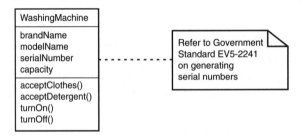

Bear in mind that a note can contain a graphic as well as text.

Classes—What They Do and How to Find Them

Classes are the vocabulary and terminology of an area of knowledge. As you talk with clients, analyze their area of knowledge, and design computer systems that solve problems in that area, you learn the terminology and model the terms as classes in the UML.

In your conversations with clients, be alert to the nouns they use to describe the entities in their business. Those nouns will become the classes in your model. Be alert also to the verbs that you hear because these will constitute the operations in those classes. The attributes will emerge as nouns related to the class nouns. After you have a core list of classes, question the clients as to what each class is supposed to do within the business. Their answers will tell you the class responsibilities.

Suppose you're an analyst building a model of the game of basketball, and you're interviewing a coach in order to understand the game. The conversation might go something like this:

Analyst: "Coach, what's basketball all about?"

Coach: "The goal of the game is to shoot the ball through the basket and score more points than your opponent. Each team consists of five players: two guards, two forwards, and a center. Each team advances the ball toward the basket with the objective of ultimately shooting the ball through the basket."

Analyst: "How does it advance the ball?"

Coach: "By dribbling and passing. But the team has to take a shot at the basket before the shot clock expires."

Analyst: "Shot clock?"

Coach: "Yes. That's 24 seconds in the pros, 30 seconds in international play, and 35 seconds in college to take a shot after a team gets possession of the ball."

Analyst: "How does the scoring work?"

Coach: "Each basket counts two points, unless the shot is from behind the three-point line. In that case, it's three points. A free throw counts one point. A free throw, by the way, is the penalty a team pays for committing a foul. If a player fouls an opponent, play stops and the opponent gets to shoot at the basket from the free-throw line."

Analyst: "Tell me a little more about what each player does."

Coach: "The guards generally do most of the dribbling and passing. They're typically shorter than the forwards, and the forwards are usually shorter than the center. All the players are supposed to be able to dribble, pass, shoot, and rebound. The forwards do most of the rebounding and intermediate-range shooting, while the center stays near the basket and shoots from close range."

Analyst: "How about the dimensions of the court? And by the way, how long does a game last?"

Coach: "In international play, the court is 28 meters long by 15 meters wide. The basket is 10 feet off the ground. In the pros, a game lasts 48 minutes, divided into four 12-minute quarters. In college and international play, it's 40 minutes divided into two 20-minute halves. A game clock keeps track of the time remaining."

This could go on and on, but let's stop and take stock of where we are. Here are the nouns you've uncovered: ball, basket, team, players, guards, forwards, center, shot, shot clock, three-point line, free throw, foul, free-throw line, court, and game clock.

Here are the verbs: shoot, advance, dribble, pass, foul, and rebound. You also have some additional information about some of the nouns—like the relative heights of the players at each position, the dimensions of the court, the total amount of time on a shot clock, and the duration of a game.

Finally, your own commonsense knowledge could come into play as you generate a few attributes on your own. You know, for example, that the ball has attributes like volume and diameter.

Using this information, you can create a diagram like the one in Figure 3.15. It shows the classes, and provides some attributes, operations, and constraints. The diagram also shows responsibilities. You could use this diagram as a foundation for further conversations with the coach, to uncover more information.

FIGURE 3.15
An initial class diagram for modeling the game of basketball.

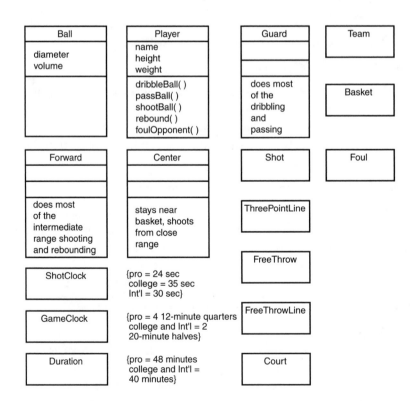

Summary

The rectangle is the UML icon for representing a class. The name, attributes, operations, and responsibilities of the class fit into areas within the rectangle. You can use a stereotype to organize lists of attributes and operations. You elide a class by showing just a subset of its attributes and operations. This makes a class diagram less busy.

You can show an attribute's type and an initial value, and you can show the values an operation works on and their types as well. For an operation, this additional information is called the signature.

To reduce the ambiguity in a class description, you can add constraints. The UML also allows you to say more about a class by attaching notes to the rectangle that represents it.

Classes represent the vocabulary of an area of knowledge. Conversations with a client or an expert in that area reveal nouns that can become classes in a model and verbs that can become operations. You can use a class diagram as a way of stimulating the client to talk more about his or her area and reveal additional knowledge.

Q&A

Q. *You mention using "commonsense" knowledge to round out the class diagram for basketball. That's all well and good, but what happens when I have to analyze an area that's new to me—where common sense won't necessarily help?*

A. Typically, you'll be thrust into an area that's new for you. Before you meet with a client or with an expert in the field, try to become a "subexpert." Prepare for the meeting by reading as much related documentation as possible. Ask your interviewee for some papers or manuals they might have written. When you've finished reading, you'll know some of the fundamentals and you'll be able to ask pointed questions.

Q. *At what point will I want to show an operation's signature?*

A. Probably after the analysis phase of a development effort, as you get into design. The signature is a piece of information that programmers will find helpful.

Q. *I've been working for my company for a long time and have in-depth knowledge of its business. Do I still have to create a class model of the business area the company works in?*

A. It's a good idea to do that. When you have to model your knowledge, you may be surprised at what you don't know.

Workshop

To review what you've learned about object-orientation, try your hand at these quiz questions. The answers appear in Appendix A, "Quiz Answers."

Quiz

1. How do you represent a class in the UML?

2. What information can you show on a class icon?

3. What is a constraint?

4. Why would you attach a note to a class icon?

Exercises

1. Here's a brief (and incomplete) description of hockey:

    A hockey team consists of a center, a goalie, two wings, and two defensemen. Each player has a stick, which he uses to advance a puck on the ice. The objective is to use the stick to shoot the puck into a goal. Hockey is played on a rink with maximum dimensions of 100 feet wide by 200 feet long. The center's job is to pass the puck to the wings, who are typically the better shooters on the team. The defensemen try to stop the opposing players from getting into position to shoot the puck into the goal. The goalie is the last line of defense, blocking opposition shots. Each time he stops the puck from getting into the goal, he's credited with a "save." Each goal is worth one point. A game lasts 60 minutes, divided into three periods of 20 minutes each.

    Use this information to come up with a diagram like the one in Figure 3.15. If you know more about hockey than I've put in the description, add that information to your diagram.

2. If you know more about basketball than I've put in Figure 3.15, add information to that diagram.

3. Go back to the conversation between the analyst and the basketball coach. Take a look at the coach's responses and find at least three areas where you could pursue additional lines of questioning. For example, at one point the coach mentions a "three-point line." Further questioning would reveal the specifics of that term.

4. Here's a preview of what's next: If you had to draw some connections among the classes in Figure 3.15, what might they look like?

HOUR 4

Working with Relationships

What You'll Learn in This Hour:

▶ How to model the connections among classes
▶ How to visualize class-subclass relationships
▶ How to show dependencies among classes

In the model that finished up the last hour, you were left with a set of classes that represent the vocabulary of basketball. Although this provides the basis for further exploration of what basketball is all about, it might be apparent to you that something's missing.

That "something" is a sense of the way the classes relate to one another. If you look at that model (refer to Figure 3.15), you'll see that it doesn't show how a player relates to the ball, how players make up a team, or how a game proceeds. It's as though you've constructed a laundry list of terms, rather than a picture of an area of knowledge.

In this hour, you'll draw the connections among the classes and fill out the picture.

Associations

When classes are connected together conceptually, that connection is called an **association**. The initial basketball model provides some examples. Let's examine one—the association between a player and a team. You can characterize this association with the phrase "a player plays on a team." You visualize the association as a line connecting the two classes, with the name of the association ("Plays on") just above the line. You show how to read the relationship with a filled triangle pointing in the appropriate direction. Figure 4.1 shows how to visualize the Plays on association between the player and the team.

When one class associates with another, each one usually plays a role within that association. You can show each class's role by writing it near the line next to the class. In the association between a player and a team, if the team is professional, it's an employer and the player is an employee. Figure 4.2 shows how to represent these roles.

You can imagine an association that you could read in the other direction: A team employs players. You can show both associations in the same diagram, with a filled triangle indicating how to read each association, as in Figure 4.3.

Associations may be more complex than just one class connected to another. Several classes can connect to one class. If you consider guards, forwards, and centers, and their associations with the Team class, you'll have the diagram in Figure 4.4.

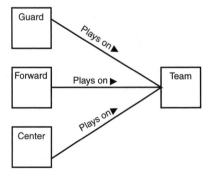

Constraints on Associations

Sometimes an association between two classes has to follow a rule. You indicate that rule by putting a constraint near the association line. For example, a Bank Teller serves a Customer, but each Customer is served in the order in which he or she appears in line. You capture this in the model by putting the word *ordered* inside curly brackets (to indicate the constraint) near the Customer class, as in Figure 4.5.

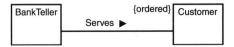

FIGURE 4.5
You can place a constraint on an association. In this example, the Serves association is constrained to have the Bank Teller serve the Customer in order.

Another type of constraint is the Or relationship, signified by {or} on a dashed line that connects two association lines. Figure 4.6 models a high school student choosing either an academic course of study or a commercial one.

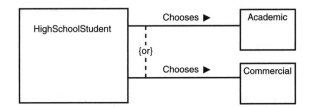

FIGURE 4.6
The Or relationship between two associations is a constraint.

Association Classes

An association can have attributes and operations, just like a class. In fact, when this is the case, you have an **association class**. You visualize an association class the same way you show a regular class, and you use a dashed line to connect it to the association line. An association class can have associations to other classes. Figure 4.7 shows an association class for the Plays on association between a player and a team. The association class, Contract, is associated with the GeneralManager class.

FIGURE 4.7
An association
class models an
association's
attributes and
operations. It's
connected to an
association via a
dashed line and
can associate with
another class.

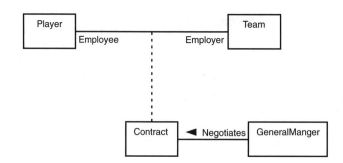

Links

Just as an object is an instance of a class, an association has instances as well. If you imagine a specific player who plays for a specific team, the `Plays on` relationship is called a **link**, and you represent it as a line connecting two objects. Just as you would underline the name of an object, you underline the name of a link, as in Figure 4.8.

FIGURE 4.8
A link is an
instance of an
association. It
connects objects
rather than
classes. In a link,
you underline the
name of the link,
just as you
underline the name
of an object.

Multiplicity

The association drawn so far between `Player` and `Team` suggests that the two classes are in a one-to-one relationship. Common sense tells you that this isn't the case, however. A basketball team has five players (not counting substitutes). The `Has` association must take this into account. In the other direction, a player can play for just one team, and the `Plays on` association must account for that.

These specifications are examples of **multiplicity**—the number of objects from one class that relate with a single object in an associated class. To represent these numbers in the diagram, you place them near the appropriate class, as in Figure 4.9. (The numbers can go either above or below the association line.)

FIGURE 4.9
Multiplicity denotes the number of objects of one class that can relate to one object of an associated class.

The multiplicity in this example is not the only type. A variety of multiplicities are possible (a multiplicity of multiplicities, so to speak). One class can relate to another in a 1-to-1, 1-to-many, 1-to-1 or more, 1-to-0 or one, 1-to-a bounded interval (for example, 1-to-5 through 10), 1-to-exactly *n* (as in this example), or 1-to-a set of choices (for example, one-to-nine or ten).

A Helpful Hint

The first time you see some of these multiplicities, the phrasing might be a little confusing. Here's a trick to help you through the confusion: Imagine double-quotes around the right-side phrase, so that one-to-one or more becomes one-to-"one or more" and one-to-a bounded interval becomes one-to-"a bounded interval." The double-quotes show the boundaries of that right-side phrase and might make the whole thing easier to understand.

By the Way

The UML uses an asterisk (*) to represent *more* and to represent *many*. In one context Or is represented by two dots, as in 1..* ("one or more"). In another context, Or is represented by a comma, as in 5,10 ("5 or 10"). Figure 4.10 shows how to visualize possible multiplicities. (Note that the phrase at the right of each multiplicity in Figure 4.10 isn't part of the UML. It's just a label I added to help clarify things.)

One-to-Zero or One

When class A is in a one-to-zero or one multiplicity with class B, class B is said to be **optional** for class A.

By the Way

Qualified Associations

When an association's multiplicity is one-to-many, a particular challenge often arises: **lookup**. When an object from one class has to choose a particular object from another in order to fulfill a role in an association, the first class has to rely on a specific attribute to select the correct object. That attribute is typically an *identifier*, such as an ID number. For example, a hotel's reservation list has many reservations, as Figure 4.11 shows.

FIGURE 4.10
Possible multiplicities and how to represent them in the UML.

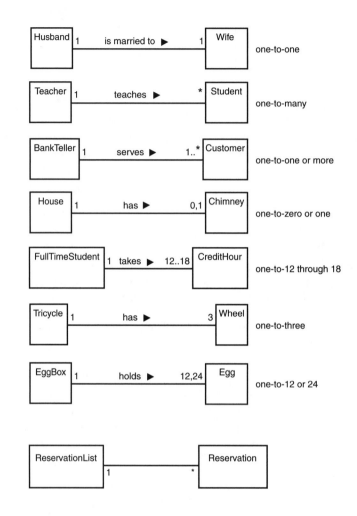

FIGURE 4.11
A reservation list and its reservations are in a one-to-many multiplicity.

When you make a reservation at a hotel, the hotel assigns you a confirmation number. If you call with questions about the reservation, you have to supply the confirmation number, so that someone looking through the reservation list can select your reservation.

In the UML, the ID information is called a **qualifier**. Its symbol is a small rectangle adjoining the class that has the "one" part in the one-to-many multiplicity. Figure 4.12 shows the representation. Although the multiplicity between ReservationList and Reservation is one-to-many, the multiplicity between confirmationNumber and Reservation is one-to-one.

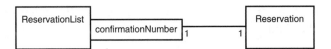

FIGURE 4.12
The UML notation for a qualifier. The idea is that when you add that little rectangle, you *qualify* the association.

Reflexive Associations

Sometimes, a class is in an association with itself. Referred to as a **reflexive association**, this can happen when a class has objects that play a variety of roles. For example, a CarOccupant can be either a driver or a passenger. In the role of the driver, one CarOccupant drives zero or more additional CarOccupants who play the role of passenger. You represent this by drawing an association line from the class rectangle back to the same class rectangle, and on the association line you indicate the roles, name of the association, direction of the association, and multiplicity as before. Figure 4.13 presents this example.

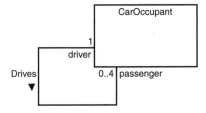

FIGURE 4.13
In a reflexive association, you draw the line from the class to itself, and you can include the roles, association name, direction of the association, and multiplicity.

Inheritance and Generalization

One of the hallmarks of object-orientation is that it captures one of the great commonsense aspects of day-to-day life: If you know something about a category of things, you automatically know some information you can transfer to other categories. If you know something is an appliance, you already know it has an on-off switch, a brand name, and a serial number. If you know something is an animal, you take for granted that it eats, sleeps, has a way of being born, has a way of getting from one place to another, and probably has a number of other attributes (and operations) you could list if you thought about it for a few minutes.

Object-orientation refers to this as **inheritance**. The UML also refers to this as **generalization**. One class (the child class or subclass) can inherit attributes and operations from another (the parent class or superclass). The parent class is more general than the child class.

The inheritance hierarchy doesn't have to end at two levels: A child class can be a parent class for still another child class. Mammal is a child class of Animal, and Horse is a child class of Mammal.

In the UML, you represent inheritance with a line that connects the parent class to the child class. On the part of the line that connects to the parent class, you put an open triangle that points to the parent class. This type of connection stands for the phrase *is a kind of*. A Mammal is a kind of Animal, and a Horse is a kind of Mammal. Figure 4.14 shows this particular inheritance hierarchy, along with some additional classes.

FIGURE 4.14
An inheritance hierarchy in the animal kingdom.

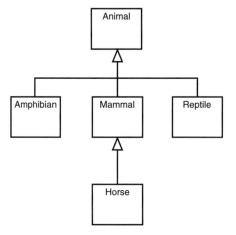

In the figure, note the appearance of the triangle and the lines when more than one child class inherits from a parent class. Setting the diagram up this way results in a less busy diagram than showing all the lines and triangles, but the UML doesn't prohibit putting all of them in the picture. Note also that you don't put the inherited attributes and operations in the subclass rectangles, as you've already represented them in the superclass.

By the Way

Child = "Is a Kind Of"

When modeling inheritance, be sure the child class satisfies the *is a kind of* relationship with the parent class. If the two don't have that kind of relationship, an association of some other kind might be more appropriate.

Child classes add to the attributes and operations they inherit. For example, a Mammal has hair and gives milk, two attributes not found in the Animal class.

A class might have no parents, in which case it's a **base class** or **root class**. A class might have no children, in which case it's a **leaf class**. If a class has exactly one parent, it has **single inheritance**. If a class has more than one parent, it has **multiple inheritance**.

Class Names Are Singular

Have you noticed that the name of a class is always singular (for example, Mammal rather than Mammals)? The *is a kind of* relationship is a good reason for this. It makes sense to say "a horse is a kind of mammal" rather than "a horse is a kind of mammals" (which makes no sense at all).

By the Way

Discovering Inheritance

In the course of talking to a client, an analyst discovers inheritance in several ways. It's possible that the candidate classes that emerge include both parent classes and child classes. The analyst has to realize that the attributes and operations of one class are general and perhaps apply to several other classes, which may add attributes and operations of their own.

The basketball example from Hour 3, "Working with Object-Orientation," has Player, Guard, Forward, and Center classes. The Player has attributes such as name, height, weight, runningSpeed, and verticalLeap. This class has operations such as dribble(), pass(), rebound(), and shoot(). The Guard, Forward, and Center inherit these attributes and operations, and add some of their own. The Guard might have the operations runOffense() and bringBallUpcourt(). The Center might have the operation slamDunk(). Based on the coach's comments about relative heights of the players, the analyst might want to place constraints on the heights of the individuals who play each position.

Another possibility is that the analyst notes that two or more classes have a number of attributes and operations in common. The basketball model has a GameClock, which keeps track of how much time remains in a game period, and a ShotClock, which tracks the time remaining from the instant one team takes possession of the ball until it's supposed to shoot the ball. Realizing that both track time, the analyst could formulate a Clock class with a trackTime() operation that both the GameClock and the ShotClock inherit.

By the Way

> **An Example of Polymorphism**
>
> Because the ShotClock tracks 24 seconds (professional) or 35 seconds (college) and the GameClock tracks 12 minutes (professional) or 20 minutes (college), trackTime() is polymorphic.

Abstract Classes

In the basketball model, the two classes I just mentioned—Player and Clock—are useful because they serve as parent classes for important child classes. The child classes are important in the model because you'll ultimately want to have instances of these classes. To develop the model you'll need instances of Guard, Forward, Center, GameClock, and ShotClock.

Player and Clock, however, will not provide any instances for the model. An object from the Player class would serve no purpose, nor would an object from the Clock class.

Classes like Player and Clock, which provide no objects, are said to be **abstract**. You indicate an abstract class by writing its name in italics. Figure 4.15 shows the two abstract classes and their children.

Dependencies

In a different kind of relationship, one class uses another. This is called a **dependency**. The most common usage of a dependency is to show that the signature of one class's operation uses another class.

Suppose you're designing a system that displays corporate forms on-screen so employees can fill them out. The employee uses a menu to select the form to fill out. In your design, you have a System class and a Form class. Among its many operations, the System class has displayForm(f:Form). The form the system displays obviously depends on which form the user selects. The UML notation for this is a dashed line with an arrowhead pointing at the class depended on, as in Figure 4.16.

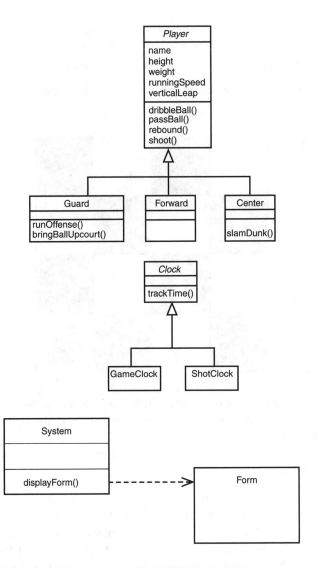

Class Diagrams and Object Diagrams

So far I've talked at length about class diagrams, but I haven't said nearly as much about object diagrams. As we end this hour on relationships, we've reached a good point to discuss how and why you visualize objects.

A *class diagram* gives general, definitional information—the properties of a class and its attributes, as well as other classes it associates with. An *object diagram*, on the other hand, gives information about specific instances of a class and how they link up at specific instants in time. ("*Instants*" and "*instances*"—that's a good way to conceptualize the purpose of an object diagram.)

Here's an example: Suppose you're looking at part of a chess game, like the chess pieces in Figure 4.17.

FIGURE 4.17
A portion of a chess game.

If you don't know anything about chess, it will be difficult for you to understand what's happening in this particular configuration of chess pieces. If you had a class diagram of chess pieces, like Figure 4.18, that diagram could help you figure out some of the general rules of chess. (The upperShape attribute is just a way of describing the physical appearance of a chess piece.)

Although this might aid your overall understanding (particularly if the diagram somehow explained knightMoveTo(), queenMoveTo(), pawnMoveTo(), and pawnCapture()), you'd still need some help comprehending the *specific* chess position in Figure 4.17. An object diagram provides the help. Figure 4.19 models the chess position in Figure 4.17, naming the links among those specific pieces.

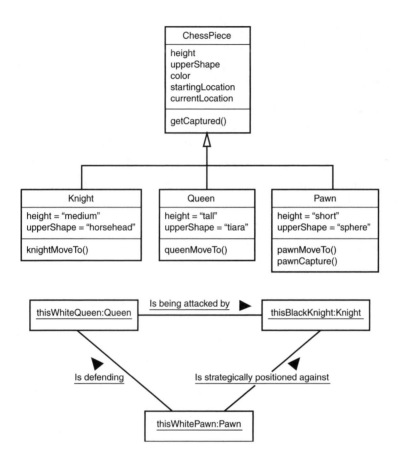

FIGURE 4.18
A class diagram of some chess pieces.

FIGURE 4.19
An object diagram that models the chess position shown in Figure 4.17.

Summary

Without relationships, a class model would be little more than a laundry list of rectangles that represent a vocabulary. Relationships show how the terms in the vocabulary connect with one another to provide a picture of the slice of the world you're modeling. The association is the fundamental conceptual connection between classes. Each class in an association plays a role, and multiplicity specifies how many objects in one class relate to one object in the associated class. Many types of multiplicities are possible. An association is represented as a line between the class rectangles with the roles and multiplicities at either end. Like a class, an association can have attributes and operations.

A class can inherit attributes and operations from another class. The inheriting class is the child of the parent class it inherits from. You discover inheritance when you find classes in your initial model that have common attributes and operations. Abstract classes are intended only as bases for inheritance and provide no objects of their own. Inheritance is represented as a line between the parent and the child with an open triangle adjoining (and pointing to) the parent.

In a dependency, one class uses another. The most common usage of a dependency is to show that a signature in the operation of one class uses another class. A dependency is depicted as a dashed line joining the two classes in the dependency, with an arrowhead adjoining (and pointing to) the depended-on class.

Class diagrams show general definitional information about classes. To model specific instances of classes at specific instants in time, use an object diagram.

Q&A

Q. *Do you ever provide a name for an inheritance relationship, as you do for an association?*

A. The UML doesn't stop you from naming an inheritance relationship, but usually it's not necessary.

Q. *When I'm modeling inheritance, can I also show other kinds of relationships in the same model?*

A. Absolutely. A model isn't constrained to showing just one kind of relationship.

Q. *In Figure 4.18, in the ChessPiece class, you show the properties color, startingLocation, and currentLocation along with the getCaptured() operation. You don't show those attributes and that operation in the Knight, Queen, or Pawn subclasses. Those classes have those features. Why don't you show them?*

A. The inheritance symbol—the open triangle with the solid line connector—implies that the subclasses have those attributes. That's what inheritance is all about. A child class has all the attributes and operations of the parent class.

Q. *While we're on the subject of Figure 4.18, let me ask you this: The subclasses show values for their two attributes. I thought that was something you show in object diagrams. What's the story?*

A. Values for attributes certainly do appear in object diagrams. Recall from Hour 3 that you have the option of showing a default value for a class's attribute.

Workshop

The quiz and the exercises are designed to firm up your knowledge of the UML in the area of relationships. Each question and exercise requires you to think about the modeling symbology you just learned and apply it to a situation. The answers to the Quiz are in Appendix A, "Quiz Answers."

By the Way

> **It's in the Cards**
>
> Here's a hint for doing exercises that involve classes: Get a set of 3×5 index cards and let one card represent one class. That is, write the name of the class at the top of the card and write attributes and operations on the lines below. This will help you conceive of a class as a tangible thing you can manipulate. Arrange the cards in the way you'll ultimately draw them in your model. It's the next best thing to having a modeling tool.

Quiz

1. How do you represent multiplicity?

2. How do you discover inheritance?

3. What is an abstract class?

4. What's the effect of a qualifier?

Exercises

1. Take the initial basketball model from Hour 3 and add links that express the relationships you covered in this hour. If you know the game of basketball, feel free to add links that represent your knowledge.

2. According to an old adage, "An attorney who defends himself has a fool for a client." Create a model that reflects this piece of wisdom.

3. Draw an inheritance hierarchy of the objects in your residence. Be sure to include any abstract classes as well as all instances.

4. Think back to the subjects you've taken in school. Model this set of subjects as an inheritance hierarchy, again with all abstract classes and instances. Include dependencies in this model. (Weren't some courses prerequisites for others?)

5. Imagine an association between the classes Dog and Person. Now imagine the same association between Cat and Person. Draw each association and attach an association class to each one. Use the association classes to show how these associations differ from one another.

6. Augment the ChessPiece class in Figure 4.18 to show the constraints on the height, upperShape, and color attributes. For upperShape, you'll have to think up some clever names for the shape at the top of Bishop, Rook, and King.

7. If you play chess and if you feel ambitious, complete Figure 4.18 to model all the chess pieces. Then create an object diagram that models the start of a chess game. Include values for all the attributes. For the location attributes, you'll have to look up the naming system for the locations on a chessboard. If you're a chess aficionado, you know that chess pieces have point values: Add that attribute to ChessPiece and the default values to the subclasses.

HOUR 5

Understanding Aggregations, Composites, Interfaces, and Realizations

---

What You'll Learn in This Hour:

- ▶ How to model classes that consist of other classes
- ▶ How to model interfaces and their connections with classes
- ▶ The concept of visibility

You've learned about associations, multiplicities, and inheritance. You're almost ready to create meaningful class diagrams. In this hour, you'll learn the final pieces of the puzzle, as you delve into additional types of relationships and other issues connected with classes. The ultimate goal is to be able to create a static view of a system, complete with all the interconnections among the system's classes.

Aggregations

Sometimes a class consists of a number of component classes. This is a special type of relationship called an **aggregation**. The components and the class they constitute are in a *part-whole* association. In Hour 2, "Understanding Object-Orientation," I mentioned that your home computer system is an aggregation that consists of a CPU box, a keyboard, a mouse, a monitor, a CD-ROM drive, one or more hard drives, a modem, a disk drive, a printer, and possibly some speakers. Along with the drives, the CPU box holds RAM, a graphics card, and a sound card (and probably some other items).

You represent an aggregation as a hierarchy with the "whole" class (for instance, the computer system) at the top and the components below. A line joins a whole to a component, with an open diamond on the line near the whole. Figure 5.1 shows the computer system as an aggregation.

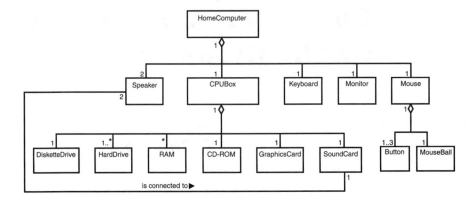

Although this example shows each component belonging to one whole, in an aggregation this isn't necessarily the case. For example, in a home entertainment system, a single remote control might be a component both of a television and of a VCR.

Constraints on Aggregations

Sometimes the set of possible components in an aggregation falls into an Or relationship. In some restaurants, a meal consists of soup or salad, a main course, and a dessert. To model this, you would use a *constraint*—the word *or* within curly brackets on a dotted line that connects the two part-whole lines, as Figure 5.2 shows.

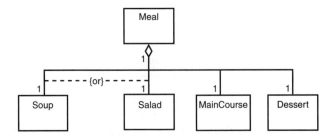

By the Way

> **Consistency in Constraints**
>
> Note the consistency between the use of {or} in Figure 5.2 (which shows a constraint on an aggregation) and the previous use of {or} in Figure 4.6 (which shows a constraint in an association).

Composites

A **composite** is a strong type of aggregation. Each component in a composite can belong to just one whole. The components of a coffee table—the tabletop and the legs—make up a composite. The symbol for a composite is the same as the symbol for an aggregation except the diamond is filled, as shown in Figure 5.3.

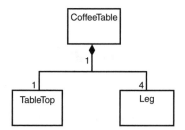

FIGURE 5.3
In a composite, each component belongs to exactly one whole. A closed diamond represents this relationship.

Composite Structure Diagram

The composite is one way to show the components of a class. If you want to give the sense of showing the class's internal structure, you can go a step further with the UML 2.0 **composite structure diagram**.

Here's an example. Suppose you're creating a model of a shirt. Figure 5.4 shows the shirt as a large class rectangle with its components nested inside. The nested diagram shows how the components of the shirt relate to one another.

The composite structure diagram focuses attention on the shirt and its internal components.

This type of diagramming isn't totally new in UML 2.0. In version 1.x this was a technique called *context diagramming*.

FIGURE 5.4
A composite structure diagram shows the components of a class as a diagram nested inside a large class rectangle.

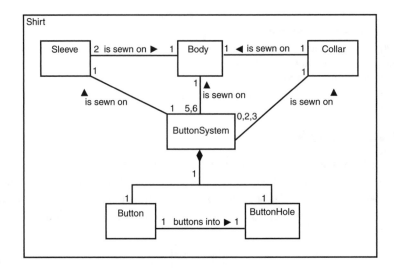

Interfaces and Realizations

In Hour 2, I mentioned *encapsulation*—the idea that an object hides its operations from other objects. When you lock your car, for example, the car doesn't show you how it performs the lockup operation. When you change channels on your TV, your TV doesn't let you see how it's done. If these operations are hidden, how do you get the car or the TV to perform them?

The car and the TV both receive a message (a request to perform an operation) through an interface. An **interface** is a set of operations that specifies some aspect of a class's behavior, and it's a set of operations a class presents to other classes.

An example will help clarify the interface concept. Every time you use a washing machine, you don't rip it apart to get to the underlying circuitry so that you can turn it on and set the time parameters. You don't get into the plumbing to start and stop the water flow. Instead, you get the washing machine to perform those operations by turning a control knob, shown in Figure 5.5. As a result of manipulating the knob, you can turn the machine on or off or set some parameter related to washing your clothes.

The control knob is the washing machine's interface. What operations does the control knob have? They're pretty simple. The control knob can close a connection or break a connection, and it can turn clockwise or counterclockwise by some number of degrees.

The control knob's operations are, in a sense, abstract. Closing or breaking a connection, turning clockwise or counterclockwise—these don't accomplish anything of value unless the control knob is attached to something. In this case it's attached to a washing machine. It's almost as if the washing machine makes the control knob's operations "real" by translating them into washing-related operations—like turning the machine on or off, or setting a parameter (the duration of the wash cycle, for example).

In UMLspeak, we'd say that the washing machine guarantees that part of its behavior will "*realize*" the control knob's behavior. For this reason, the relationship between a class and its interface is called **realization**.

Why "part of its behavior"? Because it's not the case that all of the washing machine's operations have to do with control knobs. Some operations, like acceptClothes() and acceptDetergent(), are accessible via the washing machine's drum.

Throughout all this, you might have noticed numerous references to an interface's operations, but nothing about its attributes. That's because as far as we're concerned, it doesn't have any. Yes, a control knob has a radius and thickness, and perhaps attributes like make and model. The point is that we don't care about them. When it comes to interfaces, all we're concerned with are their operations.

You model an interface the same way you model a class, with a rectangle icon. The difference is that this icon has no attributes. You'll recall that you can elide the attributes out of the representation of a class. How then do you distinguish between an interface and a class that just doesn't show its attributes? One way is to add the keyword «interface» above the name of the interface in the rectangle. Another is to put the letter *I* at the beginning of the name of any interface.

The symbol for the realization relationship between a class and its interface looks like the symbol for inheritance, except the line to the open triangle is dashed instead of solid. Figure 5.6 shows the realization between WashingMachine and ControlKnob.

FIGURE 5.6
An interface is a collection of operations that a class carries out. A class is related to an interface via realization, indicated by a dashed line with an open triangle that points to the interface.

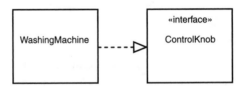

Another (elided) way to represent a class and an interface is with a small circle connected by a line to the class, as in Figure 5.7. (This is sometimes called a *lollipop diagram*.)

FIGURE 5.7
The elided way of representing a class realizing an interface.

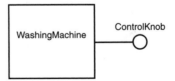

By the Way

Inheritance Versus Realization

Because of the similarity in the notation for inheritance and the notation for realization, you might take a moment to consider these two. Think of inheritance as the relationship between a parent and a child: The parent passes on physical attributes (eye color, hair color, and so on) to the child, and the child also takes on behaviors from the parent. Think of realization as something like the relationship between a teacher and a student: The teacher doesn't pass on any physical attributes to the student, but the student learns behaviors and procedures from the teacher. The student might reuse those behaviors to accomplish his or her own goals.

A class can realize more than one interface, and an interface can be realized by more than one class.

By the Way

Interfaces Everywhere

Interfaces are all around us. In fact, we're so accustomed to seeing them that we typically think of them as integral parts of whatever they happen to be attached to.

Control knobs, in particular, are part of all kinds of appliances. In addition to helping us manipulate washing machines, for example, they enable us to turn radios on and off and to adjust the volume and the reception. You can undoubtedly think of all kinds of other places where you see control knobs.

Leveraging our intuitive use of this little interface, one enterprising company markets a control knob as an input device for computers: Nashville, Tennessee-based Griffin Technology sells PowerMate, a USB-connected control knob you can program to perform just about any function you can do with a keyboard. Proud owners typically say, "It's incredibly useless—and I use it every day!"

Because we depend on the interface to get us to the washing machine's operations, we model the interaction through the interface as a dependency. In Hour 4, "Working with Relationships," you saw that the dependency symbol is a dashed line with an arrowhead. Figure 5.8 shows what I mean.

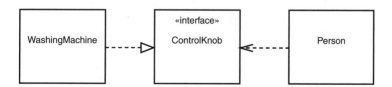

FIGURE 5.8
To model interaction with a class through its interface, use a dependency symbol.

In UML 1.x, the dependency arrow worked with both the full and elided notations for the interface. UML 2.0 introduces the "ball-and-socket" symbol for the elided version (see Figure 5.9).

FIGURE 5.9
UML 2.0's "ball-and-socket" notation for modeling interaction through an elided interface symbol.

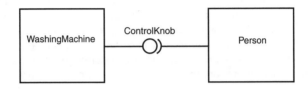

Interfaces and Ports

UML 2.0 takes the interface concept a step further by allowing you to model the connection between an interface and a class.

Think of your mouse as an interface to your computer. You can do a couple of things with it—point and click (and roll that little wheel in the middle, if you have that kind of mouse). By themselves these operations are worthless until your computer "realizes" them. That is, you can use these operations to locate the cursor and to select items.

How does the mouse connect to your computer? Follow the cable from the mouse to the back of your computer and you'll see a *port*—an access point that the mouse plugs into. Of course, your computer also has a serial port, a parallel port, and one or more USB ports. These ports are the points through which the computer interacts with its environment.

UML 2.0 provides a symbol that models these interaction points. As Figure 5.10 shows, the port symbol is a small square on the border of the class icon, and the square is connected to the interface.

FIGURE 5.10
UML 2.0's symbol for the port shows the point through which a class interacts with its environment.

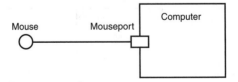

Visibility

Closely related to interfaces and realizations is the concept of visibility. **Visibility** applies to attributes or operations and specifies the extent to which other classes can use a given class's attributes or operations (or an interface's operations). Three levels of visibility are possible. At the **public** level, usability extends to other classes. At the **protected** level, usability is open only to classes that inherit from the original class. At the **private** level, only the original class can use the attribute or operation. In a television set, changeVolume() and changeChannel() are public operations, paintImageOnScreen() is a private one. In an automobile, accelerate() and brake() are public operations, updateMileageCount() is protected.

Realization, as you might imagine, implies that the public level applies to every operation in an interface. Shielding the operations via either of the other levels would make no sense, as an interface is intended for realization by a multitude of classes.

To denote the public level, precede the attribute or operation with a "+"; to denote the protected level, precede it with a "#"; and to denote private, precede it with a "–". Figure 5.11 shows the aforementioned public, protected, and private operations in a television and in an automobile.

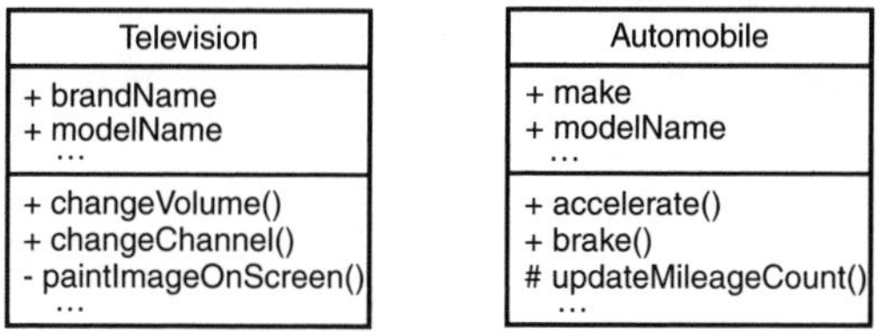

Television
+ brandName
+ modelName
...
+ changeVolume()
+ changeChannel()
- paintImageOnScreen()
...

Automobile
+ make
+ modelName
...
+ accelerate()
+ brake()
# updateMileageCount()
...

FIGURE 5.11
Public and private operations in a television, and public and protected operations in an automobile.

Scope

Scope is another concept relevant to attributes and operations and how they relate across a system. Two kinds of scope are possible. In **instance** scope, each instance of a class has its own value for the attribute or operation. In **classifier** scope, only one value of the attribute or operation exists across all instances of the class. A classifier-scoped attribute or operation appears with its name underlined. This type of scoping is usually used when a specified group of instances (and no others) has to share the exact values of a private attribute. Instance scoping is by far the more common type of scope.

Summary

To complete your knowledge about classes and how they connect, it's necessary to understand some additional relationships. An aggregation specifies a part-whole association: A "whole" class is made up of component classes. A component in an aggregation may be part of more than one whole. A composite is a strong form of aggregation, in that a component in a composite can be part of only one whole. The UML representation of aggregations is similar to the representation of composites. The association line joining a part to a whole has a diamond adjoining the whole. In an aggregation, the diamond is open; in a composite it's closed.

A composite structure diagram visualizes the internal structure of a class by showing classes nested inside that class.

A realization is an association between a class and an interface, a collection of operations that a number of classes can use. An interface is represented as a class with no attributes. To distinguish it from a class whose attributes have been elided from the diagram, the keyword «interface» appears above the interface's name or an uppercase "I" precedes the interface's name. Realization is represented in the UML as a dashed line that connects the class to the interface, with an open triangle adjoining the interface and pointing to it. Another way to represent a realization is with a solid line connecting a class to a small circle, with the circle standing for the interface.

UML 2.0 adds a symbol for the port, a point through which a class interacts with its environment. The symbol is a small square on the border of the class. The square connects to the interface.

In terms of visibility, all the operations in an interface are public, so that any class can use them. Two other levels of visibility are protected (usability extends to children of the class that owns the attributes and operations) and private (attributes and operations are usable only by the owning class). A "+" denotes public visibility, "#" denotes protected, and "–" denotes private.

Scope is another aspect of attributes and operations. In instance scoping, each object in a class has its own value of an attribute or operation. In classification scoping, one value exists for a particular attribute or operation throughout a set of objects in a class. Objects not in that set have no access to the classification-scoped value.

Q&A

Q. *Is aggregation considered transitive? In other words, if class 3 is a component of class 2 and class 2 is a component of class 1, is class 3 a component of class 1?*

A. Yes, aggregation is transitive. In the earlier example, the mouse buttons and mouse ball are part of the mouse and also part of the computer system.

Q. *Does "interface" imply "user interface" or GUI?*

A. No. It's more generic than that. An interface is just a set of operations that one class presents to other classes, one of which may (but not necessarily) be the user.

Workshop

The quiz and exercises will test and strengthen your knowledge about aggregations, composites, contexts, and interfaces. The answers appear in Appendix A, "Quiz Answers."

Quiz

1. What is the difference between an aggregation and a composite?

2. What is realization? How is realization similar to inheritance? How does realization differ from inheritance?

3. How do you model interaction through an interface?

4. Name the three levels of visibility and describe what each one means.

Exercises

1. Create a composite structure diagram of a magazine. Consider the table of contents, editorial, articles, and columns.

2. Today's most popular type of GUI is the WIMP (Windows, Icons, Menus, Pointer) interface. Using all the appropriate UML knowledge you've acquired thus far, draw a class diagram of the WIMP interface. In addition to the classes named in the acronym, include related items such as the scrollbar and cursor and any other necessary classes.

3. Construct a model of an electric pencil sharpener showing all relevant attributes and operations. What is its interface?

4. Model a computer as a class and a touchpad as its interface. List the operations of the touchpad. Also, show some of the operations in the computer that you access via the touchpad. In your model, include a class that represents the user. Use both the full representation and the elided representation from UML 2.0.

HOUR 6

Introducing Use Cases

What You'll Learn in This Hour:

- ▶ What use cases are
- ▶ The ideas behind creating, including, and extending use cases
- ▶ How to start a use case analysis

In the past three hours, you've dealt with diagrams that provide a static view of the classes in a system. You're going to ultimately move into diagrams that provide a dynamic view and show how the system and its classes change over time. The static view helps an analyst communicate with a client. The dynamic view, as you'll see, helps an analyst communicate with a team of developers, and helps the developers create programs.

The client and the development team make up an important set of stakeholders in a system. One equally important part of the picture is missing, however—the user. Neither the static view nor the dynamic view shows the system's behavior from the user's point of view. Understanding that point of view is key to building systems that are both useful and usable—that is, that meet requirements and are easy (and even fun) to work with.

Modeling a system from a user's point of view is the job of the use case. In this hour you'll learn all about what use cases are and what they do. In the next hour you'll learn how to use the UML's use case diagram to visualize a use case.

Use Cases: What They Are

I recently bought a digital camera. When I was shopping for it, I encountered a wide variety of possibilities. How did I decide which one to buy? I asked myself exactly what I wanted to do with a camera. Did I want extreme portability or did I want a larger camera with a bigger lens? Would I be taking distance shots? Did I want to take pictures and post them on the Web? Did I primarily want to make prints? If so, how large? Did I want to make short movies? With sound?

We all go through a process like this when we make a non-impulse purchase. What we're doing is a form of **use case analysis**: We're asking ourselves how we're going to use the product or system we're about to shell out good money for, so we can settle on something that meets our requirements. The important thing is to know what those requirements are.

This kind of process is particularly crucial for the analysis phase of system development. How users will use a system drives the way you design and build it.

The use case is a construct that helps analysts work with users to determine system usage. A collection of use cases depicts a system in terms of what users intend to do with it.

Think of a use case as a collection of scenarios about system use. Each scenario describes a sequence of events. Each sequence is initiated by a person, another system, a piece of hardware, or by the passage of time. Entities that initiate sequences are called **actors**. The result of the sequence has to be something of use either to the actor who initiated it or to another actor.

Use Cases: Why They're Important

Just as the class diagram is a great way to stimulate a client to talk about a system from his or her viewpoint, the use case is an excellent tool for stimulating potential users to talk about a system from their own viewpoints. It's not always easy for users to articulate how they intend to use a system. Because traditional system development was often a haphazard process that was short on up-front analysis, users are sometimes stunned when anyone asks for their input.

The idea is to get system users involved in the early stages of system analysis and design. This increases the likelihood that the system ultimately becomes a boon to the people it's supposed to help—instead of a monument to clever cutting-edge computing concepts that business users find incomprehensible and impossible to work with.

An Example: The Soda Machine

Suppose you're starting out to design a soda machine. In order to get the user's point of view, you interview a number of potential users as to how they'll interact with the machine.

Because the main function of a soda machine is to allow a customer to buy a can of soda, it's likely the users will quickly tell you that you're concerned with a set of scenarios—a use case, in other words—that you could label "Buy soda." Let's examine each possible scenario in this use case. In normal system development, remember, these scenarios would emerge through conversations with users.

FIGURE 6.1
A use case specifies a set of scenarios for accomplishing something useful for an actor. In this example, one use case is "Buy soda."

The "Buy Soda" Use Case

The actor in this use case is a customer who wants to purchase a can of soda. The customer initiates the scenario by inserting money into the machine. He or she then makes a selection. If everything goes smoothly, the machine has at least one can of the selected soda in stock, and presents a cold can of the soda to the customer.

In addition to the sequence of steps, other aspects of the scenario deserve consideration. What preconditions motivate the customer to initiate this scenario in the "Buy soda" use case? Thirst is the most obvious one. What postconditions result as a consequence of the scenario's steps? Again, the obvious one is that the customer has a soda.

Is the scenario I described the only possible one for "Buy soda"? Others immediately come to mind. It's possible that the machine is out of the soda the customer wants. It's possible that the customer doesn't have the exact amount of money the soda costs. How should you design the soda machine to handle these scenarios?

Let's turn to the out-of-soda scenario, another sequence of steps in the "Buy soda" use case. Think of it as an alternative path through the use case. The customer initiates the use case by inserting money into the machine. He or she then makes a selection. The machine does not have at least one can of the selected soda, so it presents a message to the customer, saying it's out of that brand. Ideally, the message should prompt the customer to make another selection. The machine should also offer the customer the option of getting his or her money back. At this point the customer selects another brand and the machine delivers (if it's not sold out of the new selection), or takes the option of receiving the money. The precondition is a thirsty customer. The postcondition is either a can of soda or the returned money.

Another Out-of-Soda Scenario

Of course, another out-of-soda scenario is possible: The "out of brand" message could display as soon as the machine's stock disappears and remain on until the machine is resupplied. In that case, the user might not insert money in the first place. The client for whom you're designing the machine might prefer the first scenario: If the customer has already inserted money, the tendency might be to make another selection rather than to ask the machine to return the money.

Now let's look at the incorrect-amount-of-money scenario. Once again, the customer initiates the use case in the usual way, and then makes a selection. Let's assume the machine has the selection in stock. If the machine has a reserve of appropriate change on hand, it returns the difference and delivers the soda. If the machine doesn't have a reserve of change, it returns the money and presents a message that prompts the user for correct change. The precondition is the usual one. The postcondition is either a can of soda along with change, or the returned money that was originally deposited.

Another possibility is that as soon as the machine's change reserve is depleted, a message appears informing potential customers that correct change is required. The message would remain visible until the machine's reserve is resupplied.

Additional Use Cases

You've examined the soda machine from the viewpoint of one user: the customer. Other users enter the picture as well. A supplier has to restock the machine, (Figure 6.2) and a collector (possibly the same person as the supplier) has to collect the accumulated money from the machine (Figure 6.3). This tells us we should create at least two more use cases, "Restock" and "Collect money," whose details emerge through interviews with suppliers and collectors.

FIGURE 6.2
Restocking a soda machine is an important use case.

FIGURE 6.3
Collecting the money from a soda machine is another important use case.

Consider the "Restock" use case. The supplier initiates this use case because some interval (say, two weeks) has passed. The supplier's representative unsecures the machine (probably by unlocking a lock, but that gets into implementation), pulls open the front of the machine, and fills each brand's compartment to capacity.

The representative also refills the change reserve. The representative then closes the front of the machine and secures it. The precondition is the passage of the interval, the postcondition is that the supplier has a new set of potential sales.

For the "Collect money" use case, the collector also initiates because an interval has passed. He or she would follow the same sequence of steps as in "Restock" to unsecure the machine and pull open the front. The collector then removes the money from the machine, and follows the "Restock" steps of closing and securing the machine. The precondition is the passage of the interval, and the postcondition is the money in the hands of the collector.

Notice that when we derive a use case, we don't worry about how to implement it. In our example we're not concerned with the insides of the soda machine. We don't care about how the refrigeration mechanism works, or how the machine keeps track of its money. We're just trying to see how the soda machine will look to someone who has to use it.

The objective is to derive a collection of use cases that we will ultimately show to the people who will design the soda machine and the people who will build it. To the extent our use cases reflect what customers, collectors, and suppliers want, the result will be a machine that all these groups can easily use.

Including a Use Case

In the "Restock" use case and the "Collect" use case, you'll note some common steps. Both begin with unsecuring the machine and pulling it open, both end with closing the machine and securing it. Can we eliminate the duplication of steps from use case to use case?

We can. The way to do it is to take each sequence of common steps and form an additional use case from each one. Let's combine the "unsecure" and "pull open" steps into a use case called "Expose the inside" and the "close machine" and "secure" steps into a use case called "Unexpose the inside." (OK. I've invented a word here—*unexpose*. *Hide* or *conceal* just didn't seem appropriate!) Figure 6.4 illustrates these combinations of steps.

With these new use cases in hand, the "Restock" use case starts off with the "Expose the inside" use case. The supplier's representative then goes through the steps as before and concludes with the "Unexpose the inside" use case. Similarly, the "Collect" use case starts off with the "Expose the inside" use case, proceeds as before, and finishes with the "Unexpose the inside" use case.

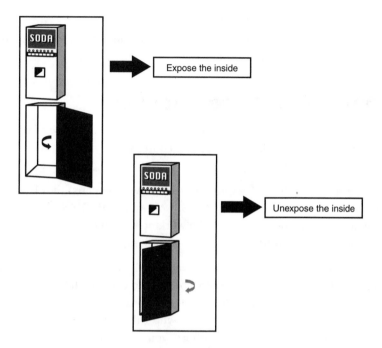

FIGURE 6.4
You can combine some of the steps that make up a use case. The combination of steps constitutes an additional use case.

As you can see, "Restock" and "Collect" include the new use cases. Accordingly, this technique of reusing a use case is referred to as **including a use case.**

More on Including

Early versions of the UML referred to *including* a use case as *using* a use case. You might still see the old way in print. The term *including* has two advantages. First, it's clearer: The steps in one use case *include* the steps of another. Second, it avoids the potential confusion of putting *using* near the *use* in *use case*. That way, we won't have to say we "promote reuse by using a use case."

By the Way

Extending a Use Case

It's possible to reuse a use case in a way other than inclusion. Sometimes we create a new use case by adding some steps to an existing use case.

Let's go back to the "Restock" use case. Before putting new cans of soda into the machine, suppose the supplier's representative notes the brands that sold well and the brands that did not. Instead of simply restocking all the brands, the rep might pull out the brands that haven't sold well and replace them with cans of the brands that have proven to be more popular. He or she would then also have to indicate on the front of the machine the new assortment of available brands.

If we add these steps to "Restock" we'll have a new use case that we can call "Restock according to sales." This new use case is an extension of the original, and this technique is called **extending a use case**.

Starting a Use Case Analysis

In our example we jumped right into use cases and focused on a few of them. In the real world, you usually follow a set of procedures when you start a use case analysis.

You begin with the client interviews (and interviews with experts) that lead to the initial class diagrams we discussed in Hour 3, "Working with Object-Orientation." This gives you some idea of the area you're working in and a familiarity with the terms you'll be using. You then have a basis for talking with users.

You interview users (preferably in a group) and ask them to tell you everything they would do with the system you're getting ready to design. Their answers form a set of candidate use cases. Next, it's important to briefly describe each use case. You also have to derive a list of all the actors who will initiate and benefit from the use cases. As you get more into this phase, you'll increase your ability to speak to the users in their language.

Use cases crop up in several phases of the development process. They help with the design of a system's user interface, they help developers make programming choices, and they provide the basis for testing the newly constructed system.

To go any further with use case analysis you're going to have to apply the UML, and that's the subject for the next hour.

Summary

The use case is a construct for describing how a system will look to potential users. It's a collection of scenarios initiated by an entity called an actor (a person, a piece of hardware, a passage of time, or another system). A use case should result in something of value for either the actor who initiated it or for another actor.

It's possible to reuse use cases. One way ("inclusion") is to use the steps from one use case as part of the sequence of steps in another use case. Another way ("extension") is to create a new use case by adding steps to an existing use case.

Interviewing users is the best technique for deriving use cases. When deriving a use case, it's important to note the preconditions for initiating the use case, and the postconditions that result as a consequence of the use case.

You should interview users after you interview clients and generate a list of candidate classes. This will give you a foundation in the terminology that you'll use to talk with the users. It's a good idea to interview a group of users. The objective is to derive a list of candidate use cases and all possible actors.

Q&A

Q. *Why do we really need the use case concept? Can't we just ask users what they want to see in a system and leave it at that?*

A. Not really. We have to add structure to what the users tell us, and use cases provide the structure. The structure comes in handy when you have to take the results of your interviews with users and communicate those results to clients and developers.

Q. *When we talk to users, are we constrained to just listing the use cases they tell us about?*

A. Definitely not. In fact, an important part of the process is to build on what users tell you and try to discover use cases they might not have thought about.

Q. *How difficult is it to derive use cases?*

A. In my experience, listing the use cases—at least the high-level ones—isn't all that difficult. Some difficulty arises when you're delving into each one and trying to get the users to list the steps in each scenario. When you're building a system that replaces an existing way of doing things, users typically know these steps so well and have used them so often they find it difficult to articulate them. It's a good idea to have a panel of users, because the discussion in the group typically brings out ideas that an individual user might have trouble expressing.

Workshop

This hour was theory rather than UML. For this workshop, the objective is to understand the theoretical concepts and apply them in several contexts. The practice will firm up the concepts for you in advance of the next hour when you'll learn how to visualize them in the UML. The answers appear in Appendix A, "Quiz Answers."

Quiz

1. What do you call the entity that initiates a use case?

2. What is meant by *including* a use case?

3. What is meant by *extending* a use case?

4. Is a use case the same as a scenario?

Exercises

1. Think of something you just purchased where you faced an array of choices. What use cases were you thinking of when you made your decision?

2. List the use cases associated with a home entertainment center.

3. For our soda machine example, create another use case that includes the "Expose the inside" and the "Unexpose the inside" use cases.

4. Use cases can help you analyze a business as well as a system. Consider a computer superstore that sells hardware, peripherals, and software. Who are the actors? What are some of the major use cases? What are some scenarios within each use case?

HOUR 7

Working with Use Case Diagrams

What You'll Learn in This Hour:

▶ How to represent a use case model
▶ How to visualize relationships among use cases
▶ How to create and apply use case models

The use case is a powerful concept for helping an analyst understand how a system should behave. It helps you gather requirements from the users' point of view. In this hour, you'll learn how to visualize the use case concepts you learned in the last hour.

As powerful as the use case concept is, use cases become even more powerful when you use the UML to visualize them. Visualization allows you to show use cases to users so they can give you additional information. It's a fact of life that users often know more than they can articulate: The use case helps break the ice. Also, a visual representation allows you to combine use case diagrams with other kinds of diagrams.

One of the objectives of the system analysis process is to generate a collection of use cases. The idea is to be able to catalog and reference this collection, which serves as the users' view of the system. When it's time to upgrade the system, the use case catalog serves as a basis for gathering the requirements of the upgrade.

Representing a Use Case Model

An actor initiates a use case, and an actor (possibly the initiator, but not necessarily) receives something of value from the use case. The graphic representation is straightforward: An ellipse represents a use case, and a stick figure represents an actor. The initiating actor is on the left of the use case, and the receiving actor is on the right. (Many modelers omit the receiving actor, and the UML 2.0 specification doesn't mention it.) The actor's name appears just below the actor. The name of the use case appears either inside the ellipse or just below it. An association line connects an actor to the use case, and represents communication between the actor and the use case. The association line is solid, like the line that connects associated classes.

One of the benefits of use case analysis is that it shows the boundary between the system and the outside world. Actors are typically outside the system, whereas use cases are inside. You use a rectangle (with the name of the system somewhere inside) to represent the system boundary. The rectangle encloses the system's use cases.

The actors, use cases, and interconnecting lines make up a **use case model**. Figure 7.1 shows the symbols.

FIGURE 7.1
In a use case model, a stick figure represents an actor, an ellipse represents a use case, and an association line represents communication between the actor and the use case.

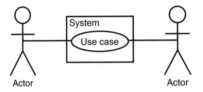

The Soda Machine Revisited

Let's apply the symbols to the example from the previous hour. As you'll recall, you developed use cases for a soda machine. The "Buy soda" use case sits inside the system along with "Restock" and "Collect." The actors are Customer, Supplier's Representative, and Collector. Figure 7.2 shows a UML use case model for the soda machine.

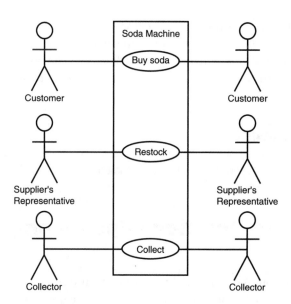

FIGURE 7.2
A use case model
of the soda
machine from
Hour 6.

Tracking the Steps in the Scenarios

Each use case is a collection of scenarios, and each scenario is a sequence of steps. As you can see, those steps do not appear on the diagram. They're not in notes attached to the use cases. Although the UML doesn't prohibit this, clarity is key in creating any diagram and attaching notes to every use case would make the diagram too busy. How and where do you keep track of the steps?

Your use case diagrams will usually be part of a design document that the client and the development team refer to. Each diagram will have its own page. Each scenario of each use case will also have its own page, listing in text form

- ▶ The actor who initiates the use case
- ▶ Assumptions for the use case
- ▶ Preconditions for the use case
- ▶ Steps in the scenario
- ▶ Postconditions when the scenario is complete
- ▶ The actor who benefits from the use case

You can also include a brief, one-sentence description of the scenario. Note that this text page is outside the boundaries of the UML. Thus, the UML doesn't specify any particular format for this.

Hour 6, "Introducing Use Cases," presented some alternative scenarios for the "Buy soda" use case. In your description, you can either list these scenarios separately ("Out-of-brand" and "Incorrect change"), or you can consider them exceptions to the first scenario in the use case. Exactly how you do all this is up to you, your client, and the users.

Another Possibility

To show the steps in a scenario, another possibility is to use a UML activity diagram (discussed in Hour 11, "Working with Activity Diagrams").

Visualizing Relationships Among Use Cases

The example in Hour 6 also showed two ways that use cases can relate to one another. One way, **inclusion**, enables you to reuse one use case's steps inside another use case. The other way, **extension**, allows you to create a new use case by adding steps to an existing use case.

Two other kinds of relationships are generalization and grouping. As is the case for classes, **generalization** has one use case inheriting from another. **Grouping** is a simple way of organizing a set of use cases.

Inclusion

Let's examine the "Restock" and "Collect" use cases from the Hour 6 example. Both begin with unsecuring the machine and pulling it open, and both end with closing the machine and securing it. The "Expose the inside" use case was created to capture the first pair of steps, and the "Unexpose the inside" use case to capture the second. Both "Restock" and "Collect" include these two use cases.

To represent inclusion, you use the symbol you used for dependency between classes—a dashed line connecting the classes with an arrowhead pointing to the depended-on class. Near the line, you add the keyword «include». Figure 7.3 shows the inclusion relationship in the use case model of the soda machine.

In the text notation that tracks the steps in the sequence, you indicate the included use cases. The first step in the "Restock" use case would be «include» (expose the inside).

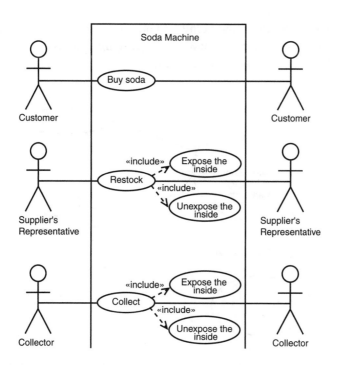

FIGURE 7.3
The soda machine
use case model
with inclusion.

Extension

Hour 6 showed that the "Restock" use case could be the basis of another use case: "Restock according to sales." Instead of just restocking the soda machine so that all brands end up with the same number of cans, the supplier's representative could take note of the brands that sold well and the brands that did not, and restock accordingly. The new use case is said to *extend* the original one because it adds new steps to the sequence in the original use case, also called the **base use case**.

Extension can only take place at specific designated points within the base use case's sequence. These points are called, appropriately, **extension points**. In the "Restock" use case, the new steps (noting the sales and designating the appropriate refills) would occur before the supplier's representative opened the machine and was ready to fill the compartments of the soda brands. For this example, the extension point is "before filling the compartments."

Like inclusion, you visualize extension with a dependency line (dashed line and arrowhead) along with a keyword. In this case the keyword is «extend». Within the base use case, the extension point appears in a compartment named "extension point" (or "extension points" if you have more than one) below the name of the use case. Figure 7.4 shows the extension relationship for "Restock" and "Restock according to sales" along with the inclusion relationships for "Restock" and "Collect."

FIGURE 7.4
A use case diagram showing extension and inclusion.

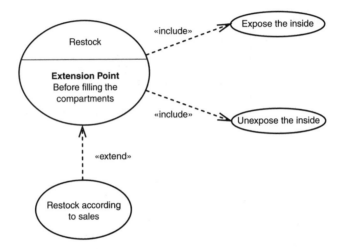

It's important to be aware that the locations of the use cases in the use case diagram don't signify anything. In Figure 7.4, for example, "Expose the inside" is above "Unexpose the inside." This does not mean that "Expose the inside" precedes "Unexpose the inside." Common sense tells you that it does, but the use case diagram doesn't take that into account.

Some have tried to number the use cases in order to show their order. This is way more trouble than it's worth, particularly when a use case is included in several others. If it's included in Use Case 3 and Use Case 4, is it Use Case 3.1? Or is it 4.1? Suppose it's the first included use case in Use Case 3, but the second in Use Case 4. Then what?

It's best to understand that the intent of the use case diagram is to show what the use cases are without specifying their order of occurrence. (In that spirit, see the accompanying sidebar "Extension, Inclusion, and Confusion.")

By the Way

Extension, Inclusion, and Confusion

In my experience, people who are used to modeling process flows (from pre-UML times) are sometimes confused by the direction of dependency arrows. The confusion often emerges when it comes to modeling extension and inclusion of use cases. This happens because process-flow veterans are used to seeing arrows that denote sequences of operations or activities: The first one in a sequence connects with the second one via an arrow that points from the first to the second.

Thus in a use case diagram that shows Use Case A including Use Case B, their tendency is to think that Use Case A takes place first, followed immediately by Use Case B. Many times—by the nature of inclusion—the opposite turns out to be true.

The key is to bear in mind that a dependency arrow doesn't specify the direction of a *process*. Instead, it specifies the direction of a *relationship*. A dependency arrow that starts at Use Case A and ends at Use Case B means that A *depends* on B, not that A *precedes* B.

Generalization

Classes can inherit from one another, and so can use cases. In use case inheritance, the child use case inherits behavior and meaning from the parent and adds its own behavior. You can apply the child wherever you apply the parent.

Suppose you're modeling a soda machine that allows a customer to buy either a can of soda or a cup of soda. In that case, "Buy soda" would be a parent use case, and "Buy a can of soda" and "Buy a cup of soda" would be child use cases. You model generalization of use cases the same way you model generalization of classes—with a solid line that has an open triangle pointing at the parent, as in Figure 7.5.

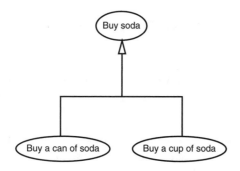

FIGURE 7.5
The generalization relationship works for use cases as well as for classes.

The generalization relationship can exist between actors, too. You might have represented both the supplier's representative and the collector as agents of the supplier. If you rename the representative as the Restocker, the Restocker and Collector are both children of the Supplier Agent, as Figure 7.6 shows.

FIGURE 7.6
Like classes and use cases, actors can be in a generalization relationship.

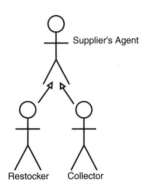

Grouping

In some use case diagrams, you might have a multitude of use cases and you'll want to organize them. This could happen when a system consists of a number of subsystems. Another possibility is when you're interviewing users in order to gather requirements for a system. Each requirement would be represented as a separate use case. You'll need some way of categorizing the requirements.

The most straightforward way to organize is to group related use cases into a package. A package, remember, appears as a tabbed folder. The grouped use cases appear inside the folder.

Use Case Diagrams in the Analysis Process

Given the example you worked with, you dived right in and applied the use case symbols. Now it's time to step back and put use cases in the context of an analysis effort.

Client interviews should start the process. These interviews will yield class diagrams that serve as the foundation for your knowledge of the system's domain (the area in which it will solve problems). After you know the general terminology of the client's area, you're ready to start talking to users.

Interviews with users begin in the terminology of the domain but should then shift into the terminology of the users. The initial results of the interviews should reveal actors and high-level use cases that describe functional requirements in general terms. This information provides the boundaries and scope of the system.

Later interviews with users delve into these requirements more closely, resulting in use case models that show the scenarios and sequences in detail. This might result in additional use cases that satisfy inclusion and extension relationships. In this phase it's important to rely on your understanding of the domain (from the class diagrams derived from client interviews). If you don't understand the domain well, you might create too many use cases and too much detail—a situation that could greatly impede design and development.

Applying Use Case Models: An Example

To further your understanding of use case models and how to apply them, let's take a look at a more complex example than a soda machine. Suppose you have to design a local area network (LAN) for a consulting firm, and you have to figure out the functionality to build into the LAN. How do you start?

Exactly What Is a LAN?

A LAN is a communication network that an organization uses over a limited distance. It allows users to share resources and information.

By the Way

Understanding the Domain

Begin with client interviews to create a class diagram that reflects what life is like in the world of consulting. The class diagram might include these classes: `Consultant`, `Client`, `Project`, `Proposal`, `Data`, and `Report`. Figure 7.7 shows what the diagram might look like.

Understanding the Users

Now that the domain is in hand, turn your attention to the users, because the objective is to figure out the kinds of functionality to build into the system.

In the real world, you would interview users. For this example you'll base your ideas on some general knowledge about LANs and about the domain. Bear in

FIGURE 7.7
A class diagram for
the consulting
world.

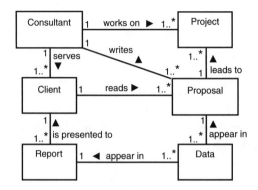

mind, however, that in real-world systems analysis, nothing can substitute for
interviews with real people.

One group of users will be consultants. Another will be clerical staff. Other potential users include corporate officers, marketers, network administrators, office
managers, and project managers. (Can you think of any others?)

At this point, it's helpful to show the users in a generalization hierarchy, as in
Figure 7.8.

FIGURE 7.8
The hierarchy of
users who will
interact with the
LAN.

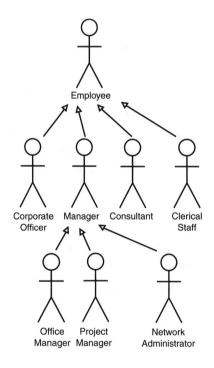

Understanding the Use Cases

What about the use cases? Here are some possibilities: "Provide security levels," "Create a proposal," "Store a proposal," "Use e-mail," "Share database information," "Perform accounting," "Connect to the LAN from outside the LAN," "Connect to the Internet," "Share database information," "Catalog proposals," "Use prior proposals," and "Share printers." Based on this information, Figure 7.9 shows the high-level use case diagram that we build.

This set of use cases constitutes the functional requirements for the LAN.

Drilling Down

Let's elaborate on one of the high-level use cases and build a use case model. One extremely important activity in a consulting firm is writing proposals, so let's examine the "Create a proposal" use case.

Interviews with consultants would probably tell you that a number of steps are involved in this use case. First of all, the initiating actor is a consultant. The consultant has to log on to the LAN and be verified as a valid user. Then he or she has to use office suite software (word processing, spreadsheet, and graphics) to write the proposal. In the process, the consultant might reuse portions of prior proposals. The consulting firm might have a policy that one corporate officer and two other consultants review a proposal before it goes to a client. To satisfy this policy, the consultant stores the proposal in a central repository accessible to the LAN and e-mails the three reviewers with a message telling them that the proposal is ready and informing them of its location. After receiving feedback and making necessary modifications (again, using the office suite software), the consultant prints out the proposal and mails it to the client. When everything's finished, the consultant logs off the network. The consultant has completed a proposal, and is the actor who benefits from the use case.

By the Way

Business Logic

When an interview reveals something like that "three reviewers" policy I just mentioned, take careful note. It means that you're starting to hear about a company's business logic—its set of rules for how it conducts itself. The more business logic you can find out, the better off you'll be as an analyst. You'll understand your client's corporate culture, and you'll be better able to understand organizational needs.

FIGURE 7.9
A high-level use case diagram of a LAN for a consulting firm.

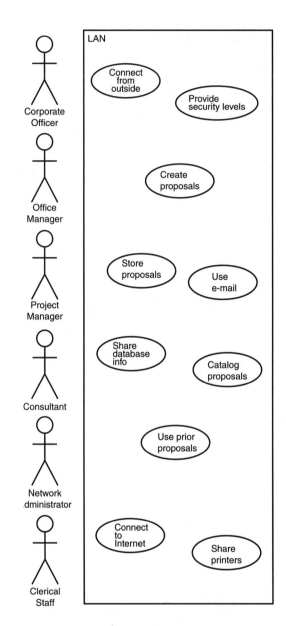

From the preceding sequence, it's clear some of the steps will be repeated from one use case to another, and thus lead to other (possibly included) use cases you might not have thought of before. Logging on and getting verified are two steps that numerous use cases can include. For this reason, you'd create a "Verify user"

use case that "Create a proposal" includes. Two other included use cases are "Use office suite software" and "Log off the network."

Additional thought about the proposal process might make you realize that the proposals written for new clients differ from the proposals written for existing clients. In fact, new-client proposals probably provide promotional information about the firm. This information usually precedes the statement of the problem. With existing clients, it's not necessary to send that kind of information. Thus, another new use case, "Create a proposal for a new client" extends "Create a proposal."

Figure 7.10 shows the use case diagram that results from this analysis of the "Create a proposal" use case.

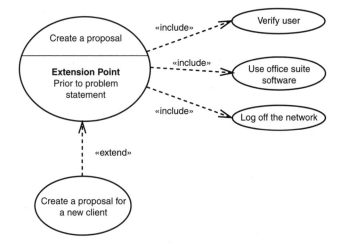

FIGURE 7.10
The "Create a proposal" use case in the LAN for a consulting firm.

This example brings home an important point—a point that was stressed before: The use case analysis describes the behavior of a system. It doesn't touch the implementation. This is particularly important here because the design of a LAN is far beyond the scope of this book!

Taking Stock of Where We Are

This is a good time to look at the overall structure of the UML because you've gone through two of its major aspects—object orientation and use case analysis. You've seen their foundations and symbols, and you've explored some applications.

In Hours 2–7, you worked with

>   Classes
>
>   Objects
>
>   Interfaces
>
>   Use cases
>
>   Actors
>
>   Associations
>
>   Generalizations
>
>   Dependencies
>
>   Realizations
>
>   Aggregations
>
>   Composites
>
>   Stereotypes
>
>   Constraints
>
>   Notes
>
>   Packages
>
>   Extensions
>
>   Inclusions

Let's try to partition this set of items into categories.

Structural Elements

Classes, objects, actors, interfaces, and use cases are five of the structural elements in the UML. Although they have a number of differences (which, as an exercise, you ought to enumerate), they are similar in that they represent either physical or conceptual parts of a model. As you proceed through Part I, you'll encounter additional structural elements.

Relationships

Associations, generalizations, dependencies, aggregations, composites, and realizations are the relationships in the UML. (Inclusion and extension are two kinds of dependencies.) Without relationships, UML models would just be lists of structural elements. The relationships connect those elements and thereby connect the models to reality.

Grouping

The package is the only grouping element in the UML. It allows you to organize the structural elements in a model. A package can hold any kind of structural element and can hold many different kinds at once.

Annotation

The note is the UML's annotation element. Notes enable you to attach constraints, comments, requirements, and explanatory graphics to your models.

Extension

Stereotypes and constraints are two constructs the UML provides for extending the language. They allow you to create new elements out of existing ones, so that you can adequately model the slice of reality your system will play in.

. . . And More

In addition to structural elements, relationships, grouping, annotation, and extension, the UML has another category—behavioral elements. These elements show how parts of a model (such as objects) change over time. You haven't dealt with these yet, but you will learn about one in the next hour.

The Big Picture

Now you have an idea of how the UML is organized. Figure 7.11 visualizes this organization for you. As you go through the remaining hours in Part I, keep this organization in mind. You'll keep adding to it as you go along, and this "big picture" will show you where to add the new knowledge you acquire.

Summary

The use case is a powerful tool for gathering functional requirements. Use case diagrams add still more power: Because they visualize use cases, they facilitate communication between analysts and users as well as between analysts and clients. In a use case diagram, the symbol for a use case is an ellipse. The symbol for an actor is a stick figure. An association line joins an actor to a use case. The use cases are usually inside a rectangle that represents the system boundary.

FIGURE 7.11
The organization of the UML, in terms of the elements you've dealt with thus far.

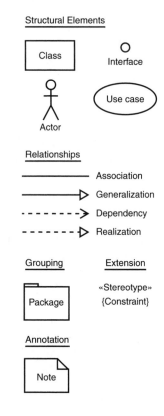

Structural Elements

Class   ○
               Interface

Actor   Use case

Relationships

———————————   Association

————————▷   Generalization

- - - - - - ->   Dependency

- - - - - - ▷   Realization

Grouping   Extension

               «Stereotype»
Package   {Constraint}

Annotation

Note

Inclusion is represented by a dependency line with the keyword «includes». Extension is represented by a dependency line with the keyword «extends». Two other relationships between use cases are generalization, in which one use case inherits the meaning and behaviors of another, and grouping, which organizes a set of use cases. Generalization is represented by the same generalization line that shows inheritance among classes. Grouping is represented by the package icon.

Use case diagrams figure heavily into the analysis process. Begin with client interviews that yield class diagrams. The class diagrams provide a foundation for interviewing users. User interviews result in a high-level use case diagram that shows the functional requirements of the system. To create use case models, drill down into each high-level use case. The resulting use case diagrams provide the foundation for design and development.

Object orientation and use cases are the two heavyweight concepts behind the UML. Now that you've seen them, you're ready for the big picture of the UML. The elements you've learned about in Hours 2–7 fall into these categories: structural elements, relationships, organization, annotation, and extension. In the next hour, you'll learn about an element in the remaining category: behavioral elements. Keeping this big picture in mind will help you as you learn more about the UML.

Q&A

Q. *I noticed that in the high-level use case diagram, you don't show associations between the actors and the use cases. Why is that?*

A. The high-level use case diagram emerges at the early stages of interviews with users. It's still more or less a brainstorming exercise at that point, and the objective is to find the overall requirements, scope, and boundaries of the system. The associations make more sense when subsequent client interviews get you deeper into each requirement and use case models take shape.

Q. *You mentioned "business logic" in connection with the use case analysis. Is this the only part of the analysis process that yields business logic?*

A. Not necessarily. You have to be alert to business logic–related information throughout the process.

Q. *Why is it important to have that "big picture" of the UML? Can't I just know when to use each type of diagram?*

A. If you understand the organization of the UML, you'll be able to handle situations you haven't encountered before. You'll be able to recognize when an existing UML element won't do the job, and you'll know how to construct a new one. You'll also know how to create a hybrid diagram (a diagram that encompasses a diverse set of UML elements) if it turns out to be the only way to clearly present a model.

Workshop

In this workshop, you'll continue with the knowledge you gained in Hour 6, using it as a foundation for the knowledge from this hour. The objective is to use your new knowledge to visualize use cases and their relationships. The answers appear in Appendix A, "Quiz Answers."

Quiz

1. Name two advantages to visualizing a use case.

2. Describe generalization and grouping, the relationships among use cases that you learned about in this hour. Name two situations in which you would group use cases.

3. What are the similarities between classes and use cases? What are the differences?

4. How do you model inclusion and extension?

Exercises

1. Sketch the diagram of a use case model for a TV remote control. Be sure to include all the functions of the remote as use cases for your model.

2. In the fourth exercise in Hour 6, you listed the actors and use cases for a computer superstore. This time, draw a high-level use case diagram based on the work you did for that exercise. Then create a use case model for at least one of the high-level use cases. In your work, try to incorporate the includes or extends relationships.

3. Consider what happens when you go shopping for groceries and other necessities in a supermarket. Create the concept for a device that eliminates some of the annoyances associated with this experience and model the use cases for that device. In your set of use cases, use inclusion, extension, and generalization wherever they're appropriate.

HOUR 8

Working with State Diagrams

What You'll Learn in This Hour:

▶ What a state diagram is and how to work with it

▶ How to work with events, actions, and guard conditions

▶ How to model substates, history states, and connection points

At the end of the last hour, I said this hour would cover a category you haven't worked with before. This new category, the **behavioral element**, shows how parts of a UML model change over time. You'll learn about a particular member of this category, the state diagram.

Each year brings new styles in clothes and cars, seasons change the color of leaves on trees, and passing years see children grow and mature. Without becoming any more like a greeting card, the point is that as time passes and events occur, changes take place in the objects around us.

This also holds true in any system. As the system interacts with users and (possibly) with other systems, the objects that make up the system go through necessary changes to accommodate the interactions. If you're going to model systems, you must have a mechanism to model change.

What Is a State Diagram?

One way to characterize change in a system is to say that its objects change their state in response to events and to time. Here are some quick examples:

When you throw a switch, a light changes its state from Off to On.

When you click a remote control, a television changes its state from showing you one channel to showing you another.

After an appropriate amount of time, a washing machine changes its state from Washing to Rinsing.

The UML **state diagram** captures these kinds of changes. It presents the states an object can be in along with the transitions between the states and shows the starting point and endpoint of a sequence of state changes.

State Diagrams Versus Blueprints

With the state diagram, the analogy between UML and a blueprint begins to break down. A blueprint shows you what a house will look like when it's finished. It doesn't show where holes will appear in the roof, where cracks will emerge in the walls, and how corrosion will become part of the plumbing. The intent of the state diagram, also referred to as a **state machine** or a **statechart**, is to show those kinds of changes.

Bear in mind that a state diagram is intrinsically different from a class diagram, an object diagram, or a use case diagram in a very important way. The diagrams you've already studied model a group of classes, objects, or use cases. A state diagram shows the states of a single object.

Some Conventions

It's customary to capitalize the initial letter of a state's name. It's also a good idea to give a state a name that ends in *ing* whenever possible (for example, *Dialing* or *Faxing*). Sometimes it's not possible (*Idle* is an example, as you'll see in a moment).

The Fundamental Symbol Set

Figure 8.1 shows the rounded rectangle that represents a state, along with the solid line and arrowhead that represent a transition. The arrowhead points to the state being transitioned into. The figure also shows the solid circle that symbolizes a starting point and the bull's-eye that symbolizes an endpoint.

Adding Details to the State Icon

The UML gives you the option of adding detail to these symbols. You can divide the state icon into two areas. The top area holds the name of the state (which you have to supply whether you subdivide the icon or not) and the bottom area holds activities that take place in that state. Figure 8.2 shows these details.

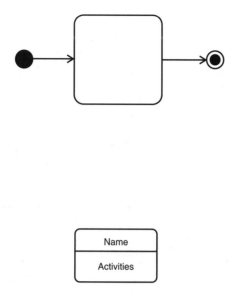

FIGURE 8.1
The fundamental
UML symbols in a
state diagram. The
icon for a state is a
rounded rectangle,
and the symbol for
a transition is a
solid line with an
arrowhead. A solid
circle stands for
the starting point
of a sequence of
states, and a bull's-
eye represents the
endpoint.

FIGURE 8.2
You can subdivide
a state icon into
areas that show
the state's name
and activities.

Three frequently used categories of activities are **entry** (what happens when the system enters the state), **exit** (what happens when the system leaves the state), and **do** (what happens while the system is in the state). You can add others as necessary.

A fax machine is an object whose states have activities. When it's sending a fax—that is, when it's in the Faxing state—the fax machine engages in the activities of adding a date stamp and timestamp to the fax and adding its phone number and the name of its owner. In other activities in this state, the machine pulls the pages through, paginates the fax, and completes the transmission.

While it's in the Idle state, the fax machine presents the date and time on a display. Figure 8.3 shows a state diagram.

Adding Details to the Transitions: Events and Actions

You can also add some details to the transition lines. You can indicate an event that causes a transition to occur (a **trigger event**) and the computation (the **action**) that executes and makes the state change happen. To add events and actions you write them near the transition line, using a slash to separate a triggering event from an action. Sometimes an event causes a transition without an associated action, and sometimes a transition occurs because a state completes an activity (rather than because of an event). This type of transition is called a **triggerless transition**.

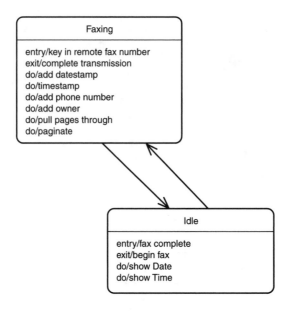

The graphical user interface (GUI) you interact with gives examples of transition details. For the moment, assume the GUI can be in one of three states:

> Initializing
>
> Working
>
> Shutting Down

When you turn your PC on, bootup takes place. Turning the PC on, then, is a triggering event that causes the GUI to transition to the Initializing state, and booting up is an activity that takes place during the transition.

As a result of activities in the Initializing state, the GUI transitions into the Working state. When you choose to shut down the PC, you generate a trigger event that causes the transition to the Shutting Down state, and eventually the PC turns off. Figure 8.4 shows the state diagram that captures these states and transitions in the GUI.

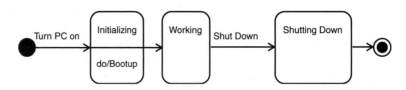

Adding Details to the Transitions: Guard Conditions

The preceding account of GUIs leaves a lot to be desired. First of all, if you leave your computer unattended or if you just sit idly by and don't type or use the mouse, a screensaver appears and rescues your pixels from potential burnout. To say this in state-change terms, if enough time passes without any user input, the GUI transitions from the Working state into a state I didn't show in Figure 8.4—the Screensaving state.

The time interval is specified in your Windows Control Panel. It's usually 15 minutes. Any keystroke or mouse movement transitions the monitor from the Screensaving state back to the Working state.

That 15-minute interval is a **guard condition**—when it's met, the transition takes place. Figure 8.5 shows the state diagram for the GUI with the Screensaving state and the guard condition added.

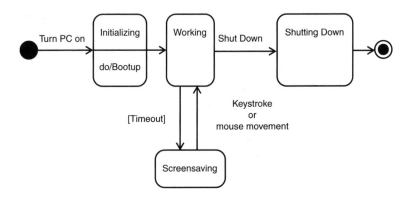

FIGURE 8.5
The state diagram for the GUI, with the Screensaving state and a guard condition.

Substates

This model of the GUI is still somewhat empty. The Working state, in particular, is a lot richer than Figures 8.4 and 8.5 indicate.

When the GUI is in the Working state, a lot is happening behind the scenes, although it might not be particularly evident onscreen. The GUI is constantly waiting for you to do something—type a keystroke, move the mouse, or press a mouse button. It then must register those inputs and change the display to visualize those actions for you onscreen—for example, by moving the cursor when you move the mouse, or by displaying an *a* when you press the *a* key.

Thus the GUI goes through changes while it's within the Working state. Those changes are changes of state. Because these states reside within a state, they're called **substates**. Substates come in two varieties: **sequential** and **concurrent**.

Sequential Substates

As the name implies, sequential substates occur one after the other. Recapping the aforementioned substates within the GUI's Working state, you have this sequence:

Awaiting User Input

Registering User Input

Visualizing User Input

User input triggers the transition from Awaiting to Registering. Activities within Registering transition the GUI into Visualizing. After the third state, the GUI goes back to the Awaiting User Input state. Figure 8.6 shows how to represent these sequential substates within the Working state.

FIGURE 8.6
Sequential substates within the GUI's Working state.

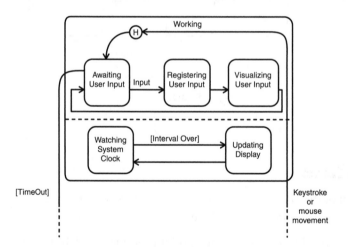

Concurrent Substates

Within the Working state, the GUI isn't just waiting for you. It's also watching the system clock and (possibly) updating an application's display after a specific interval. For example, an application might include an onscreen clock that the GUI has to update.

All this is going on at the same time as the sequence I just discussed. Although each sequence is, of course, a set of sequential substates, the two sequences are concurrent with one another. You represent concurrency with a dotted line between the concurrent states, as in Figure 8.7.

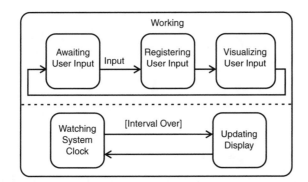

FIGURE 8.7
Concurrent sub-states proceed at the same time. A dotted line separates concurrent substates.

Separating the Working state into two components might remind you of something. Remember when I discussed aggregations and composites? When each component is part of just one whole, you are dealing with a composite. The concurrent parts of the Working state have that same kind of relationship to the Working state. For this reason, the Working state is a **composite state**. A state that consists of nothing but sequential substates is also a composite state.

History States

When your screensaver is on and you move your mouse to get back to the Working state, what happens? Does your display go back to looking as it did right after the GUI was initialized? Or does it look exactly the way you left it before the screensaver came on?

Obviously, if the screensaver caused the display to revert back to the beginning of the Working state, the whole screensaver idea would be counterproductive. Users would lose work and have to restart a session from square one.

The state diagram captures this idea. The UML supplies a symbol that shows that a composite state remembers its active substate when the object transitions out of the composite state. The symbol is the letter *H* enclosed in a small circle connected by a solid line to the remembered substate, with an arrowhead pointing to that substate. Figure 8.8 shows this symbol in the Working state.

FIGURE 8.8
The history state, symbolized by the *H* in the small circle, shows that a composite state remembers its active substate when the object transitions out of that composite state.

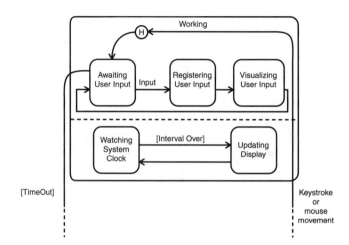

In the state diagram, I haven't dealt with windows that are opened by other windows—in other words, with substates nested within other substates. When a history state remembers substates at all levels of nesting (as the Windows Working state does), the history state is said to be **deep**. If it remembers only the highest nested substate, the history state is **shallow**. You represent a deep history by putting *H** in the circle.

New in UML 2.0

UML 2.0 has added some new state-relevant symbols called **connection points.** They represent points of entry into a state or exits out of a state.

Here's an example: Imagine a couple of the states of a book in a library. At first, it's residing on a shelf. If a borrower has called in to reserve the book, a librarian retrieves the book and brings it into the state of "Being checked out." If a borrower comes to the library, browses through the shelves, selects the book, and then decides to borrow it, it enters the Being-checked-out state, but in a different way. You can think of each way of getting to the Being-checked-out state as going through a separate **entry point**.

One more thing to be aware of: Suppose the borrower has borrowed more than some allotted limit or has a number of unpaid fines. If that's the case, the book abruptly exits—via an **exit point**—from the Being-checked-out state.

Figure 8.9 shows how to model all this in UML. Each entry point is modeled as an empty circle. The exit point is an encircled *X*. The circles are on the border of the state icon.

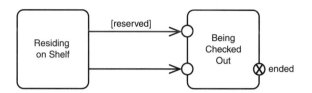

FIGURE 8.9
Entry points and an
exit point in a UML
state diagram.

Why Are State Diagrams Important?

The UML state diagram provides a variety of symbols and encompasses a number of ideas, all to model the changes that just one object goes through. This type of diagram has the potential to get very complex very quickly. Is it really necessary?

In fact, it is. It's important to have state diagrams because they help analysts, designers, and developers understand the behavior of the objects in a system. A class diagram and the corresponding object diagram show only the static aspects of a system. They show hierarchies and associations, and they tell you what the behaviors are. They don't show you the dynamic details of the behaviors.

Developers, in particular, have to know how objects are supposed to behave because they have to implement these behaviors in software. It's not enough to implement an object: Developers have to make that object do something. State diagrams ensure that they won't have to guess about what the object is supposed to do. With a clear picture of object behavior, the likelihood increases that the development team will produce a system that meets requirements.

Building the Big Picture

Now you can add behavioral elements to your big picture of the UML. Figure 8.10 presents the picture with the state diagram included.

Summary

Objects in a system change their states in response to events and totime. The UML state diagram captures these state changes. A state diagram focuses on the state changes in just one object. A rounded rectangle represents a state, and a line with an arrowhead represents a transition from one state to another.

The state icon shows the name of the state and can hold activities as well. A transition can occur in response to a trigger event and can entail an action. A transition can also occur because of an activity in a state: A transition that takes place

FIGURE 8.10
The big picture of the UML now includes a behavioral element, the state diagram.

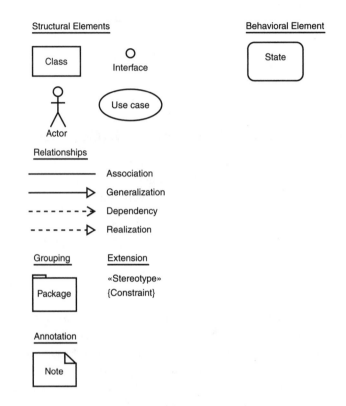

Structural Elements

Class | Interface | Actor | Use case

Relationships

——————— Association

————————▷ Generalization

– – – – – – –▷ Dependency

– – – – – –▷ Realization

Grouping

Package

Extension

«Stereotype»
{Constraint}

Annotation

Note

Behavioral Element

State

in this fashion is termed a **triggerless transition**. Finally, a transition can occur because a particular condition—a **guard condition**—holds true.

Sometimes, a state consists of substates. Substates may either be sequential (occurring one after the other) or concurrent (occurring at the same time). A state that consists of substates is called a composite state. A history state indicates that a composite state remembers its substate when the object transitions out of that composite state. A history state may be either shallow or deep. These terms pertain to nested substates. A **shallow** history remembers only the top-level substate. A **deep** history remembers all levels of substates.

UML 2.0 provides symbols for modeling **connection points**—entry points into a state and exit points out of a state.

State diagrams help analysts, designers, and developers understand the behavior of the objects in a system. Developers, in particular, have to know how objects are supposed to behave because they have to implement these behaviors in software. It's not enough to implement an object: Developers have to make that object do something.

Q&A

Q. *What's the best way to start creating a state diagram?*

A. It's much like creating a class diagram or a use case model. In the class diagram, you list all the classes and then wrestle with the interclass associations. In the state diagram, you first list the states of the object and then focus on the transitions. As you work through each transition, figure out whether a trigger event sets it off and whether any action takes place.

Q. *Must every state diagram have a final state (the one represented by the bull's-eye)?*

A. No. An object that never turns off won't have this state.

Q. *Any hints on laying out a state diagram?*

A. Try to arrange the states and transitions so that you minimize crossing lines. One objective of this diagram (and any other) is clarity. If people can't understand the models you build, no one will use them, and your efforts— no matter how thorough and insightful—will be wasted.

Workshop

The quiz and exercises will transition you into the Learned State Diagrams state. As always, you'll find the quiz answers in Appendix A, "Quiz Answers."

Quiz

1. In what important way does a state diagram differ from a class diagram, an object diagram, or a use case diagram?

2. Define these terms: *transition*, *event*, and *action*.

3. What is a *triggerless transition*?

4. What is the difference between sequential substates and concurrent substates?

Exercises

1. Suppose you're designing a toaster. Create a state diagram that tracks the states of bread in the toaster. Include necessary triggering events, actions, and guard conditions.

2. Figure 8.7 shows the concurrent substates within the GUI's Working state. Draw a diagram of the Screensaving state that includes concurrent substates.

3. Figure 8.9 shows two of the states of a library book. Using your general knowledge of libraries, expand the diagram to include the remaining states. Add appropriate substates and guard conditions.

HOUR 9

Working with Sequence Diagrams

What You'll Learn in This Hour:

▶ What a sequence diagram is
▶ How to apply a sequence diagram
▶ How to model the creation of an object
▶ How to work with some UML 2.0 additions to sequence diagrams
▶ Where sequence diagrams fit in the big picture of the UML

The state diagrams you learned about in the last hour zoom in on a single object. They show the changes an object goes through.

The UML enables you to expand your field of view and show how an object interacts with other objects. In this expanded field of view, you'll include an important dimension—time. The key idea here is that interactions among objects take place in a specified sequence, and the sequence takes time to go from beginning to end. When you create a system, you specify the sequence, and you use the UML sequence diagram to do it.

What Is a Sequence Diagram?

The **sequence diagram** consists of objects represented in the usual way (as named rectangles with the name underlined), messages represented as solid-line arrows, and time represented as a vertical progression.

Objects

The objects are laid out near the top of the diagram from left to right. They're arranged in any order that simplifies the diagram.

Extending downward from each object is a dashed line called the object's **lifeline**. Along the lifeline is a narrow rectangle called an **activation**. The activation represents an execution of an operation the object carries out. The length of the rectangle signifies the activation's duration. Duration, and time in general, are represented in a rough, ordinal way. This means that each dash in a lifeline usually doesn't stand for a specific unit of time but is intended to give a general sense of duration. Figure 9.1 shows an object, lifeline, and activation.

FIGURE 9.1
Representing an object in a sequence diagram.

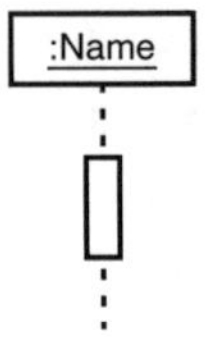

Messages

A message that goes from one object to another goes from one object's lifeline to the other object's lifeline. An object can also send a message to itself—that is, from its lifeline back to its own lifeline.

UML represents a message as an arrow that starts at one lifeline and ends at another. The shape of the arrowhead shows what type of message it is. In UML 1.x, three arrowhead shapes were available. UML 2.0 has eliminated one of those shapes and, to my way of thinking, cut down on confusion. I'll explain the messages, and then show you what UML 2.0 has eliminated.

One type of message is a **call**. This is a request from the object sending the message to the object receiving the message. The request is for the receiver to carry out one of its (the receiver's) operations. Usually, this entails the sender waiting for the receiver to carry out that operation. Because the sender waits for the receiver (that is, "synchs up" with the receiver), this message is also referred to as **synchronous.**

UML signifies this message type with a filled arrowhead at the end of a solid line. It's typically the case that a call involves a return message from the receiver, although modelers often omit the symbol for the return message. The symbol for the return message is an open-stick arrowhead with a dashed line. Figure 9.2 shows these symbols.

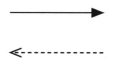

FIGURE 9.2
The UML symbol for a call and for a return.

> ### Many Happy Returns
>
> A few words about that return message symbol. First, it might be a little confusing because it closely resembles a dependency arrow. Second, as you read more about UML, you might find differing representations for a return message. Documentation from the UML 1.x era sometimes shows this symbol with the open-stick arrowhead and sometimes with the same arrowhead as the call. UML 2.0 specifies the symbol shown in Figure 9.2, and that's the one I'll use.

By the Way

Another kind of message is **asynchronous**. With this one, the sender transfers control to the receiver and doesn't wait for the operation to complete. The symbol for this message is an open-stick arrowhead, as Figure 9.3 shows.

FIGURE 9.3
The UML symbol for an asynchronous message.

> ### The Missing Arrowhead
>
> What about that extra UML 1.x arrowhead? That was an open-stick half-arrowhead. (Imagine the arrowhead in Figure 9.3 with half the arrowhead missing.) UML 1.x used it to stand for asynchronous messages. The idea was to have one kind of symbol for an asynchronous message and another for a transfer-of-control message, but the boundaries among message categories sometimes became fuzzy. I'll adopt the UML 2.0 categories and work only with the symbols in Figures 9.2 and 9.3.

By the Way

Time

The diagram represents time in the vertical direction: Time starts at the top and progresses toward the bottom. A message that's closer to the top occurs earlier in time than a message that's closer to the bottom.

Thus, the sequence diagram is two-dimensional. The left-to-right dimension is the layout of the objects, and the top-to-bottom dimension shows the passage of time.

Figure 9.4 shows the essential symbol set of the sequence diagram, with the symbols working together. The objects are laid out across the top. Each object's lifeline is a dashed line extending downward from the object. A solid line with an arrowhead connects one lifeline to another and represents a message from one object to another.

FIGURE 9.4
The symbols in a sequence diagram.

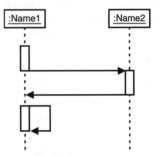

In order to bring this important UML tool to life, we'll apply it to some examples. As we do so, you'll have the opportunity to work with some object-oriented concepts that form the basis for sequence diagrams. I'll also be going back into classes, so it might seem that I'm digressing. I'm not. Trust me.

Cars and Car Keys

You might be familiar with the kind of car key that allows you to remotely lock and unlock a car. It also lets you open the car's trunk. If you have one of these keys, you know what happens when you push the "lock" button. The car locks itself, and then it blinks its lights and beeps to let you know it's finished locking its doors.

A Class Diagram

Let's capture all this in a class diagram. Figure 9.5 shows the relationships among the CarOwner, Car, and CarKey classes, as well as some other concepts.

The Car processes a message from the key and causes the appropriate behavior to take place.

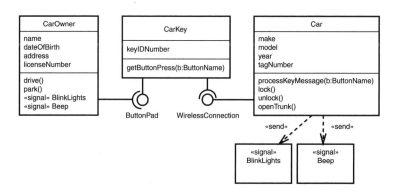

FIGURE 9.5
The relationships among CarOwner, CarKey, and Car.

Notice a couple of things about this diagram. In the CarKey class, I've shown the signature of getButtonPress(). This operation works with a button name ("lock," "unlock," or "openTrunk"). The idea is that the Car receives a message from the CarKey, processes that message, and implements the operation corresponding to the name of the pressed button.

The diagram also shows the two signals BlinkLights and Beep. You model a signal as a class with the keyword «signal» added. The dependency arrows between Car and each signal show that the Car sends these signals. Once again, the UML has no symbol for *send*, so you add the keyword «send» to the dependency arrow.

Note that the CarOwner class shows something you haven't seen before in a class icon—the two occurrences of the «signal» keyword. These show you that CarOwner is capable of receiving these signals. The signals don't request the CarOwner to do anything. Because the Car (the sender) isn't making a request when it sends those signals, it certainly isn't waiting for the CarOwner to do any-thing. Hence, the sequence diagram uses the asynchronous message symbol to model signals.

A Sequence Diagram

The class diagram in Figure 9.5 is a static view of the little world of the CarOwner, CarKey, Car, and the two signals. A sequence diagram provides a dynamic view. How? By showing the messages that pass from one of these entities to another.

Start by drawing three objects. One object is an instance of CarOwner, another is an instance of CarKey, and the third is an instance of Car. Lay them out across the top of the diagram and drop a lifeline from each one, as in Figure 9.6.

FIGURE 9.6
The beginning of a
sequence diagram.

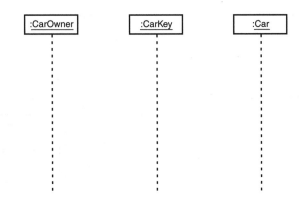

By the Way

Anonymous Objects

As you can see, none of these objects has a specific name (myCar:Car, for example). You might remember that I mentioned this possibility in a note in Hour 3, "Working with Object Orientation." These three are anonymous objects.

Next, add the arrows to model messages that go from lifeline to lifeline, as in Figure 9.7. The first message (the one highest in the vertical dimension) is a request from CarOwner to CarKey. The request is for CarKey to implement its getKeyPress() operation, registering the button the CarOwner has pressed (generically referred to as *b*). The stick arrowhead indicates that CarOwner is transferring control to CarKey.

FIGURE 9.7
Messages
complete the
sequence diagram.

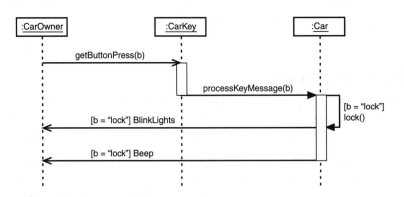

CarKey then sends a message to Car, calling on Car to implement its processKeyMessage() operation, depending on the specified button. After it processes the message from CarKey, Car sends itself a message to implement the operation that corresponds to the pressed button. Note the expression in brackets. That's a guard condition, which you just saw in Hour 8, "Working with State Diagrams." It's the UML's way of saying "if." So if the pressed button was "lock," the Car sends itself a request to carry out the lock() operation. Then Car sends its two signals to CarOwner. The first message and the signals are examples of the two usages of the stick arrowhead.

This example shows one use of a sequence diagram—modeling the interactions in a domain defined by a class diagram. The next example shows another context for applying sequence diagrams.

The Soda Machine

Let's move on to an example with a little more complexity. You'll recall that in Hour 6, "Introducing Use Cases" and Hour 7, "Working with Use Case Diagrams," you read about the use cases of a soda machine. Remember also that a use case is a name for a collection of scenarios.

The sequence diagram is useful for modeling the scenarios of a use case. In this example, you'll model scenarios of the "Buy soda" use case.

You'll begin with a class diagram, as you did in the preceding example. The class diagram will model the entities that make up a soda machine. To keep it simple, assume three components—a front, a register, and a dispenser. Engineers who make a living designing and building soda machines, of course, have a different idea of the number of components, but these components will do for this example.

In your model of the soda machine, the front

- Accepts selections and cash
- Displays prompts like "Out of selection" and "Use correct change"
- Receives change from the register and makes it available to the customer
- Returns cash
- Receives a can of soda from the dispenser and makes it available to the customer

The register

▶ Gets the customer's input (that is, the selection and the cash) from the front

▶ Updates its cash reserve

▶ Checks for change

The dispenser

▶ Checks the availability of a selection

▶ Releases a can of soda

Assume the soda machine is an aggregation of these three components. Figure 9.8 shows the class diagram.

FIGURE 9.8
Your model of a
soda machine.

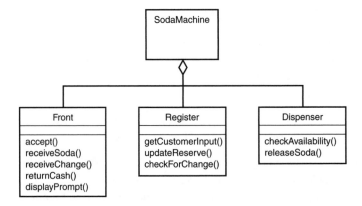

Let's model the best-case scenario of the "Buy soda" use case: The customer inserts the correct change, and the customer's selection is available. The sequence goes like this:

1. The customer inserts the money into the money slot in the front of the machine and makes a selection.

2. The money travels to the register, which updates itself.

3. Because this is the best-case scenario, an availability check reveals the soda is in stock, and the register has the dispenser release the soda to the front of the machine.

Figure 9.9 shows the sequence diagram that models these steps.

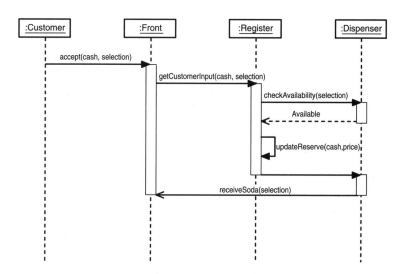

FIGURE 9.9
A sequence diagram that models the best-case scenario of the "Buy soda" use case.

This is just one scenario in this use case. In another scenario, the customer's selection might be sold out. Figure 9.10 shows a sequence diagram that models the sold-out scenario.

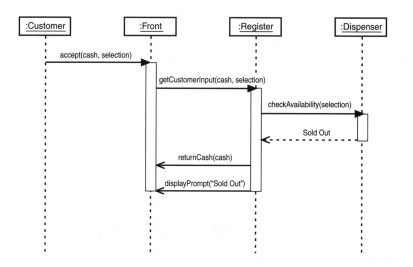

FIGURE 9.10
A sequence diagram that models the sold-out scenario of the "Buy soda" use case.

Here's another scenario. Suppose the customer does not insert the correct amount of change? Figure 9.11 shows the sequence diagram for that one.

Finally, suppose the customer does not insert the correct change, and the soda machine is out of change? The sequence diagram for that scenario is in Figure 9.12.

FIGURE 9.11
A sequence diagram for the incorrect-change scenario.

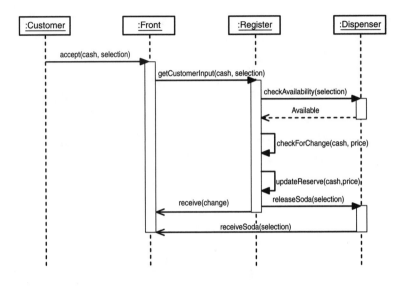

FIGURE 9.12
A sequence diagram for the incorrect-change-and-machine-is-out-of-change scenario.

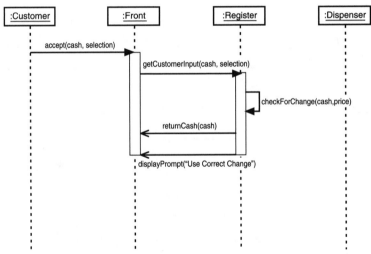

Sequence Diagrams: The Generic Sequence Diagram

So far, you've put just one scenario into a sequence diagram. When you do this, you create an **instance sequence diagram**.

If you include all of a use case's scenarios when you draw a sequence diagram, you create a **generic sequence diagram**. Let's put all our scenarios into one diagram.

We need some way of indicating conditions; one condition necessitates the messages in one scenario, another condition necessitates others. Recall from the example with cars and car keys that UML provides the guard condition to indicate *if*. This is just a bracketed statement for a condition that has to be in place to follow one path rather than another. For example, to show that an object sends a message only if the selected soda is sold out, preface that message with [sold out].

The guard conditions provide essentially the same information as the return messages. For example, [sold out] lets you know that a selection is unavailable, just as the "Sold Out" return message does. For this reason, you can remove the return messages. Keeping them around would make the diagram cumbersome.

One more idea and you'll be ready to take the plunge into a generic sequence diagram. You want to be able to show that if you fully follow one scenario's sequence of messages to its conclusion, the transaction is over, and that the remaining messages are related to other scenarios. To do this, you preface the final message in each scenario with «transaction over».

Figure 9.13 incorporates these ideas.

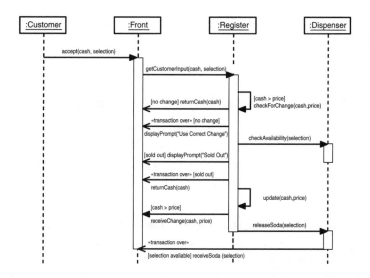

FIGURE 9.13
A generic sequence diagram for the soda machine.

Follow the diagram from top to bottom. It starts with the customer requesting the Front to accept his or her cash and selection. Next, the Front asks the Register to get the customer's input. If the cash is greater than the price of the soda, the

Register checks its cash reserve for change. If no change is available, the Register has the Front return the customer's cash and then has the Front display a prompt that says "Use Correct Change." The transaction is over.

Next on the Register's lifeline, you're in effect looking at a different scenario. The Register has the Dispenser check for the availability of the customer's selection.

If it's sold out, the Register asks the Front to display a prompt that says "Sold Out" and then has the Front return the customer's cash. Once again, the transaction is over.

Moving down the Register's lifeline, you see that if the transaction continues, the Register updates its cash reserve according to the cash and the price. If the cash is greater than the price, the Register has the Front receive the change. Then the Register asks the Dispenser to release the selected soda, the Dispenser requests the Front to receive the soda, and the transaction (happily) is over.

Are you getting the idea that behind every use case lurks one or more sequence diagrams? If so, you probably understand why a sequence diagram is a valuable thing.

As you'll see in Hour 11, "Working with Activity Diagrams," UML 2.0 offers an alternative way to combine sequence diagrams. It's called an **Interaction Overview Diagram**. Stay tuned.

Creating an Object in the Sequence

A few years ago, telecommunications giant Ericsson demonstrated a technology that enables customers to use their cell phones to buy from soda machines. A commercial during a recent Super Bowl telecast portrayed this technology in action. How would you model this interaction in a sequence diagram? What would you have to add?

Let's begin once again with a class diagram. Figure 9.14 is an expansion of Figure 9.8. Through a wireless connection, the CellPhone interfaces to the Front. The Front is smarter than before and now has the ability to process information from the Customer. In this version it acquires an additional capability—the real focus here: It creates a transaction record of the interaction between the customer and the soda machine. The machine uses this record to charge the customer's credit card for the soda. Your sequence diagram has to visualize the creation of the transaction record.

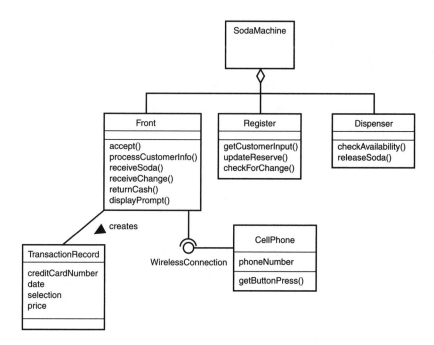

FIGURE 9.14
Expanding the class diagram from Figure 9.8 to show a cell phone as an interface to a soda machine.

On to the sequence diagram. We'll work with the best-case scenario: The customer keys his or her credit card information into the cell phone and sends it to the Front. The Front processes the information and displays an "Approved" prompt to the Customer. The Customer keys a selection into the cell phone, which sends it to the Front. In this version of the soda machine, the Front processes the information and communicates directly with the Dispenser to check availability and to instruct the Dispenser to release the soda. The rest of the scenario is just like the original best-case scenario in the twentieth-century soda machine, except for the creation of the TransactionRecord.

Figure 9.15 presents the sequence diagram. All the objects are across the top, except the TransactionRecord object. Why? Because it's not one of the objects that exists at the beginning of the sequence. You show its creation by positioning it in the vertical dimension according to when it's created. Another aspect of modeling object–creation is the «create» keyword you put on the message sent from the creator object to the created object. (Because the Register isn't involved in this sequence, it doesn't appear in the diagram.)

FIGURE 9.15
A sequence diagram that models the best-case scenario of using a cell phone as an interface to a soda machine.

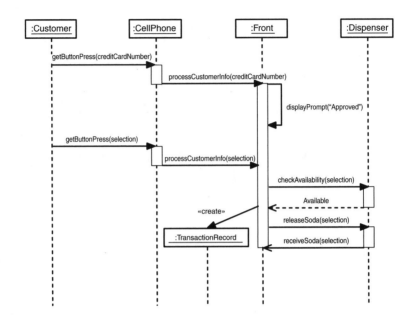

The Cell Phone: A Universal Communicator?

Several organizations around the world are working on ways to turn that little phone you're holding into a true Renaissance device. In Estonia, some people already use cell phones to interact with parking meters. Ericsson employees can use their cell phones to advance slides in PowerPoint presentations. A British company called Shazam Entertainment has developed technology that enables you to use your cell phone to automatically retrieve information about a song you're listening to. How? Just hold up your phone to the radio or stereo speaker! To read more about these projects and others, see "If Walls Could Talk, Streets Might Join In" in the September 18, 2003 *New York Times*.

While we're on the subject of object creation, we should also talk about object destruction. To show an object being destroyed, you place a large, bold *X* at the bottom of its lifeline, as in Figure 9.16. The left-hand part of the figure shows an object destroying itself (perhaps because a certain amount of time has passed). The right-hand part of the figure shows that an object can instruct another object to destroy itself. It does this by sending a message whose label is a «destroy» keyword.

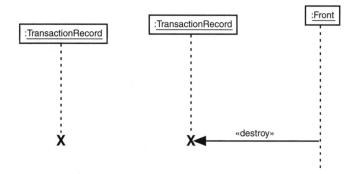

FIGURE 9.16
An object can destroy itself (left), or it can receive an instruction to be destroyed (right).

Framing a Sequence: Sequence Diagramming in UML 2.0

UML 2.0 adds a useful touch to sequence diagrams. You can now frame a sequence diagram by surrounding it with a border and adding a compartment in the upper left corner. The compartment contains information that identifies the diagram.

One of the pieces of information is an **operator**, an expression that describes the type of diagram inside the frame. For a sequence diagram, the operator is sd. Figure 9.17 shows our generic sequence diagram framed in the UML 2.0 style. Along with the operator, the compartment contains the name of the interaction (BuySoda) the diagram depicts.

Interaction Occurrences

The framing concept is helpful because you can apply it in a number of ways. Here's an example:

If you're creating instance sequence diagrams for the scenarios in a use case, you'll notice a fair amount of duplication from diagram to diagram. Framing gives you a quick and easy way to reuse part of one sequence diagram in another. You draw a frame around part of the diagram, label the frame's compartment, and just insert the frame with a label (but without the messages and lifelines) into the new diagram. This particular framed part is called an **interaction occurrence**. Its operator is ref.

Figure 9.18 shows the frame around part of the best-case scenario. The framed part is the interaction occurrence that handles the delivery of the soda. Figure 9.19 shows how to reuse that interaction occurrence in the incorrect change scenario.

FIGURE 9.17
Framing a
sequence diagram
in UML 2.0.

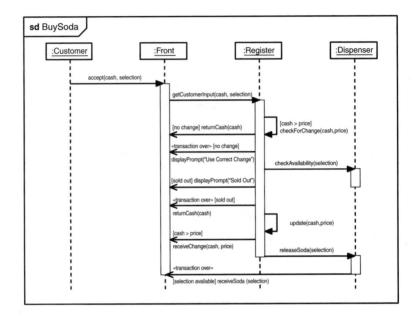

FIGURE 9.18
Framing an
interaction
occurrence in a
sequence diagram.

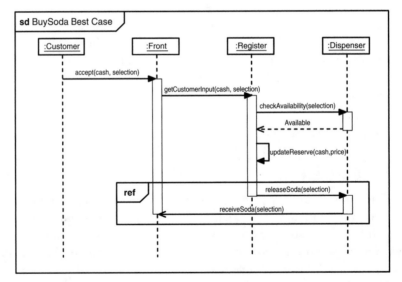

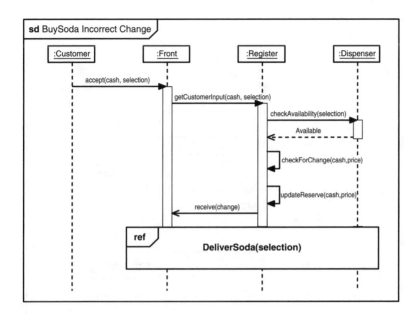

FIGURE 9.19
Reusing an
interaction
occurrence.

Combined Interaction Fragments

An interaction occurrence is a special case of an **interaction fragment—**
UML 2.0's generic name for a piece of a sequence diagram. You can combine
these interaction fragments in various ways. The operator indicates the type of
combination. To show a combination, frame the entire set of fragments, and use
a dotted line as a border between adjoining interaction fragments.

The two types of combinations I think will be the most widely used are denoted
by the alt operator and by the par operator.

In the alt combination, each fragment is an alternative and can proceed only
under certain conditions. Guard conditions indicate which fragment can take place.
Figure 9.20 shows this type of combination in the generic sequence diagram.

In contrast with the ref operator, the idea here is clarity rather than reuse. If you
compare Figure 9.20 with Figure 9.17, you'll see that the guard conditions in the
fragments eliminate the need for some of the guard conditions on the messages.
In my view, this clarifies the generic diagram and makes it easier to follow.

In the par combination, the combined fragments work in parallel and don't interfere
with one another. For example, suppose your soda machine works extremely efficiently: It returns the customer's change and delivers the selection at the same time.
This necessitates that several events happen together. Figure 9.21 shows what I mean.

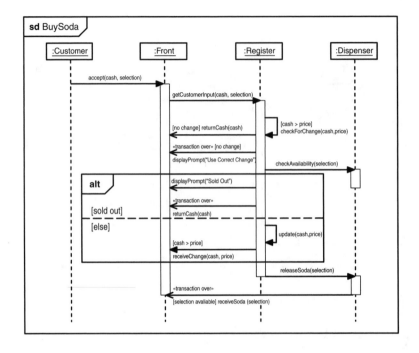

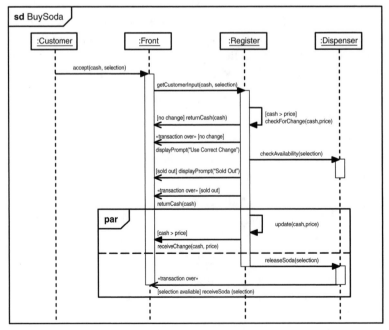

Before UML 2.0 introduced the par operator, it was difficult to show parallel events on a sequence diagram.

Building the Big Picture

You can now add one more diagram to your big picture of the UML. Because it deals with the behaviors of objects, the sequence diagram goes under the Behavioral Elements category. Figure 9.22 updates your growing picture.

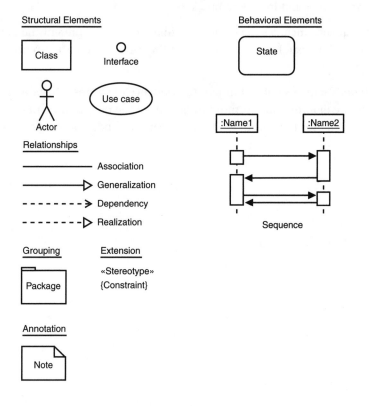

FIGURE 9.22
The big picture of the UML with the addition of the sequence diagram.

Summary

The UML sequence diagram adds the dimension of time to object interactions. In the diagram, objects are laid out across the top, and time proceeds from top to bottom. An object lifeline descends from each object.

An arrow that connects one lifeline to another represents a message that one object sends another. A message's location in the vertical dimension represents the time of its occurrence within the sequence. Messages that occur early are close to the top of the diagram, and messages that occur late are close to the bottom. A narrow rectangle on an object's lifeline represents an *activation*——an execution of one of that object's operations. An object executes an operation in response to a message it receives.

A use case diagram can show either an instance (one scenario) of a use case, or it can be generic and incorporate all of a use case's scenarios. Generic sequence diagrams often provide opportunities to represent *if* statements. Enclose each condition for an *if* statement in square brackets.

When a sequence includes the creation of an object, you represent the newly created object in the usual way. Its position in the vertical dimension represents the time it's created.

UML 2.0 adds some useful techniques for sequence diagrams. They involve framing the entire diagram and framing fragments of the diagram. Framing the fragments is helpful for reuse and for clarifying certain aspects of the diagram.

Q&A

Q. *The sequence diagram looks like it might be useful for more than just system analysis. Can I use it to show interactions in an organization?*

A. Yes, you can. The objects can be principal players, and the messages can be simple transfers of control.

Q. *Sometimes a sequence involves recursion. How can I represent recursion in a sequence diagram?*

A. To represent recursion, show an object sending a message to itself. On the activation, superimpose a smaller activation. Show the arrowhead pointing to that smaller activation.

Q. *You mentioned that the brackets in a guard condition are UML's way of saying* if. *Can I also show* while *in some way?*

A. Yes you can. Another way of thinking about *while* is that it's *if* repeated many times. From Hour 4, "Working with Relationships," remember that UML uses the asterisk to represent *many*. So in UML, "*[ ]" means *while*.

Q. *Before each sequence diagram, you started with a class diagram. Do I always have to do this?*

A. It's a good idea. If you model the classes first, you'll know which messages an object can receive.

Workshop

Now that you've stepped back and taken a long view of object interactions, step up to the plate, answer a few questions, and do a couple of exercises to firm up your knowledge of sequence diagrams. You'll find the answers in Appendix A, "Quiz Answers."

Quiz

1. Define *synchronous message* and *asynchronous message*.

2. In UML 2.0, what is an interaction fragment?

3. In UML 2.0, what does *par* mean?

4. In a sequence diagram, how do you represent a newly created object?

Exercises

General Hint: Start these exercises by creating a class diagram for each one.

1. Create an instance sequence diagram that shows what happens when you successfully send a fax. That is, model the object interactions in the best-case scenario of the "Send fax" use case of a fax machine. Include objects for the sending machine, the receiving machine, the fax, and a central exchange that routes faxes and phone calls.

2. Create a generic sequence diagram that includes unsuccessful scenarios (line busy, error on sending machine, and so on) as well as the best-case scenario from Exercise 1. Use as many UML 2.0 concepts as you can.

3. Create a sequence diagram for an electric pencil sharpener. Include as objects the user, the pencil, the insertion point (that is, the place where you put the pencil into the sharpener), the motor, and the sharpening element. What messages should you include? What are the activations? Should your diagram incorporate recursion?

HOUR 10

Working with Communication Diagrams

What You'll Learn in This Hour:

▶ What a communication diagram is

▶ How to apply a communication diagram

▶ How to model active objects, concurrency, and synchronization

▶ Where communication diagrams fit into the UML

In this hour you'll learn about a diagram that's similar to the one you covered in the last hour. This one also shows the interaction among objects, but it does so in a way that's slightly different from the sequence diagram.

Like the sequence diagram, the communication diagram shows how objects interact. It shows the objects along with the messages that travel from one object to another. So now you may be asking yourself, "If the sequence diagram does that, why does the UML need another diagram? Don't they do the same thing? Is this just overkill?"

The two types of diagrams *are* similar. In fact, they're **semantically equivalent**. That is, they present the same information, and you can turn a sequence diagram into an equivalent communication diagram and vice versa.

As it turns out, it's helpful to have both forms. The sequence diagram emphasizes the time ordering of interactions. The communication diagram emphasizes the context and overall organization of the objects that interact. Here's another way to look at the distinction: The sequence diagram is arranged according to time, the communication diagram according to space. Both deal with interactions among objects, and for that reason, each one is a type of **interaction diagram**.

What Is a Communication Diagram?

An object diagram shows objects and their relationships with one another. A communication diagram is an extension of the object diagram. In addition to the links among objects, the communication diagram shows the messages the objects send each other. You usually omit the names of the links because they would add clutter.

One way to think of the relationship between the object diagram and the communication diagram is to imagine the difference between a snapshot and a movie. The object diagram is the snapshot: It shows how instances of classes are linked together in an instant of time ("Instants and instances". . . Remember?). The communication diagram is the movie: It shows interactions among those instances over time.

To represent a message, you draw an arrow near the link between two objects. The arrow points to the receiving object. A label near the arrow shows what the message is. The message typically tells the receiving object to execute one of its (the receiver's) operations. Arrowheads have the same meaning as in sequence diagrams.

I mentioned that you can turn any sequence diagram into a communication diagram, and vice versa. Thus, you have to be able to represent sequential information in a communication diagram. To do this, you add a number to the label of a message, with the number corresponding to the message's order in the sequence. A colon separates the number from the message.

Figure 10.1 shows the symbol set for the communication diagram.

FIGURE 10.1
The symbol set for the communication diagram.

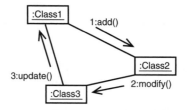

By the Way

A Change from UML 1.x to UML 2.0

If you've had some exposure to earlier versions of UML or earlier editions of this book, you'll recall the term *collaboration diagram*. UML 2.0 uses *communication diagram* instead, and that's the terminology I'll use from now on. If you use documentation or modeling tools based on UML 1.x, of course, you'll still see the older term.

Let's take advantage of the equivalence of the two types of diagrams. In order to develop the communication diagram's concepts, you'll revisit examples you worked with in the previous hour. As you do this, additional concepts will emerge.

Cars and Car Keys

We start again with the domain of cars and car keys. The class diagram in Figure 10.2 is just a refresher for you (Note it's the same as Figure 9.5 in Hour 9, "Working with Sequence Diagrams"). The idea is to remind you about the operations and signals, so you know the messages each object can receive.

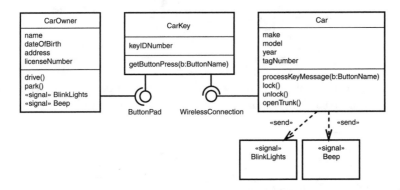

FIGURE 10.2
The domain of cars and car keys.

Next, we create an object diagram that models instances of the classes in Figure 10.2. This diagram appears in Figure 10.3 and is the foundation for a communication diagram.

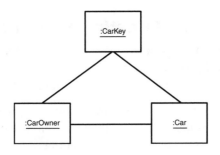

FIGURE 10.3
An object diagram that models instances of the classes in Figure 10.2.

Now you can add the messages. The messages that appeared in Figure 9.7 appear here in Figure 10.4. This figure shows one way of dealing with multiple messages that pass between two objects. As you can see, messages 4 and 5 are signals that go from the Car to the CarOwner. They have separate labels but not separate arrows.

The intent is to keep the diagram from becoming too busy. Some modeling tools, however, provide a separate arrow for each message. Bear in mind that if different kinds of messages pass between the same two objects, you have to show both arrows.

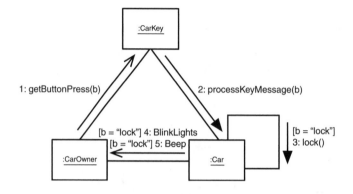

To show you the equivalence of the communication diagram and the sequence diagram, Figure 10.5 shows Figure 10.4 side by side with Figure 9.7.

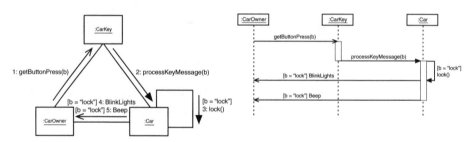

Changing States and Nesting Messages

Suppose Car has an attribute, locked, whose values are either True or False. Thinking back to Hour 8, "Working with State Diagrams," you can imagine two states, Locked and Unlocked for Car, as shown in Figure 10.6.

You can show a change of state in a communication diagram. To do that in this example, you show the value of locked in the Car object. Then, you duplicate the Car object with the new value of locked. Connect the two, and then show a message going from the first to the second. Label the message with the keyword «become».

This example gives you the chance to examine an additional concept related to communication diagrams—using the numbering system to show something about the relationships among messages. So far, you've only seen messages in sequence. It's also possible to show one message nested in another. You number the nested message by starting it with the number of the message it's nested in, then a decimal point, and then a number for the nested message. Figure 10.7 shows the state change and the nesting.

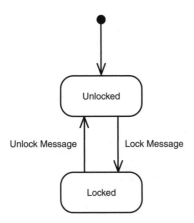

FIGURE 10.6
Modeling the Unlocked and Locked states of a car.

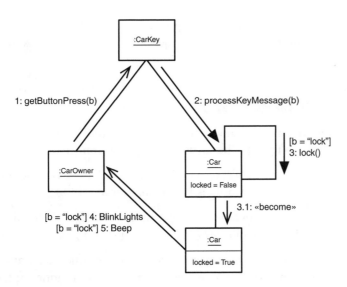

FIGURE 10.7
Modeling state changes in a communication diagram. Note the nested message (3.1: «become»)

Figure 10.8 shows an alternative technique for modeling state changes. I prefer the first way as the dotted-line arrow in the second brings to mind a dependency. People who are new to UML often find dependencies difficult to follow.

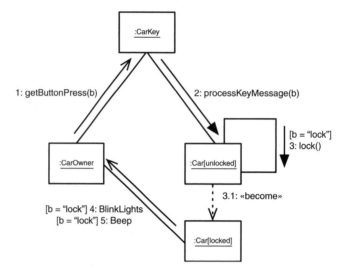

The nested message in this example might lead you to believe that messages are nested only in connection with state changes. This is not the case, as the next section shows.

The Soda Machine

Now you will move on to the soda machine example and see the communication diagrams that match up with the sequence diagrams from Hour 9.

You begin with the best-case scenario of the "Buy soda" use case. The communication diagram is straightforward, as Figure 10.9 shows.

The diagram provides another example of a nested message. The return message Available is nested in the call checkAvailability(). Thus, its number is 3.1.

I'll leave it as an exercise for you to create the communication diagrams that correspond to the remaining instance sequence diagrams for scenarios in the soda machine (Figures 9.10, 9.11, and 9.12). Instead, I'll turn my attention to the generic sequence diagram (Figure 9.13) and show you the corresponding communication diagram (Figure 10.10)

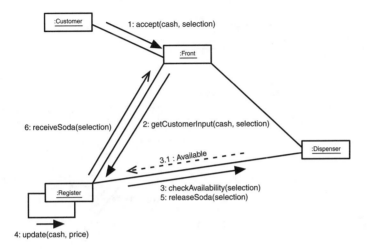

FIGURE 10.9
The communication diagram for the best-case scenario of the "Buy soda" use case.

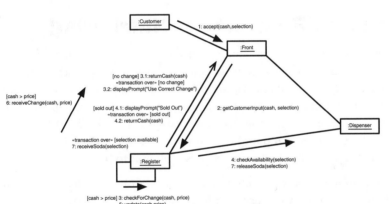

FIGURE 10.10
The communication diagram for the generic sequence diagram of the soda machine.

As you can see, the diagram is somewhat cluttered, particularly where messages pass between the Register and the Front. Several message labels are close to each other, two different kinds of messages transmit down that link, and stereotypes and guard conditions appear.

Creating an Object

To understand object creation, recall the cell-phone–enabled soda machine. The created object is the transaction record that enables the machine to charge the customer's account. Again, to model object creation, put «create» on the message label. Figure 10.11 shows the communication diagram.

FIGURE 10.11
Modeling object
creation in the
best-case
scenario in the
cell-phone–enabled
soda machine.

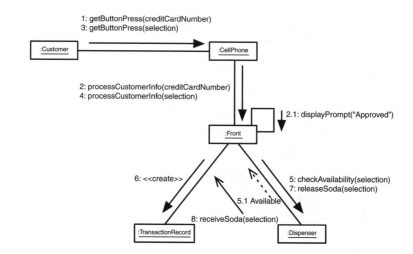

One More Point About Numbering

Sometimes, two messages come out of a decision process, and their guard conditions are mutually exclusive. How do you number them? Go back to the cell-
phone–enabled soda machine. Figure 10.11 models just the best-case scenario.
Suppose you add the possibility that the customer is not approved. This necessitates the guard condition [approved] on message 2.1 in Figure 10.11, and an
additional message with a guard condition [not approved]. In the latter case, the
transaction is over, and the Front displays a prompt to that effect.

What's the number for the additional message? It's also 2.1. Because the guard
conditions are mutually exclusive, only one path is possible. Figure 10.12 focuses
in on the relevant part of Figure 10.11 and shows the two messages.

FIGURE 10.12
Numbering the
messages for
mutually exclusive
guard conditions.

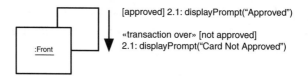

A Few More Concepts

Although you've covered a lot of ground, you haven't exhausted all the concepts
related to communication diagrams. The concepts that follow are a little esoteric,
but they might come in handy in your modeling efforts.

Multiple Receiving Objects in a Class

Sometimes an object sends a message to multiple objects in the same class. A professor, for example, asks a group of students to hand in an assignment. In the communication diagram, the representation of the multiple objects is a stack of rectangles extending *backward*. You add a bracketed condition preceded by an asterisk to indicate that the message goes to all objects. Figure 10.13 shows the details.

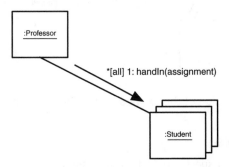

FIGURE 10.13
An object sending a message to multiple objects in a class.

In some cases, the order of message-sending is important. For example, a bank clerk serves each customer in the order that he or she appears in line. You represent this with a while whose condition implies order (such as line position = 1. . .n) along with the message and the stacked rectangles (see Figure 10.14).

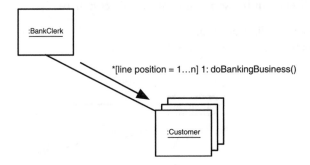

FIGURE 10.14
An object sending a message in a specified order to multiple objects in a class.

Representing Returned Results

A message can be a request for an object to perform a calculation and return a value. A customer object might request a calculator object to compute a total price that's the sum of an item's price and sales tax.

The UML provides a syntax for representing this situation. You write an expression that has the name of the returned value on the left, followed by :=, followed by the name of the operation and the quantities it operates on to produce the result. For this example, that expression would be `totalPrice:= compute (itemPrice,salesTax)`. Figure 10.15 shows the syntax on a communication diagram.

FIGURE 10.15
A communication
diagram that
includes the syntax
for a returned
result.

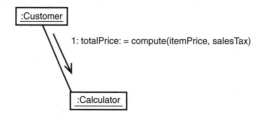

Incidentally, the right side of the expression is called a **message-signature**.

Active Objects

In some interactions, a specific object controls the flow of messages. This **active object** can send messages to passive objects and interact with other active objects. In a library, for instance, a librarian takes reference requests from patrons, looks up reference information in a database, gives information back to the patrons, assigns workers to restock books, and more. A librarian also interacts with other librarians who are carrying out the same operations. When two or more active objects do their work at the same time, it's called **concurrency**.

The communication diagram represents an active object the same as any other, except that it's border is thick and bold. (See Figure 10.16.)

FIGURE 10.16
An active object
controls the flow in
a sequence. It's
represented as a
rectangle with a
thick, bold border.

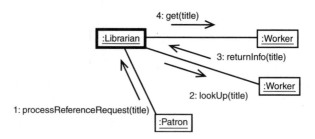

Synchronization

Another circumstance you might run into is an object sending a message only after several other (possibly nonconsecutive) messages have been sent. That is, the object must *synchronize* its message with a set of other messages.

An example will clarify this for you. Suppose your objects are people in a corporation, and they're concerned with a new product campaign. Here is a sequence of possible interactions:

1. The Senior VP of Marketing asks the VP of Sales to create a campaign for a particular product.

2. The VP of Sales creates the campaign and tells the Sales Manager to assign the campaign to a Salesperson.

3. The Sales Manager directs a Salesperson to sell the product according to the campaign.

4. The Salesperson makes sales calls to potential customers in order of their priority.

5. After the Sales Manager has issued the directive (that is, when steps 3 is complete), a corporate Public Relations Specialist has the local newspaper place an ad about the campaign.

How do you represent step 5's position in the sequence? Again, the UML provides a syntax. Instead of preceding this message with a numerical label, you precede it with the number of the message that has to be completed prior to step 5 taking place and then add a slash. If more than one message is required, use a comma to separate one list-item from another, and end the list with a slash. Figure 10.17 shows the communication diagram for this example.

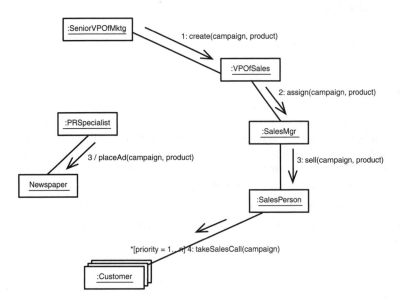

FIGURE 10.17
Message synchronization in a communication diagram.

Building the Big Picture

Now you can add the communication diagram to your picture of the UML. It's another behavioral element, as Figure 10.18 shows.

FIGURE 10.18
The big picture of the UML, including the communication diagram.

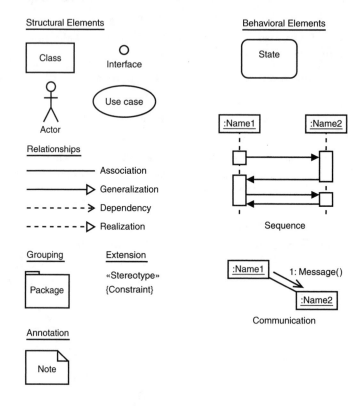

Summary

A communication diagram is another way of presenting the information in a sequence diagram. The two types of diagrams are semantically equivalent, but it's a good idea to use both when you construct a model of a system. The sequence diagram is organized according to time, and the communication diagram is organized according to the links among objects.

The communication diagram shows the associations among objects as well as the messages that pass from one object to another. An arrow near an association line represents a message, and a numbered label shows the content of the message. The number represents the message's place in the sequence of messages.

Conditionals are represented as before—by putting the conditional statement in square brackets.

Some messages are subsidiaries of others. The label-numbering scheme represents this in much the same way that some technical manuals show headings and sub-headings—with a numbering system that uses decimal points to show levels of nesting.

Communication diagrams allow you to model multiple receiving objects in a class whether the objects receive the message in a specified order or not. You can also represent active objects that control the flow of messages, as well as messages that synchronize with other messages.

Q&A

Q. *Will I really have to include both a communication diagram and a sequence diagram in most UML models I build?*

A. It's a good idea to include both. The two types of diagrams are likely to stimulate different thought processes during the analysis segment of the development effort. The communication diagram clarifies the relationships among the objects because it includes interobject links. The sequence diagram focuses attention on the sequence of interactions. Also, your client organization might include people whose thought processes differ from one another. When you have to present your model, one type of diagram might be better suited than the other for a particular individual.

Q. *In Hour 9, you showed how UML 2.0 puts frames around parts of the sequence diagram. Does UML 2.0 do anything similar for the communication diagram?*

A. You can draw a frame around a communication diagram in the same way that you draw a frame around a sequence diagram. UML 2.0 doesn't set up frames around parts of a communication diagram, however.

Q. *In this hour you showed how to model an object changing its state. Can I model this in a sequence diagram?*

A. Yes you can. You indicate an object's state by putting a state icon on its lifeline. The state icon's location on the lifeline indicates the time during which the object is in that state. To show the object changing its state, add a new state icon farther down the lifeline. Although UML allows you to take symbols from one kind of diagram and add them to another, some modeling tools do not.

Workshop

Now that you've learned about sequence diagrams and their siblings, communication diagrams, test and strengthen your knowledge with the quiz and the exercises. As always, you'll find the answers in Appendix A, "Quiz Answers."

Quiz

1. How do you represent a message in a communication diagram?

2. How do you show sequential information in a communication diagram?

3. How do you show an object changing its state?

4. What is meant by the semantic equivalence of two diagram types?

Exercises

1. In the soda machine example, I included a communication diagram equivalent to an instance sequence diagram only for the incorrect-amount-of-money scenario. Create a communication diagram that corresponds to Hour 9's generic sequence diagram for the "Buy soda" use case. That is, add the out-of-selected-soda scenario to the communication diagram in Figure 10.5.

2. Go back to Hour 4, "Working with Relationships," and examine Figures 4.17–4.19. With the knight about to move, create a communication diagram that shows the likely moves. Assume that each move is a message from one chess piece to another.

3. Create a communication diagram that's equivalent to the sequence diagram you created to model the electric pencil sharpener in Hour 9.

HOUR 11

Working with Activity Diagrams

What You'll Learn in This Hour:

▶ What an activity diagram is

▶ How to apply an activity diagram

▶ How to work with swimlanes

▶ Important concepts from UML 2.0

▶ Where activity diagrams fit into the big picture of the UML

You're about to work with a type of diagram that might seem familiar to you. This diagram shows the steps in an operation or process.

If you've ever taken an introductory course in programming, you've probably encountered the flowchart. One of the first visual models ever applied to computing, the flowchart shows a sequence of steps, processes, decision points, and branches. Novice programmers are encouraged to use flowcharts to conceptualize problems and derive solutions. The idea is to make the flowchart the foundation of the code. With its multiple features and diagram types, the UML is in some ways a flowchart on steroids.

The UML **activity diagram**, the subject of this hour, is much like the flowcharts of old. It shows steps (called, appropriately enough, **activities**) as well as decision points and branches. It's useful for showing what happens in a business process or an operation. You'll find it an integral part of system analysis.

The first four sections of this hour introduce you to the basics—the concepts from UML 1.x. Because UML 2.0 provides a fairly extensive set of activity-related model-ing techniques, I've added a section at the end that presents these newer ideas.

The Basics: What Is an Activity Diagram?

First and foremost, an activity diagram is designed to be a simplified look at what happens during an operation or a process.

Each activity is represented by a rounded rectangle—narrower and more oval-shaped than the state icon you saw in Hour 8, "Working with State Diagrams." The processing within an activity goes to completion and then an automatic transmission to the next activity occurs. An arrow represents the transition from one activity to the next. Like the state diagram, the activity diagram has a starting point represented by a filled-in circle and an endpoint represented by a bull's-eye.

Figure 11.1 shows the starting point, endpoint, two activities, and a transition.

FIGURE 11.1
Transitioning from one activity to another.

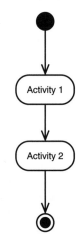

Decisions, Decisions, Decisions

A sequence of activities almost always comes to a point where a decision has to take place. One set of conditions leads to one path, another set of conditions to another path, and the two paths are mutually exclusive.

You can represent a decision point in either of two ways. (Hmmm . . . sounds like a decision.) One way is to show the possible paths coming directly out of an activity. The other is to have the activity transition to a small diamond—reminiscent of the decision symbol in a flowchart—and have the possible paths flow out of the diamond. (As an old flowcharter, I prefer the second way.) Either way, you indicate the condition with a bracketed condition statement near the appropriate path. Figure 11.2 shows you the possibilities.

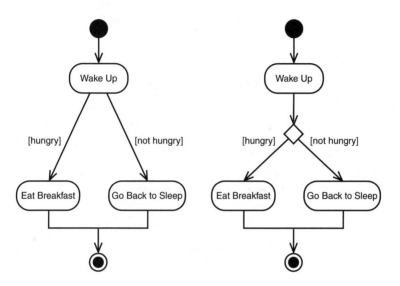

FIGURE 11.2
The two ways of showing a decision.

Concurrent Paths

As you model activities, you'll occasionally have to separate a transition into two separate paths that run at the same time (that is, concurrently) and then come together. To represent the split, you use a solid bold line perpendicular to the transition and show the paths coming out of the line. To represent the merge, show the paths pointing at another solid bold line (see Figure 11.3).

Signals

During a sequence of activities, it's possible to send a signal. When received, the signal causes an activity to take place. The symbol for sending a signal is a convex polygon, and the symbol for receiving a signal is a concave polygon. Figure 11.4 will clarify this.

In UML terms, the convex polygon symbolizes an **output event**; the concave polygon symbolizes an **input event**.

FIGURE 11.3
Representing a
transition split into
two paths that run
concurrently and
then come
together.

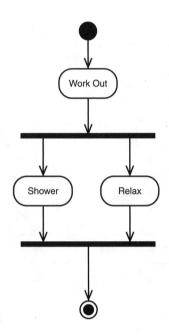

FIGURE 11.4
Sending and
receiving a signal.

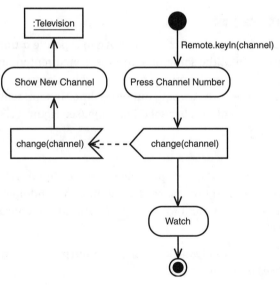

Applying Activity Diagrams

Let's look at an example that uses an activity diagram to model a process.

A Process: Creating a Document

Think of the activities that go into using an office software suite to create a document. One possible sequence of activities is

1. Open the word processing package.

2. Create a file.

3. Save the file under a unique name within its directory.

4. Type the document.

5. If graphics are necessary, open the graphics package, create the graphics, and paste the graphics into the document.

6. If a spreadsheet is necessary, open the spreadsheet package, create the spreadsheet, and paste the spreadsheet into the document.

7. Save the file.

8. Print a hard copy of the document.

9. Exit the office suite.

The activity diagram for this sequence is in Figure 11.5.

Swimlanes

One of the handier aspects of the activity diagram is its ability to expand and show who has the responsibility for each activity in a process.

Consider a consulting firm and the business process involved in meeting a new client. The activities would occur like this:

1. A salesperson calls the client and sets up an appointment.

2. If the appointment is onsite (in the consulting firm's office), corporate technicians prepare a conference room for a presentation.

3. If the appointment is offsite (at the client's office), a consultant prepares a presentation on a laptop.

4. The consultant and the salesperson meet with the client at the agreed-upon location and time.

5. The salesperson follows up with a letter.

6. If the meeting has resulted in a statement of a problem, the consultant creates a proposal and sends it to the client.

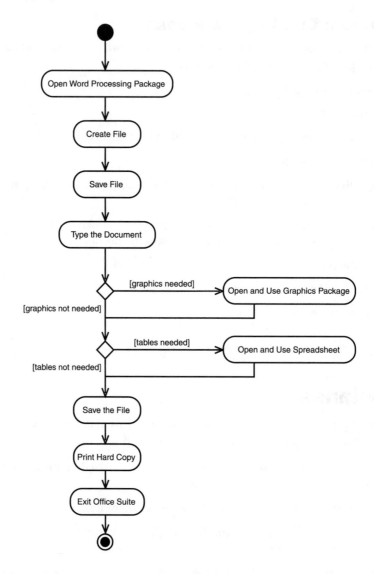

A standard activity diagram would look like Figure 11.6.

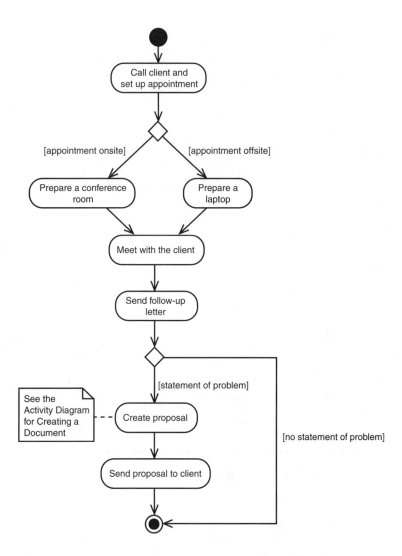

FIGURE 11.6
An activity diagram
for the business
process of meeting
a new client.

The activity diagram adds the dimension of visualizing roles. To do that, you separate the diagram into parallel segments called **swimlanes**. Each swimlane shows the name of a role at the top and presents the activities of each role. Transitions can take place from one swimlane to another. Figure 11.7 shows the swimlane version of the activity diagram in Figure 11.6.

FIGURE 11.7
The swimlane
version of the
activity diagram in
Figure 11.6 shows
the activities that
each role performs.

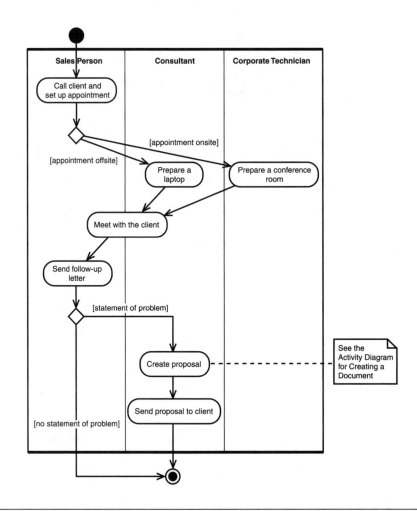

<table>
</table>

By the
Way

Using the Note Symbol

Both activity diagrams for "Meeting a new client" show creating a proposal as an
activity. In each case, that activity could attach to a note that cites the activity diagram for creating a document.

Hybrid Diagrams

Let's revisit the activity diagram for creating a document. You can refine the
activity for printing a hard copy of the document. Instead of just showing a "Print
Hard Copy" activity, you can be a little more specific. Printing takes place

because a signal containing the document's file transmits from the word processing package to the printer, which receives the signal and prints the copy.

Figure 11.8 shows that you can represent this with the symbols for signal transmission and signal reception, along with a printer object that receives the symbol and performs its print operation. This is an example of a **hybrid diagram** because it has symbols you normally associate with different types of diagrams.

New Concepts from UML 2.0

UML 2.0 has turned the magnifying glass on the activity diagram and added a number of modeling techniques. These techniques are intended to help you clarify the details of an operation or a process.

The Objects of an Activity

Newer UML concepts allow you to specify an activity's inputs and outputs. You do this with **object nodes**. I'll use an example from mathematics to illustrate this type of symbol, and carry through this example to help explain some additional UML concepts.

Have you ever seen this series of numbers? 1,1,2,3,5,8,13, . . . It's called the *Fibonacci series*, after the medieval mathematician who wrote about it 800 years ago. Each number is a "fib," so the first fib—fib(1)—is 1, fib(2) is also 1, fib(3) is 2, and so on. The rule is that each fib, except for the first two, is the sum of the preceding two fibs. (fib(8), then, is 21.)

To model the calculation of a fib as an activity, write `Calculate fib(n)` inside an activity icon. You can then connect this icon with another that represents the activity of printing the fib. Figure 11.9 shows the diagram, which includes a notation symbol containing the format for the printed message.

In order to proceed, the first activity has to have an input value for *n*. After it finishes its work, it outputs an answer, which the next activity prints. It also passes along the value of *n* so that the print activity can include that value in the printed statement.

To show an input, add a little box on the left border of the first activity and label it with the input. To show an output, add a little labeled box on the right border. These little boxes are the object nodes. An object node is also appropriate to illustrate the input to the second activity. Figure 11.10 shows object nodes added to the activity icons of Figure 11.9.

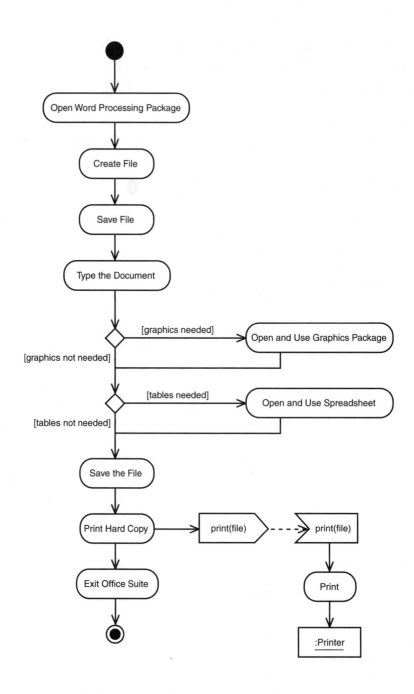

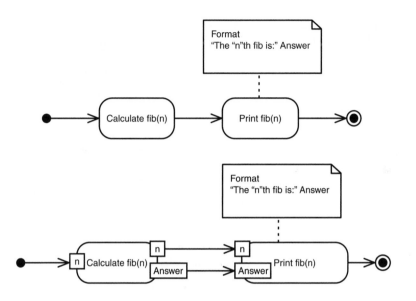

FIGURE 11.9
An activity diagram
that models the
calculation and
printing of a
Fibonacci number.

FIGURE 11.10
Adding object
nodes allows you
to specify an
activity's inputs and
outputs.

If all the object nodes make that diagram look too busy, you can use either of the
elided styles in Figure 11.11.

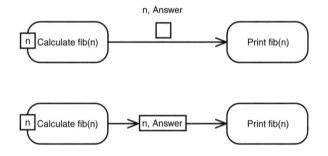

FIGURE 11.11
Two elided
equivalents for the
flow between two
of the activities in
Figure 11.10

Taking Exception

Sometimes an activity encounters an **exception**—a circumstance that's out of the
ordinary or beyond its capabilities in some way. For example, suppose your
Fibonacci calculator cannot compute beyond the one millionth Fibonacci number. If you give it a value of n that's higher than one million, it prints n along
with the message "exceeds the limit on n."

To represent this in an activity diagram, you use an arrow that resembles a lightning bolt. It begins at the activity that encounters the exception and ends at the

activity that describes what happens because of the exception. That activity is called an **exception handler**. Figure 11.12 shows how to do this.

FIGURE 11.12
Modeling an
exception and an
exception handler.

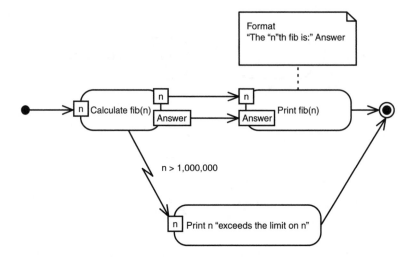

Deconstructing an Activity

UML 2.0 emphasizes the decomposability of activities. An activity can consist of a number of **actions**. The icon for an action is the same as the icon for an activity. Let's keep working with the Fibonacci series and show the actions that constitute the "Calculate fib(n)" activity.

In order to model everything that goes into calculating a fib, you'll require a few variables. You'll need a counter to keep track of whether or not the operation has reached the nth fib, a variable (let's call it Answer) to keep track of your computations, and two more to store the two fibs that you'll have to add together. (Let's call them Answer1 and Answer2.) Figure 11.13 shows the sequence of actions and decisions that make it all happen. Following UML 2.0 format, the flow of the actions is framed inside a large icon that represents the "Calculate fib(n)" activity.

It's also possible to have object nodes on actions. An object node on an action is called a **pin**. Figure 11.14 shows a fragment of the actions of the "Calculate fib(n)" activity, along with the appropriate input pins and output pins. As you can see, the symbol for a pin is smaller than the symbol for an object node on an activity, and the name is outside the pin. I'll leave it to you as an exercise to fill in the pins for the remaining actions in "Calculate fib(n)."

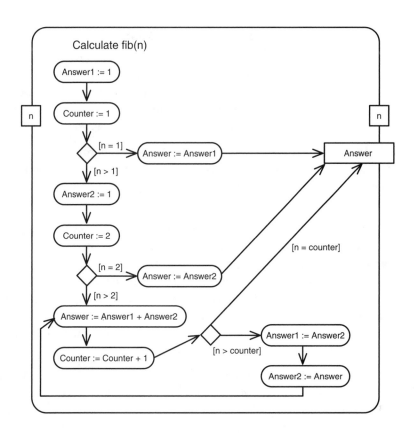

FIGURE 11.13
Modeling the actions that constitute the "Calculate fib(n)" activity.

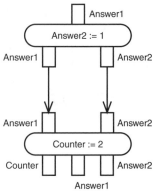

FIGURE 11.14
Part of Figure 11.13 with pins added to two of the actions.

Marking Time and Finishing a Flow

A couple of new UML symbols, shown in Figure 11.15, make activity diagrams smoother. The one on the left is intended to resemble an hourglass and shows the passage of time. The one on the right, called a **flow final node**, shows the finish of a specific sequence of activities without terminating other sequences of activities. It's the same as the exit point symbol for state diagrams you saw in Hour 8.

A good example of these symbols at work is an activity diagram that models the operation of one of my favorite possessions—a digital wristwatch that automatically resets itself early each morning. In its normal mode of operation, the watch updates its display every second.

Between 2 a.m. and 5 a.m. U.S. Eastern Time, the wristwatch goes into a different mode. Each hour on the hour (that is, at 2 a.m., 3 a.m., 4 a.m., and 5 a.m.), the watch stops displaying the time and changes its face to show it's receiving a calibration signal from the U.S. atomic clock in Ft. Collins, Colorado. When reception—which takes 3 to 6 minutes—is complete, the clock displays the recalibrated time and resumes its normal operation. If the signal is interrupted (perhaps because of atmospheric conditions), reception ends, and the watch goes back to displaying the time. Figure 11.16 models all this.

To avoid clutter, I used an elided format to show the time as an object node. This format concisely shows that an output object from one activity is an input object to the next. I've modeled signal reception time as an exception. This is reasonable when you consider that the clock keeps track of seconds. With 86,400 seconds in a day, changing the operations when only four specific seconds occur seems "exceptional." It's also an exception when the signal is interrupted, as the expectation is that the signal transmits clearly. An interrupted signal ends reception/recalibration, and it doesn't affect the rest of what the wristwatch does.

FIGURE 11.15
Two UML 2.0 symbols for activity diagrams. The one on the left models the passage of time. The one on the right shows the end of a specific sequence of activities.

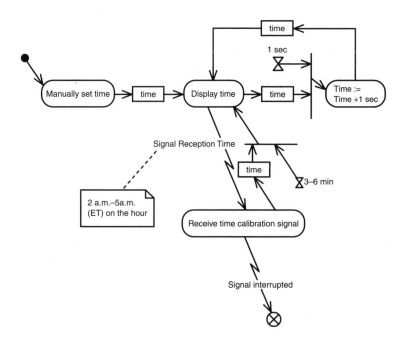

FIGURE 11.16
Modeling a wristwatch that automatically resets the time each morning by receiving a signal from the U.S. atomic clock in Colorado. If the recalibration signal is interrupted, the watch resumes displaying the time.

Special Effects

The use of objects in activity diagrams opens up still another dimension in modeling: You can use constraint notation to show the effect an activity (or an action) has on an object.

Here's an example of one kind of effect, although many are possible. If you're anything like me, you probably enjoy watching streaming video over the Internet. (I'm particularly fond of baseball games, but perhaps you have other priorities.) Let's model the transmission and reception of this type of video.

Figure 11.17 shows the model set up as a swimlane diagram. One swimlane represents the server, and the other represents the client. The server sends the video, modeled as an output object, to the client. For the client, the video is an input object. Each appearance of the word *stream* in curly brackets indicates that the attached activity is a continuous operation: "Display video" doesn't wait for "Send video" to complete before springing into action. This, of course, is why streaming media was invented. You don't wait hours for a huge multimedia file to download before you start watching and listening.

FIGURE 11.17
Modeling the effect of an activity on an object. In this case, *streaming* indicates a continuous operation: *Send video* doesn't finish before *Display video* begins.

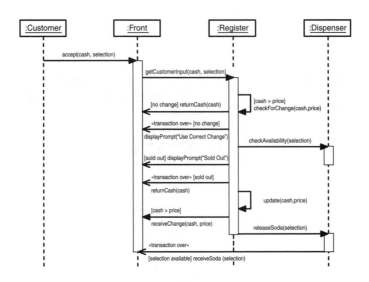

An Overview of an Interaction

In Hour 9, "Working with Sequence Diagrams," I showed you one way to combine sequence diagrams and mentioned that in Hour 11 I'd show you another. Here it is.

UML 2.0 offers the **interaction overview diagram**, a combination of modeling techniques from activity diagrams and interaction diagrams. The interaction overview diagram is an activity diagram in which each activity is. . . a separate interaction diagram!

To show you what I mean, let's return to the soda machine. Just for convenience, I've copied Figure 9.13 here as Figure 11.18. It's the generic sequence diagram for the "Buy soda" use case.

How do you represent this sequence of object interactions in activity diagram framework? In effect, you take the guard conditions out of the messages and put them on arrows that connect sequence diagrams. You also remove «transaction over» because it's no longer necessary: In this type of diagram you show that a transaction is over in the usual activity-diagram way—by pointing an arrow to the endpoint.

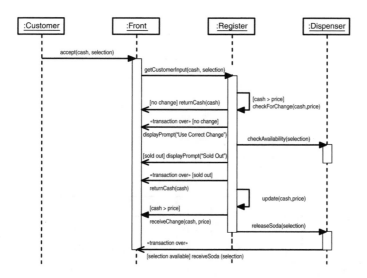

FIGURE 11.18
The generic sequence diagram for the "Buy soda" use case.

The time-intensive part of creating this diagram is the individual sequence diagrams that connect to one another. In this case, I dissected Figure 11.18 to come up with them. Figure 11.19 shows the result. By the way, I simplified things a little by assuming that change can be $0.00.

Note the frame around the whole diagram and the frame around each sequence diagram. In UML 2.0 fashion, each frame's upper left corner shows the little pentagonal compartment that holds identifying information. The *sd* in each one stands for *sequence diagram*. The large frame's pentagon shows the name of the use case and the name of the objects in the interaction. (In sequence diagrams, UML 2.0 refers to the participating lifelines, and that's the style I use here.)

The frames in this diagram might remind you that in Hour 9, I told you about *interaction occurrences*—pieces of a sequence diagram you can name and reuse. You can reuse these occurrences in interaction overview diagrams.

Go back and look at Figure 9.18, and you'll see what I mean. In the best-case scenario of "Buy soda," I compartmentalized the messages for releaseSoda(selection) and receiveSoda(selection) into an interaction occurrence, referenced it as DeliverSoda(selection), and reused it in Figure 9.19.

In our overview diagram, the referenced DeliverSoda(selection) is appropriate for the lowermost sequence diagram. Figure 11.20 zooms in on that diagram and shows the reuse of DeliverSoda(selection).

FIGURE 11.19
An interaction
overview diagram
of the "Buy soda"
use case.

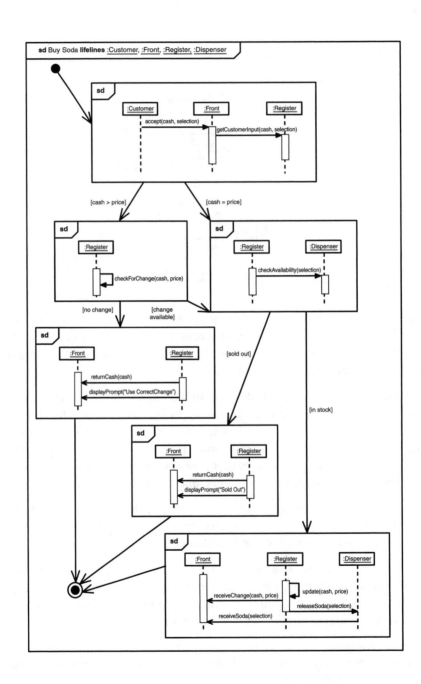

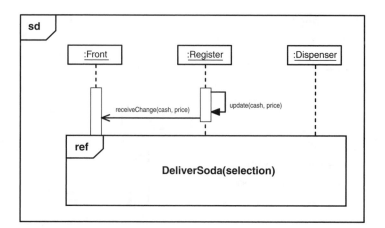

FIGURE 11.20
Reusing an interaction occurrence in one of the sequence diagrams of Figure 11.19.

Building the Big Picture

Figure 11.21 shows the growing big picture of the UML, including the activity diagram. This diagram is a behavioral element.

Summary

The UML activity diagram is much like a flowchart. It shows steps, decision points, and branches.

Each activity is represented as a rounded rectangle, more oval in appearance than the state icon. The activity diagram uses the same symbols as the state diagram for the starting point and the endpoint.

When a path diverges into two or more paths, you represent the divergence with a solid bold line perpendicular to the paths, and you represent the paths coming together with the same type of line. Within a sequence diagram you can show a signal: Represent a signal transmission with a convex pentagon and a signal reception with a concave pentagon.

In an activity diagram, you can represent the activities each role performs. You do this by dividing the diagram into swimlanes—parallel segments that correspond to the roles.

It's possible to combine the activity diagram with symbols from other diagrams and produce a hybrid diagram.

FIGURE 11.21
Your big picture of the UML now includes the activity diagram.

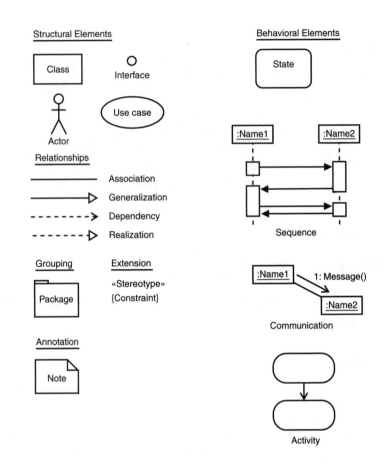

UML 2.0 adds a number of modeling techniques to the activity diagram. The latest version of UML emphasizes the component actions of an activity and the objects that activities work with and pass along to other activities.

An interaction overview diagram has the overall framework of an activity diagram and interaction diagrams as the activities.

Q&A

Q. *This is another one of those "Do I really need it?" questions. With everything that a state diagram shows, do I really need activity diagrams?*

A. My recommendation is that you include activity diagrams in your analyses. They'll clarify some processes and operations, both in your mind and in your clients'. They're also very useful for developers. It's likely that a good activity diagram will go a long way toward helping a developer code an operation.

Q. *Does the UML limit the kinds of hybrid diagrams I can create?*

A. It does not limit you. The UML is not meant to be restrictive. Although it does have syntactical rules, the idea is for analysts to build a model that conveys a consistent vision to clients, designers, and developers, not to satisfy narrow linguistic rules. If you can build a hybrid diagram that helps all stakeholders understand a system, by all means do it. Bear in mind that not all modeling tools allow you the flexibility to create hybrid diagrams.

Q. *When I look at Figure 11.12, the object nodes make it seem to me that values are moving from one activity to the next. Is that the impression these diagrams are supposed to convey?*

A. Absolutely. The idea behind activity diagrams, particularly in UML 2.0, is to show the *flow* of a **token**—a piece of information or a locus of control—through the sequence of activities. The idea for this came from a modeling technique called **Petri Nets**, which emerged in the 1960s. Adding the object nodes and pins is one way that UML 2.0 has made the activity diagram more object-oriented.

Q. *That interaction overview diagram leads me to believe that I can create an activity diagram as an intermediate step toward creating a generic sequence diagram. I'd start with activities and then substitute an interaction diagram for each one. I'd ultimately combine them into a generic sequence diagram. How does that sound?*

A. It sounds like a nice idea. It's the reverse of what I did to develop Figure 11.19, but I don't see why you couldn't work in that direction. In general, many people find it easy to use activity diagrams to start their modeling efforts, possibly because they're used to flowcharting.

Q. *I noticed that you used sequence diagrams as the parts of the interaction overview diagram. Can I use collaboration . . . excuse me . . . communication diagrams instead?*

A. Yes, you can. Either type of interaction diagram can appear in an interaction overview diagram. In fact, nothing prevents you from using both types in one overview diagram, but that would most likely confuse your audience.

Q. *The swimlane examples showed swimlanes as vertically oriented components. Can I lay them out horizontally?*

A. Yes, you can represent them either way. I like the vertical layout, but that's just my preference.

Workshop

The quiz questions and exercises will get you thinking about activity diagrams and how to use them. Answers are in Appendix A, "Quiz Answers."

Quiz

1. What are the two ways of representing a decision point?

2. What is a swimlane?

3. How do you represent signal transmission and reception?

4. What is an action?

5. What is an object node?

6. What is a pin?

Exercises

1. Create an activity diagram that shows the process you go through when you start your car. Begin with putting the key in the ignition, end with the engine running, and consider the activities you perform if the engine doesn't start immediately.

2. What can you add to the activity diagram for the business process of meeting a new client?

3. If you lay out three stones so that one stone is in one row and two are in the next row, they form a triangle. If you lay out six stones so that one is in one row, two are in the next, and three are in the next, they form a triangle, too. For this reason, 3 and 6 are called *triangle numbers*. The next triangle number is 10, the one after that 15, and so on. The first triangle number is 1. Create two different activity diagrams for a process that computes the *n*th

triangle number. For one, start with *n* and work backward. For the other, start with 1 and move forward. In your activity icon, show all the actions and pins. (You may have noticed that the *n*th triangle number is equal to [(n)(n + 1)]/2. In order to get the full benefit of this exercise, however, avoid this solution.)

4. Here's an exercise for the mathematically inclined. If you were comfortable with Exercise 3, you might like this one. If not, just move on to the next hour. (You might try diagramming what I said in these last two sentences!) In coordinate geometry, you represent a point in space by showing its *x*-position and its *y*-position. Thus, you can say that point 1's location is X1,Y1. Point 2's location is X2,Y2. To find the distance between these two points, you square X2–X1 and then you square Y2–Y1. Add these two squared quantities together, and take the square root of the sum. Create an activity diagram for an operation `distance(X1,Y1,X2,Y2)` that finds the distance between two points. Include all the actions.

HOUR 12

Working with Component Diagrams

What You'll Learn in This Hour:

▶ What a component is
▶ Components and interfaces
▶ What a component diagram is
▶ Applying component diagrams
▶ Component diagrams in the big picture of the UML

In previous hours, you learned about diagrams that deal with conceptual entities. For example, a class diagram represents a concept—an abstraction of items that fit into a category. A state diagram also represents a concept—changes in the state of an object.

In this hour, you're going to learn about a UML diagram that represents a different kind of entity: a **software component**.

What Is (and What Isn't) a Component?

A software component is a modular part of a system. Because it's the software implementation of one or more classes, a component resides in a computer, not in the mind of an analyst. A component provides interfaces to other components.

In UML 1.x, data files, tables, executables, documents, and dynamic link libraries were defined as components. In fact, modelers used to classify these kinds of items as *deployment components*, *work product components*, and *execution components*. UML 2.0 refers to them instead as **artifacts**—pieces of information that a system uses or produces.

A component, by contrast, defines a system's functionality. Just as a component is the implementation of one or more classes, an artifact (if it's executable) is the implementation of a component.

You model components and their relationships so that

1. Clients can envision the structure and the functionality in the finished system.

2. Developers have a structure to work toward.

3. Technical writers who have to provide documentation and help files can understand what they're writing about.

4. You're ready for reuse.

Let's explore that last one. One of the most important aspects of components is the potential they provide for reusability. In today's rapid-fire business arena, the quicker you bring a system to fruition, the greater your competitive edge. If you can build a component for one system and reuse it in another, you contribute to that edge. Taking the time and the effort to model a component helps reuse occur.

You revisit reuse at the end of the next section.

Components and Interfaces

When you deal with components, you have to deal with their interfaces. Early in my discussion of classes and objects, I talked about interfaces. As you might recall from Hour 2, "Understanding Object-Orientation," an object hides what it does from other objects and from the outside world. (I referred to that as *encapsulation* or *information-hiding*.) The object has to present a "face" to the outside world so that other objects (including, potentially, humans) can ask the object to execute its operations. This face is the object's *interface*.

Reviewing Interfaces

I elaborated on this idea in Hour 5, "Understanding Aggregations, Composites, Interfaces, and Realizations." As I mentioned then, an interface is a set of operations that allows you to access a class's behavior—like the control knob that enables you to get a washing machine to perform washing machine–related operations. Think of an interface as a class that only has operations—no attributes. Bottom line: The interface is a set of operations that a class presents to other classes.

In my discussion of interfaces in Hour 5, I also mentioned that the relationship between a class and its interface is called *realization*.

Wait a second. It sounds like modeling an interface is an exercise in modeling a concept. At the top of this hour, I said that when you model a component, you model something that's not conceptual but lives in a computer. What's the connection?

In fact, an interface can be either conceptual or physical. The interface a class uses is the same as the interface its software implementation (a component) uses. For you as a modeler, this means that the way you represent an interface for a class is the same as the way you represent an interface for a component. Although the UML symbology distinguishes between a class and a component, it makes no distinction between a conceptual interface and a physical one.

Here's an important point to remember about components and interfaces: You can reach a component's operations only through its interfaces. As is the case with a class and its interface, the relation between a component and its interface is called *realization*.

Here's another important point: A component can make its interface available so that other components can utilize the interface's operations. In other words, a component can access the services of another component. The component that offers the services is said to present a **provided interface**. The component that accesses the services is said to use a **required interface**.

Replacement and Reuse

Interfaces figure heavily into the important concepts of component replacement and component reuse. You can replace one component with another if the new component conforms to the same interfaces as the old one.

To illustrate replacement and interfaces, here's an example from the world of automobiles. A few years ago, a friend of mine owned a certain classic sports car from the 1960s. (I won't name the manufacturer.) He quickly discovered that one additional piece of equipment was absolutely essential—another car so he could visit the sports car in the shop! Why? The engine was, to put it mildly, "high-spirited" and constantly required repair. My friend's solution was to get a standard engine from another make of car—less powerful but more reliable—and replace the original engine. He was able to do this because the new engine, though designed and built for an entirely different automobile, just happened to interface properly with the other components of the sports car.

This is also a good illustration of reuse. You can reuse a component in another system (like the replacement engine for the sports car) if the new system can access the reused component through that component's interfaces. If you can refine a component's interfaces so that a wide array of other components can access them, you can engineer that component for reuse in development projects across your whole enterprise.

This is where modeling interfaces comes in handy. Life is easier for a developer trying to replace or reuse a component if the component's interface information is readily available in the form of a model. If not, the developer has to go through the time-consuming process of stepping through code.

What Is a Component Diagram?

A component diagram contains—appropriately enough—components, along with interfaces and relationships. Other types of symbols that you've already seen can also appear in a component diagram.

Representing a Component in UML 1.x and UML 2.0

In UML 1.x, the component diagram's main icon is a rectangle that has two rectangles overlaid on its left side. Many modelers found the 1.x symbol too cumbersome, particularly when they had to show a connection to the left side. For this reason, UML 2.0 provides a new component icon. In UML 2.0, the icon is a rectangle with the keyword «component» near the top. For continuity over the near-term, you can include the 1.x icon inside the 2.0 icon. Figure 12.1 shows these icons.

FIGURE 12.1
The component icon in UML 1.x and the two versions of the component icon in UML 2.0.

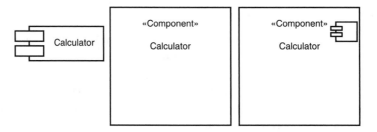

Figure 12.2 shows that if the component is a member of a package, you can prefix the component's name with the name of the package. You can also show the component's operations in a separate panel.

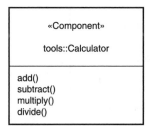

FIGURE 12.2
Adding information
to the component
icon.

Speaking of artifacts, Figure 12.3 shows a couple of ways to represent them, and it also shows how to model the relationship between a particular kind of artifact (an executable) and the component it implements. As you can see, you can place a notation symbol in the artifact icon, analogous to the UML 1.x component symbol in the component icon.

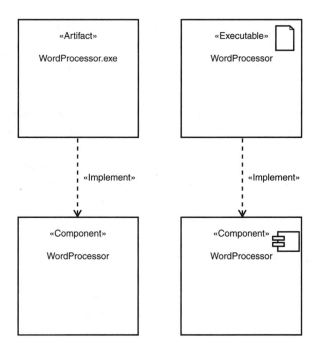

FIGURE 12.3
Modeling the rela-
tionship between
an artifact and a
component.

Representing Interfaces

A component and the interfaces it realizes can be represented in two ways. The first shows the interface as a rectangle that contains interface-related informa-tion. It's connected to the component by the dashed line and large open triangle that indicate realization. (See Figure 12.4.)

FIGURE 12.4
You can represent an interface as a rectangle that contains information, connected to the component by a realization arrow.

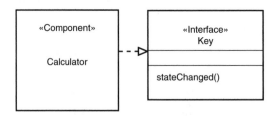

Figure 12.5 shows the second way. It's iconic: You represent the interface as a small circle connected to the component by a solid line. (Compare Figures 12.4 and 12.5 with Figures 5.6 and 5.7.)

FIGURE 12.5
You can represent an interface as a small circle connected to the component by a solid line

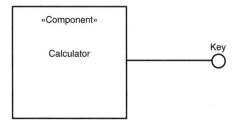

In addition to realization, you can represent dependency—the relationship between a component and an interface through which it accesses another component. As you'll recall, dependency is visualized as a dashed line with an arrowhead. You can show realization and dependency on the same diagram, as in the upper diagram of Figure 12.6. The lower diagram of Figure 12.6 shows the equivalent ball-and-socket notation that you saw in Hour 5. In the terminology I mentioned earlier, the "ball" represents a *provided interface* and the "socket" represents a *required interface*.

Boxes—Black and White

When you model a component's interfaces as in Figure 12.6, you show what UML calls an external, or "black box," view. You also have the option of showing an internal, or "white box," view. This view shows interfaces listed inside the component icon and organized by keywords. Figure 12.7 shows a white box view of the components in Figure 12.6.

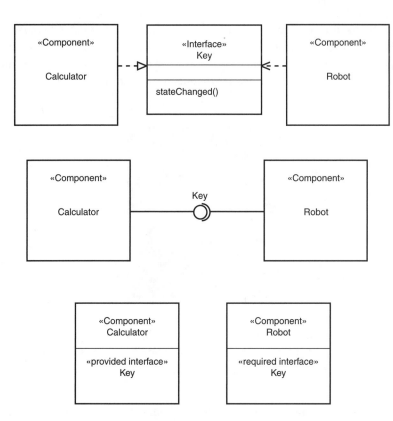

FIGURE 12.6
Two ways of show-
ing realization and
dependency in the
same diagram.

FIGURE 12.7
A white box view of
the components in
Figure 12.6.

Applying Component Diagrams

An example will get you started with component diagrams. This example models
a program from Rogers Cadenhead's *Teach Yourself Java 2 in 24 Hours, Third Edition*
(Sams Publishing, 2003). Entertaining and well-written, I highly recommend this
book if you want to (a) quickly become proficient in Java, (b) learn how to say
"Hello World" in Esperanto, and (c) find out how Rogers became the only computer author ever to be named a co-MVP in an NBA playoff game. (That last
one's a stretch, but you'll enjoy it.)

The example comes from Rogers's Hour 16 ("Building a Complex User Interface").
The Java code creates an application called ColorSlide. This is a set of three sliders that enable you to mix amounts of red, green, and blue to create a color. One
slider corresponds to each of those colors. The location of each slider determines
the amount of its color that goes into the mix. The created color appears in a
panel below the sliders.

Figure 12.8, taken from Rogers's book, shows the finished product. Of course, the figure is in shades of gray, so you can't actually see the created color. The positioning of the sliders in the figure creates North Texas Mean Green, a color that apparently holds great significance to students and alumni of the University of North Texas.

FIGURE 12.8
Rogers Cadenhead's ColorSlide application (from *Teach Yourself Java 2 in 24 Hours, Third Edition*).

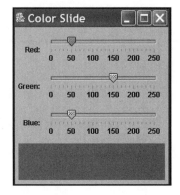

To help you understand the thought process behind this program, I'll take you through a sequence of component diagrams. The objective is for you to see how the program takes shape and at the same time learn some modeling techniques.

Figure 12.9 sets the stage by showing the packages that supply the Java elements used in the program. The acronym awt stands for "abstract windowing toolkit," a group of components that display and control a graphic user interface (GUI). The specific components for this program are Color (which displays a color), GridLayout and FlowLayout (which arrange the elements in the GUI), and Graphics and Graphics2D (which paint the GUI—that is, they render it onscreen).

The name on the tab of the other major package, swing, is a group of components that you can add to a graphic user interface. The names of the components in the package in this figure are pretty self-explanatory: JSlider is a slider, JFrame is a frame, JPanel is a panel (an area within the frame), and JLabel is a label.

The package labeled swing.event supplies the ChangeListener interface. This interface waits for state changes to occur in the GUI.

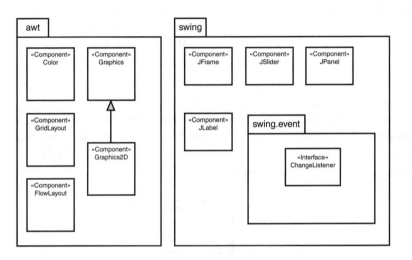

FIGURE 12.9
The packages that supply the Java ele-ments for the ColorSlide application.

Figure 12.10 shows the highest level of analysis for our components. It presents, in a general way, the idea that ColorSlide inherits from JFrame and provides ChangeListener, a required interface for a Person who interacts with ColorSlide. Interaction between ChangeListener and ColorSlide takes place through a port. The results of that interaction are sent to Color, as indicated by the arrow from the port to Color. UML 2.0 refers to the ball-and-socket connection as an **assembly connector** and to the arrow as a **delegation connector**. (The concept of connectors is new in UML 2.0.)

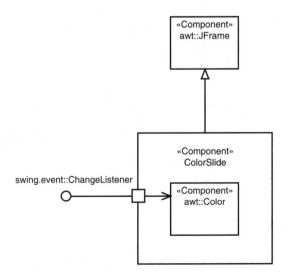

FIGURE 12.10
The initial component diagram for the ColorSlide application.

Note that the package names appear as prefixes for the component names. (Strictly speaking, awt is really java.awt and swing.event is really javax.swing.event, but I decided to cut down on the clutter.) In Java, a program **imports** packages at the beginning of the code, meaning that the programmer doesn't have to specify the package for each component throughout the program. The remaining figures reflect the import of the packages and don't include the package names.

Figure 12.11 moves to another level of analysis and shows that ColorSlide is an aggregation whose components are JSlider, JPanel, and JLabel, with the indicated multiplicities. Because the program deals with red, blue, and green, you can see why the model specifies three sliders and three labels (one label per slider). It specifies four panels because each slider has to have its own area, and the part that displays the color has to have a designated area, too.

FIGURE 12.11
The ColorSlide
application
modeled as an
aggregation of
components.

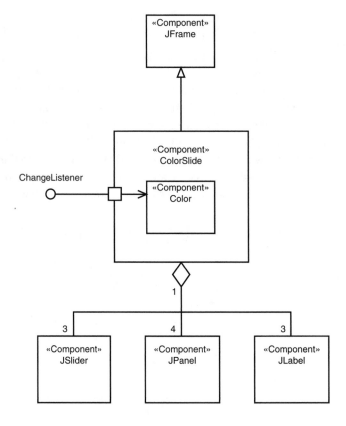

Next, Figure 12.12 takes into account the laying out of the components and the rendering of the GUI. The keyword «Arrange» shows that GridLayout and FlowLayout arrange the panels, sliders, and labels. (I won't go into the details of how they do the arranging.) The keyword «Paint» indicates that Graphics and Graphics2D handle the rendering. (Again, I'll skip the details.) These keywords aren't built into UML. I added them for clarity.

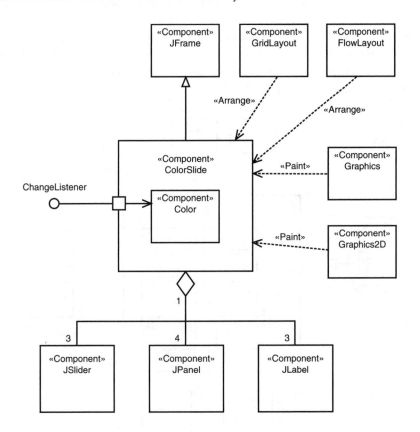

If you've been following along closely, you might have become aware of a slight disconnect. Figures 12.11 and 12.12 show JSlider as a component and ChangeListener as the interface. A user can create colors only by manipulating the sliders. Each time a slider moves, the movement causes the displayed color to change. How do you show the relationships between the sliders and the interface?

The next level of analysis provides the answer and shows that the program creates instances of the components in the GUI. To model those instances, you can use the icons for objects that you learned in Hour 3. What about those sliders? In Java, when you create an object (like an instance of a slider) you can *register* it as a change listener. In this case, registering a slider-object as a change listener means that when the slider moves, the movement is noted and the displayed color changes as a result.

Figure 12.13 shows this level of analysis and presents the objects that make up ColorSlide. The ChangeListener is a required interface for the three instances of JSlider. A delegation connector connects the port to current, an instance of Color. The canvas object is an instance of a class called ColorPanel, a child class of JPanel. For completeness, the figure shows the inheritance relationship between ColorPanel and JPanel.

FIGURE 12.13
Modeling the component-objects in the ColorSlide application.

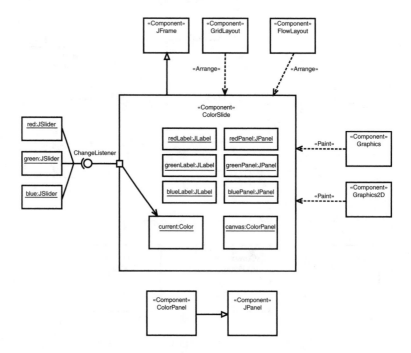

Why bother creating the ColorPanel class? How, exactly, do you register an object as an interface? How do those awt components work? You'll just have to read Rogers's book to find out.

Component Diagrams in the Big Picture

You're almost done with the big picture. Figure 12.14 includes the component diagram, which focuses on a system's software architecture. In the next hour, you'll learn how to model the hardware architecture.

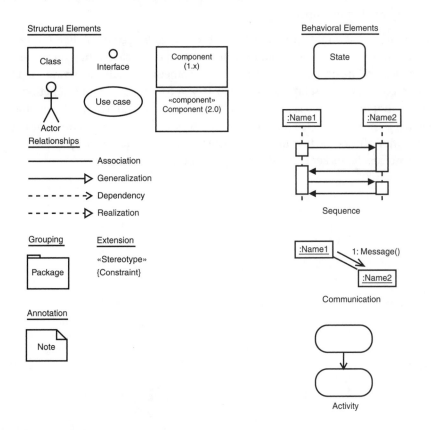

FIGURE 12.14
Your big picture of the UML now includes the component diagram.

Summary

A component is a modular part of a computer system, distinguishable from an artifact, which is a piece of information that system uses or creates. Components define a software system's functionality.

A component *provides* interfaces that allow other components to access it. For an accessing component, the interface is said to be *required*.

In UML 1.x, the component icon is a rectangle with two small rectangles overlaid on its left side. In UML 2.0, the component icon is a rectangle with the keyword «Component» near the top. For continuity in the near term, UML 2.0 recommends using a tiny 1.x component icon in the upper right corner of the new icon. The artifact icon is a rectangle with the keyword «Artifact» near the top. You can put a note symbol in its upper right corner.

You can represent an interface in either of two ways. One representation is a rectangle containing information about the interface and connected to the component with a dashed line and an empty triangle. The other is a small circle connected to the component with a solid line. In UML 2.0, you can use a ball-and-socket notation to show that an interface is provided by one component and required by another. The ball is the small circle I just mentioned. The socket is an open semi-circle connected with a solid line to another component. The ball represents a provided interface, whereas the socket represents a required interface.

Q&A

Q. *In the examples of the ball-and-socket notation, you show a provided interface on one component and a required interface on another. Can a component have one of each kind?*

A. Yes. In fact, a component can have more than one of each kind of interface.

Workshop

In this workshop, you get to solidify your knowledge about components and how to model them. You can find answers to the Quiz questions in Appendix A, "Quiz Answers."

Quiz

1. What is the difference between components and artifacts?

2. What are the two ways of representing the relationship between a component and its interface?

3. What is a *provided interface*? What is a *required interface*?

Exercises

1. Although UML 1.x is gradually giving way to UML 2.0, most existing models and many modeling tools still conform to the old standard. To give you some practice with this standard, convert Figures 12.8–12.13 to UML 1.x. This isn't just a trivial change from one icon to another: Remember that ports and connectors do not exist in UML 1.x.

2. Create a white box view of ColorSlide.

Working with Deployment Diagrams

What You'll Learn in This Hour:

▶ What a deployment diagram is

▶ Applying deployment diagrams

▶ Deployment diagrams in the big picture of the UML

So far, you've stayed mainly in the conceptual realm, turning in the last hour to models of software components. Now you will look at the hardware. As you can see, the focus has moved from items (like classes) that live in analyses, to software components, to hardware that lives in the real world.

Hardware, of course, is a prime topic in a multicomponent system. In today's world of computing, a system is likely to encompass numerous types of platforms in far-flung locations. A solid blueprint for setting up the hardware is essential to system design. The UML provides you with symbols for creating a clear picture of how the final hardware setup should look, along with the items that reside on the hardware.

What Is a Deployment Diagram?

A deployment diagram shows how artifacts (which you met in Hour 12, "Working with Component Diagrams") are deployed on system hardware, and how the pieces of hardware connect to one another. The main hardware item is a **node**, a generic name for a computing resource.

In UML 1.x, many modelers (including me) distinguished between two types of nodes—a *processor* (a node that can execute a component) and a *device* (a peripheral piece of hardware that doesn't execute components but typically interfaces in some way with the outside world). Although that distinction wasn't formalized in UML 1.x, it was useful.

UML 2.0 now formally defines a **device** as a node that executes artifacts. (Remember from Hour 12 that an executable is now classified as an artifact).

In UML 2.0 a cube represents a node (as was the case in UML 1.x). You supply a name for the node, and you can add the keyword «Device», although it's usually not necessary. I still think it's a good idea to distinguish between devices and peripherals, as you'll see. Figure 13.1 shows a node.

FIGURE 13.1
Representing a node in the UML.

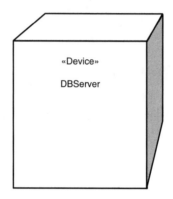

Figure 13.2 shows three ways to model the artifacts deployed on a node.

FIGURE 13.2
Three ways to model the deployment of artifacts on a node.

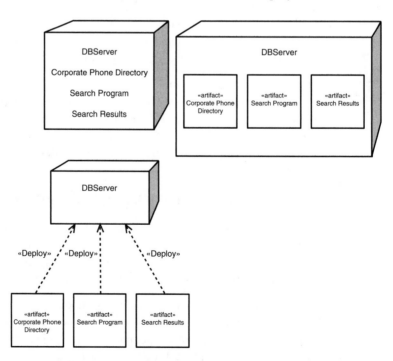

A line joining two cubes represents a connection between two nodes. Bear in mind that a connection isn't necessarily a piece of wire or cable. You can also represent wireless connections, such as infrared and satellite. Figure 13.3 shows an example of an internode connection.

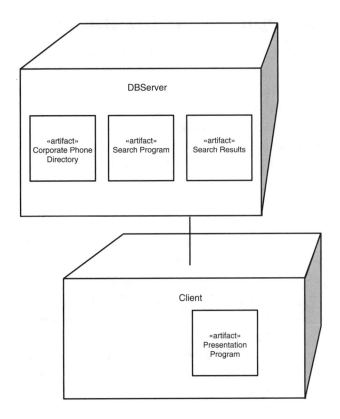

FIGURE 13.3
Representing the connection between nodes.

UML 2.0's emphasis on artifacts brings a set of new artifact-related concepts. One of these concepts is the **deployment specification**, an artifact that provides parameters for another artifact. A good example of this is the initialization command that some modem connections require. This is a string of characters that sets values for certain characteristics of the modem. Figure 13.4 shows how to model a deployment specification.

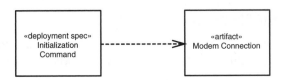

FIGURE 13.4
Representing a deployment specification and its relationship with an artifact it parameterizes.

For clarity, one could add the keyword «parameterize» to the arrow, although this keyword doesn't come with UML 2.0—that is, it's not part of the UML specification.

Applying Deployment Diagrams

A good place to start is with a home computer system, so the first example is a deployment diagram of the system I used to write this book.

As I said earlier, however, today's multiprocessor systems might connect nodes that live far away from each other. To round out the picture, then, you'll also look at examples of deployment diagrams applied to networks. I'll include examples you might find useful and adaptable to your own work. Each example includes constraints that reflect the rules of the particular network.

A Home System

In modeling my home system, I've included the devices, and I've used the node symbol to also represent peripherals. As I said earlier, the device-peripheral distinction is a useful one, and this is an example.

The way I used the node in this context is what UML 2.0 refers to as a *nonnormative* usage of the node. In UML 2.0, a node, strictly speaking, represents a piece of hardware that can compute. Because systems involve peripherals, it seems reasonable to include those peripherals in models. In order to distinguish peripherals from devices, one could add «peripheral» to each nonnormative node, but once again this is not a keyword built into UML. The nonnormative node's name (I love the alliteration) would most likely supply enough information to make that keyword unnecessary.

Figure 13.5 presents the deployment diagram. I modeled the broadband connection with my Internet service provider and their connection to the Internet. The cloud that represents the Internet and the lightning bolt that represents a wireless connection are not in the UML symbol set, but they're useful for clarifying the model. (I'll discuss this kind of symbol usage in Hour 14, "Understanding Packages and Foundations.")

A Token-Ring Network

In a token-ring network, computers equipped with **network interface cards** (NICs) connect to a central **multistation access unit** (MSAU). Multiple MSAUs are connected together in a series that looks like a ring (hence the *ring* part of the name). The ring of MSAUs combines to act as a traffic cop, using a signal called a **token** to let each computer know when it can transmit information (hence, the *token* part of the name).

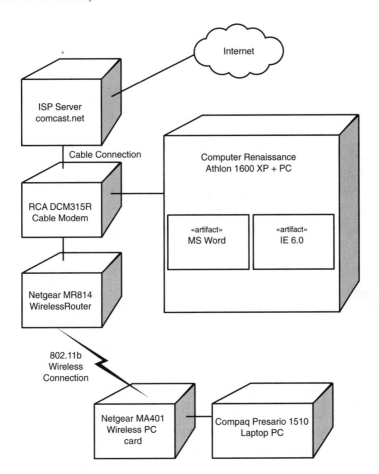

FIGURE 13.5
Deployment diagram of my home system.

When a computer *gets* the token, only that computer's information can go to the network. After it is sent, the information travels to its destination. When the information reaches its destination, an acknowledgement can go back to the computer that sent it.

In this example, shown in Figure 13.6, I've modeled a network that consists of three MSAUs and their respective computers.

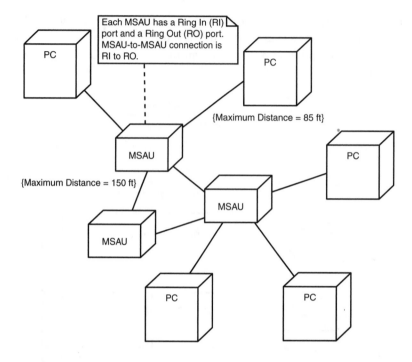

FIGURE 13.6
Deployment diagram for a token-ring network that consists of three MSAUs.

ARCnet

Like a token-ring network, an **ARCnet (Attached Resources Computing network)** involves passing a token from computer to computer. The difference is that in an ARCnet, each computer has an assigned number. This number determines the order in which the computers get the token. Each computer connects to a hub, which is either active (amplifies incoming information before passing it on) or passive (passes information without amplifying it).

Unlike the MSAUs in a token-ring network, ARCnet hubs don't move the token around in a ring. The computers really do pass the token to one another.

Figure 13.7 models an ARCnet with a passive hub, an active hub, and several computers.

Thin Ethernet

The thin ethernet is a popular type of network. Computers connect to a network cable via connection devices called T-connectors. One network segment may join another via a **repeater**, a device that amplifies a signal before passing it on.

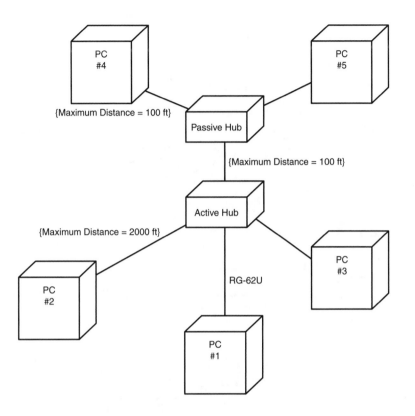

FIGURE 13.7
Deployment
diagram of an
ARCnet.

Figure 13.8 models a thin ethernet network.

The Ricochet Wireless Network

Ricochet Networks, Inc. provides a wireless modem solution for mobile Internet access. Its wireless modem plugs into a computer's serial port and broadcasts to Ricochet's proprietary network.

The Ricochet network consists of radio transmitter-receivers, each about the size of a shoebox. These microcell radios are mounted on top of streetlights a quarter- to a half-mile apart, arranged in a checkerboard pattern. Equipped with a special adapter, each microcell radio draws a small amount of power from its streetlight.

The microcell radios broadcast signals to Wired Access Points that move the information to a **Network Interconnection Facility** (**NIF**). The NIF consists of a **name server** (a database that validates connections), a **router** (a device for linking networks together), and a **gateway** (a device for translating information from one communications protocol to another). Information then moves from the NIF to the Internet.

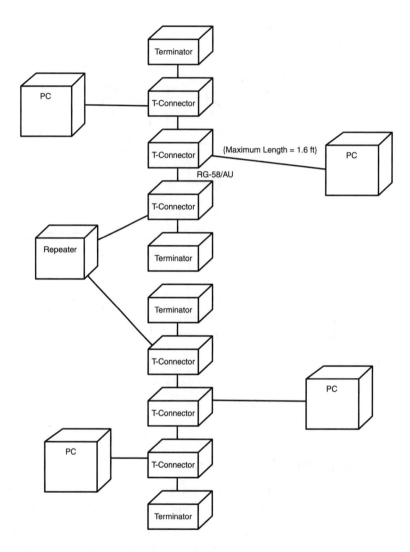

Available only in Denver and San Diego at this writing, Ricochet technology provides a nice modeling opportunity. Figure 13.9 shows the deployment diagram for
this network.

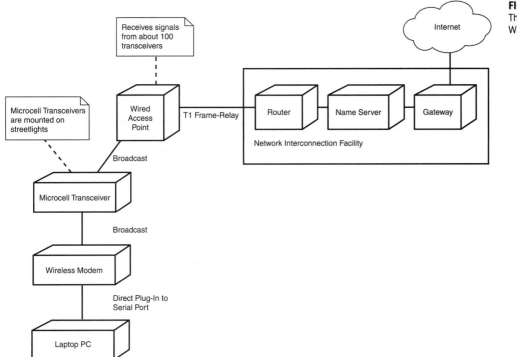

FIGURE 13.9
The Ricochet
Wireless Network.

Deployment Diagrams in the Big Picture

You've come to the end of the UML diagram set. The big picture (Figure 13.10) includes the node and the artifact and is now complete.

Summary

The UML deployment diagram provides a picture of how the physical system will look when it's all put together. A system consists of nodes, with each node represented by a cube. A line joining two cubes symbolizes a connection between two nodes. You can show the artifacts that reside on each node.

As you might imagine, deployment diagrams are useful for modeling networks. Models presented in this hour include token-ring networks, ARCnet, thin ethernet, and the Ricochet Wireless Network.

FIGURE 13.10
Your big picture of the UML includes the deployment diagram symbols and is complete.

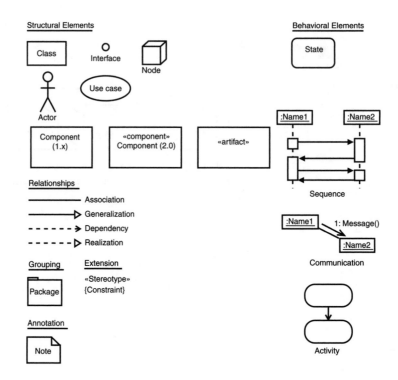

Q&A

Q. *You used a cloud to represent the Internet and said it wasn't part of the UML symbol set. Can a modeler use other symbols that aren't in the symbol set?*

A. Yes. If you do, the UML Police will not hunt you down. The idea is to use the UML to express a vision. Nowhere is this more useful than with deployment diagrams. If you have clip art that clearly shows desktops, laptops, servers, and other devices, you can use them in your diagrams. In effect, you're creating a graphic stereotype. I'll show an example of this in the next hour. (The cloud symbol, by the way, is an interesting footnote in UML lore. One of the UML creators, Grady Booch, used to represent objects as clouds in the symbol set of his modeling scheme before he became part of the UML team.)

Q. *Suppose I have clip art available for some objects but not others. Can I mix them in with the UML symbols?*

A. Yes, you can. The object is to draw diagrams that clarify a vision, not (pardon the pun) cloud it.

Workshop

Now that you've finished the set of UML diagrams, test your knowledge about how to represent hardware. The answers are deployed in Appendix A, "Quiz Answers."

Quiz

1. How do you represent a node in a deployment diagram?

2. What kinds of information can appear on a node?

3. How does a token-ring network work?

Exercises

1. Consider your home computer system to be a set of nodes. Draw a deployment diagram that includes your CPU box and peripherals. Include artifacts.

2. It's possible to connect one network to another. One way to do this is to connect each network to a router and each router to a (possibly very long) LAN-to-LAN circuit. Draw a deployment diagram of a small token-ring network connected to a small thin ethernet network.

Understanding Packages and Foundations

What You'll Learn in This Hour:

▶ Package diagrams
▶ The structure of the UML
▶ Extending the UML

If this were an academically oriented text instead of a *Teach Yourself* book, much of this hour would have appeared at the beginning of Part I rather than toward the end. I've done it this way to give you a chance to get into the trenches with the UML—to understand what the UML is and what it does. That way, you'll be ready to understand the foundations and work with them.

It's much the same as learning a foreign language. The best way to do it is to immerse yourself, as you've done in Hours 1–13 (and will do in Part II, "A Case Study"). Then you can start to pick up the rules of grammar and syntax because you'll be prepared to understand them. (Unfortunately, many academic-world foreign language courses proceed in the opposite order!)

Now that you've seen the diagrams and know how to use them, why bother with this type of hour at all? If you understand what the UML is based on, you'll be able to adapt it and extend it when you start using it in the real world. As any systems analyst can tell you, every project is different. No reference book, text, or tutorial can prepare you for every situation you'll encounter. A good grounding in the foundational concepts, however, will get you ready for most of the systems you'll have to model.

Package Diagrams

Before you begin your foray into the foundations of the UML, you'll examine one more type of diagram—the package diagram. This is a diagram that supports most of the others. A mainstay of every version of UML, the package achieves "diagram status" in version 2.0.

The Purpose of a Package

As its name implies, a package is designed to group the elements (like classes or use cases) of a diagram. Surround the grouped elements with a tabbed-folder icon and you have packaged them. If you name the package, you have named the group. In UMLspeak, the package provides a **namespace** for the grouped elements, which the package **owns**.

UML has two ways of denoting a package's contents, as Figure 14.1 shows.

FIGURE 14.1
Two ways of showing a package's contents.

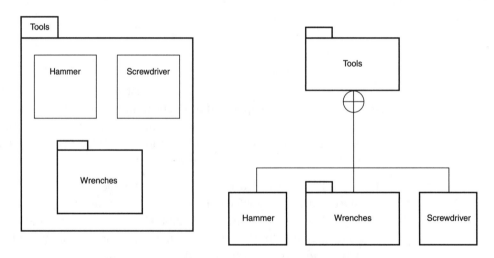

To reference an element in a package, the notation is PackageName::PackageElement (for example, Tools::Hammer). This notation is called a **fully qualified name**.

Interpackage Relationships

Packages can relate to one another in either of three ways: One package can **generalize** another, **depend** on another, or **refine** another. Figure 14.2 shows examples of generalization and dependency.

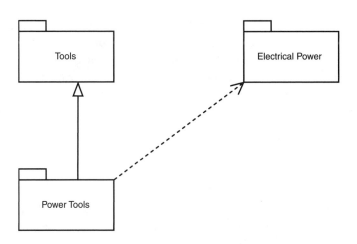

FIGURE 14.2
Generalization and dependency between packages.

You've already encountered generalization and dependency in relation to other UML elements. Refinement is all about levels of detail. One package refines another if it contains the same elements but with more detail. When you write a book, for example, you start with a proposal that briefly summarizes each chapter. Let's suppose each chapter summary is an owned element in a package called Proposal. Let's also suppose that Completed Book is a package whose owned elements are the finished chapters. In this context, the Completed Book package is a refinement of the Proposal package. Figure 14.3 shows two ways to visualize this relationship.

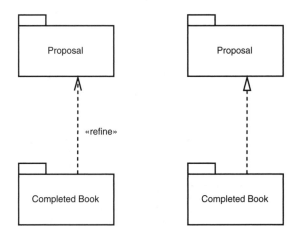

FIGURE 14.3
Two ways to visualize the refinement relationship.

The diagram on the left of Figure 14.3 shows refinement as a kind of dependency—hence the dashed-line arrow along with «refine».

The diagram on the right of Figure 14.3 includes the symbol you've used for realization—the relationship between a class and an interface. Does this mean that a class "refines" its interface? Well . . . sort of. In a sense, the operations in an interface (like turning a control knob) result in more detailed operations (like tuning a radio station) when the interface is connected with a class (in this case a radio). Incidentally, in Hour 22, "Understanding Design Patterns," you'll see this realization/refinement symbol once more.

Merging Packages

A package can merge with another. The merge relationship is a kind of dependency between the package that does the merging (the **source**) and the package that gets merged (the **target**). The result of a merge is that the source package is transformed.

Here's an example: Suppose you have one package of classes called Computers and another called Telephones. A third package, Computer Telephony, merges with each of them. Figure 14.4 shows these packages and their contents. Note that Computer Telephony is empty.

FIGURE 14.4
Modeling the merge of a package with two other packages.

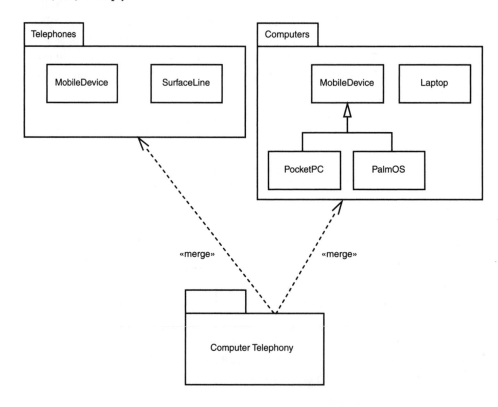

The merges transform the Computer Telephony package as in Figure 14.5. All the classes from the two target packages have been imported. Along with the fully qualified names, the inheritance relations for Laptop and SurfaceLine show the target packages in which they originated.

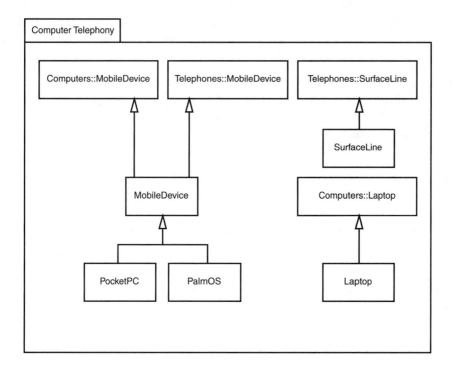

FIGURE 14.5
The transformations that result from the merges in Figure 14.4.

The inheritance relations for MobileDevice show an important point about merging: When packages merge and they contain classes with the same name, the class in the transformed package has the attributes and operations of all the same-named classes. MobileDevice in the Computer Telephony package inherits from the MobileDevice class in each target package. In effect, Computer Telephony::MobileDevice is a SmartPhone—a cell phone with computing capabilities. The inheritance relations with PocketPC and PalmOS show that a SmartPhone is available with either operating system.

Our look at the package diagram provides a nice segue into the foundations of the UML. This is because the UML is defined in terms of packages of concepts. We'll examine those packages, but first we have to turn our attention to the concepts.

A Hierarchy

Your big picture of the UML shows the categories of the diagrams and the diagrams in each category. As I mentioned in Hour 1, "Introducing the UML," you need all these diagrams because they enable you to look at a system from a number of different viewpoints. Because different stakeholders care about a system for different reasons, you have to be able to communicate a consistent vision of the system in many different ways.

Although your big picture is helpful as a way of keeping the UML's elements in mind, it won't do as a definition of the UML. The Three Amigos originally structured the UML in a formal way to ensure that the elements they created would show a clear vision of a proposed system, or a reengineered one. The foundation of UML 2.0 builds on their vision.

Let's start by examining the UML's architecture. Think of an architecture as a kind of summary shorthand for a set of decisions about the way a system is organized. Those decisions focus strongly on the system's elements—what they are, what they do, how they behave, how they interface, and how they combine.

The UML's architecture has four layers. The layers are distinguished by the generality in the elements that inhabit them. Figure 14.6 lays all this out. I've included a notation that some use to abbreviate these layers—M0 to M3.

FIGURE 14.6
A four-layer hierarchy for understanding the UML.

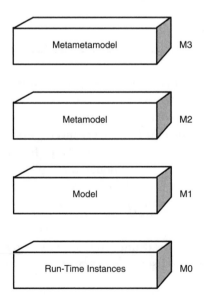

The most specific layer, M0, is called the **run-time instances layer**. This layer comes into play when a model results in the creation of code.

The next layer, M1, is called the **model layer**. The UML models you create are in this layer.

At the beginning of each hour when you learned a concept such as a class or a node, you worked in M2, the third of the four layers. This layer defines the language for specifying a model. After a little experience, you'll be familiar enough with the UML that this third layer will be second nature to you. Because this layer defines what goes into a model, it's called the **metamodel layer**. Because your big picture shows the symbols for classes, nodes, components, use cases, and so on, it pertains to the metamodel layer.

And the fourth layer (M3)? Think of it as a way of defining a language that specifies classes, use cases, components, and all the other UML elements you'll work with. Because this layer defines what goes into a metamodel, it's called the **metametamodel layer**.

An Analogy

Here's an analogy to help you understand the layers. Let's leave the world of systems modeling and talk about something a little more prosaic.

When you write a business letter, you start with your name and address. Then you include the date, the recipient's address, a salutation, the body of the letter, a closing (such as "Sincerely,"), your signature, and your typed name. In effect, you're conforming to guidelines for how to write a business letter. When you write a letter to a friend, you conform to a different set of guidelines. When you send a business memo, you use still another set.

To stay consistent with the four layers in Figure 14.6, the letter you create (say, in a word processor) is a model. The set of business letter guidelines is a metamodel. When you print the letter and send it, you have a run-time instance.

Let's move up a level. "Business letter guidelines" depend on general guidelines for correspondence. So do "friendly letter guidelines" and "business memo guidelines." Because the guidelines for correspondence ("start with a greeting," "make your ideas and feelings known to the recipient") form the basis for those metamodels, "correspondence guidelines" constitute a metametamodel.

If we think of the guidelines as packages of ideas and concepts, we can depict all this as in Figure 14.7.

FIGURE 14.7
Modeling,
metamodeling, and
metametamodeling
in the world of
letter-writing.

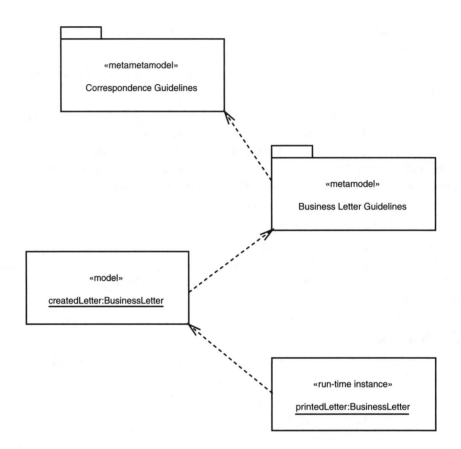

Moving On

In earlier editions of this book, I said very little about M3, the metametamodel layer. With the changes that UML 2.0 has brought and the proliferation of UML modeling tools, however, I felt it wise to explore the metametamodel layer. Although it's not a layer you'll encounter in your day-to-day modeling activities, I think you'll understand UML a little better if you're at least familiar with the foundational concepts in this layer. Knowing these concepts might also help you get conversant with a UML modeling tool, once you start using one.

So take a deep breath, and let's journey to M3.

To Boldly Go . . .

Are you a science fiction fan? A devotee of *Star Trek*, perhaps? Have you ever wondered how the bizarre inhabitants and exotic life forms from far-off planets all manage to speak perfect English to the crew of the Enterprise? (And, weirdly, to each other?)

Sometimes, sci-fi writers just ignore the language problem and have all their characters speak English regardless of their worlds of origin. The creators of *Star Trek*, however, confronted this problem and came up with the Universal Translator, a device that somehow matches up the brain waves of the speaker with the brain waves of the listener to create a matrix of information. The matrix enables the device to quickly turn words, phrases, and idioms from one language into words, phrases, and idioms from the other. In that way, everybody in the galaxy can talk to everyone else.

Why this brief excursion into the linguistics of the final frontier? If you substitute "applications on widely varying information processing systems" for "bizarre inhabitants from far-off planets," and "seamless communication" for "perfect English," you'll pretty much understand one of the early challenges that confronted the Object Management Group (Starfleet Command?): Back in the early 1990s, OMG's Prime Directive was to come up with something like a Universal Translator. The goal was to have objects based on different systems (which were potentially from different vendors) communicate smoothly and seamlessly with one another.

Bear with the *Star Trek* analogy for a moment. If you can imagine the Universal Translator as a real-life device, its architecture and infrastructure are analogous to CORBA—OMG's platform for enabling applications to work together over networks. Think back to that matrix of information that the Translator creates. The specification for what's supposed to be in that information matrix is analogous to another OMG solution—the Meta-Object Facility (MOF). MOF is OMG's way of specifying and managing information that resides on CORBA.

So . . . I've taken you from *Star Trek* to CORBA to MOF. What does this conglomeration of sci-fi and acronyms have to do with the UML? Just this: The MOF is the foundation of UML 2.0's underlying structure.

What does that mean, exactly?

Well, OMG uses the Meta-Object Facility for purposes other than specifying the nature of CORBA-related information. MOF is also OMG's template for creating modeling languages like UML.

Modeling languages like UML? Yes, just as humans have numerous languages for communicating ideas, UML is not the only possible language for creating models. It's become our standard, but other modeling languages are possible. In theory, you could learn what MOF is all about and use its concepts as the basis for creating a different modeling language.

This would be something like taking the specifications of the information matrix from the Universal Translator and using them as the basis for creating new languages for humans and other life forms to use.

Packaging the Infrastructure of UML

Let's talk about M3 more formally. In the same way we used packages in Figure 14.7 to show the layers of modeling in the world of letter writing, we can use packages to model the foundations of the UML—what the OMG refers to as the UML's **infrastructure**.

What's in those packages? Class diagrams written in MOF. These diagrams constitute specifications. (And this is why the MOF is at the foundation of the UML.) At some point, you might be wondering about MOF, so let me explain.

It all begins (in M3) with a package called the Infrastructure Library. As Figure 14.8 shows, the Infrastructure Library owns two packages, Core and Profiles. Think of the Core package as a repository of concepts for creating metamodels like UML. The Profiles package is a repository of concepts for customizing metamodels. Core holds the concepts that define UML, and Profiles holds the concepts that allow you to create variations of UML (and other metamodels) for particular domains.

FIGURE 14.8
The Infrastructure Library owns the Core and Profiles packages.

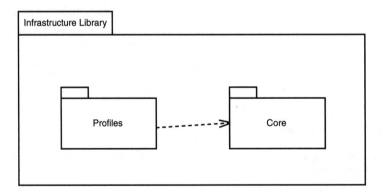

How about one more analogy? Suppose the Infrastructure Library is really a library, and suppose these "concepts" I keep talking about are books. In the "Core" section of the library, you'd find books with titles like "How to Use Oil

Paint and Canvas." You might then read this book, create your own unique style of painting, and publish your techniques for painting in that style. People could then apply these techniques to create paintings in your particular style.

In the "Profiles" section of the library, one title might be "The Human Anatomy for Painters." After reading this book, you would be able to add particular techniques to your style that would specialize it for creating paintings of people.

The Core

What's in the Core package? The Core owns four packages: Primitive Types, Abstractions, Basic, and Constructs, as Figure 14.9 shows. I'll summarize each one for you.

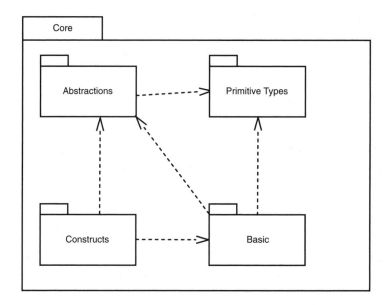

FIGURE 14.9
The contents of the Core package.

Primitive Types

Primitive Types are data types that you would use if you were creating a modeling language. The types in this package are Integer, Boolean, String, and UnlimitedNatural. That last one means any number in the infinite set of natural numbers, and it specifies that an asterisk ("*") represents infinity. In UML models, these are the numbers you see in the multiplicities at the ends of associations between classes. (And this is the origin of that asterisk that denotes *many*.) Figure 14.10 models these types.

FIGURE 14.10
The Primitive
Types package of
the Core in the
Infrastructure
Library.

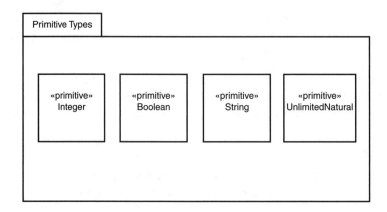

**By the
Way**

> ## A Foundational Question
>
> In looking at Figure 14.10, you might be wondering about MOF. That is, if the Infrastructure Library diagrams (which define the foundation concepts) are written in MOF, where's the definition for MOF? And then the definition of *that* definition and . . .
>
> Well, it all has to stop somewhere, and MOF is where it stops. MOF is said to be **reflective,** meaning that MOF is defined in MOF.

In the oil-painting analogy, these primitive types would correspond to properties of oil paint. You'd have to consider these properties in any rules that specify a painting style.

Abstractions

The Abstractions package owns 20 packages. Each package specifies how to set up representations of the concepts you learned about in Hours 1–13. The Elements package is the most fundamental of these packages and owns just one abstract class called, unsurprisingly, Element. We're at the metametamodel level, so it's more appropriate to refer to Element as an abstract metametaclass.

Because it generically represents any item in a model, Element is the superclass for all the other classes . . . uhmm . . . metametaclasses in the Infrastructure Library.

Other packages include Relationships, Comments, Multiplicities, and Classifiers. (A **classifier** is any element that describes structure and behavior. Classes, use cases, nodes, and actors are all examples of classifiers in the UML.)

Basic

The Basic package is a kind of baby-step into modeling. Based on classes, it's a foundation for developing complex modeling languages. If you can imagine the UML with just classes (along with their attributes and an ability to inherit from other classes), parameters (for a class's operations), packages, and the ability to specify data-types, you'll get the idea.

Constructs

The Constructs package depends on many of the Abstractions packages and on the Basic package. It combines items from those packages to add detail to elements like classes, relationships, and data types. For example, this package fleshes out the specifications for how to visualize the attributes and operations in a class. In this package, you'll also find the kinds of information you can add to an association between classes (like role-names and multiplicities).

Profiles

Let's double back and examine the Profiles package. This is the one that gives you the mechanisms for adapting a metamodel for a specific area of knowledge. Each adaptation is a separate profile.

Does a profile constitute a new metamodel? No. If you were creating a new metamodel—that is, a new modeling language—you'd begin with the Core package and work from there.

Think of a profile as a tweak of an existing metamodel—like adapting the UML to model the fields of law or education. You start with the UML and make some additions. The Profiles package gives you specifications for what you can add.

So what can you add? You're already familiar with the stereotype as a way of extending the UML. This package specifies the formal mechanisms for creating stereotypes. That is, it owns metametaclasses (classes at the metametamodel level) called Extension and Stereotype.

To give you an idea of how Extension and Stereotype work, let's say you're creating a UML profile for modeling the world of electricity. You'll want to have ways of modeling capacitors, transistors, resistors, power supplies, and other important electrical components. Because these items are hardware, you could create stereotypes of the node, the UML's symbol for a piece of hardware.

At this level, however, you don't have that block icon. Instead, you have a metametaclass called Node. If you wanted to indicate that you were creating a stereotype called `Capacitor` (something that stores electricity), your diagram would look like Figure 14.11.

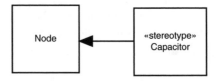

The arrow with the filled triangle represents the "extension" relationship—the association between a metaclass and a stereotype.

Capacitors (and other electronic components) often provide an interface so that you can modify their operation. For a capacitor, that interface is a control knob. (Sound familiar?) You manipulate the control knob in order to change the amount of electricity the capacitor stores. The next time you tune a radio, you might bear in mind that the knob you're turning is the interface to a capacitor. So, you might want to also create a `ControlKnob` stereotype of an interface.

When all the stereotypes are complete, they go inside a package icon that represents the profile. Figure 14.12 shows your evolving `Electricity` profile.

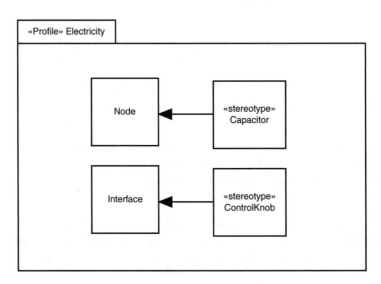

In practical terms, once these stereotypes are created you now have symbols available in your UML `Electricity` profile (that is, in your extended metamodel), which appear in Figure 14.13. (Within the UML, you can use that block icon.)

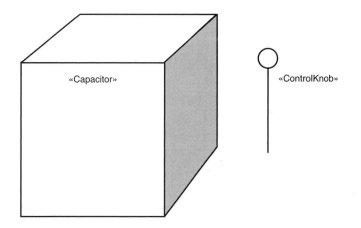

FIGURE 14.13
Symbols available
in the UML as a
result of creating
the Electricity
profile.

In even more practical terms, when you use the symbols in a model, their appearance would resemble Figure 14.14.

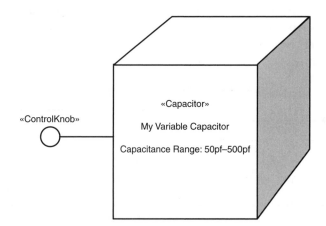

FIGURE 14.14
Using the
symbols from the
Electricity
profile.

And Now At Last . . . the UML!

Let's leave M3 and explore M2. Figure 14.15 shows the UML in the context of the ideas in previous sections—that is, it shows that the Infrastructure Library is the foundation for the UML.

FIGURE 14.15
The UML is based
on the
Infrastructure
Library.

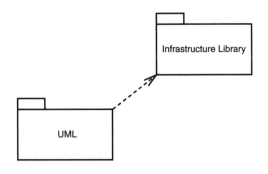

The Four Layers Again

It's also the case, of course, that the UML is the foundation for the models you create. We can restate this "foundation" business in terms of classes, metaclasses, and metametaclasses. When you create a class in your model, you have created an instance of a UML class. A UML class, in turn, is an instance of a metametaclass in the metametamodel. Going in the other direction, a runtime instance results from code based on your model. Figure 14.16 summarizes all this in terms of the four layers you've seen several times, and shows you some of the sources in the metametamodel.

FIGURE 14.16
Instances within
the four layers of
modeling.

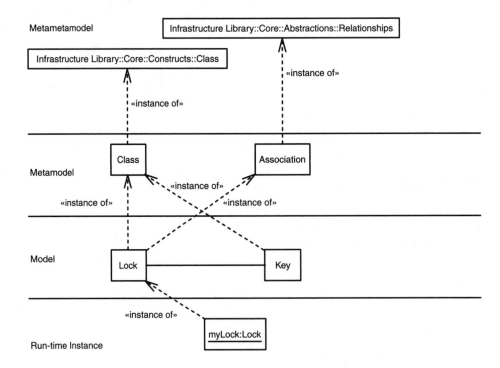

Packaging the Superstructure of the UML

Just as package diagrams model the foundation of the UML, package diagrams also model the elements within the UML—what OMG refers to as the UML's **superstructure**.

Figure 14.17 turns a magnifying glass on the UML package in Figure 14.15. It shows that the UML superstructure comprises twelve packages.

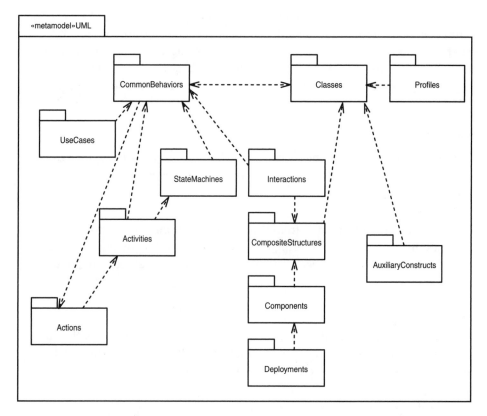

FIGURE 14.17
The superstructure of the UML.

As the names of the packages indicate, this is where you find the formal specifications for everything you learned in Hours 1–13. As you look at Figure 14.17, you'll see a couple of strange-looking arrangements of dependency arrows— two-headed dependencies and what appears to be cyclic dependency (CommonBehaviors depends on Actions, Actions depends on Activities, and Activities depends on CommonBehaviors). This diagram is set up so that a dependency arrow between two packages means that at least one element of one package depends on at least one element of the other.

Because the package names are obvious indicators of what the packages pertain to, I'll just summarize some features of the important ones. (Profiles, by the way, is a reuse of the Profiles package in the Infrastructure Library.)

Classes

Just as you'd expect, Classes contains specifications for classes and their relationships. You might recall that I mentioned these elements in connection with the Abstractions and Constructs packages of Infrastructure Library::Core. In fact, Classes reuses the specifications in those packages by merging them into Kernel, a package that represents the fundamental modeling concepts of the UML.

CommonBehaviors

In this package you'll find the specifications for how objects behave, how communication proceeds among objects, and how to model the passage of time.

UseCases

This package uses information from the Kernel and from CommonBehaviors. It specifies the diagrams for capturing a system's functional requirements. Here's where you find the formal specifications for actors, use cases, inclusion, and extension.

CompositeStructures

In addition to the specifications for composite structure diagrams (mentioned in Hour 1), this package specifies ports and interfaces. It also shows how collaborations among classes take place. You'll read more about collaborations in Hour 22.

AuxiliaryConstructs

I'll tell you about this package because the name has probably aroused your curiosity. This one is a grab bag. It deals with templates (another Hour 22 topic), techniques for visualizing the flow of information in a system, and symbols for representing models. Figure 14.18 shows the icon for a model—a package symbol with a small triangle. For good measure, AuxiliaryConstructs includes primitive types, reusing the information you saw earlier in the Infrastructure Library.

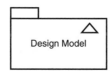

FIGURE 14.18
A package icon for representing a model.

Extending the UML

As you can see from the preceding sections, the UML has quite an extensive structure. This structure is the basis of the wide array of modeling techniques you learned in Hours 1–13.

In addition to these techniques, three mechanisms enable you to extend the UML: stereotypes, constraints, and tagged values.

Stereotypes

Appearing inside guillemets, a stereotype is intended to extend a UML element and thus create something new. Back in the section on `Profiles`, I showed how stereotyping works within the foundation of the UML. Keep in mind that you don't have to create a whole new profile in order to use stereotypes.

Stereotyping adds great flexibility. It enables you to use an existing UML element as the basis for an element you create—an element that captures some aspect of your own system or domain in ways that standard UML elements can't.

In addition to stereotypes that you create, the UML comes with an extensive set of ready-made stereotypes. I describe some of them in the subsections that follow.

Dependency

A dependency-based stereotype extends a dependency relationship between a **client** (the element the dashed arrow starts from) and a **supplier** (the element the arrow points to). Let's look quickly at some stereotyped dependencies.

An «import» dependency sits between two packages. This stereotype adds the contents of the supplier to the client's namespace (the aspect of the package that groups its constituents' names). In this hour, you've already seen «refine», another stereotyped dependency between packages.

In a «send» dependency, the client sends a signal to the supplier.

In an «instantiate» dependency, the client and the supplier are both classes. This stereotype indicates that the client creates instances of the supplier.

Class

The «metaclass» is a stereotype you encountered in the section on metamodeling. It's a class whose instances are also classes (rather than objects). Remember, a class you create in a UML model is an instance of a metaclass—a class within the UML.

A «type» is a class that specifies a domain of objects along with attributes, operations, and associations. The «type» contains no methods (executable algorithms for its operations). An object can conform to more than one type.

An «implementationClass» is the opposite of a «type». It represents the implementation of a class in a programming language. An object may not have more than one «implementationClass».

A «utility» is a named collection of attributes and operations that aren't members of that class. It's a class that has no instances.

Within a class, an operation or a method can create an instance or destroy an instance. (Perhaps you've seen **constructor** and **destructor** methods in Java.) You indicate these features by «create» and «destroy», respectively.

Package

UML has a couple of built-in stereotypes for packages. One specifies that a package holds model elements other packages can reuse. It's called «modelLibrary».

A «framework» is a stereotyped package that contains **patterns** and **templates**—UML elements geared toward reusability. I'd explain what these constructs are, but Hour 22 deals with them in detail.

Graphic Stereotypes

Sometimes you might have to bring a new symbol or two into a UML model in order to help convey a meaning. As long as everyone in your community understands and agrees on the meaning of the new symbol, it's acceptable to use it.

Deployment diagrams typically provide the greatest potential for this. Clip art of hardware is usually available and can replace the plain-vanilla cubes you learned about in Hour 13, "Working with Deployment Diagrams." When you use a picture to represent a UML icon, you create a **graphic stereotype**.

Figure 14.19 shows an example. It's a stylized version of Figure 13.7, a model of an ARCnet.

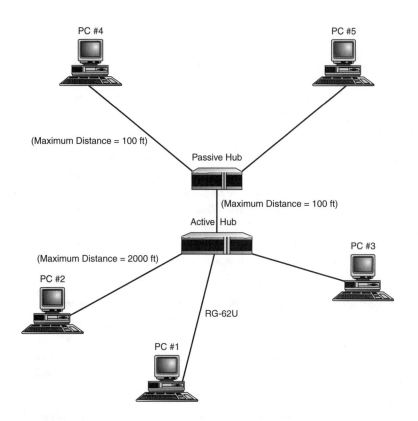

FIGURE 14.19
A graphic
stereotype-based
model of an
ARCnet.

Constraints

As you've seen, constraints supply conditions and restrictions for UML model elements. You can specify a constraint in any format as long as you write it inside braces. If, for example, a class has velocity as one of its attributes, you could apply the constraint {velocity cannot exceed the speed of light}.

Tagged Values

A tagged value is designed to explicitly define a property. It's also written inside braces. It consists of a **tag**, which represents the property to be defined, and a **value**. For example, you might attach {location = nodeName} to a component, where nodeName represents the node where the component resides.

Summary

This hour dealt with packages and with the concepts at the base of the UML. The objective was to give you an in-depth understanding that will enable you to apply the UML in real-world situations that don't always mirror textbook exercises. We covered these concepts after all the diagrams so that you would understand the elements of the language before delving into the foundations.

One way of understanding the UML is in terms of its four layers: run-time instances, model, metamodel, and metametamodel (abbreviated as M0, M1, M2, and M3). The UML models you create reside in the second layer. Code resulting from a UML model resides in the first. When you learn UML concepts, you're usually operating in the third layer. The fourth layer is one that you won't come into contact with on a daily basis, but some familiarity with its concepts can help you understand the UML and gain facility with modeling tools. In fact, vendors who create UML modeling tools have to start from this layer.

The UML provides three extension mechanisms: stereotypes, constraints, and tagged values. Stereotypes create new elements by extending existing ones. Some stereotypes are predefined in the UML. You can also create your own. Another kind of stereotype, graphic stereotyping, substitutes pictures for UML icons. Constraints indicate restrictions on model elements. A tagged value explicitly states the value of a property.

Now if I had told you all these foundational concepts at the beginning of Hour 1, would they have been comprehensible?

Q&A

Q. *I noticed that sometimes you put the name of a package on the tab of the package icon, and sometimes on the body. What's the general rule?*

A. If you're showing the elements in the package, put the name on the tab. If not, put the name on the body.

Q. *I'm a little confused about objects in the run-time instances layer. Are those the same as objects in a UML model?*

A. No, they're not. An object in your model is different from a run-time object. The object in your model is in layer M1. The run-time object is in M0.

Q. *You mentioned the four layers several times. Is that some sort of limit? Can a metamodel layering ever have more than four layers?*

A. Yes. Theoretically, there's no limit on the number of possible layers. For example, if you think of our business letter analogy, our metametamodel was "correspondence." A higher-level layer would be "written communication" which would result in metametamodels like "fiction" and "nonfiction" in addition to "correspondence." Practically speaking, however, you'll probably find few areas in life where that level of layering is appropriate.

Q. *A couple of times you mentioned "other metamodels." Is the* `Infrastructure Library` *the foundation of metamodels other than the UML?*

A. Yes. The `Infrastructure Library` is also the foundation of CWM, a language for modeling data warehouses.

Q. *That brings up another question. When do you create a profile and when do you create a new metamodel?*

A. Good question. Unfortunately, there aren't any set rules for deciding.

Q. *I understand that MOF is the foundation of UML 2.0. Has the MOF been the basis for every version of the UML?*

A. No it hasn't. UML 1.x was defined in UML.

Q. *Why the change?*

A. OMG wanted to align the UML with other OMG efforts, including future efforts (like upcoming metamodels). Giving them all a common foundation was a great way to do this.

Q. *I can see that the UML has a number of rules. Who enforces these rules?*

A. As I mentioned before, the UML Police don't come around and check your model for correctness. A modeling tool, however, gently helps you stick to the rules.

Workshop

This workshop firms up your knowledge of the UML's foundations. Use your thought processes on the quiz questions and find the answers in Appendix A, "Quiz Answers."

Quiz

1. What is a metamodel?

2. What is a classifier?

3. Why is it important to be able to extend the UML?

4. What are the UML's extension mechanisms?

Exercise

Find online pictures or clip art of devices and use them to refine the deployment diagrams you saw in Hour 13.

HOUR 15

Fitting the UML into a Development Process

What You'll Learn in This Hour:

▶ Why a development process is important
▶ Why older development methodologies are inappropriate for today's systems
▶ The GRAPPLE development process
▶ How to incorporate the UML into the process

Now that you've learned about the UML's diagrams and structure, it's almost time for the rubber to meet the road. The UML is a wonderful tool, but you don't use it in isolation. It's intended to fuel software development. In this hour, you're going to learn about development processes and methodologies as a vehicle for understanding the use of the UML in a context.

Imagine this situation: Your organization needs a new computer-based system. New hardware and software will result in a competitive advantage, and you want that advantage. Development has to start, and soon.

You're the one who made the decision to build the new system. You've put a development team in place, complete with a project manager, modelers, analysts, programmers, and system engineers. They're champing at the bit, anxious to get started.

You are, in other words, a client. What work-products will you expect to see from the team? How do you want the project manager to report to you? At the end, of course, you'll want the system up and running. Before that, you'll want indications that the team understands the problem you're trying to solve and clearly comprehends your vision of how to solve it. You'll want a look at their solution-in-progress, and you'll want an idea of how far along the team is at any point.

These are common concerns for any client and for any system development project that involves an appreciable amount of time, money, and personpower.

Methodologies: Old and New

You won't want the development team to rush off and start coding. After all, what will they code? The development team has to proceed in a structured, methodical way. The structure and nature of steps in a development effort are what I mean by a **methodology**.

Before they begin programming, the developers have to fully understand the problem. This requires that someone analyze your needs and requirements. After that analysis is done, can coding start? No. Someone has to turn the analysis into a design. Coders then work from the design to produce code, which, after testing and deployment, becomes a system.

The Old Way

This oversimplified look at a sequence of segments of effort might give you the idea that the segments should neatly occur in clearly defined chunks of time, one right after the other. In fact, early development methodologies were structured in that way. Figure 15.1 shows one way of thinking that was highly influential for a number of years. Dubbed the *waterfall* method, it specifies that analysis, design, coding, and deployment follow one another like activities in an activity diagram: Only when one is complete can the next one begin.

FIGURE 15.1
The waterfall method of software development.

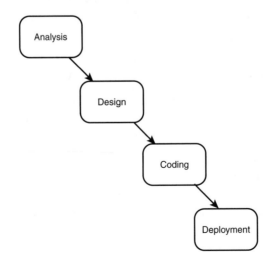

This way of doing things has some ominous overtones. For one thing, it encourages compartmentalization of effort. If an analyst hands off an analysis to a designer, who hands off a design to a developer, chances are that the three team-members will rarely work together and share important insights.

Another problem with this method is that it minimizes the impact of understanding gained over the course of a project. (Make no mistake: Understanding evolves during the life of a project—even after an analysis has turned into a design.) If the process can't go back and revisit earlier stages, it's possible that evolving ideas will not be utilized. Trying to shoehorn new insights into a project during development is difficult at best. Revisiting an analysis and a design—and then incorporating an evolved understanding—provides a much better chance of success.

A New Way

In contrast to the waterfall method, contemporary software engineering stresses continuing interplay among the stages of development. Analysts and designers, for example, go back and forth to evolve a solid foundation for the programmers. Programmers, in turn, interact with analysts and designers to share their insights, modify designs, and strengthen their code.

The advantage is that as understanding grows, the team incorporates new ideas and builds a stronger system. The downside (if there is one) is that some people like closure and want to see intermediate stages come to a discrete end. Sometimes, project managers like to be able to say something to clients like, "Analysis is complete, and we're going into design. Two or three days of design, and we'll begin coding."

That mentality is fraught with danger. Setting up artificial barriers between stages will ultimately result in a system that doesn't do exactly what a client wants.

The old way fosters another problem: It's usually the case that adherents of the waterfall method allot the lion's share of project time to coding. The net effect of this is to take valuable time away from analysis and design.

What a Development Process Must Do

In the early years of computer programming, one person could analyze a problem, come up with a solution, and write a program. In the early years of building homes (back when the world was flat), one person could build a pretty serviceable home, too.

Today it's a different story. In order to develop the kinds of complex systems today's business world demands, a team approach is necessary. Why? Knowledge has become so specialized that one person can't know all the facets of a business, understand a problem, design a solution, translate that solution into a program, deploy the executable version onto hardware, and make sure the hardware components all work together correctly.

The team has to consist of analysts to communicate with the client and understand his or her problem, designers who construct a solution, programmers who code the solution, and system engineers who deploy the solution. A development process has to take all these roles into account, utilize them properly, and allot the proper amount of time to each stage of the effort. The process must also result in a number of work-products that indicate progress and form a trail of responsibility.

Finally, the process must ensure that the stages of the effort aren't discrete. Instead, feedback must take place among the stages to foster creativity and increase the ease of building new ideas into the effort. Bottom line: It's easier to make a change to the blueprint and then make the change to the house, rather than change the house while you build the physical structure.

In arriving at a process, the temptation is to construct a set of stages that result in massive amounts of paperwork. Some commercially available methodologies do this, leaving project managers to fill out endless forms. The paperwork becomes an end unto itself.

One reason for this is the erroneous idea that a one-size-fits-all methodology is possible. Every organization is unique. An organization has its own culture, standards, history, and people. The development methodology that's right for a multinational conglomerate will probably fail in a small business, and vice versa. In trying to shoehorn a methodology to fit an organization, the misconception is that massive paper trails will somehow help.

So here's the challenge. A development process must

- Ensure that the development team has a firm understanding of the problem it's trying to solve
- Allow for a team that consists of an array of roles
- Foster communication among the team members who occupy those roles
- Allow for feedback across stages of the development effort
- Develop work-products that communicate progress to the client, but eliminate superfluous paperwork

Oh, by the way, it would be a good idea if the process produces a finished product within a short timeframe.

Process and Methodology

You'll notice that I use the words *process* and *methodology* interchangeably. Although it's possible to find some differences between the two, I'd rather not split hairs. It's been my experience that the word *methodology* has acquired a bad odor in some organizations. Mixing *process* into the discussion, I feel, somewhat alleviates the discomfort.

By the Way

GRAPPLE

To meet the multifaceted challenge of creating a development process, I present the Guidelines for Rapid APPLication Engineering (GRAPPLE). The ideas within GRAPPLE aren't original. They're a distillation of the ideas of a number of others. The Three Amigos created the Rational Unified Process, and prior to that, each Amigo had his own process. The ideas in those processes are similar to GRAPPLE. Steve McConnell's book, *Rapid Development* (Microsoft Press, 1996), contains a number of best practices that pertain to . . . well . . . rapid development.

The first word in GRAPPLE's name, *Guidelines*, is important: This isn't a methodology written in stone. Instead, it's a set of adaptable, flexible ideas. Think of it as a simplified skeleton of a development process. I present it as a vehicle for showing the UML within a context. With a little tweaking here and there, GRAPPLE can work in a variety of organizations (but maybe not all). It leaves room for a creative project manager to add his or her own ideas about what will work in a particular organization and to subtract the built-in steps that won't.

A Little Context

Before I discuss GRAPPLE, here's a question you might be asking: "Why are you telling me about this in a book about the UML?"

Here's the answer: If I don't tell you about a development process and provide a context for using the UML, all I've done is show you how to draw diagrams. The important thing is to show why and when you'd use each one.

In Part II, "A Case Study," you'll go through a test case that applies GRAPPLE and the UML.

By the Way

RAD³: The Structure of GRAPPLE

GRAPPLE consists of five segments. I use *segments* rather than *stages* to get away from the idea that one "stage" has to be complete before the next one starts. (I resisted the temptation to call them *pieces*. "Five easy pieces" was just too cute.) Each segment, in turn, consists of a number of *actions*. Each action produces a *work-product*, and each action is the responsibility of a particular *player*.

In many cases, the project manager can combine the work-products into a report that he or she presents to the client. The work-products, in effect, serve the same purpose as a paper trail without bogging down the project in paperwork.

To adapt GRAPPLE, a project manager could add actions to each segment. Another possibility is to drill down a level deeper and subdivide each action into subactions. Still another possibility is to reorder the actions within each segment. The needs of an organization will dictate the course to follow.

GRAPPLE is intended for object-oriented systems. Thus the actions within each segment are geared toward producing work-products of an object-oriented nature.

The segments are

1. Requirements gathering

2. Analysis

3. Design

4. Development

5. Deployment

This acronymizes nicely to RADDD, or RAD³. After the third segment, the project manager combines the work-products into a design document to give to the client and the developers. When all the RAD³ segments are complete, all the work-products combine to form a document that defines the system.

Before all these segments start, you assume the client has made a business case for the new system. You also assume the members of the development team, particularly analysts, have read as much relevant documentation as possible.

Let's examine each segment more closely, with an eye toward showing the parts of the UML that fit into each one.

Requirements Gathering

If you were to try and assign a relative importance to each segment, this one is a good candidate for *numero uno*. If you don't understand what the client wants, you'll never build the right system. All the use case analysis in the world won't help if you don't understand the essentials of the client's domain and the problem he or she wants you to solve.

Discover Business Processes

It's a good idea to begin the development effort by gaining an understanding of the client's business processes, specifically the one(s) you're trying to enhance with the proposed system. To gain this understanding, an analyst typically interviews the client or a knowledgeable client-designated person and asks the interviewee to go through the relevant process(es) step-by-step.

An important outcome is that the analyst gains a working vocabulary in a subset of the client's terminology. The analyst uses this vocabulary when interviewing the client in the next action.

The work-product for this action is an activity diagram or a set of activity diagrams that captures the steps and decision points in the business process(es).

Perform Domain Analysis

This action is like the example of the conversation with the basketball coach from Hour 3, "Working with Object-Orientation." It can take place during the same session as the preceding action. The objective is to gain as solid an understanding as possible of the client's domain. Note that this action and the preceding one are about concepts; they're not about the system you're going to build. The analyst has to get comfortable in the client's world, as he or she will ultimately be the client's emissary to the development team.

The analyst interviews the client with the goal of understanding the major entities in the client's domain. During the conversation between the client and the analyst, another team member takes notes (optimally, on a laptop computer equipped with a word processing package), and an object modeler constructs a high-level class diagram. If you can have more than one team member take notes, by all means do so.

The object modeler listens for nouns and starts by making each noun a class. Ultimately, some nouns will become attributes. The object modeler also listens for verbs, which will become operations of the classes. At this point, a computer-based modeling tool becomes extremely valuable.

The work-product is a high-level class diagram and a set of meeting notes.

By the
Way

> **To Tape or Not to Tape?**
>
> Should you tape these interviews or should you just rely on your meeting notes? This is a question that crops up frequently. When you tape an interview, the temptation is to not listen as closely or not take notes as rigorously. (After all, you can always listen to the tape later.) If you do decide to tape, my advice is to forget the tape recorder, and take notes as though the recorder weren't there.
>
> Tape recording can be a useful tool when you're training a new object modeler. An experienced modeler can compare the new modeler's diagrams with the taped discussion and check for completeness.

Identify Cooperating Systems

Seventeenth-century poet John Donne wrote, "No man is an island, entire of itself." If he were writing today, it would have been "No person is a land-mass surrounded entirely by water, entire of him- or herself." He might also have written "No system is an island . . . ," and so on.

Donne would have been right on all counts. Today's business systems don't typically emerge in vacuums. They have to work with others. Early in the process, the development team finds out exactly which systems the new system will depend on and which systems will depend on it. A system engineer takes care of this action, and produces a deployment diagram as the work-product. The diagram shows the systems as nodes, with lines of internode communication, resident components, and intercomponent dependencies.

Discover System Requirements

This one is extremely important. You might have guessed that because it has *requirements* in its name. In this action, the team goes through its first **Joint Application Development (JAD)** session. Several more occur throughout the course of GRAPPLE.

A JAD session brings together decision-makers from the client's organization, potential users, and the members of the development team. A facilitator moderates the session. The facilitator's job is to elicit from the decision-makers and the users what they want the system to do. At least two team members should be taking notes, and the object modeler should be refining the class diagram derived earlier.

The work-product is a package diagram. Each package represents a high-level area of system functionality (for example, "Assist with customer service"). Each package groups a set of use cases (for example, "Retrieve customer history" and "Interact with customer").

The complexity of the system determines the length of the session. It's almost never less than half a working day, and it can last as long as a full workweek. The client's organization has to make a commitment to invest the necessary time.

Why use a JAD session to develop the system requirements? Why not interview each individual? As you'll recall, I said the last part of the challenge for a development process is to turn out a system in a short timeframe. Individual interviews can take weeks or even longer, if people's schedules conflict. Waiting for individual interview results eats up time and, with it, the potential competitive advantage of quickly completing the system. Individual interviews will probably contain conflicting views, and more time gets wasted as the team tries to resolve the conflicts. Grouping everyone together creates a whole that exceeds the sum of the parts, and the interplay among JAD participants results in a symbiosis that's beneficial for everybody.

Present Results to Client

When the team finishes all the Requirements actions, the project manager presents the results to the client. Some organizations might require the client's approval at this point in order for development to proceed. Other organizations might require a cost estimate based on the results. The work-product, then, will vary according to the organization.

Analysis

In this segment, the team drills down into the results of the Requirements segment and increases its understanding of the problem. In fact, parts of this segment begin during the Requirements segment, as the object modeler begins refining the class diagram during the Requirements JAD session.

Understand System Usage

This action is a high-level use case analysis. In a JAD session with potential users, the development team works with the users to discover the actors who initiate each use case from the Requirements JAD session, and the actors who benefit from those use cases. (An actor, remember, can be a system as well as a person.) A facilitator moderates the session, and two team members take notes. After a few projects, the facilitator for this session will likely evolve into a use case analyst.

The team also tries to develop new use cases. The work-product is a set of use case diagrams that shows actors and any stereotyped dependencies («extends» and «includes») between use cases.

Flesh Out Use Cases

In this action, the development team continues its work with the users. The objective is to analyze the sequence of steps in each use case. This JAD session can be a continuation of the previous JAD session. Beware: This is usually the most difficult JAD session for the users. They're probably not accustomed to breaking down an operation into constituent steps and exhaustively enumerating all those steps. The work-product is a text description of the steps in each use case.

Refine Class Diagrams

During the JAD sessions, the object modeler listens to all the discussions and continues to refine the class diagram. At this point, the object modeler should be filling in the names of associations, abstract classes, multiplicities, generalizations, and aggregations. The work-product is a refined class diagram.

Analyze Changes of State in Objects

The object modeler further refines the model by showing changes of state wherever necessary. The work-product is a state diagram.

Define Interactions Among Objects

Now that the team has a set of use case diagrams and a refined class diagram, it's time to define how the objects interact. The object modeler develops a set of sequence diagrams and collaboration diagrams to depict the interaction. State changes should be included. These diagrams form the work-product for this action.

Analyze Integration with Cooperating Systems

Proceeding in parallel with all the preceding steps, the system engineer uncovers specific details of the integration with the cooperating systems. What type of communication is involved? What is the network architecture? If the system has to access databases, a database analyst determines the architecture (physical and logical) of those databases. The work-products are detailed deployment diagrams and (if necessary) data models.

Design

In this segment, the team works with the results of the Analysis segment to design the solution. Design and Analysis should go back and forth until the design is complete. Some methodologies, in fact, combine Analysis and Design into one stage.

Develop and Refine Object Diagrams

Programmers take the class diagram and generate any necessary object diagrams. They flesh out the object diagrams by examining each operation and developing a corresponding activity diagram. The activity diagrams will serve as the basis for much of the coding in the Development segment. The work-products are the object diagrams and the activity diagrams.

Develop Component Diagrams

Programmers play a major role in this action. The task here is to visualize the components that will result from the next segment and show the dependencies among them. The component diagrams are the work-product.

Plan for Deployment

When the component diagram is complete, the system engineer begins planning for deployment and for integration with cooperating systems. He or she creates a deployment diagram that shows where the components will reside. The work-product is a diagram that's part of the deployment diagram developed earlier.

Design and Prototype User Interface

This involves another JAD session with the users. Although this is part of Design, this session can be a continuation of the prior JAD sessions with users—an indication of the interplay between Analysis and Design.

The user interface should allow for completion of all use cases. In order to perform this action, a GUI analyst works with the users to develop paper prototypes of screens that correspond to groups of use cases. The users position post-it notes that represent screen components (pushbuttons, check boxes, drop-down lists, menus, and so on). When the users are satisfied with the positioning of the components, developers build screen prototypes for the users' approval. The work-products are screen shots of the screen prototypes.

Design Tests

Use cases enable the design of tests for the software. The objective is to assess whether or not the developed software performs as it's supposed to—that is, it does what the use cases specify. Preferably, a developer or test specialist from out-side the development team uses the use case diagrams to develop test scripts for automated test tools. The test scripts constitute the work-product.

Begin Documentation

It's never too early to begin documenting the system for the end-users and for sys-tem administrators. Documentation specialists work with the designers to begin storyboarding the documentation and arriving at a high-level structure for each document. The document structure is the work-product.

Development

Here's where the programmers take over. With enough analysis and design, this segment should go quickly and smoothly.

Construct Code

With the class diagrams, object diagrams, activity diagrams, and component dia-grams in hand, the programmers construct the code for the system. The code is the work-product from this action.

Test Code

Test specialists (not the developers) run the test scripts to assess whether or not the code is doing what it should. The test results are the work-products. This action feeds back into the preceding action and vice versa, until the code passes all lev-els of testing.

Construct User Interfaces, Connect to Code, and Test

This action draws on the user-approved prototype user interfaces. The GUI spe-cialist constructs them and connects them to the code. Further testing ensures that the interfaces work properly. The functioning system, complete with user inter-faces, is the work-product.

Complete Documentation

During the Development segment, the documentation specialist works in parallel with the programmers to ensure timely delivery of all documentation. The docu-mentation is the work-product for this action.

Deployment

When development is complete, the system is deployed on the appropriate hardware and integrated with the cooperating systems. The first action in this segment, however, can start long before the Development segment begins.

Plan for Backup and Recovery

The system engineer creates a plan for steps to follow in case the system crashes. The plan, the work-product for this action, specifies what to do to back up the system and to recover from the crash.

Install Finished System on Appropriate Hardware

The system engineer, with any necessary help from the programmers, deploys the finished system on the appropriate computer(s). The work-product is the fully deployed system.

Test Installed System

Finally, the development team tests the installed system. Does it perform as it's supposed to? Does the backup and recovery plan work? Results of these tests determine whether further refinement is necessary, and the test results make up the work-product.

Celebrate

Self-explanatory. The team invents ad hoc work-products for this action.

The GRAPPLE Wrap-up

If you step back and look at the segments and actions in GRAPPLE, you'll see that the movement is from general to specific—from the unrefined to the refined. It begins with a conceptual understanding of the domain, moves to high-level functionality, drills down into use cases, refines models, and designs, develops, and deploys the system.

You'll also notice that more actions were in the Analysis and Design segments than in the Development segment. This is, pardon the pun, by design. The idea is to spend as much time as you can in up-front analysis and design so that coding proceeds smoothly. It might seem like heresy, but in the ideal world, coding is just one small part of system development. The more you analyze, the closer you come to the ideal.

GRAPPLE, as I said, is a simplified skeleton of a development process. I didn't touch on the details of important issues like levels of testing. I also left out some important nuts and bolts: Where and how does the team maintain the work-products-in-progress? How does the team handle the all-important issue of configuration management?

I didn't address these topics because they're tangential to our discussion of the UML. The short answer for these nuts-and-bolts issues is to embrace the technology. Work-products (finished or in-progress) can reside in a repository that lives on the organization's LAN. One option is to have a hierarchy of directories that the team members can access. A safer option is to install a centralized repository package that tracks checkout and check-in of work-products and permits only one person at a time to check out an editable copy of an item. This is the foundation of a solution for configuration management. Repository technology is advancing steadily, and several choices are available.

The next hour begins Part II, a case study that applies the UML and GRAPPLE.

Summary

A development methodology structures the segments and activities in a system development project. Without a methodology, chaos would reign, developers wouldn't understand the problem they were trying to solve, and systems wouldn't meet the needs of their users. Early methodologies forced a "waterfall" sequence of analyze, design, code, and deploy.

This kind of sequential methodology can compartmentalize development, so that a development team might not take advantage of the increased understanding that results during the life of a project. It also typically allots the major share of project time to coding and thus takes valuable time away from analysis and design.

This hour presented GRAPPLE (Guidelines for Rapid APPLication Engineering), a skeleton development process. GRAPPLE consists of five segments: Requirements gathering, Analysis, Design, Development, and Deployment. Each segment consists of a number of actions, and each action results in a work-product. UML diagrams are work-products for many of the actions.

Part II applies GRAPPLE and the UML to a case study.

Q&A

Q. *Is the waterfall method ever appropriate?*

A. If the scope of the proposed system is very small (admittedly, a subjective call), you might get away with a sequential methodology. For modern object-oriented system development, however, a methodology that encourages the continuing interplay among segments of development is likely to produce a better result.

Q. *In the preceding answer, you mention object-oriented system development. Suppose the proposed system isn't object-oriented?*

A. Even with non–object-oriented systems (as in the case of many mainframe-based projects), the ideas you learned in this hour are appropriate. JAD sessions, up-front analysis and design, and interplay among development segments will still work. You would have to adapt GRAPPLE (for instance, by eliminating classes and class modeling), but that's the idea: It's a set of flexible guidelines rather than a methodology written in stone.

Workshop

Now that you know about methodologies, test your knowledge with these quiz questions. Appendix A, "Quiz Answers," supplies the answers.

Quiz

1. What are some typical concerns of a client?

2. What is meant by a development methodology?

3. What is the waterfall method? What are its weaknesses?

4. What are the segments of GRAPPLE?

5. What is a JAD session?

PART II

A Case Study

HOUR 16 Introducing the Case Study   **267**

HOUR 17 Performing a Domain Analysis   **285**

HOUR 18 Gathering System Requirements   **307**

HOUR 19 Developing the Use Cases   **325**

HOUR 20 Getting into Interactions and States Charges   **339**

HOUR 21 Desinging Look, Feel, and Deployment   **351**

HOUR 22 Understanding Design Patterns   **367**

HOUR 16

Introducing the Case Study

What You'll Learn in This Hour:

▶ The scenario for the case study

▶ Discovering and modeling business processes

▶ Tips on interviewing

Now that you've had some UML experience and exposure to a skeleton development methodology, you're going to see how the UML is applied in a development effort. This hour begins Part II, a case study that applies the UML in the context of the GRAPPLE process.

Getting Down to Business

The noted multinational (and fictional) conglomerate LaHudra, Nar, and Goniff, Inc. has surveyed the world of restaurants and come to some startling conclusions: People like to eat out, but they don't enjoy some parts of the experience.

"You know," said LaHudra, "I could have predicted the results from our survey. When I go out to eat, I hate it when I give the waiter my order and he disappears for an hour. Go out to a classy place, and you expect better treatment than that."

"That's true," said Nar. "Sometimes I change my mind after I order and I want to get a hold of the waiter. Or I have a question . . . or something . . . and I can't find the guy."

Goniff chimed in: "I agree. But still, the dining-out experience is a lot of fun. I like it when someone waits on me. I like the idea of a kitchen staff preparing a meal for me. Our survey results show that most people feel that way, too."

"Isn't there some way we can retain the essential experience but enhance it some-how?"

"How?" asked Nar.

"I know how!" said LaHudra. "With technology."

And that's when they decided to have one of their corporate software develop-ment teams build the restaurant of the future.

GRAPPLEing with the Problem

The development team members are all strong proponents of GRAPPLE. They understand that most of the project time will be devoted to analysis and design. That way, coding will take place quickly and efficiently, and the likelihood of a smooth installation and deployment will increase.

The effort has to start with requirements gathering and with an understanding of the restaurant domain. As you'll recall from the last hour, the requirements-gathering segment consists of these actions:

▶ Discovering business processes

▶ Performing domain analysis

▶ Identifying cooperating systems

▶ Discovering system requirements

▶ Presenting results to client

In this hour, you'll cover the first action.

Discovering Business Processes

LaHudra, Nar, and Goniff don't do anything in a small way. They're ready to take on the world of restaurants, and they've put together a new LNG Restaurants Division. They've hired a number of experienced restaurateurs, waiters, chefs, and maintenance people.

All they're waiting for is the technological backbone for the restaurant of the future. Then they'll launch their first restaurant, complete with the technology to increase the pleasure of dining out.

The development team members are lucky. They're starting with a blank piece of paper. All they have to do is understand the business processes and the domain, and then they're on their way.

The business process analysis starts with an analyst interviewing a restaurateur. During the interview, a note-taker is sitting by, typing away at a laptop. At the same time, a modeler is working at a whiteboard, drawing and modifying an activity diagram that the analyst, the note-taker, and the restaurateur can all see.

In the subsections that follow, we'll go through an interview for each business process in a restaurant. The goal is to produce activity diagrams that model the processes.

Serving a Customer

"Thanks for taking the time to do this," said the analyst.

"My pleasure," said the restaurateur. "What exactly do you want to know?"

"Let's start with a single business transaction. What happens when a customer walks into a restaurant?"

"It works like this: If the customer has a coat on, we help him or her take it off and store it in our cloakroom, and then we give the customer a coat-check ticket. We can do that for a hat, too. Then we . . ."

"Just a second. Let's backtrack. Suppose there's a waiting line. Do they get in line first, or leave their name up front, or . . ."

"No. We try to make them feel as comfortable as possible right off the bat. Then we worry about lines, if there are any. If, in fact, there's a waiting list, we ask the customer whether or not they made a reservation. We always try to honor those in a timely way and seat people with reservations as quickly as possible. If there's no reservation, they leave their name and then they have the option of going to our cocktail lounge and having a drink before dinner. They don't have to do that, of course. They can sit and wait in a well-appointed waiting area."

"Interesting. They haven't even sat down yet to order a meal, and several decision points have already been reached."

Let's stop for a moment and take stock of where we are. The activity diagram of the business process now looks something like Figure 16.1.

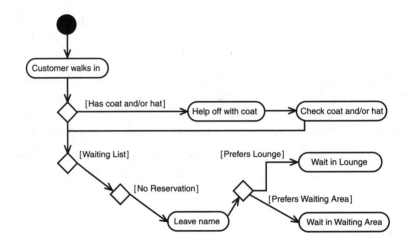

FIGURE 16.1
The beginning stages of the activity diagram for the restaurant business process "Serving a customer."

Back to the interview.

The analyst's job is to proceed with the business process.

"Okay. After the waiting-list customer's turn comes up, or the reservation customer has arrived, it's time to seat that customer, right?"

"Right. But, now that I think of it, it's not quite that simple. The table has to be ready. It has to be clean, of course, so a busser gets rid of the tablecloth from the previous customer and sets the table. When it's ready, the maitre d' walks the customer to the table and calls for a waiter."

"'Calls for'?"

> **Tip 1: Pursue Definitions**
> Notice what the analyst does here. The restaurateur has used a new term ("new" within the context of the interview), and the analyst pursues the definition.
> Knowing when and how to do this is part of the art of interviewing, and experience is the best teacher.

"Yes. That's not too involved because waiters have their designated serving areas, and they generally know when a table is ready. They sort of hover in the area, and they usually see the maitre d' gesturing for them."

"What happens next?"

"Well, the waiter takes over from here. He shows each diner a menu, and he asks them whether they want to order drinks while they decide. Then he calls over an assistant who brings a tray of bread and butter and pours a glass of water for each person in the party. If someone orders a drink, the waiter goes and gets it."

"Just a second. You said 'he.' Is the person who waits on tables always a man?"

"No. I just say that out of force of habit. Sorry."

"Okay. How about if we use the neutral term 'server'? I also notice that the customer has a couple of opportunities to order a drink."

"That's true. If a customer is waiting for a table and they're in the lounge with a drink, they can bring the drink to the table if they haven't finished it by the time the table is ready. By the way, we always reserve the right to refuse service to someone who's obviously had one too many."

Tip 2: Detect Business Logic
The interviewer isn't just a passive listener after asking a question. Here, the analyst has put together a common theme from some earlier answers and asked a question based on something cropping up a few times (the opportunity to order a drink).
The answer contains a piece of business logic, a rule that the business follows in a particular situation. In this case, the business logic pertains to refusing service to an inebriated customer.

By the Way

"Glad to hear it. We're back at the table with the diners deciding on a menu choice."

"Yes. We always have some daily specials that aren't on the menu, and the waiter . . . uh, server . . . recites those to the customers."

"You know what I've noticed happens a lot? People ask the server what they recommend, and the servers usually seem pretty honest—they'll tell you if one dish is better than another. Is that something you encourage?"

"Yes, I do. Certainly our servers eat at our restaurant, and they have their opinions on what they like and don't like. If they really, really don't like a particular dish, we want them to tell the chef before they tell the customer, but I don't mind if they express a preference. Of course, we don't want our servers telling the customers the food stinks, but expressing a preference for one dish over another is okay."

"Understood. All right, let's summarize. The customer and . . . Well, it's actually a party isn't it? . . . The party leaves their coats, possibly sits in the lounge if they're waiting for a table, gets seated, possibly orders drinks, gets served bread and water, and looks at the menu."

Tip 3: Stop and Summarize

It's a good idea to stop and summarize from time to time. It helps you check your understanding, gives you the opportunity to use the domain's terminology, and usually gives the interviewee a comfort level that you've been listening intently to him or her.

"Right. The server comes back with any drinks, and the customers drink while they read the menu. The server allows them five to ten minutes to make a selection and then comes back. The server comes back sooner, of course, if they've made up their minds sooner."

"How does the server know to come back sooner?"

"Well, they have to somehow get his attention. The server's usually in the area of the table, unless he's back in the kitchen getting an order or talking with the chefs for some reason."

"Area?"

"Yes. Each server is assigned an area that consists of a number of tables. One area is designated as the smoking area, the rest are for non-smokers."

"How do you determine who serves in what area?"

"We rotate the servers through all the different areas."

"Let's get back to the serving process. The diners make their selections, the server writes them down, and then . . ."

"And then notifies the chef. The server does that by writing the selection on a form he gives the chef."

"What's on the form?"

"The table, the selection, and—this is extremely important—the time."

"Why is that so important?"

"Because the kitchen is usually (we hope) a very busy place, and the chef often has to prioritize his efforts in terms of the time an order arrives."

"Can that get complicated?"

"Actually, it gets a little more complicated down the line."

"How so?"

"Most meals consist of an appetizer before the main course. Most people like to have the main course hot. So the chef prepares the appetizers—many are already made, like some of the salads—and the server brings them out to the party. The challenge is to bring out the main course for everyone in the party at the same time and have it hot. I say 'challenge' because people at the table typically finish their appetizers at different times. The whole thing has to be coordinated."

"Hmmm . . . This sounds like a separate process. Let's have it be a whole different discussion—from the chef's point of view."

"Okay. That sounds like a good idea."

"We're at the point where the chef is cooking the main course. By the way, how does our diagram look to you?" (See Figure 16.2.)

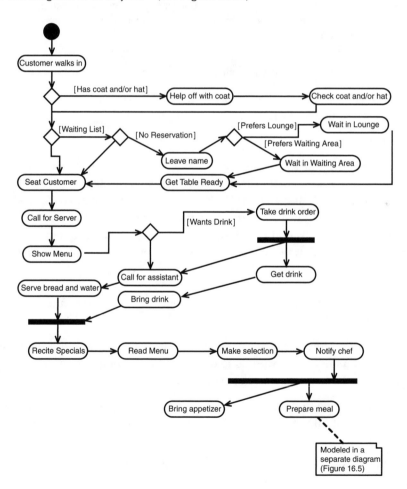

FIGURE 16.2
The intermediate stages of the activity diagram for the restaurant business process "Serving a customer."

"I think you've got it. Anyway, the chef cooks the main course, and the server picks it up when the people in the party are finished with their appetizers. The server brings it to the table. The people eat their meals, and the server comes over at least once to check on things."

> ### Tip 4: Discuss Complex Processes Separately
>
> The analyst has made an important decision—to put off the discussion of a sequence that will probably turn out to be a separate process. Recognizing when to do this comes with experience.
>
> A good rule of thumb is, if the interviewee uses words such as *complex* and *complicated*, or answers "yes" when you ask whether something's about to get complicated, you're probably facing a set of steps that will require its own model. Let the interviewee talk a bit before you make the decision on this.

"Suppose a customer isn't satisfied with something about the meal?"

"Then we do our best to make sure they are, even if it costs us some money. It's better to lose a little money than to lose a customer."

"Nice concept."

"Thanks. When the diners finish their meals, the server comes by and asks whether they want dessert. If they do, the server provides a dessert menu and takes their orders. If not, he asks if they want coffee. If they do, the server brings coffee and cups, and pours it for them. If they don't want anything, the server brings the check. After a few minutes, he comes by and collects cash and/or credit cards. He brings change and/or credit card receipts, the customers leave a tip, pick up their coats, and leave."

"Is that it?"

"Not quite. The server calls a busser over to clean the table, set it, and get it ready for the next party."

"Since that doesn't involve the customer, I'm going to consider that a separate process, albeit a brief one. I wanted to ask you a couple of questions. First, how does the server know when the people are finished?"

"He stays in his area and glances over at each table. With experience, he knows about how long it takes to eat a meal, so he can anticipate when to be near the table. You have another question?"

"Yes. Earlier you said the server might be back in the kitchen talking to the chef for some reason. Why does that happen?"

"Sometimes a customer wants to know how long it will be before the meal comes out. In cases like that, the customer summons the server, who goes back and asks the chef. When he finds out, he comes back and tells the customer."

"You know, I never realized all the things that go into serving a customer in a restaurant."

"Funny you should say that. Until you asked me to spell out all the steps, I never thought that much about it. I think your diagram captures everything I said, and it's a useful picture for clarifying my own thinking." (See Figure 16.3.)

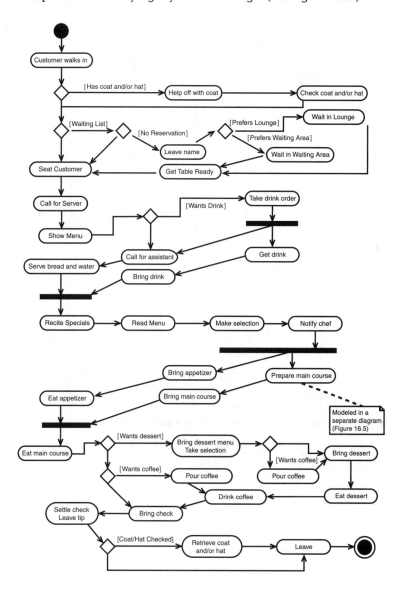

FIGURE 16.3
The full activity diagram for the restaurant business process "Serving a customer."

As you learned in Hour 11, "Working with Activity Diagrams," you can turn an activity diagram into a swimlane diagram. When you model a business process, this is a good thing to do because the swimlane diagram shows how each role figures into the process. Figure 16.4 is a swimlane diagram for the business process "Serving a customer."

FIGURE 16.4
A swimlane diagram for "Serving a customer."

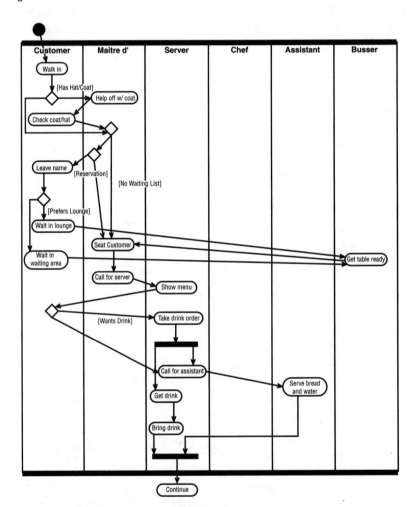

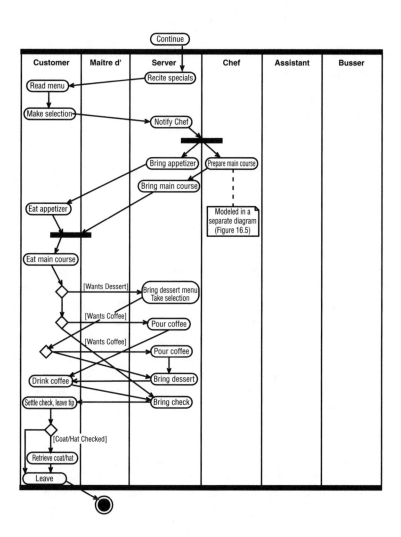

Preparing the Meal

Remember that first separate business process the interview revealed? Let's rejoin the analyst and the restaurateur and explore the process of "Preparing the meal."

"When we were talking before," said the analyst, "you mentioned that most meals provide an appetizer before the main course, and that most people prefer the main course hot. You mentioned the challenge of bringing out the main course for everyone in a party at the same time and still having it hot, and you mentioned the importance of coordination. Could you elaborate?"

"Certainly," said the restaurateur. "People in a party almost always finish their appetizers or salads or soups at different times. We have to coordinate to bring out hot main courses to everyone. The coordination takes place between the server and the chef. The chef receives the order from the server and starts preparing the appetizers and cooking the main course. When the appetizers are finished, the server comes back to the kitchen, gets the main courses, and brings them out to the table."

"And the server knows the appetizers are done because . . . ?"

"Because he checks the kitchen from time to time. Now, here's where the coordination comes in: The chef, after giving the appetizer to the server, relies on the server to let him know when everyone in the party is almost finished with their appetizers before he puts the final touches on the main course. The server stays in his or her designated area and keeps an eye on the table. At the appropriate time, the server goes back to the kitchen, tells the chef the party is just about ready for the main course, and the chef finishes preparing it. A skillful chef, working with a group of assistants, balances the meal preparation for a number of parties at once. The goal is to have the main course ready as soon as everyone in the party is ready for it."

"Does it always happen exactly on time?"

"No, not always. But with a little experience and common sense, you get it right more often than not. What sometimes happens is that one slow eater in a group isn't quite ready when we bring out the main course, but that's a minor glitch."

"Got it. What do you think of our diagram for this process?" (See Figure 16.5.)

As was the case with the previous business process, a swimlane diagram is appropriate, as Figure 16.6 shows.

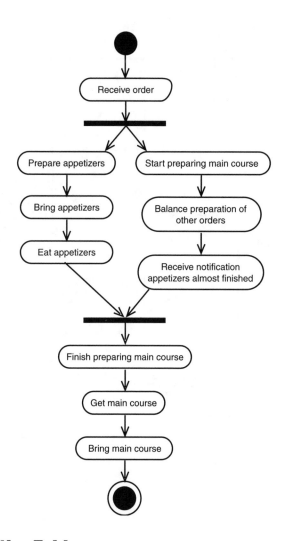

FIGURE 16.5
An activity diagram for "Preparing a meal."

Cleaning the Table

"Let's get back to that other separate process—the one where the busser cleans the table," said the analyst.

"That one involves a little coordination, too. The server first makes sure everyone has left and then calls for the busser to come and take care of the table. On a busy night, this has to happen quickly. We don't have as many bussers as we have servers, so sometimes this is a haphazard process. The bussers aren't always nearby, so the server might have to hunt for one."

FIGURE 16.6
A swimlane
diagram for
"Preparing a meal."

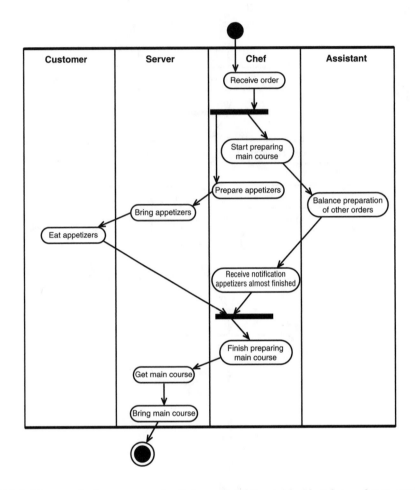

"I think I know what you mean by 'take care of the table,' but how about getting a little more specific?"

"Sure. In the restaurants I run, we have a new tablecloth for every party. So the busser has to remove the used tablecloth, bundle it up, and bring a fresh set of silverware and cloth napkins to the table. He folds the napkins and arranges the silverware and a plate for each position at the table. Then he brings the bundled-up tablecloth to a room in back of the kitchen. We pack them up and send them to the laundry the next day."

Figure 16.7 shows the activity diagram for this process.

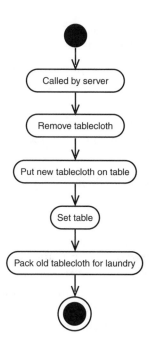

FIGURE 16.7
An activity diagram
for "Servicing a
table."

Lessons Learned

If you're an aspiring analyst, remember these lessons from this "interview":

▶ It's good to stop and summarize from time to time to test your understanding, practice with the terminology, and make the interviewee comfortable.

▶ Always get the interviewee to explain any terminology that you think is unfamiliar. Don't worry about looking unknowledgeable. The reason you're there is to acquire knowledge and learn the terminology. After all, you're going to have to use the new vocabulary when you get into the domain analysis.

▶ Every so often, you'll be able to ask a question based on a theme you discern in the answers to some preceding questions. Keep your mind and ears open for opportunities to ask questions like this. Business logic often emerges in the answers.

▶ Take note when rules of business logic come out. Maintain a record of these rules. They'll probably come in handy later. (You never know—someday you might want to build an automated decision tool that relies on these rules.) Of course, a running record should appear in the meeting notes.

▶ If you sense part of the process becoming complicated and convoluted, consider setting off the complication as a separate business process. It will be easier to model, and the resulting model will be clearer than if you try to lump everything together into one process.

▶ Get the interviewee's feedback on the activity diagram. Make any modifications that he or she suggests.

You've been through a lot in this hour, and you got a look at some valuable techniques. As you gain experience, you'll come up with some techniques of your own.

In the next hour, you'll learn about domain analysis.

Summary

This hour introduced the scenario for a case study that applies the UML in a development effort. In the scenario, the fictional conglomerate LaHudra, Nar, and Goniff decides to incorporate computer technology into the restaurant of the future. As an analyst, your job is to understand the business processes involved, understand the domain, and gather the requirements—actions in the first segment of GRAPPLE.

The newly created LNG Restaurants Division supplies you with the domain experts you'll require to understand the business processes.

The content of this hour was largely devoted to the dialog in an interview and how that might proceed. Interspersed notes provided hints about how to conduct the interview. The objective was to show you how to map the interview results into a UML model.

In the next hour, you'll learn about analyzing a domain.

Q&A

Q. *Is it always the case that the actions within a segment proceed in the order that you listed them?*

A. No. Sometimes it might make sense to go in a different order. For example, you might want to discover system requirements before you identify cooperating systems. Also, bear in mind that some actions might not even be necessary for some projects, and some actions can take place in conjunction with others. The G in GRAPPLE means *Guidelines*. It doesn't stand for "Gee, I always have to do it exactly like this."

Q. *Is it necessary to have a single interviewer for finding out the business processes from a client or an expert? Will two work better than one?*

A. Usually it's a good idea to have one person at a time talk to the expert, so that he or she doesn't feel confronted by an inquisition. You might consider changing interviewers halfway through a session. The second interviewer might have originally been one of the note-takers and can switch roles with the first interviewer.

Q. *Are there any special considerations for interview notes?*

A. Make sure you have the date, time, place, and participants carefully listed at the beginning. You never know when you'll need that information, and you don't want to have to rely on memory for it. Also, try to capture as much as you possibly can within the notes. It's almost like being a court stenographer. If you try to outline as you go along, you're going to miss something.

Q. *Won't you miss something if you try to get everything?*

A. Absolutely—which is why you're better off with more than one note-taker. One is sure to pick up what another one misses. Remember, the notes you take will be part of a document you give to the client. The more complete the notes, the easier to trace the evolution of an idea.

Workshop

To really get the hang of all this, follow along with the quiz questions and exercises. The answers are in Appendix A, "Quiz Answers."

Quiz

1. Which UML diagram is appropriate for modeling a business process?

2. How can you modify this diagram to show what the different roles do?

3. What is meant by *business logic*?

Exercises

1. Try applying the principles from this hour to a different domain. Suppose LaHudra, Nar, and Goniff have engaged you to head up a development team to build a system for their corporate library. Start the requirements-gathering segment by understanding and modeling the business processes involved. For this one, you'll have to rely on your own knowledge of libraries. Hold on to your notes for your solution because you'll use this library example in the exercises for the hours that follow in Part II, "A Case Study."

2. Go back over the interviews in this hour. What pieces of business logic emerged?

3. Although the activity diagrams in this hour are sufficient for describing business processes, you might want to try your hand at applying a technique from UML 2.0. Take a look at Figure 16.5. What object nodes would you include?

HOUR 17

Performing a Domain Analysis

What You'll Learn in This Hour:

▶ Analyzing the interview

▶ Developing the initial class diagram

▶ Creating and labeling associations between classes

▶ Finding multiplicities

▶ Deriving composites

▶ Filling out the classes

In this hour, you'll continue with the conceptual analyses in the Requirements gathering segment of GRAPPLE.

The first two actions in GRAPPLE are concerned with the domain rather than with the system. Nothing in the preceding hour referred to the proposed system, and nothing in this hour will either. Indeed, in the scenario thus far, no specific system has been proposed. The development team has only a nebulous assignment from LaHudra, Nar, and Goniff to use technology to enhance the dining-out experience.

The objective in the last hour and in this one is to achieve an understanding of the domain. That means you have to know the specific processes you're trying to enhance and the nature of the world those processes operate in. In our scenario, uncovering the business processes has jump-started the development team's knowledge. As a result, the team members have a vocabulary they can use to communicate further with the LNG Restaurants Division. This is of utmost importance because the team now has a foundation for growing and evolving its knowledge over the course of the project.

Analyzing the Business Process Interview

The development team will have additional interviews with the restaurant experts, but first they work within the context of the business-process interview. The objective is to produce an initial class diagram. An object modeler does this by either working with the team during the interview or by going over the results of the interview. At this point the modeler looks for nouns, verbs, and verb phrases. Some of the nouns will become classes in the model, and some will become attributes. The verbs and verb phrases can become either operations or the labels of associations.

Examine the results of the interview from the previous hour. What nouns and verbs did the restaurateur use?

Here are the nouns:

> customer, coat, cloakroom, coat-check ticket, hat, line, waiting list, reservation, name, cocktail lounge, drink, dinner, waiting area, table, busser, tablecloth, maitre d', waiter, serving area, diner, menu, assistant, tray, bread, butter, glass, water, person, party, server, menu choice, selection, daily special, restaurant, chef, dish, kitchen, order, smoking area, form, time, appetizer, main course, dessert, dessert menu, coffee, cup, check, cash, credit card, change, credit card receipt, tip, silverware, napkin, room, laundry

Notice that each noun is in its singular form.

The verbs and verb phrases are

> has, help, store, give, get in line, honor, seat, leave, sit, wait, come up, get rid of, set, walk, call for, hover, see, gesture, show, ask, order, decide, call over, bring, pour, order, go, get, wait, bring, finish, reserve, refuse, recite, recommend, encourage, like, tell, express, look, come back, drink, read, allow, make a selection, get attention, get an order, talk, assign, designate, determine, notify, write, prioritize, consist of, prepare, bring, finish, coordinate, cook, pick up, eat, come over, check on, cost, lose money, lose a customer, come by, want, take an order, pour, collect, leave, call, get ready, glance, anticipate, talk, come out, summon, go back, find out, tell, prefer, finish, coordinate, receive, check, rely, stay, keep an eye on, take care of, hunt for, remove, bundle up, fold, arrange, pack up, send

When you first note all the nouns and verbs, keep your mind open and include everything. Would a modeler ultimately use all these words in the model? No.

Common sense dictates which ones to keep and which ones to eliminate. Further interaction with the restaurateur will also help.

Developing the Initial Class Diagram

Put yourself in the role of the modeler and start developing the class diagram. Here's where the aforementioned common sense comes into play. Start by eliminating some of the nouns.

Recall from the interview that *waiter* and *server* are synonymous. Thus, you can eliminate one of these terms. The interviewer and the interviewee decided on *server*, so you can eliminate *waiter*. *Customer* and *diner* are also synonymous, so you can eliminate another noun. Try sticking with *customer*. *Person* seems a little too generic, so you can eliminate that one, too. *Menu choice* and *selection* seem to say the same thing, so eliminate one of them. *Selection* seems more descriptive (although this is a matter of opinion), so keep that one for this example.

Can you eliminate any others? Some nouns are more appropriate as attributes rather than classes. In your list, *name, time,* and *reservation* fit that category. Another noun, *laundry,* isn't physically part of the restaurant, so you can eliminate it.

Here's the other side of the coin: It's also possible to add classes. If you examine the interview, you'll see that the restaurateur referred to "designated areas" and "rotating the servers." Who does the designating and rotating? Clearly another class, *manager,* belongs on your list. That class might not have emerged during the original interview simply because the analyst was focusing on the customer, the server, the chef, and the busser.

Adding a class (and as you'll see later, adding abstract classes) reflects the evolution of understanding as the effort proceeds.

After filtering out the synonyms and attributes and adding the new class, here's the list of nouns that can become classes:

> customer, coat, cloakroom, coat-check ticket, hat, line, waiting list, cocktail lounge, drink, dinner, waiting area, table, busser, tablecloth, maitre d', serving area, menu, assistant, tray, bread, butter, glass, water, party, server, selection, daily special, restaurant, chef, dish, kitchen, order, smoking area, form, appetizer, main course, dessert, dessert menu, coffee, cup, check, cash, credit card, change, credit card receipt, tip, silverware, napkin, room, manager, reservation

You can use these classes to build the class diagram in Figure 17.1, capitalizing the first letter of each class name. If the class name has more than one word, put all the words together and capitalize the first letter of each constituent word.

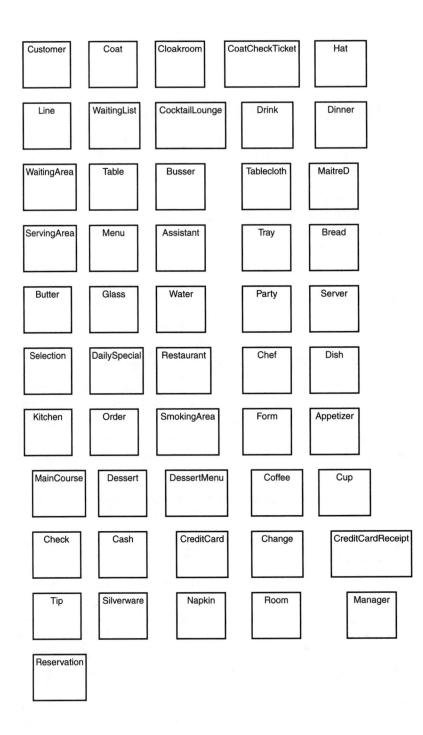

FIGURE 17.1
The initial class diagram for the restaurant domain.

Grouping the Classes

Now you can try to form some meaningful groups. One group consists of people: customer, party, busser, maitre d', assistant, chef, server, and manager. This group could stand some subdivision because all of its members, except the customer and the party, are employees. So you're left with customer, party, and the employee group.

Another group consists of food items: drink, dinner, bread, butter, water, daily special, dish, appetizer, main course, dessert, and coffee.

A third group consists of utensils: glass, silverware, tray, cup, napkin, and table-cloth.

The fourth group holds payment items: coat-check ticket, check, cash, change, credit card, credit card receipt, and tip.

Another group consists of areas within the restaurant: waiting area, smoking area, cocktail lounge, cloakroom, kitchen, serving area, table, and room. *Room* refers to the room that holds the tablecloths (and presumably other items) that the restaurant sends out to the laundry. To make the last one more descriptive, call it *laundry room*.

Finally, you can group restaurant forms together: menu, dessert menu, coat-check ticket, check, and form. The last one is the form the server gives the chef when the order goes into the kitchen. To be more descriptive, call it *order form*.

Notice that a couple of these last items fall into two groups (forms and payment items). This, as you'll see, is acceptable.

What do you do with these groups? Each group name can become an abstract class—a class that generates no instances of its own but serves as a parent for subclasses. Thus, the abstract class `RestaurantArea` has `CocktailLounge`, `ServingArea`, `Table`, `WaitingArea`, `Cloakroom`, and `Kitchen` as its children.

You can modify the class diagram from Figure 17.1 and produce the diagram in Figure 17.2.

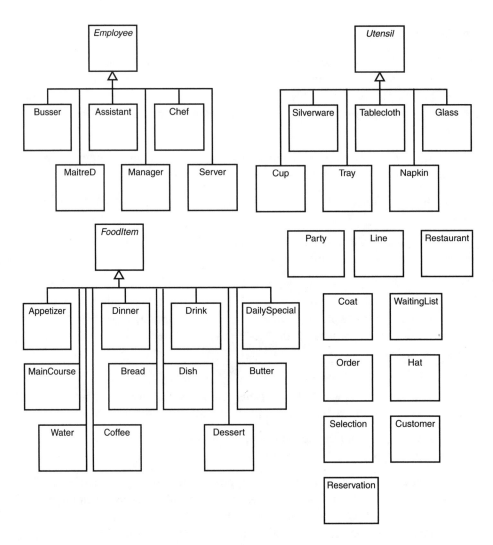

FIGURE 17.2
Abstract classes partition the class diagram into meaningful groups.

Forming Associations

Next, create and label associations among some of the classes. The verbs and verb phrases can help with the labeling, but don't limit yourself to the ones from the interview. Labels that are somewhat more descriptive might suggest themselves.

One strategy is to focus on a few of the classes and see how they associate with one another, and then move on to another group until you've exhausted the set of classes. After that, you'll develop aggregations and composites. Finally, you'll incorporate verbs and verb phrases as class operations.

Associations with Customer

Begin with the Customer class. Which classes associate with Customer? Reservation is an obvious one. Another one is Server. Some others are Menu, Meal, DessertMenu, Dessert, Order, Check, Tip, Coat, and Hat. Figure 17.3 shows the associations.

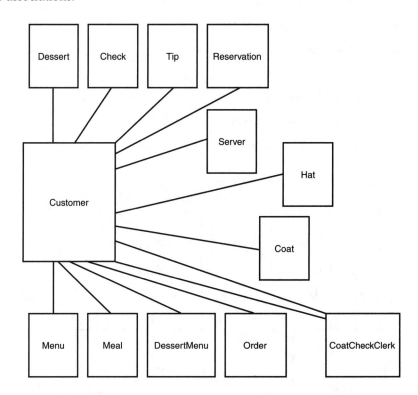

FIGURE 17.3
Initial associations with the Customer class.

At this point, you can make some decisions. Is it necessary to include Coat and Hat? After all, you're focusing on serving a meal. After some discussion, the development team would probably conclude that these classes should stay in the model because your field of interest includes the whole dining-out experience. This leads you to add another class, CoatCheckClerk, because someone has to check the coat and hat for the customer.

Try labeling the associations by generating phrases that characterize the associations. Here are some phrases that immediately come to mind:

▶ The Customer makes a Reservation.

▶ The Customer is served by a Server.

▶ The Customer eats a Meal.

▶ The Customer eats a Dessert.

▶ The Customer places an Order.

▶ The Customer selects from a Menu.

▶ The Customer selects from a DessertMenu.

▶ The Customer pays a Check.

▶ The Customer leaves a Tip.

▶ The Customer checks a Coat with a CoatCheckClerk.

▶ The Customer checks a Hat with a CoatCheckClerk.

Figure 17.4 shows the labeled associations.

FIGURE 17.4
Labeled associations with the Customer class.

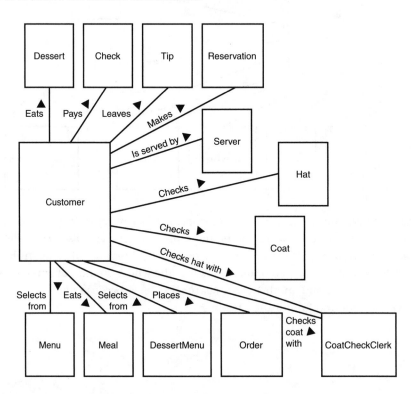

Now you can turn your attention to multiplicities. A multiplicity, remember, is part of an association: It indicates how many instances of class B associate with a single instance of class A.

In most of the bulleted phrases, the Customer is involved with one instance of the other class. The second phrase is different from the others. It has a passive voice ("is served by") rather than the active voice in the other phrases (for example, "pays" and "leaves"). This suggests that something different might be happening with this association. If you turn it around and examine the association from the Server's point of view ("The Server serves a Customer"), it's apparent that a Server can serve many Customers.

The final two phrases map to a kind of association you haven't encountered before:

▶ The Customer checks a Coat with a CoatCheckClerk.

▶ The Customer checks a Hat with a CoatCheckClerk.

How do you model this?

This kind of association is called a **ternary association**. *Ternary* indicates that three classes are involved. You model this kind of association by connecting the associated classes with a diamond, and you write the name of the association near the diamond, as in Figure 17.5. In a ternary association, the multiplicities indicate how many instances of two classes are involved when the third class is held constant. In this example, one Customer can check zero or more Coats with one CoatCheckClerk. (It's possible to have more than three classes in an association. For the sake of generality, the UML refers to *n*-ary associations.)

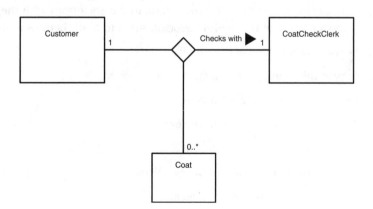

FIGURE 17.5
A ternary association.

In the next subsection, you'll see another way to handle this.

Figure 17.6 shows all labeled Customer associations with the multiplicities included.

FIGURE 17.6
Including the
multiplicities in the
associations with
the Customer
class.

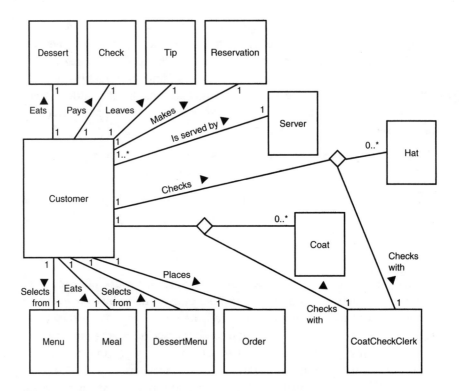

Associations with Server

That Customer-Server association is a nice segue into associations with the server. One way to model many of the Server associations is to treat them as ternary:

▶ The Server takes an Order from a Customer.

▶ The Server takes an Order to a Chef.

▶ The Server serves a Customer a Meal.

▶ The Server serves a Customer a Dessert.

▶ The Server brings a Customer a Menu.

▶ The Server brings a Customer a DessertMenu.

▶ The Server brings a Customer a Check.

▶ The Server collects Cash from a Customer.

▶ The Server collects a CreditCard from a Customer.

This will undoubtedly clutter up the model and make it difficult to comprehend. A more efficient way is to examine these associations, use the minimum number of labels, and attach appropriate association classes.

The Server's job is apparently to take and bring requested items. You attach an association class called RequestedItem, and in that class you specify what is taken or brought. To do that, you give the association class an attribute called itemType and make it an enumerated type. The possible values of the attribute are the possible items that the Server can bring or take.

Figure 17.7 shows this in action.

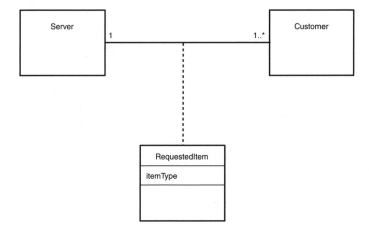

FIGURE 17.7
Using an association class in the Server associations.

The Server also associates with an Assistant and a Busser, as Figure 17.8 shows.

Associations with Chef

The Chef associates with Assistants, with the Server, and with the Meal, as in Figure 17.9. The association class Order models the order the Server brings to the Chef, and its attribute (which can be an enumerated type) shows the order's status.

Associations with Busser

As Figure 17.10 shows, the Busser has two associations. One indicates that the Server calls the Busser, and the multiplicities indicate that more than one

Server can call a Busser. The other association shows that a Busser sets more than one Table.

FIGURE 17.8
Additional associations with the Server.

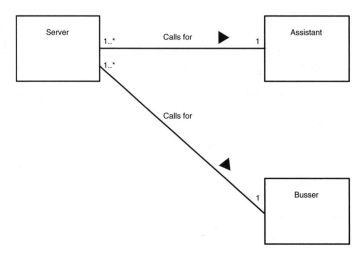

FIGURE 17.9
Chef associations with Assistant, Server, and Meal.

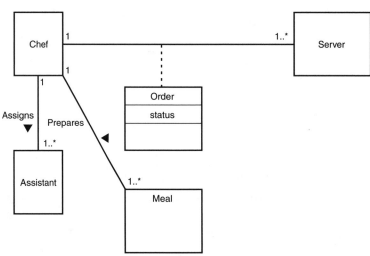

Associations with Manager

Manager is the new class you derived during the domain analysis. This class associates with many of the others, and you would develop these phrases:

▶ The Manager operates the Restaurant.

▶ The Manager monitors the Employees.

► The Manager monitors the Kitchen.

► The Manager interacts with the Customer.

Figure 17.11 models these associations.

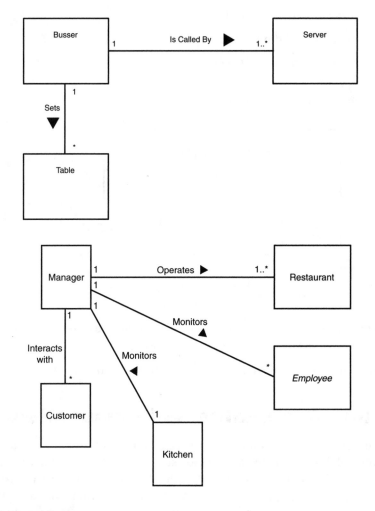

FIGURE 17.10
Busser associations with Server and Table.

FIGURE 17.11
Associations with the Manager.

A Digression

One school of thought holds that you should eliminate nouns that are roles in associations and just have a general class such as Employee. In the association, you would put the role name near the appropriate end of the association.

In some contexts (such as a payroll system), that works well. In this one, it probably won't. Consider these associations:

▶ The Server brings to the Customer.

▶ The Server takes from the Customer.

▶ The Server brings to the Chef.

▶ The Server takes from the Chef.

▶ The Server summons the Busser.

The diagram looks like Figure 17.12.

FIGURE 17.12
Modeling with the Employee class.

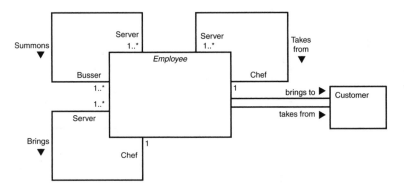

As you can see, the class icons in the diagram become dense and unclear, and you haven't even included the association classes.

In all things modeling-related, let comprehensibility be your guide.

Forming Aggregates and Composites

You've been forming and naming abstract classes and associations, and another organizational dimension awaits. The next step is to find classes that are components of other classes. In this domain, that shouldn't be difficult. A Meal, for instance, consists of an Appetizer, a MainCourse, a Drink, and a Dessert. The Appetizer and Dessert are optional. Also, the components are in a specific order, and you want that order preserved in your model.

Here are some other composites:

▶ An Order consists of one or more MenuSelections.

▶ A Restaurant consists of a Kitchen, one or more ServingAreas, a
WaitingArea, a CocktailLounge, and a LaundryRoom.

▶ A ServingArea consists of one or more Tables.

▶ A Party consists of one or more Customers.

In each case, the component is a member of only one aggregate, so Figure 17.13
models all these as composites.

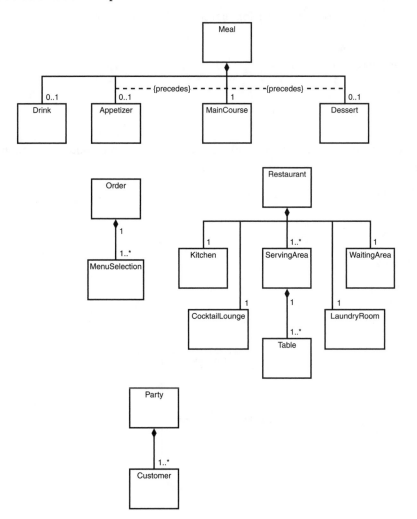

FIGURE 17.13
Composites in the
restaurant domain.

Filling Out the Classes

Further interviews and sessions will prove helpful for fleshing out your classes. Bear in mind that from here on in, an object modeler will sit in on all sessions, work with a computer-based modeling tool and refine the model on the fly. You can begin the refinement now by adding some attributes and operations.

Your most important classes appear to be Customer, Server, Chef, Manager, and Assistant. Check is another important class.

Customer

What are the obvious attributes for Customer? Here are a few:

- ▶ name
- ▶ arrivalTime
- ▶ order
- ▶ serveTime

How about the operations? Your verb list can guide you (but shouldn't limit you). Some Customer operations are

- ▶ eat()
- ▶ drink()
- ▶ beMerry (just kidding!)
- ▶ order()
- ▶ pay()

Figure 17.14 shows the Customer class.

FIGURE 17.14
The Customer class.

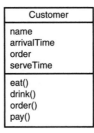

Customer
name arrivalTime order serveTime
eat() drink() order() pay()

Employee

Server, Chef, Manager, and Assistant are all children of the abstract class Employee. Thus, you assign attributes to Employee and the child classes inherit them. Some of these attributes are

- ▶ name
- ▶ address
- ▶ socialSecurityNumber
- ▶ yearsExperience
- ▶ hireDate
- ▶ salary

For the Assistant, things get a little more complicated. First, you'll need a separate attribute called worksWith because an Assistant can help either the Server or the Chef. This attribute will be an enumerated type.

Operations will be specific to each child class. For the Server, the following operations seem appropriate and appear in Figure 17.15:

- ▶ carry()
- ▶ pour()
- ▶ collect()
- ▶ call()
- ▶ checkOrderStatus()

For the Chef:

- ▶ prepare()
- ▶ cook()
- ▶ prioritize()
- ▶ createRecipe()

For the Assistant:

- ▶ prepare()
- ▶ cook()

▶ serveBread()

▶ serveWater()

The Manager operations include

▶ monitor()

▶ operateRestaurant()

▶ assign()

▶ rotate()

FIGURE 17.15
The Employee
class and its
children.

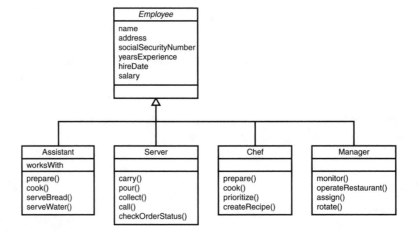

Check

The Check is obviously an important class because it contains the information on collecting money for the meal. Its attributes are

▶ mealTotal

▶ tax

▶ total

Because total is the sum of mealTotal and tax, it's a **derived variable**. To show this in the model, you precede total with a slash. (See Figure 17.16.). The Check's operations are computeTotal(mealTotal,tax) and displayTotal().

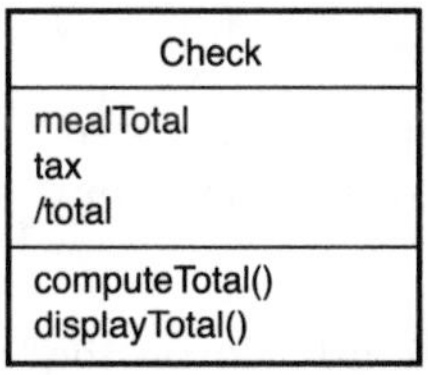

```
┌─────────────────────────┐
│          Check          │
├─────────────────────────┤
│ mealTotal               │
│ tax                     │
│ /total                  │
├─────────────────────────┤
│ computeTotal()          │
│ displayTotal()          │
└─────────────────────────┘
```

FIGURE 17.16
The Check class.

General Issues About Models

At this point, you've gathered a lot of information. Here are a few hints to help you keep it all organized:

Model Dictionary

When you're putting together interview results, business processes, and domain analyses, keep a **model dictionary**. This is a glossary of all the terminology in the model. It will help you maintain consistency and avoid ambiguity.

For example, in the restaurant domain, the term *menu* is prominent. This term means one thing to a restaurateur, but it means something else to a GUI developer. *Server* is another term fraught with danger: a restaurateur thinks *waiter* or *waitress*, a system engineer thinks something else entirely. If you have definitions everyone agrees on, or if you are at least aware of the potential for confusion, you'll avoid a lot of problems down the road. Most modeling tools allow you to build a dictionary as you create your model.

Diagram Organization

Another hint pertains to diagram organization. It's not a good idea to have every detail of your class model in one huge diagram. You'll need a master diagram that shows all the connections, associations, and generalizations, but it's best to elide attributes and operations from this picture. You can turn the spotlight on selected classes by putting them in separate diagrams. Modeling tools typically enable you to organize your diagrams by linking them appropriately.

Lessons Learned

What have you learned from going through the domain analysis?

- ▶ The business process interview provides the foundation for the domain analysis

▶ The nouns in the business process interview provide the candidate classes

▶ Eliminate nouns that are attributes, nouns that are synonymous with other nouns in the list, and nouns that represent classes out of the domain's scope.

▶ Be alert for opportunities to add classes that might not have emerged during the business process interview.

▶ Use some of the verbs or verb phrases from the interview as labels for associations.

▶ Group classes together and use the group names as abstract classes.

▶ Group classes into aggregates and/or composites.

▶ Rename the classes for clarification.

▶ Remember that some associations may be ternary (that is, involve three classes).

▶ Use common sense to name associations and to set multiplicities.

In the next hour, you'll move out of the conceptual realm and into system-related issues.

Summary

This hour continued the conceptual analysis that began in the previous hour. The business process interview results provide the foundation for the domain analysis. The nouns, verbs, and verb phrases in the interview are the candidates for the initial class diagram that defines the restaurant domain. Common sense tells you which ones to use and which ones to eliminate. It's possible that you'll add classes as you do your analysis.

The object modeler adds substance to this diagram by deriving abstract classes, associations, and multiplicities. Deriving aggregates and/or composites helps organize the model. Additional interviews and sessions will be necessary to completely flesh out the model, but it's possible to begin adding attributes and operations at this point.

Q&A

Q. *How will I know which classes to eliminate from the candidate class list?*

A. By using common sense, eliminate redundant class names and be aware of names that are attributes. Eliminate class names that are out of the scope of the domain you're analyzing. Remember that you can add classes, too.

Workshop

This workshop tests the all-important skill of domain analysis—as embodied in the creation and development of a class diagram. The answers are in the domain of Appendix A, "Quiz Answers."

Quiz

1. How do you make use of the nouns derived from the interview with an expert?

2. How do you use the verbs and verb phrases?

3. What is a ternary association?

4. How do you model a ternary association?

Exercises

1. Revisit the Customer's ternary associations with the CoatCheckClerk. Use an association class to model these associations in a more efficient way.

2. If you've closely followed the interview and the domain analysis, you might come up with some classes that didn't appear in either. One is the Cashier. Form an association between the Server and the Cashier. Use an association class if necessary. If you can think of some other classes, incorporate them into the domain analysis.

3. The Restaurant composite (in Figure 17.13) includes only "physical" classes—areas such as the Kitchen and the CocktailLounge. You might argue that a Restaurant also consists of people. Revisit the Restaurant composite and include the employees in the diagram. Does including the employees turn the composite into an aggregate?

4. In addition to attributes and operations, I pointed out in Hour 3, "Working with Object Orientation," that you can represent a class's responsibility. For the Server class, add a responsibility panel and fill it in with a description of the Server's responsibility.

5. Turn your attention to the association classes in Figures 17.7 and 17.9. For each one, I said that the attribute is an enumerated type. Model these enumerated types.

6. Continue with the library domain from the first exercise in Hour 16, "Introducing the Case Study," and develop a class diagram.

HOUR 18

Gathering System Requirements

What You'll Learn in This Hour:

- ▶ Envisioning the system
- ▶ The Joint Application Development (JAD) session
- ▶ Organizing system requirements
- ▶ The use of use cases

Messrs. LaHudra, Nar, and Goniff are impressed. They've seen the output of their development team, and they know the effort is headed in the right direction. Everyone seems to have a good understanding of the restaurant domain—so good, in fact, that the restaurateurs in the LNG Restaurants Division say the diagrams have crystallized their own thinking about restaurant operations.

Now it's time for the team to work on the technical backbone for the restaurant of the future. They've got business processes and class diagrams. They can begin coding, right? Wrong. They're not even close to writing a program. First, they have to develop a vision of the system.

Most projects begin with statements like "Construct a database of customer information and make it user-friendly so that clerks can use it with a minimum of training" or "Create a computer-based helpdesk that resolves problems in under a minute." Here, the development team has started with the vague mission to "Use technology to build the restaurant of the future." They have to envision this technology-based restaurant so they can start figuring out how restaurant personnel will work in it. They're working at a level that a development team usually doesn't get to, but LaHudra, Nar, and Goniff have faith in them.

The team will use its business process knowledge and newly acquired domain knowledge to see where an infusion of technology enhances the dining-out experience. Let's listen in on a team meeting. The players are an analyst, a modeler, a restaurateur, a server, a chef, and a system engineer. A facilitator runs the meeting.

The facilitator begins by distributing copies of Figure 18.1, the business process diagram for "Serving a customer," and Figure 18.2, the business process diagram for "Preparing a meal."

Developing the Vision

Facilitator: "Looking at our business process diagrams, I think we can all see a number of places where computer-based technology will help. I'll keep a running list here on the whiteboard. Who wants to start?"

FIGURE 18.1
The business process diagram for "Serving a customer."

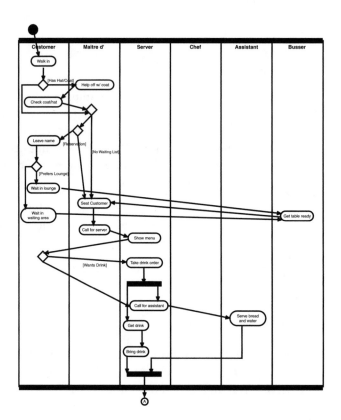

Analyst: "Yes. Apparently the restaurant business, like almost any other, depends on the movement of information. If we can speed that movement along—some thing technology is really good at—we'll meet our goal."

Restaurateur: "I'm not sure I understand. What do you mean by 'the movement of information?' I always thought my business was about the movement of food."

System Engineer: "I think I can help. When the customer places an order, he's giving information to the server. (By the way, let's all agree that a 'server' is someone who waits on tables, not a major piece of hardware in a client/server system.) When the server relays the order to the chef, he's moving the information along."

Facilitator: "Where else do we see information move?"

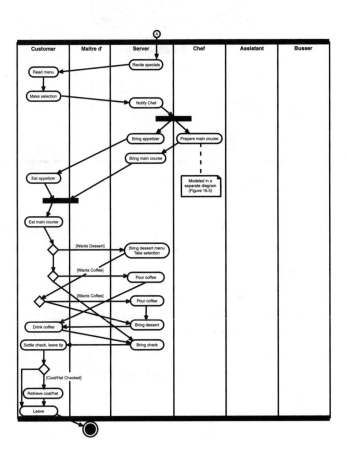

FIGURE 18.1
Continued

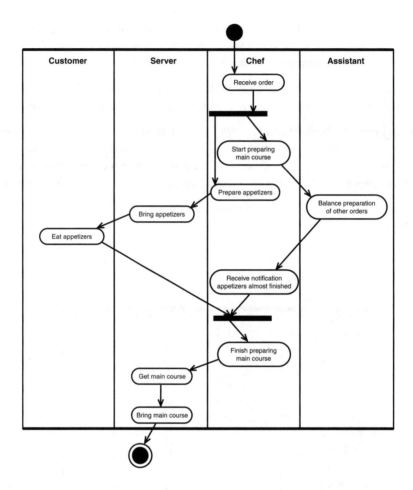

Server: "I think I'm seeing the picture. When a customer asks me to track down where his order is and I ask the chef, that's information movement, isn't it?"

Analyst: "Absolutely."

Chef: "Movement, shmovement. No offense, but I'm never all that thrilled when a server comes in and asks me how long it's going to take until I'm finished preparing a meal. It takes as long as it takes, and I can't be bothered."

Facilitator (smoothing things over with the chef, so she'll stay involved): "Maybe we can figure out a way to minimize that aggravation. Any other points of information movement?"

Restaurateur: "How about when the server recites the daily specials? Or when he answers a question about something on the menu?"

Facilitator: "Definitely."

Chef: "Sometimes I answer questions, too. People send the server back to the kitchen to ask about a particular recipe. I either relay the info through the server, or if it's not too busy, I come out and talk to the customer. They love that."

Server: "I'll tell you about a kind of information movement I'm never happy about: A customer places an order, I go back and pass it along, and then fifteen minutes later when I'm back in the kitchen for something else, I hear we're out of the ingredients for that order. I have to go back and ask the customer to order something else. That usually irritates the customer—and it irritates me because it cuts into my tip."

Analyst: "I wonder whether we should add that to the business process . . ."

Facilitator (keeping the meeting focused, and avoiding saying the maddening "Yes, but . . ."): "Maybe. I think you'll agree that's a separate meeting."

Analyst: "Yes. I didn't mean to take us off-track."

Facilitator (stopping and summarizing): "Let's see where we are. According to my list here, information transfer takes place when

▶ The customer places an order.

▶ The server relays the order to the chef.

▶ The customer asks the server to track the status of an order.

▶ The server recites the daily specials.

▶ The server answers a question about something on the menu.

▶ The chef answers questions about a recipe."

Analyst: "I know it's not in any of our business process diagrams, but doesn't the customer sometimes have a question about something on the check? When the server answers that, we're talking about information movement."

Facilitator: "We sure are. Anything else from the business processes?"

System Engineer: "I think I see one. How about all that coordination that takes place between the server and the chef? You know, when they make sure that the main course comes out hot after everyone in the party finishes their appetizers? That's quite a bit of information moving around."

Analyst: "I agree. The information is flowing a couple of different ways there."

Restaurateur: "You've given us only two business process diagrams. I recall we created one more."

Facilitator: "You're right. Here's the one for 'Servicing a table.'" (See Figure 18.3.)

FIGURE 18.3
The business process diagram for "Servicing a table."

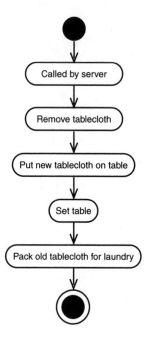

Analyst: "It looks like there's only one instance of information transfer going on here, but I bet it's an important one: The server calls for the busser to let him or her know that it's time to clean up the table."

Restaurateur: "Yes, that's extremely important. You can't seat a new party until their table is ready. If the cleanup doesn't start and end as soon as possible, we'll have a lot of hungry—and angry—customers stacking up in the lounge and the waiting area."

Modeler: "I've been working on my class diagrams while I've been listening to all of you. Can I ask a question? Would it be a good idea if our system—whatever it's going to look like—allowed us to assess our overall efficiency in serving our customers?"

Restaurateur: "Sure. That way we'd know where and how to improve. What did you have in mind?"

Modeler: "In our `Customer` class, we have one attribute called `arrivalTime` and another called `serveTime`. I want to add a derived attribute called `waitDuration`, which would be the difference between `arrivalTime` and `serveTime`. What do you think?"

Restaurateur: "That's a nice idea. Then we'd know how we're doing with our customers."

Analyst: "Yes, you would. You'd have a lot of data to play with—like `waitingTime` as a function of the time of day, or as a function of how many servers were working at the time—things like that."

Modeler: "Here's another possibility. Suppose we have another attribute called `departureTime` and a derived attribute called `mealDuration` that would be the difference between `serveTime` and `departureTime`?"

Facilitator: "With apologies to our friend the chef here, I'd say you're really cooking. Any other ideas?"

Modeler: "As long as we're working with time-based attributes, how about some attributes in the `Server` class, the `Waiter` class, and the `Chef` class that tell the manager how long each employee is taking to get the job done?"

Restaurateur: "Uhhh . . . No. That whole idea of monitoring performance doesn't sit well with employees—or with me, for that matter. It's not that they want to slack off: They don't. They just don't want to feel like Big Brother's looking over their shoulder with a stopwatch and that their jobs are in jeopardy if they don't save a second here and a second there. If you keep everybody happy, you'll run a better restaurant, and customers will sense that, too."

Chef: "I agree. As I said before: When you're preparing a meal, it takes as long as it takes. I don't want to look at a bunch of printouts and have a manager tell me I have to take 4.5 minutes less to prepare a Trout Almandine."

Server: "And I don't want to hear about taking too long to come back with dessert menus when the customers have finished the main course. There's just too much going on."

Modeler: "Okay. I'll scrap that idea. In fact, now that you mention it, I ought to remove *monitor* as an operation from the `Manager` class. In the meantime, here's what the `Customer` class looks like now." (See Figure 18.4.)

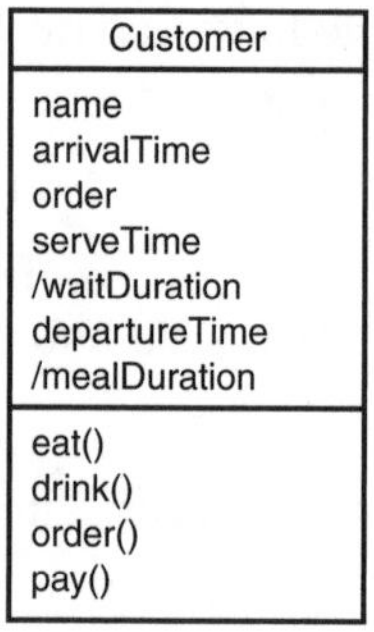

FIGURE 18.4
The updated
Customer class.

Customer
name
arrivalTime
order
serveTime
/waitDuration
departureTime
/mealDuration
eat()
drink()
order()
pay()

By the Way

A Few Good Points

The modeler's ideas show that she is constantly updating the class diagrams.

The discussion between the modeler, the restaurateur, and the server shows a crucial point: Having business people participate in system development is an absolute must. Without input from the restaurateur, the chef, and the server, the development effort would have spent time and money implementing some performance-monitoring features that ultimately would be self-defeating. Employees would have reacted negatively, causing repercussions for the system and eventually for the restaurant.

Facilitator: "From what I'm hearing, it sounds like we can distinguish between two kinds of speedup. One involves speeding up information transfer, and the other involves speeding up how each employee performs a task. The sense of the group seems to be that the second one is an annoyance, but the first one is good. Am I right?"

(All agree)

Analyst: "Now that we've settled that, can we move on to some ideas about what the system should specifically do?"

Facilitator: "Sure. Ideas, anyone?"

Server: "When I'm moving all this information, I sure cover a lot of ground in the course of an evening. Sometimes I have to work an area that's far from the kitchen. Schlepping around back and forth is what takes time, not to mention shoe leather."

Analyst: "Sounds like we have to come up with something that eliminates, or at least alleviates, the schlepp factor. Then we'll speed up information transfer."

Facilitator: "'Schlepp factor?'"

Analyst: "Yes. Our system has to somehow keep the servers from walking around so much. Obviously they have to walk to the kitchen to get the order and bring it back to the table, but suppose that's the only time they have to go back there? And suppose they go back to the kitchen just in time to get the order?"

System Engineer: "I think we're onto something. How about if we had something like a local area network that connects the servers to the kitchen? And the bussers? Then the information would move around very quickly."

Analyst: "I hate to be overly analytical about this, but a *local area network*? They'd be tripping over wires to get to the terminals. Instead of walking constantly to the kitchen, the servers would be constantly running around to get to a terminal. That just sounds like technology for the sake of technology. What does that save?"

System Engineer: "If we do it the way you just said it, I agree we'd save nothing. We might even make matters worse. But that's not what I had in mind."

Analyst: "Well, then? The suspense is killing me."

System Engineer: "Suppose each server and busser carries a terminal around—a handheld PC. And suppose we set up a network that involves no wires. We can have a desktop terminal in the kitchen and one in the manager's office.

Analyst: "Hmmm . . . I like your style. The system you're talking about would resolve a number of issues. Like when the party decides on their orders, the server could tap them into his handheld PC, and the order would go to a terminal in the kitchen. That eliminates the step, and the steps, of walking from the serving area to the kitchen."

Server: "I love it. How about when the party is almost finished with their appetizers, I let the kitchen know by pressing something on the handheld PC? That saves me from having to go back and tell the chef to finish preparing the main course."

Chef: "Then I'd get the message in the kitchen. In fact, all my assistants would get the message at the same time, and we could have the messages displayed on a big screen or two or three. I wouldn't have to keep track of which assistant was cooking what meal and tell them how far along they ought to be. They could take that responsibility for themselves."

System Engineer: "And when the order is finished, you folks in the kitchen could send a message to the server's handheld PC to let him know. He doesn't have to keep coming back and checking. Incidentally, we can refer to a handheld PC as just a 'handheld.'"

Server: "That's beautiful. I could also send a signal to a busser to come clean up a table. I wouldn't have to run around and hunt for one. That would speed everything up."

Restaurateur: "How are you all going to make this happen?"

System Engineer: "Let's not worry about that right now."

Facilitator: "So we're all set, then? Our system will be a wireless local area network with handheld computers for the servers and bussers and desktop computers in the kitchen and the manager's office. We're just missing one thing."

Analyst: "What's that?"

Facilitator: "A cool name for the system."

Chef: "How about 'MASTER CHEF'?"

Facilitator: "What do the letters stand for?"

Chef: "I dunno. I just like MASTER CHEF."

Analyst: "How about Wireless Interactive Network for Restaurants? It comes out as WINER."

Facilitator: "I'm not sure about the connotation."

System Engineer: "How about keeping it short and sweet: 'Wireless Interactive Network'—*WIN*."

Chef: "I like it."

Analyst: "Me, too. It's hard to argue with WIN."

Facilitator: "Can we all agree on WIN? Okay. I think our work here is done."

Setting Up for Requirements Gathering

The team passes the results of their meeting to the corporate bigwigs. LaHudra can't believe his good fortune in stumbling into a great new area. Nar is overwhelmed by it all. Goniff sees visions of dollar signs dancing before his eyes. They give the team the go-ahead to proceed.

Now that the team has a vision for the system, can the programmers program and the systems engineers engineer? Absolutely not. The team must center the WIN system around the users' needs, not around nifty technology. Although they have a few insights from the team meeting, they still haven't exposed the WIN concept to a group of employees and managers to get feedback and ideas from the users' point of view.

The next GRAPPLE action does just that. In a Joint Application Development (JAD) session, the team will gather and document system requirements. With these in hand, they will be able to make some estimates about time and money.

The JAD session takes place in a conference room. Led by a facilitator, it's called a "joint" session because it includes members of the development team along with potential system users and domain experts. The development team members in this meeting are two analysts who are doubling as note-takers, a modeler, two programmers, and a system engineer. The potential users are three servers, two chefs, two restaurateurs, and two bussers.

The objective of this meeting is to produce a package diagram that shows all the major pieces of functionality for the system. Each package will represent one piece and will contain use cases that detail what the functionality piece is all about.

Let's go to the session.

The Requirements JAD Session

Facilitator: "First, I want to thank you all for coming to our session. These sessions can take a lot of time, but they can also be a lot of fun. What we're trying to do is gather the requirements for a system called WIN—Wireless Interactive Network."

"The WIN concept is pretty straightforward. The way we envision it, servers carry handheld computers and use them to communicate with the kitchen and with bussers. Bussers also carry these computers and use them for communication. The kitchen will have a desktop terminal and one or more screens. The manager will also have one in her office. Here's a picture of what I'm talking about." (See Figure 18.5.)

Facilitator (continuing): "We hope to install WIN in LNG Restaurants, and we want it to help you do your jobs. In order for that to happen, we need you to tell us what you want the system to do. In other words, if the system were in place, what would you use it to do?

"We'll be asking that question over and over again. At the end of the session, we'll have an organized set of requirements that everyone will be happy with. Think of it as a high-level organized wish list. We'll use those requirements as a

FIGURE 18.5
The WIN system.

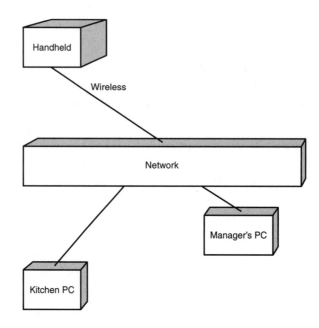

step toward building a blueprint that programmers will use to create the system. One thing I'd like you to keep in mind: We need insights and ideas from every one of you, no matter what your job title is."

Analyst 1: "Can we start by figuring out what the major pieces of functionality should be?"

Facilitator: "Sure can. Group, how should we proceed?"

Restaurateur 2: "Well, I wasn't in on the preliminary discussions, but I think this is a good idea. Can we organize it according to, say, areas in the restaurant? You know, the serving areas need one set of requirements, the kitchen needs another, the waiting area another, and so forth?"

Facilitator: "That's a possibility."

Analyst 2: "When I look at the business process diagrams, it seems to me we already have an organization."

Programmer 1: "What's that?"

Analyst 2: "By job. The chef has to do one set of things, the server has to do another, and so on."

Facilitator: "Sounds good. Can we agree on organizing by job?"

(All agree)

Facilitator: "All right! From the business process diagrams and the class diagrams, the jobs we have are *server, chef, busser, assistant,* and *manager.*"

Restaurateur 2: "Didn't you leave out a couple? How about *coat-check clerk* and *bartender?*"

Restaurateur 1: "Ooh. How did we skip those?"

Facilitator: "I'll add those to our list, and I'll use the UML package symbols to keep track." (See Figure 18.6.)

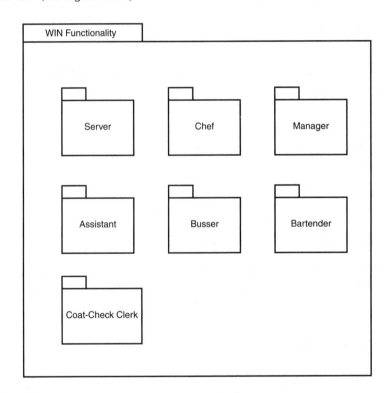

FIGURE 18.6
The packages of functionality for WIN.

Modeler: "I'm on it. I just added some information to our class diagrams. The CoatCheckClerk class was in already. I elaborated on it and added the Bartender."

Restaurateur 2: "I wondered what you've been doing there on your laptop. Could you show us these, uh, 'classes'?"

Modeler: "Sure. Here they are." (See Figure 18.7.)

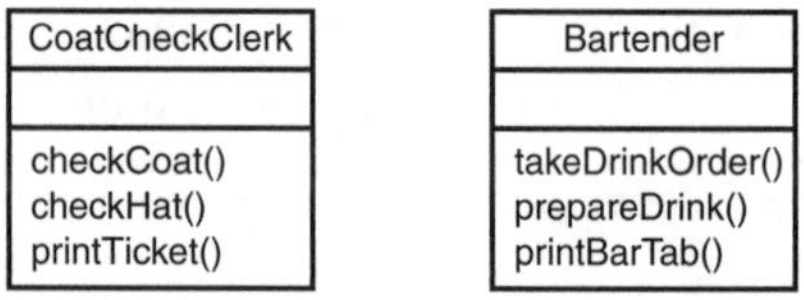

FIGURE 18.7
The
CoatCheckClerk
class and the
Bartender class.

CoatCheckClerk
checkCoat() checkHat() printTicket()

Bartender
takeDrinkOrder() prepareDrink() printBarTab()

Restaurateur 2: "Interesting. Maybe when we take a break you can explain to me what it all means."

Facilitator: "Now that we have the major pieces, does anyone have a preference as to where to start?"

Server 1: "How about with the server part?"

Facilitator: "Sounds good. All right, what kinds of functionality would you want to see in this package? Remember, group, just because we're doing a piece that happens to not coincide with your particular job, you can still participate. Everyone's insights are welcome."

Server 2: "I'd like to be able to take an order on my little computer and pass it to the kitchen."

Facilitator: "Okay. What else?"

Server 1: "Can I find out the status of an order?"

Chef 2: "Can I notify a server when the order is done?"

Facilitator: "Yes and yes. You'll notice that I'm writing these in as labeled ellipses. We refer to these as *use cases*. We'll be asking some of you to come back and help us analyze those use cases, but that's another meeting."

The Outcome

The JAD session continued on for the rest of the day. When the participants were finished, they had a set of requirements that appear as use cases arranged in the packages.

For the Server package, the use cases were

- ▶ Take an order
- ▶ Transmit the order to the kitchen
- ▶ Change an order
- ▶ Receive notification from kitchen

- ▶ Track order status
- ▶ Notify chef about party status
- ▶ Total up a check
- ▶ Print a check
- ▶ Summon an assistant
- ▶ Summon a busser
- ▶ Take a drink order
- ▶ Transmit drink order to lounge
- ▶ Receive acknowledgment
- ▶ Receive notification from lounge

For the Chef package, the use cases were

- ▶ Store a recipe
- ▶ Retrieve a recipe
- ▶ Notify the server
- ▶ Receive a request from the server
- ▶ Acknowledge server request
- ▶ Enter the preparation time
- ▶ Assign an order

The use cases for the Busser were

- ▶ Receive a request from the server
- ▶ Acknowledge a request
- ▶ Signal table serviced

The use cases for the Assistant were

- ▶ Receive a request from the server
- ▶ Receive a request from the chef
- ▶ Acknowledge a request
- ▶ Notify request completed

For the Bartender,

- ▶ Enter a drink recipe
- ▶ Retrieve a drink recipe
- ▶ Receive notification from the server
- ▶ Receive a request from the server
- ▶ Acknowledge a request
- ▶ Notify request completed

And for the Coat-check clerk,

- ▶ Print a coat check
- ▶ Print a hat check

Figure 18.8 shows how all this looks in the UML.

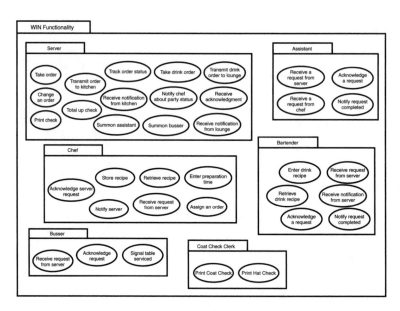

The modeler kept evolving the class diagrams by adding the two classes and associations, as shown in Figure 18.9.

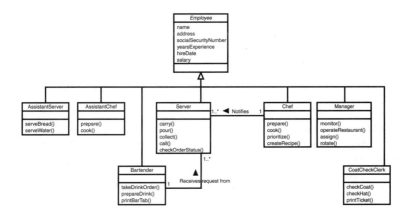

FIGURE 18.9
The newly added
class information.

Now What?

The design document the team will deliver to its client is growing by leaps and bounds. It includes business processes, class diagrams, and a set of functionality packages.

Now does the team start coding? No way. In the next hour, they start analyzing the contents of the packages.

Summary

In the context of a team meeting, the development team has generated a vision for the computer-based system in the restaurant of the future. The team members decided that speeding up information movement is the key to the success of the system, and they've come up with ways for technology to do that.

In a JAD session, the development team meets with potential users and domain experts to gather the requirements for the system. The result is a package diagram in which each package represents a major piece of functionality. Use cases inside a package elaborate on the functionality.

Q&A

Q. *Can some of the JAD session participants be the same people who participated in the earlier team meeting?*

A. Yes. In fact, that's advisable. They might remember crucial details that might not come through clearly in the meeting notes.

Q. *I notice that Messrs. LaHudra, Nar, and Goniff don't participate in these meetings. Does anyone from that level ever take part in meetings and JAD sessions?*

A. These particular individuals don't. In some organizations, however, upper management participates actively at least for part of a session. It's hard to get a high-level executive for an entire JAD session.

Q. *Is it always the case that you'll organize system functionality by roles, as in this domain?*

A. No, not always. This just turned out to be convenient for this domain. In fact, you could probably come up with an alternative way of doing it for the restaurant world if you really put your mind to it. Another type of system might demand a different kind of cut. For example, a helpdesk might have Call Receiving, Problem Resolution, and Call Return as the packages. Again, within each package, you'd have a set of use cases.

Workshop

Test your knowledge of requirements gathering and find the answers in Appendix A, "Quiz Answers."

Quiz

1. How does the development team represent system requirements?
2. Does class modeling stop after the domain analysis?
3. What is the schlepp factor?

Exercise

1. Continue on with the Library domain from the exercises in Hours 16, "Introducing the Case Study," and 17, "Performing a Domain Analysis." What are the major packages of functionality? What are the constituent use cases?

HOUR 19

Developing the Use Cases

What You'll Learn in This Hour:

▶ The care and feeding of use cases

▶ Specifying descriptions, preconditions, and postconditions

▶ Specifying steps

▶ Diagramming the use cases

The use cases from the package diagram in Hour 18, "Gathering System Requirements," give a good picture of what the system will have to do. The team will have to analyze and understand each one. They've moved gradually from understanding the domain to understanding the system. The use cases have provided the bridge.

If you're getting the idea that the system development project is use case driven, you have a good understanding of the whole process.

Notice that at no point in the JAD session did the development team discuss how the system would accomplish all the activities specified in the panoply of use cases. The idea was just to enumerate all the possible use cases. As the use cases are fleshed out in this hour, notice how the components of the WIN system start to materialize. At this point in the development effort, the system begins to take center stage.

Now, put yourself in the shoes of the development team, and we'll deal with part of this collection of use cases.

The Care and Feeding of Use Cases

To analyze the use cases, you have to run another JAD session. The discussion in this JAD session is intended to derive an analysis for each use case.

A word of caution: The use case JAD session is usually the most difficult one, as it calls for the participants—potential users of the finished system—to become analysts. In their own niche, each one is a domain expert, and you have to tap into their expertise. Typically, they're not used to either verbalizing or analyzing what they know. They probably haven't been part of a system design effort before, and they may be uncomfortable trying to specify what a system should do to help them carry out their work.

In order to alleviate the strain, it's best to organize the JAD session so that the team deals with one group at a time—for instance, just the servers. That way, the others won't sit idly by as the servers analyze their use cases. The overall domain experts, the restaurateurs, can show up to lend a hand with all the groups. A cross-section of the users would be appropriate when dealing with the Customer package.

The use cases are numerous. Just to keep this hour manageable, we'll focus on the first eight use cases for the Server package. After you see how these analyses are done, you'll be able to deal with the remaining Server use cases, as well as the use cases for the other packages, on your own. (See the exercises in the Workshop at the end of this hour.)

The Use Case Analysis

Remember (from Hour 7, "Working with Use Case Diagrams"): Each use case is a collection of scenarios, and each scenario is a sequence of steps. For each scenario in each use case, you'll want to show

- ▶ A brief description of the scenario
- ▶ Assumptions for the scenario
- ▶ The actor who initiates the use case
- ▶ Preconditions for the use case
- ▶ System-related steps in the scenario
- ▶ Postconditions when the scenario is complete
- ▶ The actor who benefits from the use case

(In your analysis, you can also include any exception conditions or alternative flows. I've kept the scenarios simple for this example, however.)

No specific way of laying out a use case analysis is correct. The items listed typically provide a complete picture of a use case.

In your design document (the document you give your client and the programmers), each of these use case analyses will have a separate page. You'll probably want to include a diagram of the use case, complete with actors, on this page.

The system-related steps in the scenario are extremely important. They'll show how the system is supposed to work. When the JAD session participants tell you these steps, they're describing, in effect, what the system will ultimately look like. After this JAD session, you should have a good idea about the components of the system.

The assumptions are important, too. In the list of assumptions, you can list design considerations, as you'll see.

This is what I meant by the system development project being use case driven. The use cases will ultimately create the path to the system.

The Server Package

The Server class seems to figure in the greatest amount of activity. This isn't surprising because the Server interacts with virtually every other class.

The Server use cases are

- ▶ Take an order
- ▶ Transmit the order to the kitchen
- ▶ Change an order
- ▶ Track order status
- ▶ Notify chef about party status
- ▶ Total up a check
- ▶ Print a check
- ▶ Summon an assistant
- ▶ Summon a busser
- ▶ Take a drink order
- ▶ Transmit a drink order to lounge
- ▶ Receive acknowledgment

▶ Receive notification from lounge

▶ Receive notification from kitchen

Take an Order

Let's begin with "Take an order." The team relies on experienced servers for a description, assumptions, preconditions, steps, and postconditions. The package and subpackage already indicate the initiating actor (Server) and the benefiting actor (Customer).

A good one-sentence description might be, "The server enters the customer's order into the handheld device and transmits it to the kitchen." The assumptions are that a customer wants a meal, the customer has read the menu, and the customer has made a selection. Another assumption is that the server's handheld has a user interface dedicated to order entry.

The preconditions are that the customer has been seated and has read the menu. The postcondition is that the order is entered into WIN.

The steps in the use case are

1. On the handheld computer, the server activates the user interface for order entry.

2. The order-entry user interface appears.

3. The server enters the customer's menu selection into WIN.

4. The system transmits the order to the kitchen PC.

Although the assumption is that an order entry interface exists, you haven't yet specified how that interface will look or how the physical act of entering the order will proceed. You don't know yet what the kitchen PC's user interface will look like, nor have you said anything about the technical details of transmitting an order.

The point is that as you state your design assumptions, you're starting to get a handle on what the system is supposed to do, and you'll start to crystallize your thoughts on how to do it. The steps in the use cases force you to come up with assumptions about the components of the system. Remember that the use cases are intended to show how the system looks to a user.

Transmit the Order to the Kitchen

Ready for another? This one will be included in (that is, used by) at least two use cases—the previous one and "Change an order."

The description is, "Take an order entered into the handheld, put it on the wireless network, and send it to the kitchen PC." The assumptions are that you'll have a means of communicating the order (via a wireless network), and again, that you have an order-entry interface. Do you have to repeat this assumption? You do. Each use case will eventually appear on a separate page in the design document, which will serve as a reference about the system. For clarity, the assumptions should appear on each use case, even if you have to repeat them from use case to use case.

The precondition is an order entered into a handheld. The postcondition is that the order has arrived in the kitchen. The benefiting actor is the customer.

The steps are

1. A button-click in the order-user interface indicates "Send to kitchen."

2. WIN transmits the order over the wireless LAN.

3. The order arrives in the kitchen.

4. The order-entry user interface on the handheld indicates that the order arrived in the kitchen.

Obviously, you have to change your use case diagram for the customer subpackage. It has to show the «include» dependency between this use case and "Take an order" and between this use case and "Change an order." Figure 19.1 shows the updated use case diagrams for the Server package.

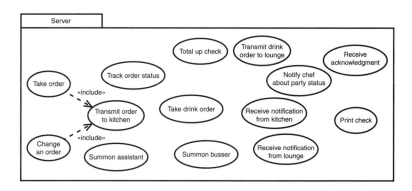

FIGURE 19.1
The updated use case diagrams for the Server package.

Change an Order

While we're on the subject, let's move to "Change an order." The description is, "Modify an order already entered into WIN." The assumption is that an order has already been placed and sent to the kitchen and that, subsequently, the customer wants to change that order. You also assume that WIN has a database of orders showing the server who entered each order and the table the order came from, that the server can access the database from the handheld, that WIN can make transmissions from the handheld to the kitchen PC and back, and that the handheld has a user interface screen for changing an order.

The precondition is the previously placed order. The postcondition is that the modified order has arrived in the kitchen. The benefiting actor is the customer.

The steps in this use case are

1. On the handheld computer, the server activates the user interface screen for changing an order.

2. The user interface brings up a list of existing orders in the kitchen placed by this server.

3. The server selects the order to be changed.

4. The server enters the modification to the order.

5. The system transmits the order to the kitchen PC.

   (Step 5 includes the previous use case "Transmit the order to the kitchen.")

Track Order Status

As you might recall, earliest discussions about the restaurant of the future included finding out when a customer's order will come out of the kitchen. This use case does just that. Implementing it in the system will go a long way toward facilitating the server's job.

The description is, "Track the status (time to completion) of an order already entered into WIN." The assumption is that an order has already been placed, has been sent to the kitchen, and that the customer wants to know how much longer it will take for the food to arrive. You repeat two of the previous design assumptions: a database of orders and the capability to transmit messages back and forth between the handheld and the kitchen PC. You also assume a user-interface screen on the handheld for tracking orders and a user-interface screen on the kitchen PC for the same purpose.

The precondition is the previously placed order. The postcondition is that the order status has arrived at the server's handheld. The benefiting actor is the customer.

The steps are

1. On the handheld computer, the server activates the user-interface screen for tracking an order entry.

2. The user interface brings up a list of existing orders in the kitchen that this server has placed.

3. The server selects the order to be tracked.

4. The system transmits a tracking message to the kitchen PC.

5. The kitchen PC receives the message.

6. The chef brings up the tracking order interface on the kitchen PC.

7. The chef enters a time estimate for the order's completion.

8. The system transmits the time estimate back to the server's handheld.

Notify Chef About Party Status

Starting with this use case, I'll use subheadings within these subsections to indicate the aspects of the use case analysis, and I'll use bullets to set off phrases within those subheadings—with two exceptions: I'll still number the steps, and I won't use bullets for the description.

Description

Via the network, the server tells the chef that a customer is almost finished with the appetizer.

Assumptions

▶ The server is in the customer's serving area.

▶ The server can gauge the customer's progress.

▶ The system has a user-interface screen for customer status.

▶ The system transmits messages from handheld to kitchen PC and vice versa.

Preconditions

▶ The customer is partially finished with the appetizer.

Postconditions

▶ The chef has initiated the final stages of completing the main course.

Steps

1. On the handheld computer, the server activates the interface screen for customer status.

2. The user interface brings up a list of the tables in the server's serving area.

3. The server selects the table of interest.

4. The server sends an "almost finished with appetizer" message about this table to the kitchen PC.

5. The kitchen PC receives the message.

6. The server receives an acknowledgment from the kitchen PC.

This last step uses the "Receive acknowledgment" use case, which is in the Server package. Figure 19.2 shows a diagram for the "Notify chef about party status" use case. (In somewhat traditional style, Figure 19.2 shows the benefiting actor. Many modelers now don't bother to show this actor in a use case diagram.)

FIGURE 19.2
The use case diagram for "Notify chef about party status."

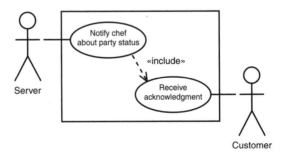

Benefiting Actor

▶ Customer

Total Up a Check

Here's an important use case. Without it, a restaurant wouldn't make any money!

Description

Add up the items in the order.

Assumptions

- ▶ There is a database of orders accessible to the server's handheld.
- ▶ Each item in the order is attached to its price.

Preconditions

- ▶ The party has completed its meal.

Postconditions

- ▶ The bill is totaled.

Steps

1. The server brings up a list of active orders on the handheld.
2. The server selects the appropriate order.
3. The server clicks a button on the handheld to total the check.
4. The system calculates the total from the prices in the order.

Benefiting Actor

- ▶ Customer

Print a Check

Although this one may seem trivial, it's an important part of the transaction.

Description

Print the totaled check.

Assumptions

- ▶ A (wireless) networked printer is located in the serving area.

Preconditions

▶ A totaled check

Postconditions

▶ A printed check

Steps

1. The server clicks a button on the handheld to print the check.

2. The networked printer in the serving area prints the check.

3. The server clicks a button on the handheld to remove this order from the list of active orders.

Benefiting Actor

▶ Customer

Summon an Assistant

This one is important because assistants help keep everything flowing smoothly.

Description

Request an assistant to clean the table for the next customer.

Assumptions

▶ The system allows wireless communication between two mobile employees.

▶ The system has a user interface screen for sending a message to an assistant.

Preconditions

▶ An empty table that must be cleaned and reset

Postconditions

▶ The assistant has come to the table to clean and reset it.

Steps

1. The server activates the interface for sending a message to an assistant.

2. The server receives an acknowledgment from the assistant.

As in the "Notify chef about party status" use case, the last step uses the "Receive acknowledgment" use case.

Benefiting Actor

▶ Assistant

Analyzing this use case as well as the use cases in the Assistant package, might lead you to believe that splitting the Assistant class into two classes, AssistantServer and AssistantChef, is a good idea. (It just makes things cleaner.) Could they be children of an abstract Assistant class? They could, but you probably wouldn't gain much from setting up this abstract class.

Creating these two new classes necessitates revisiting the domain analysis. You have to rework the class diagrams, particularly the diagram for Employee, as Figure 19.3 shows.

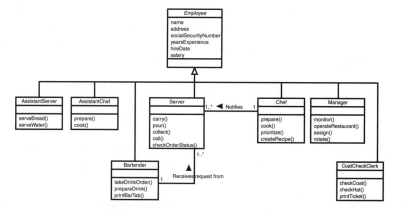

FIGURE 19.3
The updated class diagram for Employee.

You would also have to update your package diagrams to include an Assistant Server package and an Assistant Chef package.

This is an example of how the segments of GRAPPLE feed each other. The knowledge gained during use case analysis has helped you evolve the domain analysis.

Remaining Use Cases

The remaining use cases in the Server package are roughly analogous to the ones you just analyzed. I leave it to you as an exercise to finish the analyses for this package. (See Exercise 2 in the "Workshop.")

Components of the System

One important aspect of the use case analysis is that you begin to reveal the components of the system. Before you leave this hour, take note of the components that have emerged through your analysis of the use cases in the Server package. You'll find them in the "Assumptions" section of each use case analysis. (Additional components will become apparent when you do the exercises.)

On the software side, it's obvious that a number of user interface screens are necessary. WIN will need handheld-based user interfaces for order entry, order change, order status tracking, customer status, and sending messages to an assistant. For good measure, something like an interface "home page" will be necessary to keep all these other interface screens organized. WIN will also need a user interface on the kitchen PC to enable the chef to see and track each order. In general, any of these user interfaces should display that home page, accept user input, and display messages. If the restaurant wants to really delight its customers, all the user interfaces should be capable of tracking an order and tracking a customer's status. That way, anyone who has access to WIN will be able to answer a customer's questions and be sensitive to that customer's status.

It also seems that you'll need a database to contain all the orders. Each record will contain the table number, the order, the time the order went in, the server, whether the order is active, and more.

Of course, you'll also need an order processor that works behind the interfaces to create orders, send them where they're supposed to go, and register them in the database.

Figure 19.4 shows a class diagram that models the interfaces, the database, and the order processor. It also shows some of their operations. This will come in handy in the next hour when you examine the interactions among these components.

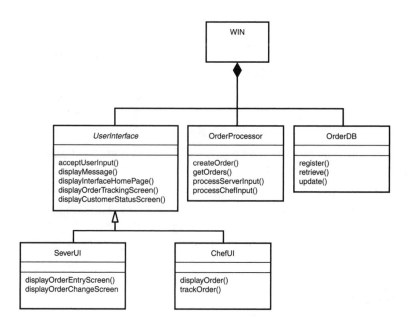

FIGURE 19.4
Modeling the
components of
WIN.

On the hardware side, you'll need a wireless network, handheld computers for the mobile employees (servers, assistant servers, and bussers), and a desktop PC in the kitchen and another in the lounge. You'll need a networked printer in each serving area. You'll probably need a palmtop and a printer for the coat-check clerk, too.

The order processor and the database of orders have to reside on a computer. One possibility is to have a central machine that holds the order processor and the database and makes them accessible to all other machines on the network. The wireless network, then, would allow wireless communication among the hand-held computers and desktop PCs and this central computer.

A rather involved design document is starting to take shape. In the next hour, you'll delve even further into the use cases.

Summary

It's not enough to list all the use cases. A development team has to understand each one in great detail in order to begin to understand the system. In this hour, accordingly, you went through the intricacies of use case analysis.

A use case analysis involves specifying a description of the use case, deriving the preconditions and postconditions, and specifying the steps. One important aspect of the use case analysis is that the components of the system begin to emerge.

Q&A

Q. *In the initial segment of GRAPPLE, I notice you skipped over the action "Identify cooperating systems." Why is that?*

A. As you'll remember, this development team started with a blank piece of paper. No cooperating systems existed. The next system that someone devises for LNG Restaurants, however, might have to access WIN in some way.

Q. *In this hour, you modified the use case diagrams and the class diagram. Does this usually happen?*

A. Yes. You can never be hesitant about making changes as your knowledge evolves. The original list of use cases captured all the knowledge at one point in the effort, and it represents a snapshot at that point. The modified diagrams represent the development team's latest thinking.

Workshop

The workshop for this hour tests your knowledge on fleshing out use cases. To see the fleshed-out answers, turn to Appendix A, "Quiz Answers."

Quiz

1. What are the parts of a typical use case diagram?

2. What does it mean for a use case to include (or use) another use case?

Exercises

1. Draw the use case diagram for "Summon an assistant."

2. Analyze the remaining use cases in the Server package, and draw use case diagrams.

3. Analyze the use cases in the Chef package, and draw use case diagrams.

4. Do the same for the Bartender, Assistant, and Busser packages.

5. Examine Figure 19.4. What additional interface classes should the model include? What would their operations be?

HOUR 20

Getting into Interactions

What You'll Learn in This Hour:

▶ Listing the working parts of the system

▶ Analyzing interactions among the working parts

▶ Modifying use cases

The use-case analysis in the last hour goes a long way toward making the WIN system a reality. The analysis still isn't far enough along to begin coding the system, however.

Analyzing the use cases has helped conceptualize the working parts of the system. Although you now know a lot about the use cases, you still have to model how those working parts will interact with one another and how (and when) they change state. Passing this information to the programmers will make their jobs a lot easier. They will have a clearer vision of how to code classes and make them work together.

The Working Parts of the System

One way to start is to enumerate the system components suggested in each package of use cases. Although you didn't explicitly analyze all the use cases in all the packages in the last hour, you can still extract the system components those use cases assume. In a real development effort, of course, a development team would have analyzed all the use cases before moving on.

The Server Package

At the end of the last hour, you enumerated the software parts of the system based on your analysis of the first nine use cases in the Server package: On the handheld

PCs, WIN will need user interface screens for order entry, order change, order-status tracking, customer status, and message sending. A user interface main screen will also be necessary. Your analysis revealed the need for an order-tracking user interface screen on the kitchen PC. WIN will require a database to hold all the orders.

In addition, the use cases you didn't analyze might suggest other system components. To refresh your memory, those use cases were

- Summon a busser
- Take a drink order
- Transmit drink order to lounge
- Receive acknowledgment
- Receive notification from lounge
- Receive notification from kitchen

The use cases suggest some straightforward components. The first one tells you something in the Server's user interface (like a dedicated screen) has to enable the server to summon a busser. The second tells you that a screen is necessary for taking a drink order (analogous to the screen for taking a meal order). The user interface has to be able to receive an acknowledgment (to show, for example, that a busser has received a request) and to receive a message from the lounge that a drink is ready.

Given the job of a server, it's not surprising that the main components in this package are user interface screens concerned with order taking and with message sending and receiving.

The Chef Package

The use cases in the Chef package are

- Store a recipe
- Retrieve a recipe
- Notify the server
- Receive a request from the server
- Acknowledge server request
- Enter the preparation time
- Assign an order

What components do these use cases suggest? Again, they follow in a straightforward manner.

The Busser Package

The use cases for the Busser are

- ▶ Receive a request from the server
- ▶ Acknowledge a request
- ▶ Signal table serviced

The Assistant Server Package

As you'll recall, in the last hour you split the Assistant package into Assistant Server and Assistant Chef. The use cases for the Assistant Server would be

- ▶ Receive a request from the server
- ▶ Acknowledge a request
- ▶ Notify request completed

The Assistant Chef Package

The use cases for the Assistant Chef would be

- ▶ Receive a request from the chef
- ▶ Acknowledge a request
- ▶ Notify request completed

One might argue that a separate computer for an assistant chef isn't necessary because he or she works in close proximity with a chef in the kitchen. If the kitchen is very large, however, electronic communication might be a good idea.

The Bartender Package

The use cases for the Bartender are

- ▶ Enter a drink recipe
- ▶ Retrieve a drink recipe
- ▶ Receive notification from the server

▶ Receive a request from the server

▶ Acknowledge a request

▶ Notify request completed

These use cases are analogous to the Chef package's use cases, and the software components they suggest are analogous to the Chef's components. The hardware is analogous, too: Behind a bar, a desktop would make more sense than a hand-held would.

You'll need a database of drink recipes and user interface screens that allow easy access to this database for entering and retrieving a recipe. The bartender's user interface has to show a notification from a server (that a customer's table is ready) and a request from a server for a drink. The bartender has to be able to send an acknowledgment that a request was received and also to notify the server that a drink is ready.

The Coat-Check Clerk Package

The Coat-Check Clerk's use cases are

▶ Print a coat check

▶ Print a hat check

The software components in the coat-check clerk's handheld should include a user interface screen that enables him or her to print the appropriate check. The check should include the time and a description of the article. You will probably also want the system to have a database of checked items.

Interactions in the System

At this point in the project, the task is to show how the system components interact in order to complete each use case. (Remember what I said earlier: Behind every use case lurks a sequence diagram.) You'll model the interactions for a couple of the use cases in the Server package. The set of use cases is too big for you to look at all of them. In a real-world project, however, a development team does just that.

Take an Order

Start with the "Take an order" use case. From Hour 19, "Developing the Use Cases," the steps are

1. On the handheld computer, the server activates the user interface for order entry.

2. The order entry user interface appears.

3. The server enters the customer's menu selection into WIN.

4. The system transmits the order to the kitchen PC.

In the model you developed in the last hour, this use case includes the "Transmit the order to the kitchen" use case, whose steps are

1. A button-click in the order user interface indicates "Send to kitchen."

2. WIN transmits the order over the wireless LAN.

3. The order arrives in the kitchen.

4. The order-entry user interface on the handheld indicates that the order arrived in the kitchen.

A sequence diagram will show this interaction nicely. (So will a collaboration diagram, which I ask you to create in Exercise 1.) Preparing the diagram forces you to focus your thinking in several ways.

First, when the server takes the customer's order, the server, in effect, creates something—an order! That order is an object in the WIN system. (It's also an instance of a class, Order, from your domain analysis in Hour 17, "Performing a Domain Analysis.") The chef will use it as a guideline for initiating and carrying out a set of actions. The server will total up a check that corresponds to it. The customer will pay the check. This created order, then, is an important item.

Also, if you examine the use cases "Change an order" and "Track order status" (as you will in a moment), you'll see references to a list of orders. This list has to come out of a database of orders—a database I alluded to at the end of Hour 19. It has to get into that database in the course of this use case. Remember also that the order processor operates behind the scenes.

You can focus your thinking in still another way. In the included use case, the term "kitchen" is a little vague. Because you're modeling software components, you have to refine what you mean here. Envisioning how this all might work leads one in a common-sense way to conclude that the order must somehow show up in the chef's user interface in the kitchen PC. How it does that is not your concern at this point, of course.

After you think these ideas through, the "Take an order" use case looks something like this:

1. On the handheld computer, the server activates the user interface for order entry.

2. The order entry screen appears.

3. The server enters the customer's menu selection into the order entry screen.

4. The order processor creates an order.

5. The order processor transmits the order to the chef's interface.

6. The order processor enters the order into the database of orders.

7. The order processor lets the server know that the order has been sent to the kitchen and that it's registered in the database of orders.

To create the sequence diagram that captures your thinking for this use case, you'll build on the class model at the end of Hour 19. The operations of the classes in that model are the set of messages you can include in your sequence diagram.

Figure 20.1 shows the sequence diagram. Just to recap what you learned earlier about sequence diagrams, the objects laid across the top of the diagram represent the components in this use case. The dashed line descending from each object is that object's *lifeline*, and time proceeds vertically downward. The little rectangles on the lifelines are called *activations*. Each activation represents the period of time during which an object is performing an action. An arrow from one lifeline to another represents a message that goes from one object to another. The type of arrowhead denotes the type of message. The Order object is created during this use case. For that reason, it's lower than the other objects, and the message pointing to it has a «create» stereotype.

Change an Order

Here's another one. From the last hour, the steps in the "Change an order" use case are

1. On the handheld computer, the server activates the user interface screen for changing an order.

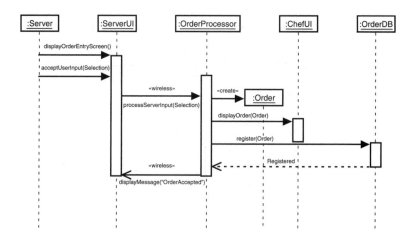

FIGURE 20.1
The sequence
diagram for "Take
an order."

2. The user interface brings up a list of existing orders in the kitchen placed by this server.

3. The server selects the order to be changed.

4. The server enters the modification to the order.

5. The order processor transmits the updated order to the kitchen PC.

Again, preparing the diagram helps you refine your thinking and modify the use case slightly. After step 5, the system should enter the modified order into the database of orders.

The new use case should thus be

1. On the handheld computer, the server activates the user interface screen for changing an order.

2. The user interface brings up a list of existing orders in the kitchen placed by this server.

3. The server selects the order to be changed.

4. The server enters the modification to the order.

5. The order processor transmits the updated order to the kitchen PC.

6. The order processor enters the new order into the database of orders.

Figure 20.2 shows the sequence diagram that corresponds to this use case.

FIGURE 20.2
The sequence diagram for "Change an order."

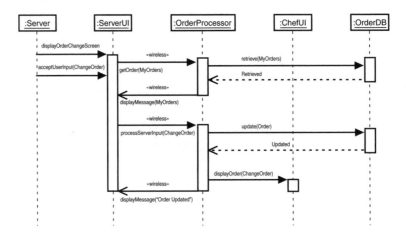

Track Order Status

Try one more case before you finish. As you read in Hour 19, the "Track order status" use case consists of these steps:

1. On the handheld computer, the server activates the user interface screen for tracking an order entry.

2. The user interface brings up a list of existing orders in the kitchen placed by this server.

3. The server selects the order to be tracked.

4. The system transmits a tracking message to the kitchen PC.

5. The kitchen PC receives the message.

6. The chef brings up the tracking order interface on the kitchen PC.

7. The chef enters a time estimate for the order's completion.

8. The system transmits the time estimate back to the server's handheld.

As you work through this, you might decide that the tracking message to the kitchen PC (that is, to the chef's user interface) could be to display the order-tracking screen with the desired order highlighted. That would eliminate the need for step 6. Also, you would replace "system" (the term in your original use case) with "order processor."

Finally, you might want to interview a few chefs and ask how they come up with the time estimate in step 7. Perhaps you can develop a software package that would help.

Figure 20.3 does the honors for this use case.

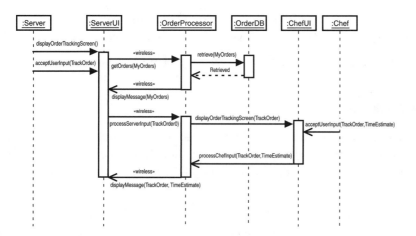

FIGURE 20.3
The sequence diagram for "Track an order."

Implications

Seeing all the results so far, Messrs. LaHudra, Nar, and Goniff are ecstatic.

"This is going to change the entire nature of the restaurant business," said Nar.

"I agree we're onto something," said LaHudra, "but what do you mean 'change the entire nature of the restaurant business'?"

"Yes, what do you mean?" asked Goniff.

"Well, if you think about it," Nar continued, "the whole job of the server is going to change, and so is the job of the chef. The servers won't be running around as much as they do now. They'll be information resources for the customers because they'll always be in their designated serving areas. They'll go to the kitchen and the bar only when they have to. Through their handheld computers, they'll become monitors of the order-preparation process and managers of their areas. They'll be more like lifeguards than traditional waiters. In fact, they'll be able to actually sit down while they work in their areas because work won't involve running around so much anymore."

"And the chefs?"

"They'll become more managerial, too. They'll use their computers to assign orders to assistant chefs and coordinate what goes on in a kitchen. This will be great for large kitchens and large restaurants, now that we're moving information around instead of people."

"Hmmm . . . That has a nice ring to it," said LaHudra. "Apparently, when you move information more, you can get away with moving people less. Not bad."

"Not bad at all," said Goniff, already plotting the next expansion of the business.

Summary

After the use case analysis, a development team turns its attention to the system components the use cases suggest. What are they? How do they interact? This hour showed how to answer these questions in the context of developing the WIN system.

The objective of this effort is to provide information to the programmers—information that facilitates their efforts. The results of this analysis should make it easy for programmers to code the system objects and the ways those objects communicate with one another.

After you model interaction among components, the system is much closer to becoming a reality. As you model the interactions, you may find that it's appropriate to modify the use cases at the base of these interactions.

Q&A

Q. *You've shown modification of use cases in several places here. Realistically, does that ever happen in a project?*

A. It absolutely does. Granted, the examples here may seem a bit contrived: For instance, you probably would have known about the database in the first use case before you ever got this far. The point is to show you that as your knowledge evolves, the model evolves along with it.

Q. *Why would the original use cases fail to capture all the nuances in the first place?*

A. Because they're the results of JAD sessions with system users, not system developers. You'll notice all the additions and changes were system-related, not business-related. After you finish the sessions with the potential users and have a chance to analyze the use cases, it's not uncommon for modifications like these to emerge.

Q. *As I look at the sequence diagrams, I see that the arrowheads for the messages aren't alike. Why is that?*

A. The filled arrowhead represents a call from one object to another, where the sender is waiting for the receiver to do something. The open-stick arrowhead represents a message where the sender has transferred control to the receiver and isn't waiting for anything.

Q. *Also in the sequence diagrams, sometimes those activation rectangles are long and sometimes they aren't. Can you explain?*

A. Those rectangles represent an object performing one of its operations— typically as a response to a message from another object. The height of the rectangle corresponds roughly to the length of time the operation takes. The longest rectangles in these figures are for the Server UI. The Server has sent a message to the Server UI to display a particular screen. The long rectangle shows that the screen remains visible.

Q. *One more question about the sequence diagrams. I see that in the first two, the OrderDB is at the extreme right. In the third one it's in a different place. Is that OK?*

A. Yes. Bear in mind that the left-right position of an object in the top row doesn't mean anything. In fact, all the diagrams start with a message from the leftmost object—the Server. But, the Server doesn't have to be in that position to kick off the sequence of messages. It's good form to do it that way, but it's not absolutely necessary.

Workshop

Here's where you get your chance to spread your wings on modeling interactions among system components. After you have answered the questions, interact with Appendix A, "Quiz Answers," to find the answers. Incidentally, you might want to use the components listed in this hour to help you go above and beyond the listed exercises and make additional sequence diagrams and collaboration diagrams.

Quiz

1. How do you represent an object that's created during the course of a sequence diagram?

2. How is time represented in a sequence diagram?

3. What is a *lifeline*?

4. In a sequence diagram, how do you show an *activation*, and what does it represent?

Exercises

1. Develop a collaboration diagram equivalent to the sequence diagram for the Server, use case "Take an order."

2. Create a sequence diagram for the use case "Take a drink order."

3. Select at least one use case in the Chef package and develop a sequence diagram. Use the list of components mentioned in this hour. Are any additional ones necessary?

4. Use your imagination on this one: The use cases in the Coat-Check Clerk package seem pretty simple. Can you embellish each one by adding a step or two? Would any additional components be helpful? Draw a sequence diagram for one of these use cases.

5. Take a look at the three sequence diagrams. Do you see any repetitions from one to another? If so, use the UML 2.0 techniques from Hour 9, "Working with Sequence Diagrams," to reuse the repeated information from one diagram to another.

HOUR 21

Designing Look, Feel, and Deployment

What You'll Learn in This Hour:

▶ Some general principles of GUI design

▶ The GUI JAD session

▶ From use cases to user interfaces

▶ UML diagrams for GUI design

▶ Mapping out system deployment

You've come through a lot of use case–driven analysis. In this hour, you're going to look at two aspects of system design. Both are ultimately traceable to use cases, and both are extremely important to the final product. **Graphical user interfaces** (GUIs) determine system usability. **Deployment** turns the system's planned physical architecture into a reality.

Some General Principles of GUI Design

User interface design, equal parts art and science, draws upon the vision of the graphic artist, the findings of the human factors researcher, and the intuitions of the potential user. After much experience with WIMP (Windows, Icons, Menus, Pointing device) interfaces, some general principles have emerged. Here are some of the major ones:

1. Understand what the user has to do. User interface designers typically perform a **task analysis** to understand the nature of the user's work. Your use case analysis roughly corresponds to this.

2. Make the user feel in control of the interaction. Always include the capability for the user to cancel an interaction after it's started.

3. Give the user multiple ways to accomplish each interface-related action (like closing a window or a file) and forgive user errors gracefully.

4. Because of cultural influences, our eyes are drawn to the upper left corner of a screen. Put the highest priority information there.

5. Take advantage of spatial relationships. Screen components that are related should appear near one another, perhaps with a box around them.

6. Emphasize readability and understanding. (Words for all of us to live by!) Use the active voice to communicate ideas and concepts.

7. Even though you might have the capability to include upwards of umpteen gazillion colors on a screen, limit the number of colors you use. Limit that number severely. Too many colors will distract the user from the task at hand. It's also a good idea to give the user the option of modifying the colors.

8. If you're thinking of using color to denote meaning, remember it's not always easy for a user to see an association between a color and a meaning. Also, bear in mind that some users (about 10% of adult males) have color confusion, and they may find it difficult to distinguish one color from another.

9. As is the case with color, limit your use of fonts. Avoid italics and ornate fonts. "Haettenschweiler" is a font name that's fun to say, but it doesn't always promote ease of use.

10. Try to keep components (like buttons and list boxes) the same size as much as possible. If you use different-size components, a multiplicity of colors, and a variety of fonts, you'll create a patchwork that GUI specialists call a "clown-pants" design.

11. Left-align components and data fields—line them up according to their left-side edges. This minimizes eye movements when the user has to scan the screen.

12. When the user has to read and process information and then click a button, put the buttons in a column to the right of the information or in a row below and to the right of the information. This is consistent with the natural tendency (in our culture) to read left to right. If one of the buttons is a default button, highlight it and make it the first button in the set.

These dozen principles aren't the only ones, but they give you an idea of what's involved in designing a GUI. The challenge is to convey the proper information in an uncomplicated, straightforward, intuitive visual context.

Figure 21.1 shows what happens when you put some of these principles into action. Figure 21.2 shows what happens when you don't.

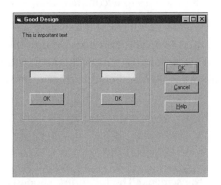

FIGURE 21.1
Applying GUI design principles.

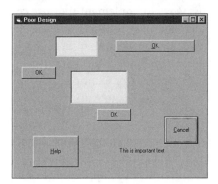

FIGURE 21.2
The result of not applying GUI design principles.

By the way, if you're creating Web pages, check out GUI honcho Jakob Nielsen's highly informative www.useit.com for more information on user interface design.

The GUI JAD Session

Although this doesn't directly connect to the UML, it's a good idea to talk about how potential users determine the GUI. Once again, a Joint Application Development (JAD) session is in order.

For this session, you recruit potential users of the system. For WIN, you'd recruit servers, chefs, assistant servers, assistant chefs, bussers, and coat-check clerks. The development team players should include programmers, analysts, modelers, and a facilitator. The objective is to understand the users' needs and implement an interface based on their ideas—an interface that enables the system to integrate smoothly into business processes. The old way of developing a system—writing a program from scratch, molding the behavior of the users so they can interact with it, and modifying business processes to accommodate it—is extinct.

To keep the session efficient, you'd schedule the users in groups according to their roles. You'd plan the length of each session according to the number of use cases in each role's package. This is just a rough guideline, of course, as some use cases are more complex than others. Remember, too, that new use cases might emerge as you design the GUI.

The users' participation in the session is a two-part affair. In the first part, they derive the user interface screens. In the second, they approve prototypes generated by the development team.

How do the users derive the screens? The facilitator suggests a use case to start from, and the users discuss ways to implement that use case via the system. When they're ready to start talking at the level of a specific screen, the users work with paper mockups. The facilitator provides a large sheet of easel paper in landscape view (long dimension as the horizontal) to represent the screen. Post-it notes represent the GUI components (for example, pop-up menus, buttons, combo boxes, and list boxes). The users' task is to work as a group to position the components appropriately.

When they reach agreement on which components should be on a screen and where those components should be located, development team members create prototype screens. As they work, they use appropriate GUI principles outlined in the preceding section. Then, they present those screens on computers, and the users make any necessary modifications.

The point of all this, of course, is to have users (rather than developers) drive the process as much as possible. That way, the system will work optimally in the real world of everyday business activities.

From Use Cases to User Interfaces

Use cases describe system usage. Therefore, the user interface has to serve as a means of implementing the use cases.

Think of a use case's sequence diagram as one view of a use case. If you could "rotate" that view in three dimensions so that the leftmost part of the sequence diagram sticks out of the page and faces you, you'd be looking at the user interface that takes the user into the sequence. (See Figure 21.3.)

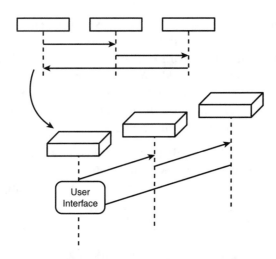

FIGURE 21.3
Rotating the sequence diagram orients the user interface toward you.

Let's examine the use cases in the Server package and show how they map into the WIN user interface. Here are those use cases once again:

▶ Take an order

▶ Transmit the order to the kitchen

▶ Change an order

▶ Track order status

▶ Notify chef about party status

▶ Total up a check

▶ Print a check

▶ Summon an assistant

▶ Summon a busser

▶ Take a drink order

▶ Transmit drink order to lounge

▶ Receive acknowledgment

▶ Receive notification from lounge

▶ Receive notification from the kitchen

The Server interface has to accommodate all these use cases.

One way to begin is to partition the set of use cases into groups. Three groups are sufficient. One group deals with orders ("Take an order," "Change an order," "Track order status," and "Take a drink order"). Another group deals with checks ("Total up a check" and "Print check"). A third is concerned with sending and receiving messages ("Notify chef about party status," "Summon an assistant," "Summon a busser," "Transmit drink order to lounge," "Receive acknowledgment," and "Receive notification from lounge").

You might want to start with a main screen that takes the server to screens for all the other groups of use cases. You'd want to be able to navigate from one group to any other group. Within a group, you'd want to navigate to any use case within the group. Figure 21.4 shows a first cut at the main screen. This will have to go on a handheld, so it will probably be scaled down in some ways.

FIGURE 21.4
First cut at a
Server main
screen.

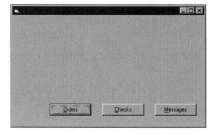

Your JAD session might arrive at the convention that navigation within a group will be done by buttons on the right of the screen, whereas navigation between groups will be accomplished via buttons at the bottom of the screen. Figure 21.5 shows a first cut at one of the Server interface screens—the screen for the orders-related use cases.

This screen opens in the Take Order mode. The large white box will be a scrollable copy of the dinner menu with check boxes that the server clicks to indicate a customer's selections. (When you deal with the interface, remember you're dealing with the world of restaurants and be extra careful about how you use the word *menu*.) Clicking OK creates the order and sends it to the kitchen PC. Clicking a button on the right brings its associated capabilities to the screen.

Clicking a bottom-row button brings up a separate group of capabilities. The Message button, for example, brings up the screen in Figure 21.6. By the way, the user interface doesn't have to be just visual. This interface incorporates a sound signal to notify the server that a message has arrived. He or she clicks the Read button to read a scrollable list of messages.

FIGURE 21.5
Screen for orders-
related use cases.

FIGURE 21.6
Screen for mes-
sage-related use
cases.

UML Diagrams for GUI Design

The UML makes no specific recommendations regarding diagrams for GUI designs. Earlier, however, I hinted at a possibility: Recall from Hour 8, "Working with State Diagrams," that I presented an example that dealt with state changes in a GUI. Although that example drilled deeper into the mechanics of GUIs than you have to at this point, it suggests that state diagrams are useful when you discuss user interfaces.

You'd use a state diagram to show the flow of a user interface. Figure 21.7 shows how the high-level screens in the Server interface connect with one another.

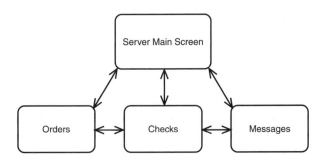

FIGURE 21.7
A state diagram for
high-level screen
flow in the Server
interface.

Because a particular screen consists of a number of components, a class diagram of a composite is appropriate for modeling a screen. Figure 21.8 shows a composite diagram that corresponds to the screen in Figure 21.5.

FIGURE 21.8
A class diagram that corresponds to the screen in Figure 21.5.

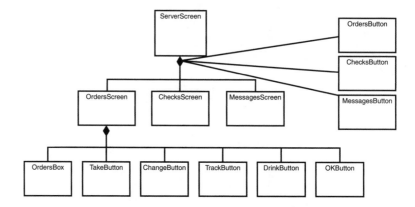

Mapping Out System Deployment

After the GRAPPLE analysis segment has produced the general concept of the WIN system, a system engineer will start thinking about how the physical architecture should look. He or she will start considering alternative network topologies and how to implement them in a wireless way. The system engineer will also start figuring out which software artifacts belong on which nodes in the network. This design segment doesn't have to wait for analysis to be complete. Its actions can proceed in parallel with actions in other GRAPPLE segments, such as the design of the GUI.

The key is for the project manager to track all the actions in all the segments.

The Network

Remembering the different types of LANs available (from Hour 13, "Working with Deployment Diagrams"), the system engineer has a number of choices. The objective is to pick the one that integrates most smoothly with wireless connectivity for the handheld computers.

To understand some of the decisions the system engineer has to make, let's delve a little into Wireless LANs (WLANs). A radio transceiver called an **access point** sits at a fixed location and communicates with wireless-enabled devices. The access point can connect to a LAN (of the standard, everyday garden-variety wired type). Multiple access points increase the WLAN's range and the number of users that can access it.

The system engineer has to decide how many access points to have in the restaurant, the type and layout of the wired network, and whether to have handhelds with built-in WLAN capability or handhelds that require PC cards for wireless networking.

For this exercise, suppose the system engineer decides on a thin ethernet for the LAN (see Hour 13).

The Nodes and the Deployment Diagram

You've already enumerated the nodes in your system. The servers, assistant servers, and bussers will have handheld computers. Let's assume the system engineer chooses a handheld device that requires a PC card.

The kitchen, cloakroom, and cocktail lounge will have desktops. Each desktop will connect to a printer. In addition, each serving area will have a desktop connected to a printer so the server can print checks and retrieve them without walking too far. (A server's print server, so to speak.)

To illustrate the deployment, the system engineer delivers the initial deployment diagram shown in Figure 21.9. It will ultimately have to be fleshed out, but this is a good start.

Next Steps

The development team has traveled the road from use cases to user interfaces to WLANs. What's next?

First, the analysts clean up the model. They look through the model dictionary and clear up any ambiguities. They make sure that all terminology is used consistently throughout all diagrams and that problems with terms like *menu* and *server* haven't crept in. When all appropriate analysis and design parts of GRAPPLE are complete, the team compiles its results into a design document and hands off copies to the client and to the programmers.

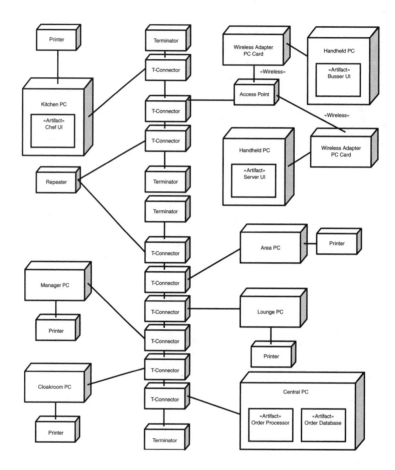

It then falls to the programmers to start turning the design into code, which is beyond the scope of this book. The code will be tested, rewritten according to the results of the tests, and retested—a process that will continue until the code passes all tests. The use case analysis forms the basis for the tests.

Document specialists begin creating documentation for the system, and they create training materials as well. A good document creation effort should proceed like a good system development effort—with careful planning, analysis, and testing—and should begin early in the development process.

With a solid analysis and design and an informative, well-organized design document, these next steps should proceed smoothly all the way through deployment.

The main idea is to focus intense efforts on analysis and design. That way the developer confronts as few challenges as possible during implementation and the result of the project is a system that fully meets the client's needs.

And Now a Word from Our Sponsor

Messrs. LaHudra, Nar, and Goniff couldn't be more thrilled with the way the development effort has gone. The development team has kept them posted throughout the process and has given them UML-based blueprints that show where the project is headed. They're even happy with the System Engineer's strategic thinking on which mobile device to use.

The whole effort has fired up their imaginations, impelling them to look for new ways to harness technology—both inside and outside the restaurant world. They've come to the realization that most business processes involve the movement of information. To the extent that technology accelerates that movement, it provides a potentially huge competitive advantage.

Empowering a Sales Force

Outside the restaurant world, the three entrepreneurs see the potential of reusing the wireless LAN ideas for a mobile sales force inside a huge work area. Reuse shouldn't be difficult, as all the modeling information is intact.

One application of this idea might be in the gigantic home supply stores that cater to do-it-yourself types. (Places where "hardware" has a different connotation than the one in this book.) Salespersons on the floor of that kind of store would benefit from a handheld device that accesses product information through a wireless LAN. A system like this would help the salesperson answer questions about where the product is located in the store, whether it's in stock, and how someone would use it.

This has some intriguing implications for both salesperson and customer. The customers would always be sure they're getting the latest and most accurate information from the salespeople. A new salesperson trained in the use of the system could quickly start working with minimal training about the stock.

LaHudra, Nar, and Goniff will soon invade the world of home improvement.

By the Way

No Strings Attached

Although LaHudra, Nar, and Goniff are obviously trailblazers, they're no longer alone in their visions for mobile devices and wireless LANs.

For example, tablet PCs have already invaded the restaurant world. One restaurant is using a tablet PC as a digital wine list that links wirelessly to information about its wines. The next time you hear a sommelier describe a wine as "somewhat impetuous, with an amusing insouciance and a brisk bouquet," he or she might just be relying on a tablet PC and a wireless LAN.

Of course, "Internet hotspots" in restaurants and coffee houses are also popular. Bring your wireless-enabled laptop, have a snack, and read your e-mail via the restaurant's WLAN.

And what about servers using wireless handhelds to send orders to the kitchen? When I dreamed up the whole thing for the first edition of this book, I thought we'd really see this kind of futuristic restaurant someday. Apparently, "someday" is now. Zozobra, a restaurant in Israel, took the pencils and pads out of the hands of its waiters and gave them wireless handheld computers instead. By all accounts, waiters and customers couldn't be happier.

Expanding in the Restaurant World

This mobile sales force idea isn't enough for LaHudra, Nar, and Goniff. They want to do nothing less than use technology to revolutionize the entire restaurant business. They believe they can build WIN-based restaurants in major cities throughout the world. They feel the technology will expedite the dining experience and make it more convenient for everyone to eat out.

Goniff, ever on the lookout for new ways to make a buck, had been thinking about this for a while (at least since the end of Hour 20, "Getting into Interactions"!).

"Fellas," said he to his partners, "if we build restaurants in all the major cities, we can take technology to the next step and move information all over."

"How so?" asked Nar, always a little slow on the uptake.

"Think about it. If we're international, we can go on the Web and . . . "

LaHudra interjected: "Just a second. We're already on the Web. We get hits all day on www.lahudranargoniff.com, don't we?"

"Let me finish, LaHudra. We can use the Web to get people to come into all these restaurants. We'll use the Web to give them a free sandwich."

"What???!!!" asked Nar and LaHudra simultaneously, and incredulously.

"Work with me on this. We devote a page of our Web site to our restaurants division. Someone hits that page, supplies his name and a bunch of other information, and gets to select the sandwich of his choice. If our database shows he hasn't done this before, he gets to go to another page where he can print out a coupon for a sandwich. He takes the coupon into the nearest restaurant. He gets the sandwich, eats it, loves it, and comes back as a paying customer."

"Nice, but the Web goes everywhere," said Nar. "Suppose somebody doesn't live near one of our restaurants but still wants the sandwich?"

"Wait! I know!" said LaHudra. "They can use their credit card to pay a nominal shipping fee on the Web site, and our closest restaurant will send it right to their house in an inexpensive cold container. They can put the sandwich in the microwave and warm it up. That way, they can have a LaHudra-Nar-Goniff experience wherever they are. Then, when they happen to travel to a city that has one of our restaurants, they're likely to eat there."

"By the way, what about that 'other information' they entered when they printed the coupon?" asked Nar.

"I'm way ahead of you," said Goniff. "We use that information to e-mail them promotional information about our other businesses, according to their demographics—if they indicate it's OK to do that, of course.

"Now where's that development team? We've got work to do."

Summary

When your project moves into the Design segment, two items to focus on are the user interface and the system deployment. Both are ultimately use case–driven, and both are extremely important.

User interface design depends on artistic vision and scientific research. A number of principles of user interface design have emerged after years of work with WIMP interfaces. This hour presented some of them. Keep them in mind as your development team designs GUIs.

Use cases drive the design of the user interface. The system has to enable the user to complete every use case, and the user interface is the gateway into the use cases.

In parallel with a number of project efforts, the team's system engineer maps out the physical architecture. The architecture is use case–driven because system usage ultimately determines the physical nature and layout of the system. The system engineer provides a UML deployment diagram that shows the nodes, the software components that live in each node, and the internodal connections. Although deployment issues show up late in the GRAPPLE process, there's no reason to hold back on starting to think about deployment. As shown in this hour, fundamental issues can arise that require resolution.

After the system is modeled, the modeling information can be reused in a variety of contexts. The model can fuel a multitude of new business ideas.

Q&A

Q. *After the users have developed a paper prototype, is it really necessary to go to the trouble of creating a screen and showing it to them? After all, they've created the paper screen and positioned the paper components. Can't they just wait to see the screen on the working system?*

A. You absolutely have to show the users a real screen—"real" in the sense that it's on a computer. First of all, users are likely to see things on the screen they didn't see on paper. Another reason—related to the first—is that the dimensions of post-it notes only approximate the dimensions of onscreen components (relative to the larger sheet that represents the screen). Placing the post-its results in some distortion of the spatial relationships among the onscreen components. The screen is likely to look somewhat different from the paper prototype. Also, screen shots become valuable parts of your design document.

Q. *I know this isn't directly related to the UML, but one of the GUI principles you mentioned is to give a user multiple ways to accomplish interface-related actions. Why is that important?*

A. This is important because you can't predict all the contexts in which a user will perform an action. Sometimes the user will be using a keyboard-intensive application, and a keystroke combination will be more appropriate than a mouseclick. At other times the user will be using the mouse, and a mouseclick will be more appropriate. Providing multiple ways of accomplishing the same thing makes the interaction that much easier for the user.

Q. *Speaking of questions not directly related to the UML, why the "active voice" GUI principle?*

A. Studies show that people have an easier time understanding the active voice than the passive. Also, the active voice typically requires fewer words and thus takes up less precious screen real estate than the passive voice does. Users (as well as publishers and editors) appreciate it if your directions say, "Click the Next button to continue" rather than "The Next button should be clicked by you in order for the process to be continued."

Q. *I've got one more unrelated question. Where can I find out more about WLANs?*

A. To find out more about WLANs, visit www.wlana.org, the Web site of the Wireless LAN Association (WLANA). WLANA is a consortium of corporations that market WLAN components.

Workshop

This workshop tests your knowledge of issues related to designing a system's look and feel and to mapping out the system's physical architecture. Design your answers well, and then interface with Appendix A, "Quiz Answers."

Quiz

1. What is a task analysis?

2. Which analysis that we've already done is roughly equivalent to a task analysis?

3. What is a clown-pants design?

4. Give three reasons for limiting the use of color in a GUI.

Exercises

1. Use a UML state diagram to model the chef's user interface.

2. Use pencil and paper to design at least one of the screens for the chef's user interface. Start by grouping the use cases, and then stick to the JAD session conventions. If you have access to Visual Basic or another visual screen design tool, try using it to complete this exercise.

3. Play the role of system engineer and research alternatives (other than the selected PC card and access point) for implementing the WLAN with hand-held devices.

4. Suppose the development team had decided to use palmtops instead of handhelds. Play the role of system engineer again and list all the implications of this choice. Research potential ways of implementing the WLAN with Palm OS–based devices or with Pocket PCs. Modify Figure 21.9 accordingly.

Understanding Design Patterns

What You'll Learn in This Hour:

▶ How to parameterize a class

▶ The thought process behind design patterns

▶ Applying a design pattern

▶ Using your own design pattern

▶ The advantages of design patterns

Now that you've learned the fundamentals of the UML and you've seen how to use it in the context of a development project, we end Part II with a look at applying the UML to support a useful idea—design patterns.

In the preceding 21 hours, you covered a variety of topics. From class diagrams to sequence diagrams, from state diagrams to JAD sessions, the goal was to get you ready to apply the UML in frequently occurring, real-world situations.

Now we change direction a bit. In this hour, I'll delve into a popular application of the UML. This application, the representation of design patterns, captures the essence of solutions that have worked repeatedly in real-world projects and situations.

Parameterization

In Hour 2, "Understanding Object-Orientation," I mentioned that a class is a template for creating objects. I said you could think of a class as a cookie-cutter that stamps out new objects. An object, you'll recall, is an instance of a class.

To further refresh your memory, return once again to the washing machine example. Specifying the washing machine class—or to be notationally correct, the WashingMachine class—as having the attributes brandName, modelName, serialNumber, and capacity, and the operations acceptClothes(), acceptDetergent(), and turnOn() gives you a way to create new objects in the WashingMachine class. Each time you want to create an object, you assign values to the attributes.

As it happens, the UML enables you to move a step higher. It gives you a mechanism for creating classes in a way that's analogous to creating objects. You can set up a class so that when you assign values to a subset of its attributes, you create a class rather than an object. This kind of class is called a **parameterized class**. Its UML representation appears in Figure 22.1. The dashed box in the upper right corner holds the parameters to which you assign values in order to generate the class. Just for the record, these are called **unbound parameters**. When you assign values to them, you **bind** them to those values. The T in the dashed box is a classifier that indicates the class is a template for creating other classes.

FIGURE 22.1
The UML icon for a parameterized class.

Here's an example: Suppose you set up LivingThing as a parameterized class. The unbound parameters could be genus and species, along with the attributes name, height, and weight as shown in Figure 22.2.

FIGURE 22.2
LivingThing as a parameterized class.

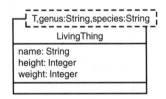

If you bind genus to *homo*, and species to *sapiens*, you create a class called Human. The class name is bound to T. Figure 22.3 shows one way of representing the binding. This particular style is called **explicit binding** because it explicitly shows the generated class in a relationship with the parameterized class, and it provides the generated class with its own name.

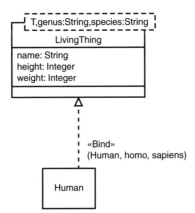

FIGURE 22.3
Explicitly binding
the LivingThing
parameterized
class.

The connection between Human and LivingThing is the realization arrow you saw earlier in connection with interfaces. Recall that an interface has simple operations and
that connecting an interface with a class brings "reality" to those operations.
Somewhat analogously, Human brings reality to the specifications of LivingThing.
Notice I said "somewhat." In order to show the special nature of this relationship, you
add «Bind», along with the parenthesized list of bindings.

Another binding style is called **implicit binding**. With this you don't show the
relationship, and the bindings appear in an angle-bracketed list in the name of
the generated class. Figure 22.4 shows this.

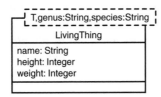

FIGURE 22.4
Implicitly binding
the LivingThing
parameterized
class.

LivingThing<Human,homo,sapiens>

In either case, you can then assign values to name, height, and weight to create
objects in the Human class.

Design Patterns

It's possible to expand on the parameterization idea. Any UML classifier can be parameterized. In fact, a group of collaborating classifiers can be parameterized, and that leads off in an intriguing direction.

After several decades of increasingly widespread use, object orientation has resulted in a number of robust solutions to frequently recurring problems. These solutions are called **design patterns**. Because design patterns have grown out of the object-oriented world they're easy to conceptualize, diagram, and reuse. Because we now have the UML, we have a common modeling language to explain and disseminate them.

The first book to popularize design patterns is entitled, unsurprisingly, *Design Patterns* (Addison-Wesley, 1995). Its authors—Erich Gamma, Richard Helm, Ralph Johnson, and John Vlissides—have become widely known as the "Gang of Four."

A design pattern is essentially a solution—a design—that has emerged through practical experience with a number of projects, and that development teams have found to be applicable in a variety of contexts. Each design pattern describes a set of communicating objects and classes. The set is customized to solve a design problem in a specific context.

In their book, the Gang of Four cataloged and characterized 23 fundamental design patterns. They partitioned these patterns into three categories according to each pattern's *purpose*: (1) **Creational** patterns that concern themselves with the process of object creation, (2) **Structural** patterns that deal with the composition of objects and classes, and (3) **Behavioral** patterns that specify how classes or objects interact and apportion responsibility. They further partition their design patterns in terms of whether they apply to objects or classes. They refer to this criterion as **scope**, and most patterns' scope is at the object level.

Each design pattern has four elements: (1) a *name* that enables you to describe a design problem in a word or a phrase, (2) a *problem* that defines when to apply the pattern, (3) a *solution* that specifies the elements that make up the design and how they collaborate, and (4) the *consequences* of applying the pattern.

Now you come to that "intriguing direction" I mentioned earlier: Within a model, you can represent a design pattern as a parameterized collaboration in the UML. The design pattern is expressed in a general way, with generic names for the collaborators. Assigning domain-specific names makes the pattern applicable to a specific model. The parameterized collaboration helps you visualize the specificity within the context of the pattern.

Chain of Responsibility

Let's examine one design pattern, and you'll see what I mean.

The Chain of Responsibility is a behavioral pattern that applies to a number of domains. This pattern deals with the relationship between a set of objects and a request. You apply this pattern when more than one object can handle a request. The first object in the chain gets the request and either resolves it or moves it along to the next object in the chain until one can handle it. The original requesting object doesn't know which object will handle its request. The object that ultimately handles the request is said to be an **implicit receiver**.

Restaurants are set up this way, and so are car dealerships when they finance auto purchases. In a restaurant, a customer typically doesn't send a request directly to a chef and isn't usually acquainted with the chef the request is going to. Instead, the customer gives an order to a server and the server gets it to the chef, who might fulfill the order or pass it along to an assistant chef. (That's how it happens at the LaHudra, Nar, & Goniff restaurants, anyway.) In an automobile dealership, the dealer passes a loan application to several financial institutions until one decides to offer a loan.

Now that you've seen the Chain of Responsibility design pattern in a couple of contexts, you're ready to understand it in the abstract. The participants in this pattern are a `Client`, an abstract `Handler`, and concrete `Handler`s that are children of the abstract `Handler`. The `Client` initiates a request. If a (concrete) `Handler` can take care of that request, it does so. If not, it passes the request along to the next concrete `Handler`. Figure 22.5 shows how this structure looks.

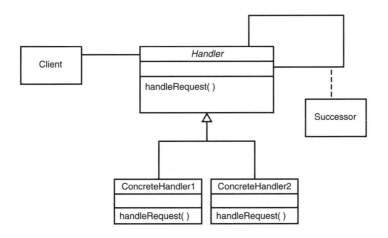

FIGURE 22.5
The structure of the Chain of Responsibility design pattern.

The idea behind this pattern is to free an object from having to know which other object fulfills its request. It gives you additional flexibility when you assign responsibilities to objects. The downside is that the pattern gives no guarantee that any object will handle the request. For example, it's possible that no financial institution will offer a car loan in response to a loan application.

Note the reflexive association on the abstract Handler class. The Gang of Four intended to show that you have the option of having the Handler implement the successor link. (In some contexts, the objects know how to find their own successors.) I decided to represent that implementation with an association class, as in Figure 22.5, to allow the further option of adding attributes to the successor.

Chain of Responsibility: Restaurant Domain

In the restaurant domain, the abstract Handler is the Employee class, and concrete Handlers are the Server, the Chef, and the Assistant Chef. The Customer is the Client, who might initiate a request, like placing an order, and doesn't know who will ultimately fulfill it.

Substituting domain-specific names into Figure 22.5 gives you Figure 22.6.

FIGURE 22.6
The Chain of
Responsibility
design pattern in
the restaurant
domain.

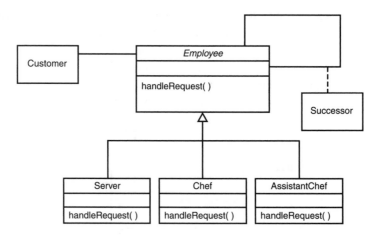

Figure 22.6, while a useful diagram, doesn't show how the domain-specific names fit into the pattern. To show the context, you use a parameterized collaboration as in Figure 22.7.

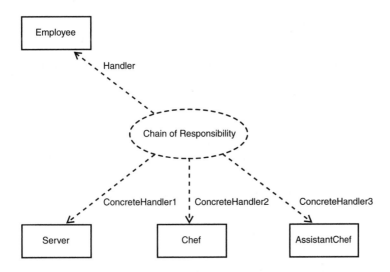

FIGURE 22.7
A parameterized collaboration for representing the Chain of Responsibility in a restaurant.

In Figure 22.7, the dashed oval represents the collaboration that is the design pattern, hence the name inside the oval. The surrounding boxes represent the collaborators. The dependencies show that the collaboration depends on the collaborators. The label on a dependency tells which role the depended-on collaborator satisfies within the pattern. The collaboration has been parameterized with the addition of the domain-specific class names.

Chain of Responsibility: Web Browser Event Models

When developing interactive Web pages, a designer has to consider the event model of the browser that will open it. In Internet Explorer (IE), you write JavaScript or VBScript code for reacting to an event like a button click. This code, called an **event handler**, specifies the changes, if any, that occur when the button is clicked.

In an HTML document, you can divide a page into areas called DIVs, and subdivide a DIV into forms. You can position a button inside a form. Does this sound strangely like a composite? That's because it is. Each element is a component of the document, and some components are components of other components. Gamma, Helm, Johnson, and Vlissides list the Composite as one of their design patterns, and note that it's often used in conjunction with the Chain of Responsibility pattern. The component-composite relationship implements the successor links. When I showed you the class diagram for the Chain of

Responsibility, I mentioned parenthetically that in some contexts the objects know how to find their own successors. This is one of those contexts.

When the button is positioned in a form inside a DIV whose document opens in IE, the button-click event starts with the button, is passed along to the form, then to the DIV, and finally to the containing document. Each of these elements can have its own button-click event handler to react to the click event.

If a document-resident script dynamically specifies which element's event handler fires, the script is an instance of the Chain of Responsibility design pattern. Figure 22.8 shows the class diagram, and Figure 22.9 shows the parameterized collaboration for this design pattern applied to the IE event model. Incidentally, this model is called *event bubbling*.

FIGURE 22.8
Class diagram for the Chain of Responsibility in a Web page that opens in IE.

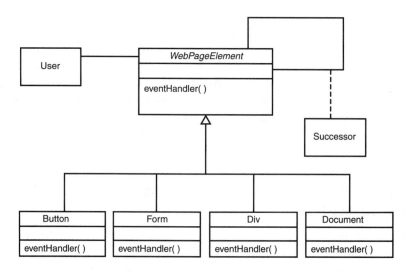

Netscape Navigator has an event model, too. Known as *event capturing*, its model is the exact opposite of IE's. In Navigator, the highest-level element (the document) gets the event first and passes it along until it ends up at the element from which it originated. How would you change the class diagram in Figure 22.8 to model the Navigator event model? (The Exercise at the end of this hour asks you to do just that.)

Your Own Design Patterns

While the Gang of Four became justly famous for their catalog of design patterns, they didn't mean to imply that their patterns were the only ones possible. On the contrary, their intent was to encourage the overall discovery and use of patterns.

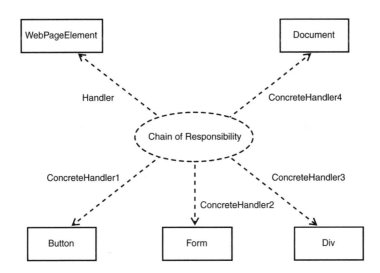

FIGURE 22.9
Parameterized collaboration for the Chain of Responsibility in a Web page that opens in IE.

Just to give you an idea of how these patterns emerge, remember your work in Hour 11, "Working with Activity Diagrams." During that hour, you saw an example dealing with Fibonacci numbers and an exercise concerning triangle numbers.

What were the common features? Each one started with an initial value or set of values, followed a rule to accumulate numbers, and ended with the nth number in a series.

Let's refer to this pattern as "Series Calculator." Although you could implement this as one object, you'll make it a set of collaborating objects to illustrate some concepts about design patterns.

The Series Calculator has three participants, InitialValue (which can hold one or more values), AccumulationRule, and FinalValue. Figure 22.10 shows the class diagram for this pattern. The starting value is in the attribute first. If a second starting value is necessary, as in the case of Fibonacci numbers, it's specified in an attribute called second. Sometimes, as in the case of factorials, the pattern will need a value for the zeroth term. The algorithm for AccumulationRule is implemented in the operation accumulate(). The number of terms to calculate is in the attribute nth in AccumulationRule.

In the collaboration, InitialValue creates the list of starting values, AccumulationRule accepts this list from InitialValue, and applies the rule the requisite number of times, and FinalValue accepts the result and prints it. Figure 22.11 shows the interaction.

FIGURE 22.10
The class structure for the Series Calculator design pattern.

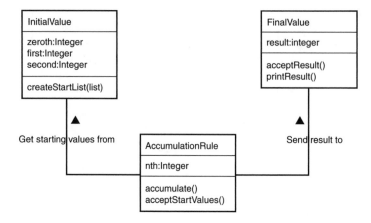

FIGURE 22.11
The interaction within the Series Calculator design pattern.

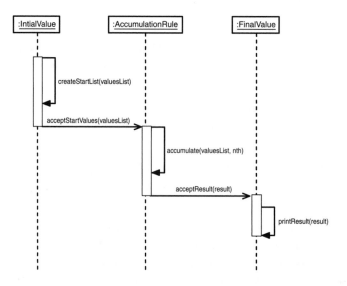

To apply this design pattern to the triangle numbers series, adopt some triangle-numberish names for the classes to show the parameterized collaboration in Figure 22.12. (This collaboration, of course, avoids the "trivial" solution I pointed out at the end of Exercise 3 in Hour 11.)

For good measure, show the parameterized collaboration for a Factorial calculator seen in Figure 22.13.

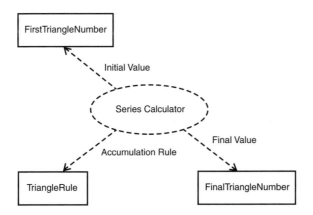

FIGURE 22.12
The parameterized collaboration for a Triangle Number calculator.

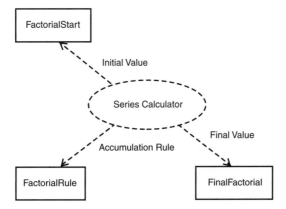

FIGURE 22.13
The parameterized collaboration for a Factorial calculator.

The Advantages of Design Patterns

Design patterns are useful in a number of different ways. First, they promote reuse. If you express a solid design as a pattern, you make it easy for you and others to work with it again. Also, they give you a clear, concise way of speaking and thinking about a set of classes or objects that work together to solve a problem. This increases the likelihood that you'll use the pattern as a component of a design. Finally, if you use patterns in your design, you'll probably find it easier to document the system you build.

Summary

A parameterized class has unbound parameters. Binding these parameters results in the creation of a class. You can parameterize any UML classifier. A parameterized collaboration serves as the representation of a design pattern—a solution that's useful in a variety of domains.

One design pattern, the Chain of Responsibility, deals with objects passing a request from one to another until one object can handle it. This pattern comes from *Design Patterns*, the best-known book on design patterns.

Your own design patterns emerge from work you did in Hour 11 on activity diagrams. You can create a design pattern for a calculator that computes the nth value in an arithmetic series. This pattern's participants are `InitialValue`, `AccumulationRule`, and `FinalValue`.

Design patterns afford a number of advantages. They enable designers to easily reuse proven solutions, incorporate solid components into designs, and clearly document the systems they create.

Q&A

Q. *How difficult is it to discover design patterns?*

A. It's not a question of difficulty; it's more a matter of experience. As you progress in your career as an analyst and a designer, you'll see certain regularities occur again and again. After a while, you'll think in terms of those regularities. Studies show that experts in a particular domain think in terms of patterns and apply those patterns in most situations they encounter. It's the basis of their seemingly smooth, effortless performance.

Q. *Are patterns useful only for design?*

A. No. Patterns can emerge anywhere in the development process or in any field of endeavor. The Gang of Four was inspired by the work of an architect who discerned recurring patterns in the designs of buildings.

Workshop

The quiz questions and exercises in this workshop get you thinking about some of the UML's advanced features. Advance to Appendix A, "Quiz Answers," for the answers.

Quiz

1. How do you represent a parameterized class?

2. What is *binding* and what are the two types of binding?

3. What is a *design pattern*?

4. What is the Chain of Responsibility design pattern?

Exercise

Change the class diagram in Figure 22.8 so that it visualizes the Netscape Navigator event model. As I pointed out earlier this hour, an event in Navigator starts at the document level and is passed along until it winds up at the element from which it originated. The originating element may be buried several levels deep in the HTML document.

PART III

Looking Ahead

HOUR 23 Modeling Embedded Systems   **383**

HOUR 24 Shaping the Future of UML   **403**

HOUR 23

Modeling Embedded Systems

What You'll Learn in This Hour:

▶ Embedded systems concepts

▶ Modeling an embedded system in the UML

As in Hour 22, "Understanding Design Patterns," you're going to look at a particular application of UML. In this hour, you'll learn about computer systems that don't sit on desks, laps, or palms. Instead, they're embedded deep inside venues like planes, trains, and automobiles.

Back to the Restaurant

LaHudra and his intrepid partners, Nar and Goniff, have been raking in the profits from their LNG Restaurants Division. The service is so good and the meals so tasty that people are coming from miles around to sample the delicious fare in an efficient and friendly atmosphere.

Two flaws have marred their otherwise good fortune. As they read over the monthly reports, these ominous trends stood out. "Take a look at this," said Nar, handing the printouts to Goniff and LaHudra. "We're making a boatload of money, but we should be making more. The waiters . . . uhm . . . servers seem to be dropping more than their fair share of dishes."

"Yes, I noticed that, too," said Goniff. "Every time they drop a dish full of food, the chef has to prepare another meal, and we have to pay for a new dish."

"Does it really make a difference if a few of our waiters have butterfingers?" asked LaHudra.

"It most certainly does," replied Goniff. "A couple of dishes here, a couple there, pretty soon we're talking real money. But something else about the servers is bothering me even more."

"What's that?" asked Nar.

"These reports show they call in sick a lot. It's a good thing we've got all this technology in the restaurants. It helps us when we have to work shorthanded; we can usually get by with the servers who do show up covering larger service areas than they typically do."

"Let's find out what's wrong," said LaHudra.

The Mother of Invention

The three partners interviewed several of the servers who had frequently called in sick over the previous two months, and they made an astounding discovery: The dropped dishes and the sick days were related. The servers had been handling and grasping their handheld computers so much that their wrists began to weaken. Just as loose lips sink ships, weak wrists drop dishes. What's more, their wrists had often become so painful they couldn't come in to work.

"Can't we help these people somehow?" asked a disconsolate Nar.

"And in the process, maybe help ourselves?" countered an opportunistic Goniff.

"Maybe there's some way we can help them strengthen their grip and their wrists," said LaHudra.

"Well, what should we do," asked Goniff, "buy each of them a grip strengthener?"

"We could do worse," said LaHudra, "but I don't know how effective those little hand grippers really are. It might take forever for our people to strengthen their wrists by using them."

"Still, the idea is a good one," said Nar. "Maybe we just need a better grip strengthener than the ones you can buy in a store."

"Really? How would we make a better grip strengthener?" LaHudra asked.

He didn't have long to wait for an answer. Nar was on one of his patented rolls.

"As I recall, lots of people believe that the best and most efficient form of exercise is one that creates the greatest challenge when your muscles are working their hardest. If we can create a gripper that increases its resistance as the forearm muscles work harder, I bet we can strengthen our servers' wrists in half the time they'd need with a regular gripper."

"Exactly how do we do that?" wondered the perpetually pragmatic LaHudra.

"The same way we revolutionized the restaurant business," said Nar, "with technology."

"Wait a second," said LaHudra, "we did what we did in the restaurants by adding computers. Do you seriously mean to tell me that we're going to add a computer to a grip-strengthening device?"

"Why not?" said Nar.

"Why not indeed," Goniff chimed in. "I'm with you, Nar. And when we've finished creating this gizmo, we can market it. I've got the perfect name: How about the LNG 'GetAGrip'?"

"I think I'm going to like it," said LaHudra, cautiously.

"I like it already," bubbled Nar, enthusiastically. "Where's that development team?"

Fleshing Out the GetAGrip

The WIN development team reassembled. Their new mission was to implement the vision of the GetAGrip, a "smart" wrist/forearm strengthening device that provides variable resistance during the repetitions of an exercise: The more the muscles work, the harder it should be to squeeze the GetAGrip.

In the course of realizing the vision, the team did some research to find out how to measure how hard a muscle is working. They learned about electronic signals from active muscle fibers. These signals, called EMGs (short for *electromyographic* signals), are the basis for fascinating devices that allow handicapped people to manipulate electronic equipment.

By the Way

Working with EMG Signals

This isn't an excursion into science fiction. In the early '90s, neuroscientist David Warner at the Loma Linda University Medical Center placed electrodes on a boy's face and connected them to a computer. The boy, completely paralyzed from the neck down in an auto accident, was able to move objects on the computer screen by tensing some of his facial muscles.

To learn more about this exciting area, read Hugh S. Lusted and R. Benjamin Knapp's article, "Controlling Computers with Neural Signals," in the October, 1996 issue of *Scientific American*.

In the time since I wrote about this in the original edition, Lusted moved on to found SGS Interactive, a company that interfaces computers with biosensors. One of their products is a sensor you strap on your arm, connect to a computer, and voilà: you're ready to arm wrestle a similarly plugged-in opponent . . . over the Internet! Read all about it at www.sgspartners.com.

The team concluded that they could capture these EMGs via a small, inexpensive surface electrode placed on the forearm. pass the captured EMGs through a computer, and then use them as a basis for the computer to adjust resistance in a hand-gripping device. This involves real-time data capture and analysis because the adjustments have to occur as soon as the muscle contracts.

One design possibility is to put the surface electrode on the forearm, connect it to a desktop computer, and have the desktop analyze the EMGs and make the necessary resistance adjustments in the hand gripper. The upside of this design is that it makes it possible to display all kinds of data onscreen, print informative progress reports, and analyze trends. The downside, however, is that the exerciser is tethered to a computer.

Another possibility is to embed a computer chip directly into the gripping device so that the exerciser is free to move around while he or she uses the GetAGrip. Figure 23.1 shows how this design would look. In each repetition of the exercise, the exerciser grips the squeeze bar and moves it toward the base bar.

The upside of the embedded design is that the exerciser can use a device like this almost anywhere (if the computer is battery powered). The downside, of course, is the loss of all the potential information that a desktop could store and display.

JAD sessions revealed that everyone would be much happier with the second design, and this takes us into the wonderful world of embedded systems.

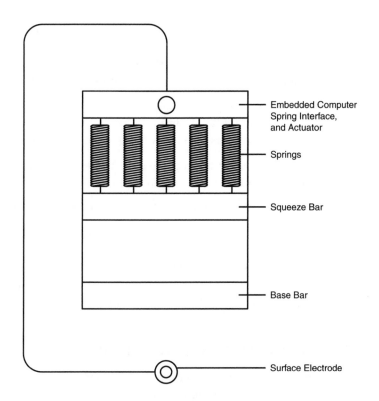

FIGURE 23.1
The embedded system version of GetAGrip.

Embedded Computer
Spring Interface,
and Actuator

Springs

Squeeze Bar

Base Bar

Surface Electrode

What Is an Embedded System?

Of course, you know that computers are everywhere. What you might not know is just how much territory "everywhere" encompasses. The computers you see all around you are just the tip of the iceberg. Many of them lurk below the surface, in places you can't easily see. They're inside appliances, cars, airplanes, factory machinery, biomedical devices, and more. Fairly powerful processors live inside printers.

All of these not-readily-visible-to-the-naked-eye computers are examples of **embedded systems**. Wherever you have a "smart" device, you have an embedded system.

Embedded systems don't have keyboards and monitors that interact with us. Instead, each one is a chip that sits inside a device (like a home appliance), and the device doesn't look like a computer at all. The embedded system decides what that device should do.

If you use a system of this type, you don't get the sense of working with a computer. Instead, you're just interacting with the device. If you never know the computer chip is inside, all the better. When you're toasting a slice of bread, you don't care that an embedded computer chip is distributing the heat—you just want your bread toasted.

When you finish working with a desktop, you turn it off. An embedded system doesn't usually have that luxury. After it's in place, an embedded system has to go on working for days or even years (as in a pacemaker, for example).

If a word processor or a spreadsheet has a glitch and crashes your desktop, you reboot. If the software in an embedded system fails, the results can be disastrous.

So an embedded system doesn't do computing in the usual sense. It's in place to help some other type of device do its work. The other device is the one that interfaces with the user and with the environment.

As you might imagine, programming an embedded system is not for the squeamish. It requires a lot of knowledge about the device the system will live in—what kinds of signals it sends out, what kind of timing parameters it has, and more.

Embedded Systems Concepts

Let's take a closer look at embedded systems and what they typically have to do. The subsections that follow deal with some of the more important embedded system concepts.

Time

If you go back over the discussion thus far, you'll see that time figures prominently in the embedded systems world. In fact, time is the basis of categorizing embedded systems as either **soft** or **hard**.

A soft system does its work as quickly as possible without having to meet specific deadlines. A hard system also has to work as quickly as possible, as well as finish its tasks according to strict deadlines.

Threads

In the embedded systems world, a **thread** (also called a **task**) is a simple program. It's a piece of an application, and it performs some meaningful job within that application. It tries to get the full attention of the CPU. **Multitasking** is the process of sheduling the CPU to work with many threads and switching its attention from one to the other.

Each thread has a number that denotes its priority within the application program, and it is usually in one of six states:

- **dormant**—it's in memory and hasn't been made available to the operating system.
- **ready**—it can run, but the thread that's running has a higher priority.
- **delayed**—it has suspended itself for a specified amount of time.
- **waiting for an event**—some event has to happen for it to run.
- **running**—it has the attention of the CPU.
- **interrupted**—because the CPU is taking care of an interrupt.

Figure 23.2 shows a UML state diagram that presents these states and the inter-state transitions. Notice the absence of a start symbol and a termination symbol. This tells you the thread moves from state to state in an infinite loop.

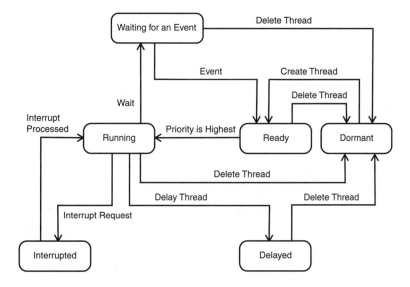

FIGURE 23.2
States of a thread in an embedded system application.

By the way, you might be wondering what an "interrupt" is. Read on to find out.

Interrupts

An **interrupt** is an important little item in an embedded system. It's a hardware-based mechanism that tells the CPU an asynchronous event has happened. An event is asynchronous if it appears unpredictably (that is, "out of sync"). In the GetAGrip, for example, EMG signals arrive asynchronously.

When the CPU recognizes an interrupt, it saves what it was doing and then invokes an **ISR** (Interrupt Service Routine) that processes the event. When the ISR finishes its job, the CPU goes back to what it was doing when the interrupt happened.

After processing an interrupt, what the CPU goes back to is determined by the type of operating system that runs the CPU, as you'll see in a moment.

Interrupts are important because they enable a CPU to disengage from whatever thread it's working on and process events as they happen. This is tremendously significant for a real-time system that has to respond to environmental events in a timely fashion.

Because timeliness is so crucial, embedded systems have to worry about the time course of an interrupt and its processing, even though that time might seem infinitesimal. The CPU has to take some time from when it's notified about an interrupt until it starts saving what it was doing (that is, its **context**). That's called the **interrupt latency**. The **interrupt response** is the time between the arrival of the interrupt request and when the CPU starts the ISR. After the ISR finishes, the **interrupt recovery** is the time it takes the CPU to get back to where it was—its context—when the interrupt occurred.

One type of interrupt is special: the **clock tick**. A sort of system heartbeat, the clock tick occurs at regular intervals specific to an application (typically between 10 and 200 microseconds). Clock ticks determine an embedded system's time constraints. For example, a thread in the delayed state remains in that state for a specified number of clock ticks.

Operating System

A real-time operating system (RTOS) acts as a traffic cop among threads and interrupts, and mediates the communication between threads and between an interrupt and a thread. The *kernel* is the part of the RTOS that manages the time the CPU spends on individual threads. The kernel also determines which thread executes next. As I mentioned before, each thread has a priority assigned to it.

The kernel schedules the CPU in either a **preemptive** or a **nonpreemptive** fashion, depending on what it has the CPU deal with after an ISR. With a nonpreemptive kernel, when an ISR finishes executing, the CPU goes back to the thread it was working on when the interrupt request arrived. A nonpreemptive kernel is said to engage in **cooperative multitasking**. Figure 23.2 applies to a nonpreemptive kernel.

With a preemptive kernel, on the other hand, when an ISR finishes, the priority of threads in the ready state determines which thread the CPU is scheduled to tackle next. If a thread in the ready state has a higher priority than the interrupted thread, the CPU executes the higher priority task rather than the one it was working on when the interrupt request arrived. Thus, the higher priority task **preempts** the interrupted task. Figure 23.3 shows the modification to two of the states in Figure 23.2, in order to model the preemptive kernel.

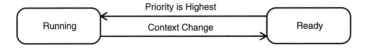

FIGURE 23.3
Modification of transitions between two of the states in Figure 23.2 to reflect what happens in a preemptive kernel.

It's helpful to model the two types of kernels as sequence diagrams. Figure 23.4 shows the classes whose instances interact in these diagrams.

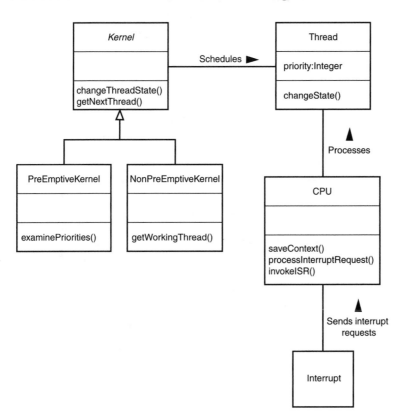

FIGURE 23.4
Instances of these classes interact in the sequence diagrams that follow.

Figure 23.5 models the nonpreemptive kernel, and Figure 23.6 models the preemptive kernel. In Figure 23.5, I've used the **duration constraint**, a new time-related modeling element in UML 2.0. The idea is to visualize the terms I mentioned before in the section on interrupts. Within the curly braces, *d* stands for *duration*.

FIGURE 23.5
Sequence diagram for the nonpreemptive kernel.

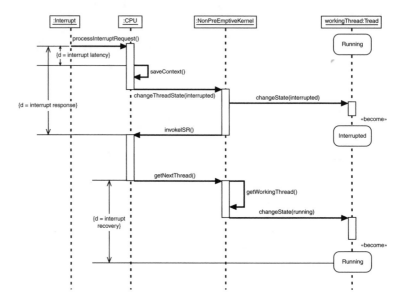

FIGURE 23.6
Sequence diagram for the preemptive kernel.

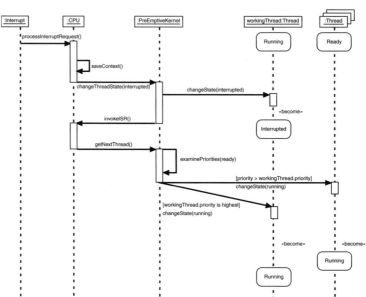

Each diagram is an example of a hybrid diagram, as I've superimposed state icons onto the lifelines of the thread objects. These icons represent states from Figure 23.2. Note that «become» on each lifeline indicates an object transition from one state to the next.

Although we've covered a lot of ground here, bear in mind that we've just scratched the surface of embedded systems.

Modeling the GetAGrip

Back to the task (thread?) at hand—to start creating a model of the GetAGrip. Although it's not the case that all embedded systems are object oriented, you can still use object orientation to model the system and its interactions with the outside world.

From the section on embedded systems, it's clear that you have to consider timing, events, state changes, and sequences.

Classes

As is the case with any other type of system, you'll begin with classes. To understand the class structure, start with a summary description of the GetAGrip and how it works. This summary would have resulted from a domain analysis.

Here's the description: The GetAGrip consists of a surface electrode, a CPU, a kernel, an actuator (to carry out the CPU's adjustment commands), and a set of five springs. The actuator connects to the springs via a mechanical interface. The surface electrode captures asynchronous EMG signals from the user's muscles and passes them to the CPU. Each EMG causes an interrupt request, which the CPU services with an ISR. Software in the CPU analyzes the signals. When the analysis is complete, the CPU sends a signal to an actuator to adjust the tension in the springs. The actuator specifies the adjustment by manipulating the mechanical interface with the springs and the interface adjusts the tension.

Figure 23.7 shows a class diagram that summarizes the preceding paragraph. The CPU continuously receives and analyzes signals and then directs adjustments. It also performs general housekeeping duties within the system.

Note the use of association classes to model `EMGSignal` and `AdjustMessage`. This allows you to focus on the properties of these classes and use those properties in your modeling efforts. For example, the system will be interested in the exact time a signal arrives and how strong it is, so `arrivalTime` and `amplitude` would seem to be reasonable attributes for the `EMGSignal`. Also, the `EMGSignal` will undoubtedly have complex characteristics that are beyond the scope of this discussion.

FIGURE 23.7
A model of the
GetAGrip.

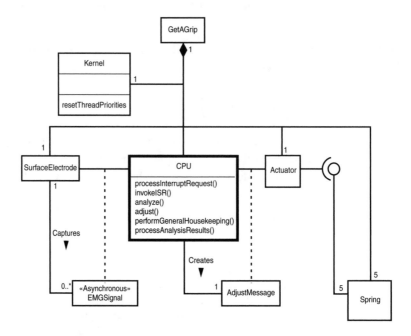

For `AdjustMessage`, the attributes `generationTime` and `adjustmentAmount` seem reasonable.

Figure 23.8 shows the attributes for these classes.

FIGURE 23.8
A closer look at
`EMGSignal` and
`AdjustMessage`.

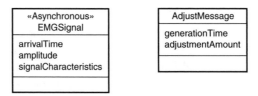

Use Cases

The JAD session I referred to earlier (which resulted in the design decision for an embedded system rather than a desktop) also resulted in a number of use cases, as depicted in Figure 23.9.

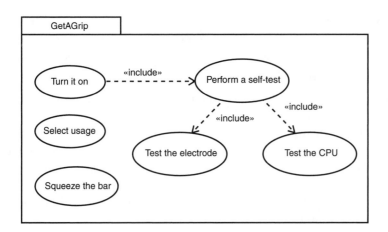

FIGURE 23.9
Use cases for
GetAGrip.

These use cases determine the capabilities to build into the system. "Turn it on" includes "Perform a self-test" which, in turn, includes "Test the electrode" and "Test the CPU."

"Select usage" refers to a number of different ways to set up the GetAGrip—ways that never occurred to Mr. Nar when he dreamed up this device. For example, the JAD participants said they'd like the option of setting "negative" repetitions— limited resistance when they squeeze the bars together, maximal resistance as they release them.

This means you have to add an attribute to AdjustMessage to reflect the system usage. You can call it usageAlgorithm and give it the possible values increasingTension and negativeRep. Figure 23.10 shows the modified AdjustMessage class.

FIGURE 23.10
The modified
AdjustMessage
class.

Interactions

Direct your attention to "Squeeze the bar," and assume that the exerciser has selected the originally conceived mode—increasing resistance with increasing muscular activity. In this part of the model, you have to make sure that you consider time constraints and state changes. Assume that a clock tick interval is 20 microseconds and that the time from receiving a signal to sending an adjustment message must take no longer than 10 clock ticks.

One more assumption: suppose that the kernel works preemptively. This necessitates a few modeling decisions. First, in order to reflect the kernel's operation, we'll treat the CPU's analyze(), adjust(), and generalHousekeeping() operations as threads and assign them priorities.

To show them this way in the model, you have to treat them as classes—something you don't usually do with operations. This is an example of an advanced UML concept called **reification**—treating something as a class (or an object) that isn't usually treated that way. When you do that, you add richness to your model because your reified classes have relationships with other classes, have attributes of their own, and become structures that you can manipulate and store. In this case, reification allows you to show thread priorities as attributes and use the threads in your interaction diagrams.

Figure 23.11 shows the class structure for the GetAGrip threads. In this model, threads know how to change their states and downgrade their priorities.

FIGURE 23.11
Class structure for the GetAGrip threads.

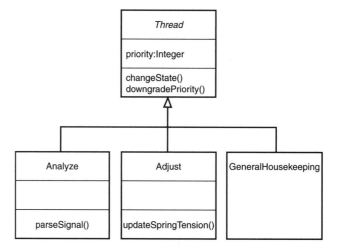

How should you prioritize the threads? When an interrupt request arrives, the CPU has to stop what it's doing, remember its context, and service the interrupt with an ISR. The processISR() operation grabs the EMGSignal's amplitude and the other complex signal characteristics and places them in memory for analyze() to work on. The analyze() operation, then, has to have the highest priority. The adjust() operation should follow. The generalHousekeeping() operation should have the lowest priority.

Here's an example of how all this would play together preemptively: If the CPU is in the middle of carrying out some general housekeeping operations and a signal arrives, the signal interrupts what the CPU is doing. The CPU executes `processISR()` and extracts the appropriate values from the signal. What happens next? Going back to the general housekeeping would be unproductive. Instead, the CPU executes the highest priority operation, `analyze()`, followed by `adjust()`. Presumably, each thread downgrades its priority accordingly after it does its work, and the kernel resets all the priorities after the adjustment is complete.

Figure 23.12 shows the sequence diagram for the "Squeeze the bar" use case. Once again, I've used the domain constraint. The first one shows the duration of a clock tick. The second indicates the upper limit (in terms of clock ticks) from the reception of a signal until the CPU is notified that the **Adjust** thread has done its job.

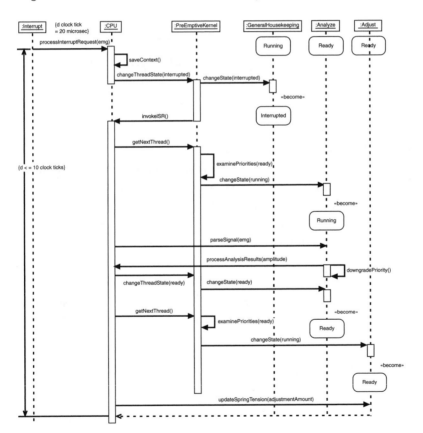

FIGURE 23.12
Sequence diagram for "Squeeze the bar."

This diagram follows the sequence up until the adjustment message is processed by the `Adjust` thread. At the end of this hour, Exercise 4 gives you an opportunity to add to this diagram.

At this point, a timing diagram (new in UML 2.0) is appropriate. Figure 23.13 shows the time course of the Adjust thread's state changes, given the duration constraints in Figure 23.12. In creating this diagram, I assumed that Figure 23.12 represents a scale—that is, that the distance delineated by the second duration constraint represents 10 clock ticks.

FIGURE 23.13
A timing diagram that models the time course of state changes in the Adjust thread.

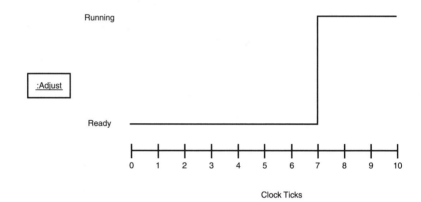

General State Changes

In addition to changes of state within an interaction, you can examine systemwide state changes. Generally, we expect that the GetAGrip will be either in the Working state or the Waiting state (between sets of an exercise, for example). It can also be in the Off state. As you might imagine, the Working state is a composite. Figure 23.14 presents the details.

Deployment

How will GetAGrip look once it's implemented? Figure 23.15 is a deployment diagram that shows the parts of the system, along with a battery that supplies the power.

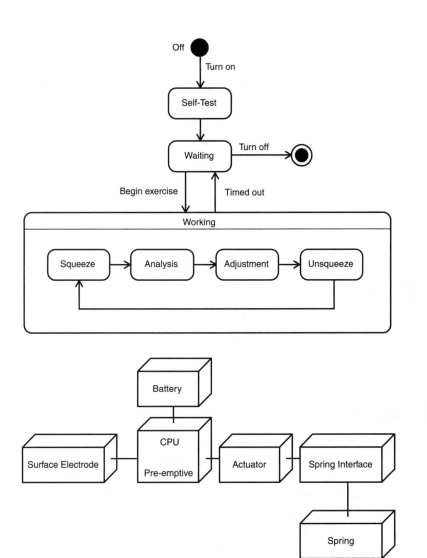

FIGURE 23.14
GetAGrip state changes.

FIGURE 23.15
A deployment diagram for GetAGrip.

Flexing Their Muscles

When the partners received the UML diagrams for the GetAGrip, the wheels started turning.

"This is a concept we can expand on," said Goniff.

"How so?" asked Nar.

"Think about it. How many muscles are there in the human body? We can build a smart exercise device that covers lots of them."

"Really?" asked Nar again, enthralled.

"Sure," said Goniff. "If we take the electrode-CPU-springs concept a step or two further, we can develop a smart, portable barbell that people could take with them when they travel. It wouldn't weigh very much because lightweight springs would provide the resistance and the CPU would provide the smarts. We could call it 'GetABuild.'"

"Yeah," said Nar, "or we could go in another direction and make a separate machine for each body part."

"Sure. Something like 'GetAChest.'"

"Or 'GetAnArm.'"

"Or 'GetALeg.'"

"How about 'GetALegUp'!"

At this point, LaHudra couldn't take it anymore.

"I've got one for the both of you," he said to his partners.

"What's that?" they asked in unison.

"Get a life."

Summary

An embedded system is a computer that lives inside another type of device, like an appliance. Programming an embedded system requires a great deal of knowledge about the characteristics of the device the system resides in. An embedded system can be *soft*, meaning that it doesn't have to meet deadlines, or *hard*, meaning that it does.

Time, threads (simple programs that are parts of an application), and interrupts (hardware devices that let a CPU know an event has occurred) are important embedded system concepts. One particular interrupt, the clock tick, occurs at regular intervals and acts as a system heartbeat.

A real-time operating system (RTOS) directs traffic among threads and interrupts. The kernel is the part of the RTOS that manages the time the CPU spends on individual threads. The kernel's scheduler determines which thread will execute next. A kernel might be preemptive (in which a higher-priority thread preempts an interrupted lower-priority thread when an interrupt service routine finishes) or nonpreemptive (in which the interrupted thread resumes after the interrupt service routine finishes).

We applied these concepts by modeling a "smart" exercise device that varies its resistance as a function of how hard a muscle is working.

Q&A

Q. *You mentioned "smart" systems. Do these embedded systems ever include anything like Artificial Intelligence?*

A. Absolutely. One subfield of AI, called "fuzzy logic," is at the heart of numerous kinds of embedded systems.

Q. *Is one type of RTOS more appropriate than another for certain types of embedded systems applications?*

A. Yes. One type I didn't elaborate on, the superloop, is the simplest RTOS. It's often embedded in high-volume applications like toys. The preemptive kernel is the RTOS of choice for hard systems.

Workshop

I've embedded some questions here to test your newfound knowledge, and I've embedded the answers in Appendix A, "Quiz Answers."

Quiz

1. What is an embedded system?

2. What is an asynchronous event?

3. In terms of embedded systems, what is a "hard" system? What is a "soft" system?

4. What happens in a "preemptive kernel"?

Exercises

1. Imagine an embedded system for a toaster. Assume that the toaster has a sensor that looks at a slice of bread as it's toasting and can sense how dark it is. Assume also that you can set how dark you want the toast. Draw a class diagram of this system. Include the sensor, CPU, and heating element (and the slice of bread!).

2. Draw a sequence diagram for the embedded toaster system. Justify your choice of a preemptive or a nonpreemptive kernel. Just for the heck of it, draw a deployment diagram too.

3. Draw a communication diagram equivalent to Figure 23.12.

4. Refine Figure 23.12 so that the Adjust thread finishes in the Ready state, the General Housekeeping thread finishes in the Running state, and the priorities are reset.

5. After you finish Exercise 4, create a timing diagram that traces the state changes in the Analyze thread. Base this diagram on the duration constraints in Figure 23.12. Assume that the vertical distances in Figure 23.12 and in your solution represent a scale.

HOUR 24

Shaping the Future of the UML

What You'll Learn in This Hour:

▶ Extensions for business

▶ Lessons from the business extensions

▶ Modeling GUIs

▶ Modeling expert systems

Here we are in the final hour. It's been a long haul, but in the process you've seen a lot of the UML. In the last two hours, you've looked at applications in hot areas. In this hour, you'll wrap it all up with a current UML extension and a look at some other areas for applying the UML.

You read about UML extensions and profiles in Hour 14, "Understanding Packages and Foundations." The goal of this hour is to start you thinking about how you would apply the UML in your domain and perhaps ultimately develop a domain-specific profile. Like any language, the UML is evolving. Its future depends on how modelers like you use and extend it.

Extensions for Business

One popular extension is a set of stereotypes designed to model a business. The stereotypes abstract some of the major ideas of what a business is all about. You can visualize them in terms of UML symbols you already know or as specialized icons (created by UML Amigo Ivar Jacobson). The intent is to model business-world situations rather than to serve as the basis for software construction.

Within a business, one obvious class is a **worker**. In the context of this UML extension, a worker acts within the business, interacts with other workers, and participates in use cases. A worker can be either an **internal worker** or a **case worker**. An internal worker interacts with other workers inside the business, and a case worker interacts with actors outside the business. An **entity** doesn't initiate any interactions, but it does participate in use cases. Workers interact with entities.

Figure 24.1 shows the customary UML notation for these stereotypes, along with the specialized icons. For each one, I've included an example from the restaurant domain.

FIGURE 24.1
Stereotypes for business modeling.

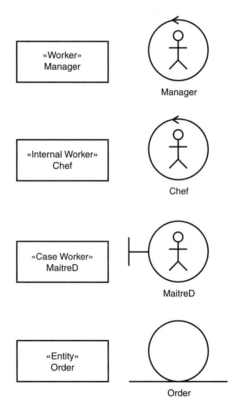

The business extensions include two association stereotypes—**communicates** and **subscribes**. The first stereotype is for interactions between objects. The second describes an association between a source (called a **subscriber**) and a target (called a **publisher**). The source specifies a set of events. When one of those events occurs in the target, the source receives a notification.

Entities combine to form **work units**, which are task-oriented sets of objects. Work units, classes, and associations combine to form **organization units**. An organization unit, which can include other organization units, corresponds to an organization unit of the business.

By the way, for another take on UML extensions for modeling businesses and business processes, see *Business Modeling with UML* by Hans-Erik Eriksson and Magnus Penker (John Wiley & Sons, 2000).

Lessons from the Business Extensions

The business extensions teach some valuable lessons. First, it's apparent that with a little imagination, it's possible to come up with simple icons and representations that capture fundamental aspects of a domain. The operative word is "simple." Second, the representations help you think about, and create solutions in, a domain.

We'll consider these lessons as we try and move the UML into two important modeling efforts—graphic user interfaces and expert systems.

Graphic User Interfaces

A hallmark of contemporary software packages, the graphic user interface (GUI) is here to stay. GRAPPLE and other development methodologies devote a JAD session to the development of an application's GUI.

In a design document, you typically include screen shots to show your client and your developers what the GUI will look like to the users. For several reasons, you still might want a specialized diagram to model a GUI.

Connecting to Use Cases

The primary reason has to do with use cases. Like most parts of a development effort, GUI development is use case–driven. In fact, the GUI connects directly to use cases because it's the window (pardon the pun) through which the end-user initiates and completes use cases. It might be difficult to use screen shots to capture the relationship between screens and use cases.

Another reason is that you might want to capture the evolution in the thought process as the GUI takes shape. In GRAPPLE, GUI development starts when end-users participating in the JAD session manipulate post-it sticky notes (which represent onscreen controls) on large sheets of paper (which represent screens). It would be helpful to have a type of diagram that directly captures the results of these manipulations—one that a modeler could easily change when the JAD participants modify the design.

A diagram that shows the connections of the screens to the use cases will help the JAD participants remember what each screen is supposed to do when they're laying out the screen components. Showing the use case connections will also help ensure that all use cases are implemented in the final design.

Modeling the GUI

A typical UML model would present a particular application's window as a composite of a number of controls, as in Figure 24.2.

FIGURE 24.2
A UML model of a window.

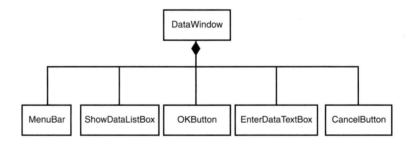

You can use attributes to add the spatial location of each component—a horizontal location and a vertical location, both measured in pixels. Another pair of attributes could represent the component's size (height and width). It's easier to comprehend those parameters, however, if you visualize them. You can specify that a package will represent a window and that the location and size of objects within the package reflects their location and size in the window. Figure 24.3 shows this.

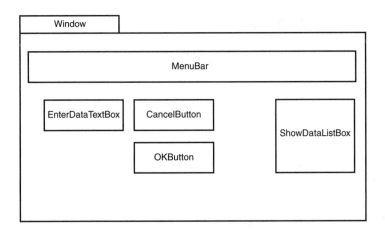

FIGURE 24.3
A model of a window that shows the locations of components.

Figure 24.4 is the hybrid diagram that adds the finishing touch by showing the connections with use cases.

This type of modeling doesn't preclude showing screen shots. Instead, it can be a helpful addition—a schematic diagram that keeps the big picture in view.

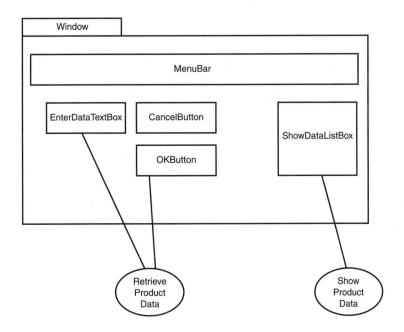

FIGURE 24.4
Modeling a window and showing how onscreen components connect to use cases.

Expert Systems

Expert systems experienced a surge in popularity in the 1980s. Something of a curiosity when they first appeared, today they're part of the mainstream of computing.

An expert system is designed to capture the insights and expertise of a human expert in a specific domain. It stores that expertise in a computer program. The intent is to use the expert system to answer repetitive questions so the human expert doesn't have to or to store the expertise so that it's available when the expert is not.

Components of an Expert System

The expertise resides in the expert system's **knowledge base** as a set of **if-then** rules. The **if-part** of each rule describes some real-world situation in the expert's domain. The **then-part** of each rule indicates the course of action to take in that situation. How does the expertise get into the knowledge base? A **knowledge engineer** holds extensive interviews with an expert, records the results, and represents the results in software. It's similar to the interview that takes place in a domain analysis, although knowledge-engineering sessions are typically more extensive.

The knowledge base isn't the only component in an expert system. If it were, an expert system would merely be a laundry list of *if-then* rules. What's needed is a mechanism for working through the knowledge base to solve a problem. That mechanism is called an **inference engine**. Another necessary piece of the puzzle is a **work area** that stores the conditions of a problem the system has to solve, creates a record of the problem, and displays the solution. One more component, of course, is the user interface for entering the problem conditions. Condition entry may proceed via checklist, question-and-multiple-choice-answer, or in extremely sophisticated systems via natural language. Figure 24.5 shows a class diagram of an expert system.

To interact with an expert system, a user enters the conditions of a problem into the user interface, which stores them in the work area. The inference engine uses those conditions to go through the knowledge base and find a solution. Figure 24.6 presents a sequence diagram for this process.

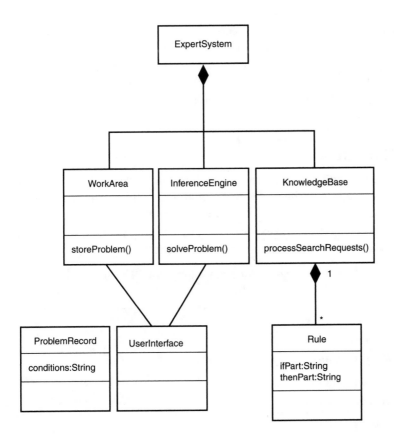

FIGURE 24.5
A class diagram of an expert system.

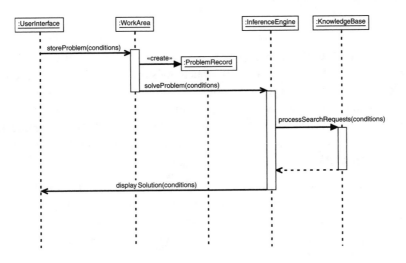

FIGURE 24.6
Interactions in an expert system.

If you can form an analogy between an expert system and a human, you've pretty much got it: The work area is roughly analogous to a person's short-term memory, the knowledge base is like the long-term memory, and the inference engine is the problem-solving process. When you "rack your brain" to come up with an answer to a sticky problem, you're doing something like what an expert system does.

An Example

An inference engine usually goes through its knowledge base ("racks its brain") in one of two ways, and the best way to explain is with an example. Suppose you have an expert system that captures the expertise of a plumber. If you had a leaky faucet, you'd use the expert system by entering the details of the leak into the system. The inference engine would do the rest.

Two of the rules in the knowledge base might look like this:

Rule 1:

IF you have a leaky faucet

AND the faucet is a compression faucet

AND the leak is in the handle

THEN tighten the packing nut

Rule 2:

IF the packing nut is tight

AND the leak persists

THEN replace the packing

Without getting into the specifics of the plumbing world, suffice it to say that these two rules are obviously related—notice the similarity between the then-part of Rule 1 and the if-part of Rule 2. That similarity is the basis for working through the knowledge base, which typically has many, many more than two rules. The inference engine might start with a potential solution, like "replace the packing" from Rule 2, and work backward to see whether the specifics of the problem demand that solution.

How does the inference engine work backward? It looks at the if-part of the rule that has the solution and tries to find a rule whose then-part matches it. In the two-rule example, that's easy—Rule 1 has a matching then-part. In industrial-strength applications, it's not so easy because a knowledge base might store hundreds, even thousands, of rules.

After the inference engine has found a rule, it checks to see whether the conditions in the if-part match the conditions of the problem. If they do, the engine keeps moving in the same direction—a matching if-part, check the if-part, another matching if-part, and so forth. When the inference engine runs out of rules, it asks the user for more information. The point of all this is that if the path through the rules is successful (that is, matches the conditions of the problem), the expert system offers the original potential solution as the solution to the problem. If not, the system tries a new path.

This technique of trying a solution and seeing whether the associated conditions match the conditions of the problem is called **backward chaining**—"backward" because it starts with then-parts and proceeds to examine if-parts.

As you can imagine, another technique starts with if-parts and matches then-parts, and it's called **forward chaining**. Here's how it works: The user enters the conditions of the problem, and the inference engine finds a rule whose if-part matches the conditions. It checks that rule's then-part and looks for a rule whose if-part matches that then-part. In this example, suppose Rule 1's if-part matches the problem conditions. The inference engine checks Rule 1's then-part and then looks for a rule with a matching if-part. Again, this is easy with only two rules. When the system runs out of rules to match, it offers the then-part of the final rule as the solution. The *forward* in *forward chaining* refers to this movement from if-parts to then-parts.

If you were to model an expert system as in Figure 24.5, it would be helpful to add a stereotype that indicates the type of chaining the inference engine performs. You would add either «forward chaining» or «backward chaining» to the composite ExpertSystem class.

Chaining

Both kinds of chaining are examples of the Chain of Responsibility design pattern you saw earlier. In each one, the system searches for a rule's successor.

Just as the Chain of Responsibility sometimes ends without finding a successor, an expert system doesn't always come up with a solution.

By the Way

Modeling the Knowledge Base

What can the UML add to all this, and why would we want it to? One of the sticking points in expert system development is the lack of a solid standard for a visual representation of the knowledge base rules. A UML-based representation would go a long way toward standardizing the field and toward encouraging good documentation practices. It's not enough for the knowledge to reside in a software representation in a knowledge base—the rules should all be in a document as well.

Another sticking point is that use case analyses are rarely done in the course of developing an expert system. A use case analysis, complete with UML use case diagrams, might help determine the best type of inference engine to use in an expert system implementation. The deployment diagram is still another possible point of UML applicability to expert system development. Although they were once stand-alone devices, expert systems today typically have to fit into a corporate computing structure and interact smoothly with other systems. Deployment diagrams can be used to show where an expert system resides and how it depends on (and feeds into) other areas of information technology. Given that an actor in a use case diagram can be another system, the deployment diagram and the use case diagram can work together to provide views of an expert system in a corporate context.

Let's focus on the knowledge base. How can you represent a knowledge base in the spirit of the UML? One possibility, of course, is to represent each rule as an object. Have one of the attributes be the if-part, another be the then-part, and add attributes as necessary. Figure 24.7 shows this arrangement.

FIGURE 24.7
Representing rules as objects.

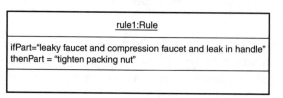

Although this is eminently doable (and many developers do it), I believe rules are important enough to warrant their own representation—and not only because they serve as the foundation of knowledge bases in expert systems. The growing emphasis on knowledge management within organizations and institutions calls out for a unique way to represent rules.

What would that unique representation look like? First, you'd want to make sure you show something that gives the contents of a rule's if-part and the contents of its then-part. In order to make this representation useful, you'd also want to somehow visualize the connections among rules.

This can all get very thorny very quickly. Industrial-strength rules tend to have a lot more information than the two plumbing rules I showed you, and the rules tend to proliferate. You have to balance these proliferations against the need for simplicity.

Let's first create a simple icon to represent a rule. Begin with a box divided by a centered vertical line. The left half of the box represents the if-part and the right half the then-part. Within each part, you'll write a meaningful summary of the contents. Figure 24.8 shows what I mean, using the two plumbing rules as an example.

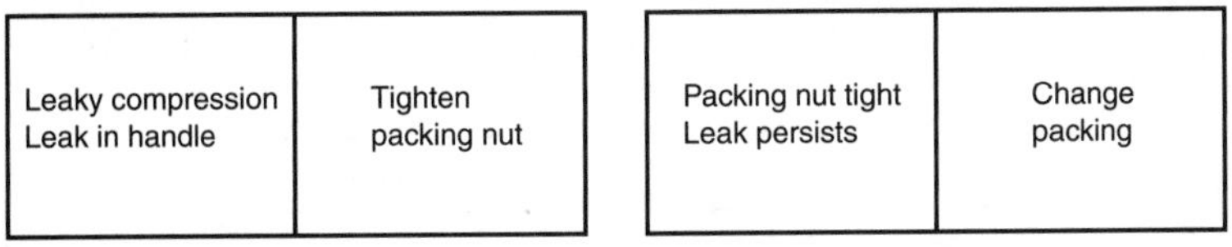

Leaky compression Leak in handle	Tighten packing nut

Packing nut tight Leak persists	Change packing

FIGURE 24.8
The two plumbing rules cast into a visual representation.

Now you have to incorporate some identification information for each rule. Across the top of each box, add a compartment that holds a numerical identifier. This accomplishes two things: (1) It makes each rule unique and (2) It shows where to go in a rules catalog for a complete description and explanation of the rule. If a rule is part of a subgroup of rules (as in a "faucet" subset of the plumbing knowledge base), you can treat the subgroup as a package. You then add the package information to the identifier in the UML's usual way—have the package name precede a pair of colons that precede the identifier. Figure 24.9 shows this addition.

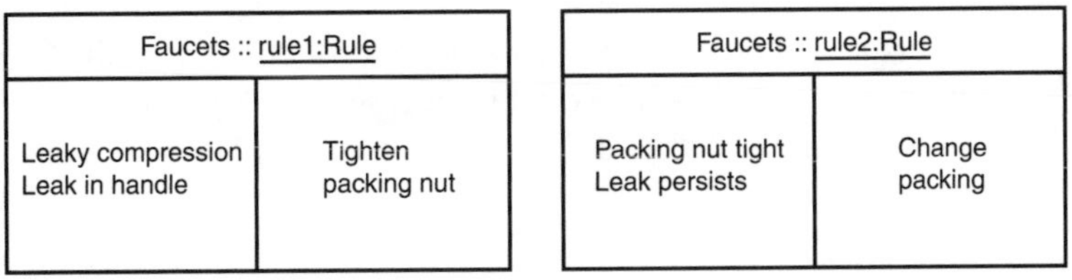

Faucets :: rule1:Rule	
Leaky compression Leak in handle	Tighten packing nut

Faucets :: rule2:Rule	
Packing nut tight Leak persists	Change packing

FIGURE 24.9
Adding an identifier to each rule.

Represent the relation between the two as a line between the then-part of Rule 1 and the if-part of Rule 2. Figure 24.10 shows the connection.

FIGURE 24.10
Connecting the then-part of one rule to the if-part of the other.

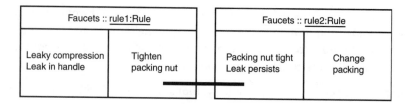

Unlike the two-rule set in this example, a rule in a real expert system is usually related to more than one other rule. If the related rules aren't nearby—either in the knowledge base or in the documentation—it will be helpful to have a way of showing the relationship even when you can't draw connecting lines.

Compartments at the bottom of the icon will do the trick. If you put them below the compartments you already have, you can show identifiers for other rules, as in Figure 24.11. The lower compartment on the left identifies rules whose then-parts connect to this rule's if-part. The lower compartment on the right identifies rules whose if-parts connect to this rule's then-part.

FIGURE 24.11
Compartments at the bottom of the rule icon identify related rules.

Faucets :: rule1:Rule		Faucets :: rule2:Rule	
Leaky compression Leak in handle	Tighten packing nut	Packing nut tight Leak persists	Change packing
10, 11, 15, Pipe ::22	2, 6, Washer ::22	2, 13, Pipe ::15	17, 18, 31

As is the case with class diagrams, compartments within the rule icon could be elided depending on the purpose of the diagram. The idea is to concisely show the connections among rules as well as their content and thus clearly communicate the nature of the knowledge base.

The model for the expert system is more drastic than the model for the GUI in that it proposes a new *view element* (the rule icon) for the UML. The model for the GUI, on the other hand, is a hybrid diagram that consists of current UML elements.

Web Applications

Since the first edition of this book appeared, a number of analysts have created sets of UML extensions for important domains. In this section, we examine one for Web application development.

Simply put, a Web-based system allows an end-user with a browser (a software application on a client computer) to access and view a document that resides on a host computer (a server). A **Web application** augments a Web-based system by adding business functionality, like the ability to add selections to a shopping cart and to complete transactions via credit card.

The **Web Application Extension** (**WAE**) to the UML is the brainchild of Rational's Jim Conallen. This profile includes about a dozen graphic stereotype icons, additional stereotyped associations, attributes, and some "well-formedness" rules for combining all these elements to create a model.

Each element is associated with zero or more tagged values. Recall from Hour 14 that a tagged value is a bracketed string consisting of a tag, an equal sign (=), and a value. Its purpose is to provide important information about an element. In the WAE, for example, the tagged value for a Web page shows the path that specifies the Web page on the Web server.

While you're on the subject, Figure 24.12 shows the WAE icon for a Web page.

FIGURE 24.12
The WAE icon for a Web page.

Notice the similarity between this icon and the UML icon for a note. The folded corner is designed to reinforce the notion of a page. Keep in mind that conceptually a Web page is a class with attributes and operations, and a specific Web page is an object. (See Exercise 1.)

Figure 24.13 shows WAE icons for three types of pages that can appear in a Web application: a server page, a JavaServer Pages (JSP) page, and an Active Server Page. Figure 24.14 shows three more: client page, frameset, and servlet.

FIGURE 24.13
The WAE icons for (left to right) server page, JSP page, and Active Server Page.

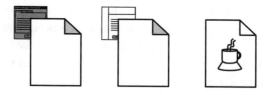

The WAE has icons for structures other than pages. For example, when you surf the Web you often see pages whose components allow you to enter information into the page (check boxes, radio buttons, combo boxes, and more). A collection of these components for a particular page is called a **form**, and Figure 24.15 shows the WAE icon for a form.

The WAE is much richer than the description in this section. For further details and updates, see Jim Conallen's *Building Web Applications with UML Second Edition* (Addison-Wesley, 2003). To download WAE icons and use them in a UML modeling tool like Rational Rose or Visio, visit www.wae-uml.org.

That's All, Folks

We've come to the end of the road. Now that you have a bag full of UML tricks, you're ready to go out on your own and apply them to your domain. You'll find that as you gain experience, you'll add to that bag of tricks. You might even come up with some suggestions for adding to the UML. If you do, you'll be carrying on a grand tradition.

Just after the beginning of the twentieth century, the renowned mathematician Alfred North Whitehead pointed out the importance of symbols and their use. A symbol, he said, stands for the presentation of an idea: The importance of a symbol is that it quickly and concisely shows how an idea fits together with a complex set of other ideas.

In the first decade of the twenty-first century, Whitehead's observations still ring true for the world of system development. Carefully crafted symbols show us the thought processes and complexities behind the wonderful systems we propose to build, and help us ensure their efficient performance when we build them.

Summary

As modelers extend and mold the UML to fit their needs, they'll shape its future. In this hour, you looked at an extension for business modeling and saw some ways of applying the UML to other areas. We also examined the Web Application Extension (WAE), which is a UML extension for modeling Web applications.

Taking a lesson from the business extension's simplicity, we explored ways for modeling GUIs and expert systems. To model a GUI, we set up a hybrid diagram that shows the spatial relationships of screen components and their connections with use cases. This has the advantages of showing the evolution of a GUI as it takes shape and keeping the appropriate use cases within the focus of attention.

In an expert system the *if-then* rule is the building block of the knowledge base, the component that contains the knowledge of a human domain expert. We suggested a diagram that visualizes the rules and their interrelationships. In this diagram, a box divided into compartments models the rule. One compartment contains the rule identifier, another summarizes the if-part, another the then-part, and two others show related rules. Links to nearby rules appear as connecting lines between appropriate parts of the rules.

The WAE encompasses a set of stereotyped icons, stereotyped associations, attributes, and rules for modeling a Web application. Many of the icons are designed to reinforce the idea of a page.

Q&A

Q. *Although in principle it looks like an expert system isn't particularly difficult to model, it seems like it would be an extremely hard program to write.*

A. It would be if you had to create one from scratch. Fortunately, most of the programming is done for you in a package called an *expert system shell*. All its components are ready-made; you just add the knowledge. Extracting the knowledge from a human expert is not always an easy task, however.

Q. *Haven't vendors of expert system shells come up with a notation for representing rules?*

A. Yes, and that's the problem. No single notation is standard. This field typifies the statement (attributed, I think, to famed computer scientist Edsger Dijkstra): "The great thing about standards is that there are so many of them."

Workshop

The questions in this workshop test your knowledge about applying the UML to GUIs and expert systems. The answers to the quiz questions are in Appendix A, "Quiz Answers."

Quiz

1. What are the advantages of our model of a GUI?

2. What are the components of an expert system?

3. What expert system features does our diagram encompass?

Exercises

1. Visit the home page of Sams Publishing (www.samspublishing.com) and use the WAE Web page icon to model that page. Next, model the page without using the WAE icon—that is, with a standard UML icon.

2. Imagine that an appliance manufacturer wants to create a Web-based expert system that provides troubleshooting information. When something goes wrong, an appliance owner would be able to go to this Web site, enter the symptoms, and receive advice on how to proceed. Perform a use case analysis, and use the information on expert systems and the WAE from this hour to create a rudimentary model of the Web site.

PART IV

Appendixes

A Quiz Answers   **421**

B Working with a UML Modeling Tool   **435**

C A Summary in Pictures   **457**

APPENDIX A
Quiz Answers

Hour 1

1. Why is it necessary to have a variety of diagrams in a model of a system?

Any system has a variety of stakeholders. Each type of UML diagram presents a view that speaks to one or more of these stakeholders.

2. Which diagrams give a static view of a system?

These diagrams provide a static view: class, object, component, and deployment.

3. Which diagrams provide a dynamic view of a system (that is, show change over time)?

These diagrams provide a dynamic view: use case, state, sequence, activity, and collaboration.

4. What kinds of objects are in Figure 1.5?

The objects in Figure 1.5 are anonymous objects.

Hour 2

1. What is an object?

An object is an instance of a class.

2. How do objects work together?

Objects work together by sending messages to one another.

3. What does multiplicity indicate?

Multiplicity indicates the number of objects of one class that relate to one object of an associated class.

4. Can two objects associate with one another in more than one way?

Yes. Two persons, for example, can be associated as friends and also as co-workers.

5. What is inheritance?

Inheritance is a relationship between two classes. One of the classes has all the attributes and operations of the other, and it also adds its own. The class that supplies the attributes and operations is the superclass. The class that has all those attributes and operations and adds its own is the subclass.

6. What is encapsulation?

Encapsulation means that when an object carries out its operations, it hides what it's doing. That is, the object doesn't let you see how it does what it does.

Hour 3

1. How do you represent a class in the UML?

You use a rectangle to represent a class. The class's name is inside the rectangle, near the top.

2. What information can you show on a class icon?

You can show the class's attributes, operations, and responsibilities.

3. What is a constraint?

Represented by text enclosed in curly brackets, a constraint is a set of one or more rules that a class follows.

4. Why would you attach a note to a class icon?

You attach a note to a class icon to add information that's not in the attributes, operations, or responsibilities. You might, for example, want the user of the model to refer to a particular document that contains additional information about the class.

Hour 4

1. How do you represent multiplicity?

At one end of the association line, you put the number of objects from the class at that end that relate to one object in the class at the other end.

2. How do you discover inheritance?

In the list of classes in your initial model, find two or more classes that share attributes and operations. Either another class in your initial model will be the parent of these classes, or you will have to create a parent class.

3. What is an abstract class?

An abstract class is a class that serves as the basis for inheritance but provides no objects.

4. What's the effect of a qualifier?

The effect of a qualifier is to reduce a one-to-many multiplicity to a one-to-one multiplicity.

Hour 5

1. What is the difference between an aggregation and a composite?

Both an aggregation and a composite specify a part-whole association between component classes and a whole. In an aggregation, a component may be part of more than one whole. In a composite, a component can be part of only one whole.

2. What is realization? How is realization similar to inheritance? How does realization differ from inheritance?

Realization is the relationship between a class and an interface. The class is said to *realize* the operations in the interface. Realization is similar to inheritance in that a class takes operations from its interface and can inherit procedures from its parent class. Realization is different from inheritance in that a class takes no attributes from its interface but can inherit attributes from its parent class.

3. How do you model interaction through an interface?

You model interaction through an interface as a dependency.

4. Name the three levels of visibility and describe what each one means.

If a class's attributes and operations have public visibility, another class may use them. If they have protected visibility, a child (or other descendant) class may use them. If they have private visibility, only the owning class can use them. An interface's operations have public visibility.

Hour 6

1. What do you call the entity that initiates a use case?

The entity that initiates a use case is called an actor.

2. What is meant by *including* a use case?

Including a use case means that some of the steps in a scenario in one use case are the same as the steps from another use case. Instead of listing all those same steps, we just indicate the use case they're part of.

3. What is meant by *extending* a use case?

Extending a use case means to add steps to an existing use case. You do that to create a new use case.

4. Is a use case the same as a scenario?

No. A use case is a collection of scenarios.

Hour 7

1. Name two advantages to visualizing a use case.

With visualization, you can (1) show use cases to users and get them to tell you additional information and (2) combine them with other kinds of diagrams.

2. Describe generalization and grouping, the relationships among use cases that you learned about in this hour. Name two situations in which you would group use cases.

In generalization, one use case inherits the meaning and behaviors of another. Grouping is the organization of a collection of use cases into packages.

3. What are the similarities between classes and use cases? What are the differences?

Similarities: Both are structural elements. Both can inherit.

Differences: The class consists of attributes and operations. The use case consists of scenarios, and each scenario consists of a sequence of steps. The class provides a static view of the parts of the system, whereas the use case provides a dynamic view of behavior. The class shows the inside of the system. The use case shows how the system looks to an outsider.

4. How do you model inclusion and extension?

You use a dependency arrow for both inclusion and extension. For inclusion, you label the arrow with the keyword «include». For extension, you label the arrow with the keyword «extend».

Hour 8

1. In what important way does a state diagram differ from a class diagram, an object diagram, or a use case diagram?

A state diagram models the states of just a single object. Class diagrams, object diagrams, and use case diagrams model a system, or at least part of a system.

2. Define these terms: *transition, event,* and *action.*

A transition is a change from one state to another. An event is an occurrence that causes a transition to occur. An action is an executable computation that results in a state change.

3. What is a *triggerless transition*?

A triggerless transition is a transition that occurs because of activities within a state, rather than in response to an event.

4. What is the difference between sequential substates and concurrent substates?

Substates are states within a state. Sequential substates occur one after the other. Concurrent substates occur at the same time.

Hour 9

1. Define synchronous message and asynchronous message.

When an object sends a synchronous message, it waits for an answer before moving on. When it sends an asynchronous message, it doesn't wait for an answer.

2. In UML 2.0, what is an interaction fragment?

An interaction fragment is a part of a sequence diagram.

3. In UML 2.0, what does par mean?

The par operator signifies that combined interaction fragments work in parallel and don't interfere with each other.

4. In a sequence diagram, how do you represent a newly created object?

A newly created object is represented by an object rectangle positioned in the timeline (that is, along the top-to-bottom dimension) so that its location represents the time it was created in the sequence. You also add «create» to the message arrow that points to the created object.

Hour 10

1. How do you represent a message in a communication diagram?

By placing an arrow near the association line that joins two objects. The arrow points to the receiving object.

2. How do you show sequential information in a communication diagram?

By attaching a number to the label of a message arrow. The number corresponds to the sequential order of the message.

3. How do you show an object changing its state?

One way is to show, in the object, the attribute that corresponds to the state along with the value of the attribute when the object is in that state. Link that object with a copy of the object. In the copy, show the value of the attribute in the new state. Along the link, place a message whose label is «becomes». The message goes from the original state to the new state.

Here's another way: Inside an object's rectangle, indicate its state inside brackets next to the name of the object. Add a copy of the object and show the changed state. Connect the two with a dashed line arrow with an open-stick arrowhead pointing to the changed state. Label the arrow with «becomes».

4. What is meant by the semantic equivalence of two diagram types?

The two types of diagrams present the same information, and you can turn one into another.

Hour 11

1. What are the two ways of representing a decision point?

One way is to show a diamond with branches coming out of it. The other is to show branches coming directly out of an activity. Either way, put a bracketed condition on each branch.

2. What is a swimlane?

In an activity diagram, a swimlane is a segment that shows the activities a particular role performs.

3. How do you represent signal transmission and reception?

Use a convex pentagon to show signal transmission and a concave pentagon to show signal reception.

4. What is an action?

An action is a component of an activity.

5. What is an object node?

An object node is a piece of information that's an input to an activity or an output from an activity. In UML 2.0, activity diagrams typically show the flow of objects through a sequence of activities.

6. What is a pin?

A pin is an object node for an action.

Hour 12

1. What is the difference between components and artifacts?

Components are modular, replaceable parts of a system. They define a system's functionality. Artifacts are pieces of information that a system uses or creates.

2. What are the two ways of representing the relationship between a component and its interface?

You can represent the interface as a rectangle (like a class icon) and the connection with the component as a dashed line with an empty triangle that points to the interface. Alternatively, you can use a small circle to represent the interface, connected by a solid line to the component.

3. What is a *provided interface*? What is a *required interface*?

A provided interface is an interface that one component makes available so that other components can use its services. When another component uses these services, it goes through a required interface. Thus, the same interface is provided by one component and required for another.

Hour 13

1. How do you represent a node in a deployment diagram?

A cube represents a node in a deployment diagram.

2. What kinds of information can appear on a node?

Information on a node can include the node name, package name, and components deployed on the node.

3. How does a token-ring network work?

Computers in a token-ring network connect to multistation access units (MSAUs) connected in the form of a ring. The MSAUs pass a signal called a token around the ring. The position of the token indicates which computer can send information at any moment.

Hour 14

1. What is a metamodel?

A metamodel is a model that defines the language for expressing a model. The UML is an example of a metamodel.

2. What is a classifier?

A classifier is any element that defines structure and behavior.

3. Why is it important to be able to extend the UML?

When you start to use the UML to model real systems, you'll run into situations that are richer and more complex than the ones you find in textbooks and references. If you can extend the UML, you'll be able to reflect the nature of those real-world situations.

4. What are the UML's extension mechanisms?

The UML's extension mechanisms are stereotypes, constraints, and tagged values.

Hour 15

1. What are some typical concerns of a client?

Does the development team understand the problem? Do the team members understand the client's vision of how to solve it? What work-products can the client expect from the development team? How will the project manager report to the client? How far along is the team at any point?

2. What is meant by a development methodology?

A development methodology sets the structure and nature of steps in a system development effort.

3. What is the waterfall method? What are its weaknesses?

In the waterfall method, analysis, design, coding, and deployment follow one another sequentially. One major weakness is the compartmentalization of effort, which often prevents team-members from working together and sharing insights. Another weakness is that it minimizes the impact of knowledge gained during the course of the project. Still another is that the waterfall method typically allots most of the project time to coding and shortchanges analysis and design.

4. What are the segments of GRAPPLE?

The segments of GRAPPLE are Requirements gathering, Analysis, Design, Development, and Deployment.

5. What is a JAD session?

A JAD (Joint Application Development) session brings together decision-makers from the client's organization, potential end-users of the system, and members of the development team. Some GRAPPLE JAD sessions pair the development team with just the users.

Hour 16

1. Which UML diagram is appropriate for modeling a business process?

The UML activity diagram is the one for modeling business processes.

2. How can you modify this diagram to show what the different roles do?

You can use the activity diagram to create a swimlane diagram. Each role is at the top of a swimlane.

3. What is meant by *business logic*?

Business logic is a set of rules the business follows in specific situations.

Hour 17

1. How do you make use of the nouns derived from the interview with an expert?

Nouns become candidates for class names and attribute names.

2. How do you use the verbs and verb phrases?

Verbs and verb phrases become candidates for operations and for names of associations.

3. What is a ternary association?

A ternary association involves three classes.

4. How do you model a ternary association?

You model a ternary association by linking each of the three classes to a diamond. You write the name of the association near the diamond. Multiplicities in a ternary association reflect the number of instances of any two classes associated with a constant number of instances of the third.

Hour 18

1. How does the development team represent system requirements?

The team uses the UML package diagram along with use cases to represent system requirements.

2. Does class modeling stop after the domain analysis?

Class modeling continues to evolve after the domain analysis.

3. What is the schlepp factor?

This is the term I whimsically applied to the server having to walk around all over the restaurant. I just wanted to see if you were paying attention.

Hour 19

1. What are the parts of a typical use case diagram?

The parts of a typical use case diagram are the initiating actor, the use case, and the benefiting actor. Many modelers leave out the benefiting actor, but you should include this actor in your design document.

2. What does it mean for a use case to include (or use) another use case?

   Including a use case means that one use case incorporates the steps of another use case.

Hour 20

1. How do you represent an object that's created during the course of a sequence diagram?

   You represent a created object by placing it below the level of the other objects. You'll increase clarity if you also add «create» to the message leading to that object.

2. How is time represented in a sequence diagram?

   Time is represented as proceeding in the downward direction.

3. What is a *lifeline*?

   The lifeline is a dashed line descending from an object. It represents the existence of an object over time.

4. In a sequence diagram, how do you show an *activation,* and what does it represent?

   An activation is represented as a small narrow rectangle on an object's lifeline. It represents the time period during which the object performs an action.

Hour 21

1. What is a task analysis?

   A task analysis is an analysis that a GUI designer carries out in order to understand what the user will do with the application associated with the GUI.

2. Which analysis that we've already done is roughly equivalent to a task analysis?

   The use case analysis is roughly equivalent to the task analysis.

3. What is a clown-pants design?

   A clown-pants design is a GUI design that incorporates an excessive number of colors, component sizes, and fonts.

4. Give three reasons for limiting the use of color in a GUI.

Three reasons to limit the use of color in a GUI are

▶ The association of a color with a meaning may not be as obvious to the user as it is to the designer.

▶ Too many colors will distract users from the task at hand.

▶ Part of the user population may have some trouble distinguishing between colors.

Hour 22

1. How do you represent a parameterized class?

The icon for a parameterized class is the standard class icon with a small box superimposed on the upper right corner. The small box consists of dashed lines.

2. What is *binding* and what are the two types of binding?

Binding is the attachment of a value to a parameter. The two types of binding are *explicit* and *implicit*.

3. What is a *design pattern*?

A design pattern is a proven solution to a design problem. It's usable in a variety of situations, and you represent it in the UML as a parameterized collaboration.

4. What is the Chain of Responsibility design pattern?

In the Chain of Responsibility design pattern, a client object initiates a request and passes it to the first in a chain of objects. If the first object can't handle the request, it passes it to the next. If that one can't handle the request, it passes it to the next, and so forth until an object can handle the request.

Hour 23

1. What is an embedded system?

An embedded system is a computer system that resides inside some other kind of device, like a home appliance.

2. What is an asynchronous event?

An event is asynchronous if you can't predict its occurrence.

3. In terms of embedded systems, what is a *hard* system? What is a *soft* system?

A hard system has to meet time deadlines, but a soft system does not.

4. What happens in a preemptive kernel?

In a preemptive kernel, after an ISR executes, the CPU doesn't return to the interrupted thread if a higher priority thread is in the ready state. Instead, it executes the higher priority thread.

Hour 24

1. What are the advantages of our model of a GUI?

This model can capture the thought processes in the evolution of a GUI, and it keeps attention on the use cases connected with each screen.

2. What are the components of an expert system?

The components of an expert system are a knowledge base, a work area, and an inference engine.

3. What expert system features does our diagram encompass?

The diagram shows the parts of a rule, associated rules, and the relationships among rules.

APPENDIX B

Working with a UML Modeling Tool

As you followed along with the book's discussion and did the exercises, you probably used pencil and paper to create your diagrams. If you had to do that in your project-related modeling efforts, you'd quickly hit a number of snags. In addition to drawing those troublesome lines, circles, ellipses, and rectangles, you'd have a difficult time when you wanted to move them around and change the layout of a finished diagram.

Fortunately, technology comes to the rescue. A number of tools are available to help you create UML models.

What You Should Find in a Modeling Tool

One fundamental feature of a UML modeling tool is a palette of UML elements. You use that palette to create diagrams by selecting elements from the palette and then dragging and dropping them onto a drawing page. Once you've added your elements, "rubber-band" diagramming allows you to create a connection between two elements and have the connection adjust accordingly when you drag those elements around the screen.

Another important feature is the use of dialog boxes for editing. That is, if you want to modify an element in a diagram, you should be able to somehow access a dialog box for that element and enter information into its fields. Because of those dialog boxes, one thing you find when you work with a modeling tool is that the model consists of more than just the diagrams: Much of the model's information resides in the dialog boxes that sit behind the diagrams.

Still another practical consideration is that the tool should allow you the flexibility to format the onscreen information in various ways.

Possibly the most important feature of a UML modeling tool is what I call its **dictionary.** This is a record of all the elements you create and all their features. In addition to keeping track of your creations, the dictionary is important because it enables you to reuse them from diagram to diagram. In other words, if you create a class for one diagram, you should be able to use it again by selecting it from the dictionary and dragging-and-dropping it onto another.

Finally, some high-end (read "expensive") modeling tools allow you to generate code from your models.

When I wrote the earlier editions of this book, only a few UML modeling tools were available, and I discussed three of them.

Since those earlier editions, the number of modeling tools has grown substantially. Two that come to mind, for example, are Together, a recent acquisition of Borland, and Poseidon, a product of Gentleware.

Rather than survey the entire field, I thought that this time around, I'd give you a feel for what it's like to work with a modeling tool: I'll take you through some steps with one of them—Microsoft Visio Professional Edition. If you're familiar with Visio, that's helpful. If not, that's OK, too.

Working with UML in Visio Professional Edition

One of the best-known diagramming tools, Visio Professional Edition adds a number of UML-related capabilities that turn it into a surprisingly strong modeling tool. UML is just one of Visio's capabilities.

I'll walk you through the creation of a class diagram, an object diagram, and a sequence diagram. As I do, I'll point out the features of this tool.

To give you an idea of where you're headed, I'll start by showing you the diagrams I'm going to create. The diagrams will form a rudimentary model of our solar system. Because I'm focusing on the tool rather than on the UML, I'll keep the diagrams simple.

Because our particular solar system is an instance of a planetary system, you'll begin with a class model of a planetary system as shown in Figure B.1.

Figure B.2 is an object diagram of Earth and the sun. If you're feeling ambitious, you can fill in the remaining planets.

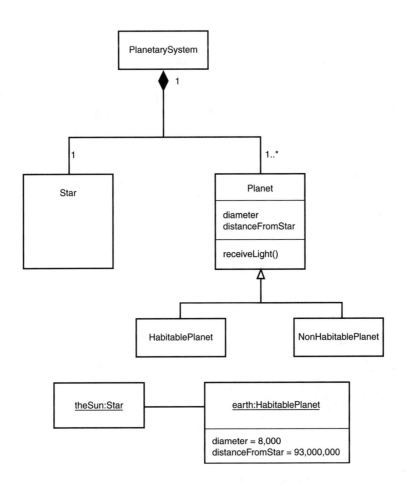

FIGURE B.1
A class model of a planetary system.

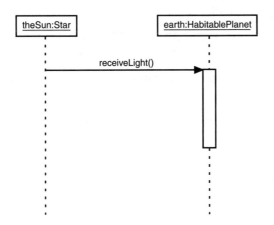

FIGURE B.2
An object model of Earth and the sun.

The sequence diagram (Figure B.3) shows just one message from the sun to Earth. (I told you I'd keep it simple.)

FIGURE B.3
A sequence diagram showing one interaction between the sun and Earth.

Getting Started

Figure B.4 shows Visio ready for UML modeling. The large white area is the Drawing page. Model Explorer (upper left) is Visio's dictionary. Visio's palette of UML elements is in the lower left. It's called "Shapes," and it consists of a number of tabbed pages. Each tabbed page supplies the icons for a specific UML diagram. When Visio opens in the UML, the UML Static Structure tabbed page is visible. This one enables you to create class diagrams and object diagrams.

FIGURE B.4
Visio ready for UML modeling.

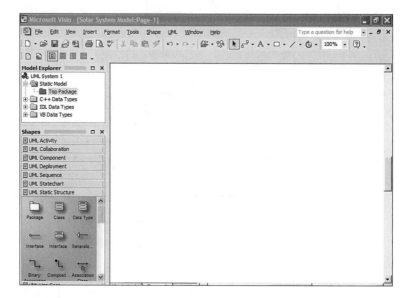

Just to get you in the mood, I'll write this as if you have Visio Professional and you're working along.

The Class Diagram

The first step is to select a class icon from UML Static Structure and drop it on the Drawing page. This causes the Drawing page to resemble Figure B.5.

Next, with the class selected on the Drawing page you type **PlanetarySystem** to rename the class. (Figure B.6)

Model Explorer reflects the addition of the new class. (Figure B.7)

Now you can add the Planet class, as in Figure B.8.

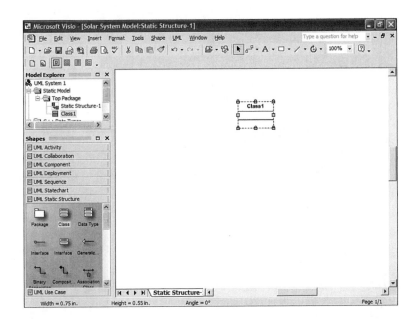

FIGURE B.5
Starting the class
diagram.

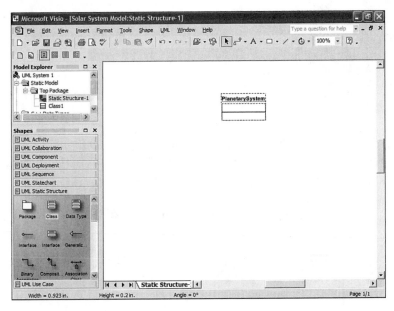

FIGURE B.6
Renaming the
class.

FIGURE B.7
The
PlanetarySystem
class in Model
Explorer.

FIGURE B.8
Adding the Planet
class.

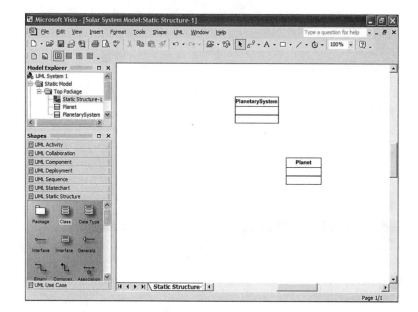

For this class, you'll add the two attributes and the operation from Figure B.1, and you'll make Planet an abstract class. To do this, double-click on the Planet class to bring up the UML Class Properties dialog box (Figure B.9).

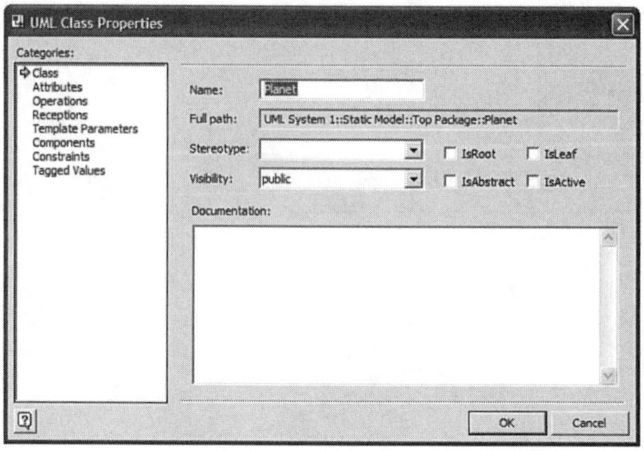

FIGURE B.9
The UML Class
Properties dialog
box.

The first step is to click the IsAbstract checkbox. Next, select Attributes from the Categories field on the left to open the Attributes table in this dialog box (Figure B.10).

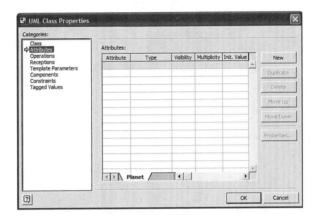

FIGURE B.10
The Attributes table for the `Planet` class.

Type **diameter** and **distanceFromStar** into this table. Then select Operations from the Categories field to open the Operations table, into which you type **receiveLight**, as shown in Figure B.11.

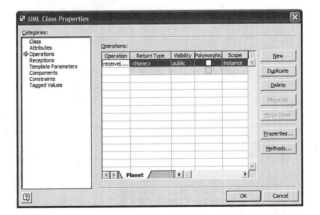

FIGURE B.11
The Operations table for the `Planet` class.

Clicking OK gives you the abstract `Planet` class with its attributes and its operation, as in Figure B.12.

Note the minus sign to the left of each attribute and the plus sign to the left of the operation. These are the visibilities. To make the diagram less busy, you can take them out of the diagram. In order to do that, right-click on the `Planet` class to bring up the popup menu in Figure B.13.

FIGURE B.12
The abstract class
Planet with its
attributes and
operation.

FIGURE B.13
Right-clicking a
model element
pops up this menu.

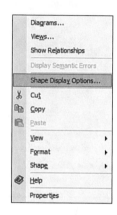

Selecting Shape Display Options opens the UML Shape Display Options dialog box in Figure B.14.

FIGURE B.14
The UML Shape
Display Options
dialog box.

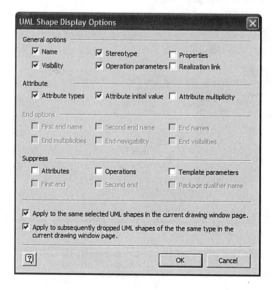

Unchecking the Visibility checkbox and clicking OK makes the Planet class look like Figure B.15. By the way, if you look closely at Figure B.14, you'll notice the checks in the two bottom checkboxes. Checking these boxes specifies that your choices in this dialog box determine the appearance of any subsequent elements of this type in this diagram.

FIGURE B.15
The Planet class
without the
visibilities.

Note that the Planet class and its attributes and operation are now in Model Explorer (Figure B.16).

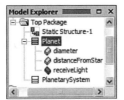

FIGURE B.16
Model Explorer
records the
attributes and
operation of the
Planet class.

The next order of business is to drag and drop the remaining classes into the diagram so that the Drawing page resembles Figure B.17.

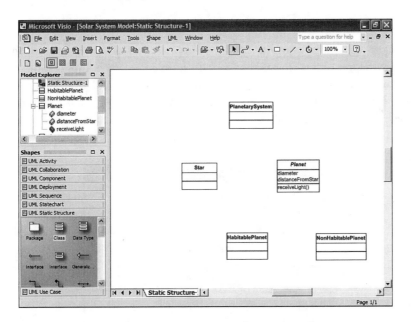

FIGURE B.17
All the classes in
the model.

Of course, you're not through yet. You have to add the composition relationship and the inheritance relationship. Start with the composition. Dragging a composition from Shapes into the Drawing page, connecting the filled diamond to Planetary System, and connecting the other end (the "tail") to Star result in Figure B.18.

FIGURE B.18
Starting the
composition.

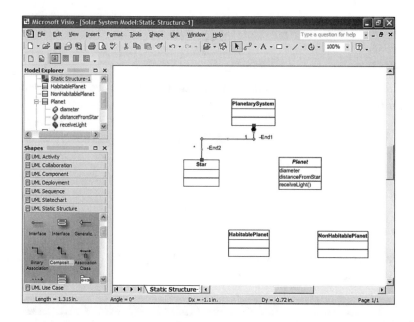

As you can see, you have multiplicities, visibilities, and default names for the
ends of the composition. To take the default names and visibilities (-End1 and
-End2) out of the diagram, right-click on the composition and select Shape
Display Options from the popup menu. This time, in the UML Shape Display
Options dialog box (Figure B.19), uncheck First End Name, Second End Name,
and End Visibilities.

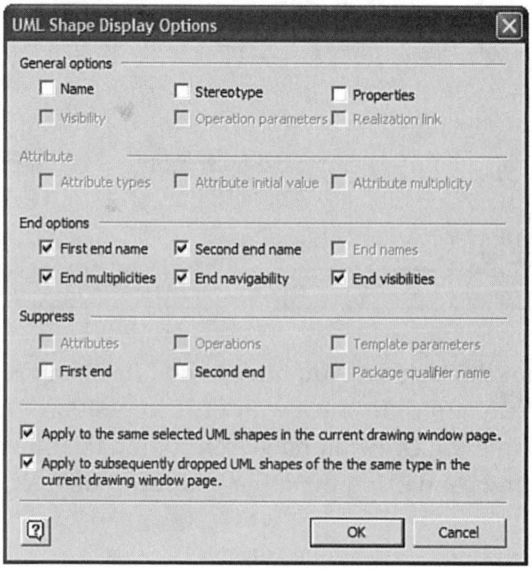

FIGURE B.19
The UML Shape
Display Options
dialog box for the
composition
symbol.

Now you have to take care of the multiplicity for the Star class. Double-clicking
on the composition symbol opens the UML Association Properties dialog box
(Figure B.20).

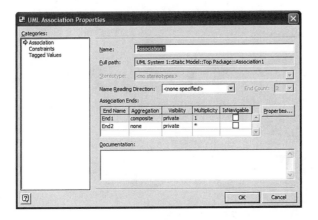

In the Association Ends table, select End2 and click in its cell in the Multiplicity column. Clicking the down arrow in that cell reveals a list of possible multiplicity expres-
sions for End2. If you select 1 from that list and click OK, you'll have the desired multiplicity (Figure B.21).

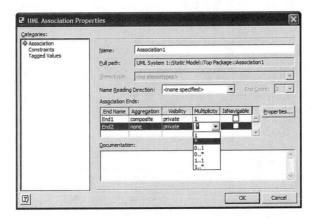

Dragging and dropping another composition symbol, superimposing the diamond
on the first, and connecting the tail to the Planet class gives you Figure B.22. The
default multiplicity ("many," as denoted by the asterisk) is appropriate.

FIGURE B.22
Completing the
composition.

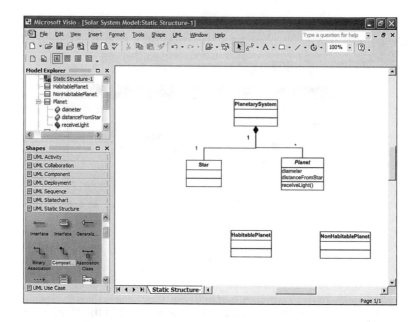

Finally, you'll add the inheritance relationships. Drag and drop a generalization symbol from Shapes and connect the triangle indicator to Planet and the tail to HabitablePlanet. Do the same thing with another generalization symbol, superimposing the triangle on the first and connecting the tail to NonHabitablePlanet. When you're finished, the Drawing page shows the completed class diagram (Figure B.23).

FIGURE B.23
The completed
class diagram.

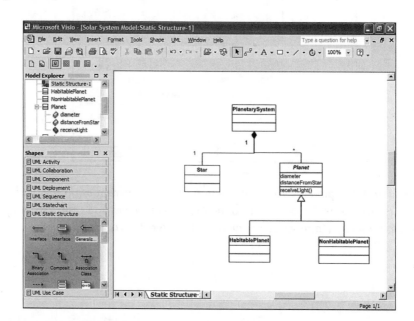

As I mentioned earlier, however, when you use a modeling tool, the information is not just in the diagrams. It's also in the dialog boxes that sit behind the diagrams. You're at a point where I can give you an example. If you double-click on HabitablePlanet, the UML Class Properties dialog box appears. Clicking on Attributes in the Categories field opens the Attributes table, as shown in Figure B.24.

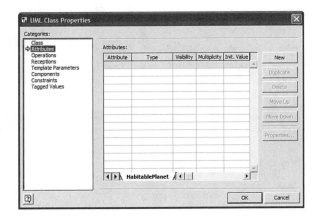

FIGURE B.24
The Attributes table for the HabitablePlanet class.

At the bottom of the Attributes table, you see a tab. This tab indicates that you're looking at the page of attributes for HabitablePlanet. That page, of course, is empty because you didn't specify any attributes for this class. But HabitablePlanet inherits a couple of attributes from Planet, and this table shows them. The tabs are scrollable, and if you scroll, you'll see a tab for Planet. Clicking on this tab opens the page of attributes for Planet (Figure B.25).

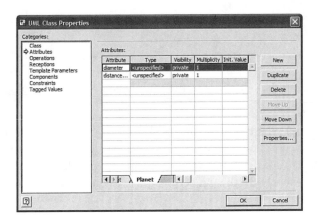

FIGURE B.25
The Attributes table for the Planet class opens up in the dialog box for HabitablePlanet.

So, because of the inheritance indicator in the diagram, the dialog box for the subclasses shows the attributes for the class from which they inherit. (Visio does this for operations as well.)

The Object Diagram

To get started on the object diagram, right-click in Model Explorer on the package icon labeled Top Package. A sequence of popup menus enables you to open a new Static Structure Diagram. From UML Static Structure in Shapes, select an Object icon and drop it on the Drawing page. Figure B.26 shows what the Drawing page looks like after this.

FIGURE B.26
The Drawing page after with a newly added Object icon.

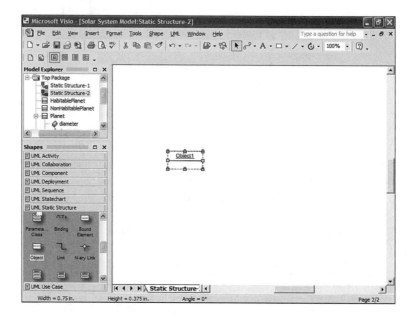

Double-clicking on the object opens the UML Object Properties dialog box (Figure B.27).

In the Name field, type **theSun** to change from the default name (Object1). You also have to indicate that theSun is an instance of the Star class. To do this, click in the Class field and click the down arrow. This opens a list of classes you created. Figure B.28 shows how the dialog box looks when you do all this.

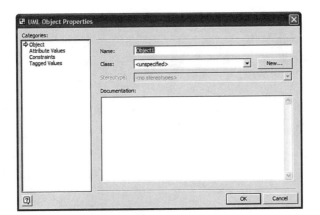

FIGURE B.27
The UML Object Properties dialog box.

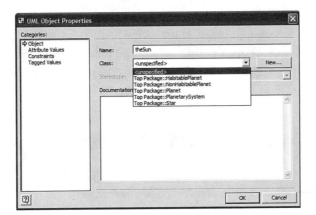

FIGURE B.28
The UML Object Properties dialog box, with the object renamed and the list of the classes.

Selecting Star from the list of classes and clicking OK makes the object appear as in Figure B.29.

FIGURE B.29
The renamed sun-object showing the name of its class.

Next, the same series of steps creates an earth-object. Figure B.30 shows the UML Object Properties dialog box after renaming the object and selecting its class.

FIGURE B.30
The UML Object
Properties dialog
box after renaming
the earth-object
and selecting its
class.

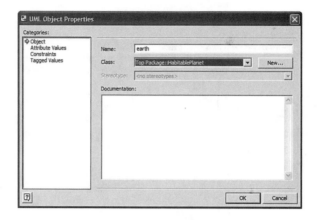

Selecting Attribute Values from the Categories field opens the Attribute Values
table. In this table you fill in the values for the `diameter` and
`distanceFromTheStar` properties that `HabitablePlanet` inherits from `Planet`
(Figure B.31). Remember, you didn't put those attributes into the `HabitablePlanet`
class. The modeling tool supplies them for you here because of the inheritance
relationships you set up in the class diagram.

FIGURE B.31
Supplying values
for an object's
attributes.

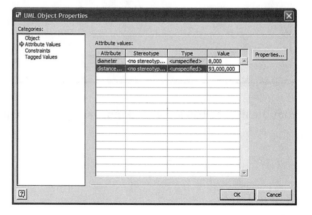

As the figure shows, I supplied the values (8,000 and 93,000,000) in the Values
column. Clicking OK makes the earth-object appear as in Figure B.32.

FIGURE B.32
The renamed
earth-object along
with the values of
its attributes.

All that's left is to add the link between the two objects. Drag a link symbol from UML Static Structure to the Drawing page and connect an end to each object. The names End1 and End2 show up when you do this, but right-clicking on the link and working with Shape Display Options enables you to remove them from the diagram. The completed object diagram appears in Figure B.33.

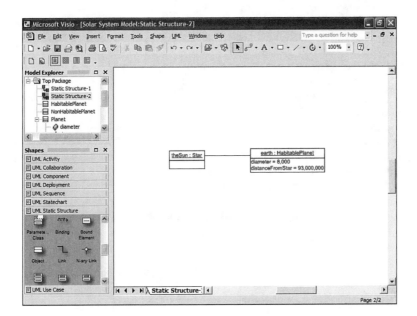

FIGURE B.33
The completed object diagram.

The Sequence Diagram

Let's finish up. Once again, right-clicking in Model Explorer (on the Top Package icon) and selecting from a sequence of popup menus opens a new Drawing page and opens the UML Sequence tab in Shapes.

From UML Sequence, dragging an Object Lifeline icon and dropping it on the Drawing page makes Visio look like Figure B.34.

As you did with the Object diagram, rename the icon and show its class. Double-clicking on the icon opens the UML Classifier Roles dialog box (Figure B.35).

After renaming the object in the Name field and selecting its class from the list of your classes in the Classifier field, this dialog box appears as in Figure B.36.

FIGURE B.34
Starting the
sequence diagram
with an Object
Lifeline icon.

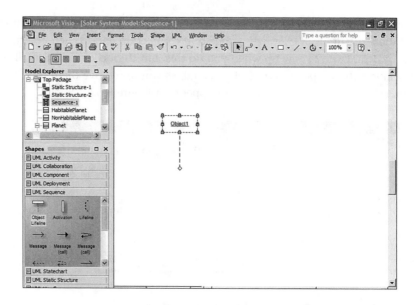

FIGURE B.35
The UML Classifier
Roles dialog box.

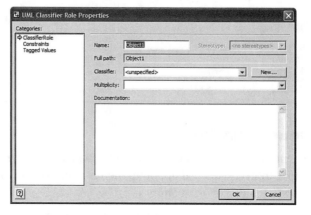

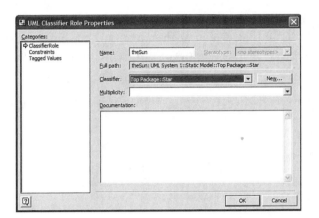

FIGURE B.36
The UML Classifer
Roles dialog box
after renaming the
object and
selecting its class.

Clicking OK makes the Object Lifeline icon look like Figure B.37.

FIGURE B.37
The appearance of
the Object Lifeline
after renaming
the object and
selecting its class.

Right-clicking and working with Shape Display Options allows you to show the
class name. Following a similar series of steps with another Object Lifeline icon
(to represent Earth) results in Figure B.38.

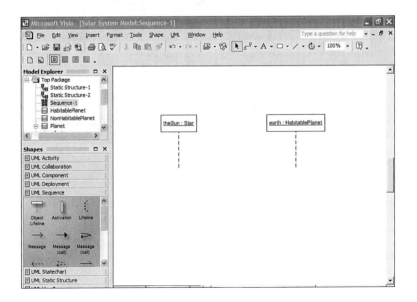

FIGURE B.38
Two Object Lifeline
icons, showing the
names and classes
of the objects.

Now it's time for the message from the sun-object to the earth-object. Select a Message symbol from UML Sequence, drag it to the Drawing page, connect the tail to the sun-object's lifeline and the arrowhead to the earth-object's lifeline (Figure B.39).

FIGURE B.39
Connecting the two lifelines with a message.

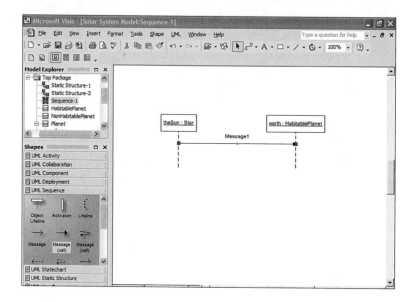

To change from the message's default label, double-click on the message icon to open (you guessed it) the UML Message Properties dialog box (Figure B.40).

FIGURE B.40
The UML Message Properties dialog box.

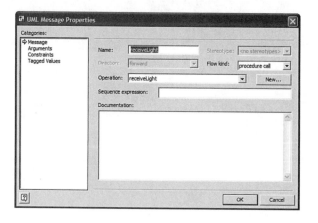

With only one possible operation, the name (in the Name field) and the operation that the message requests from the earth-object are already selected. (Had you specified more operations for this class in your class diagram, you would have chosen from a list of operations here.) Clicking OK puts that operation on the message, as in Figure B.41.

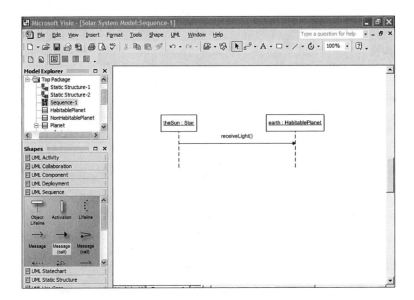

FIGURE B.41
The relabeled message connecting the two lifelines.

Dragging and dropping an Activation symbol completes the diagram (Figure B.42).

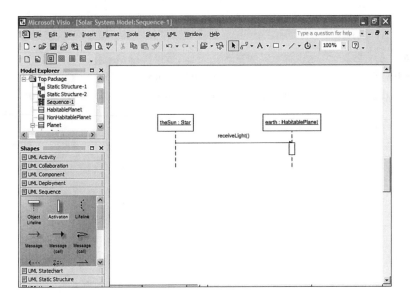

FIGURE B.42
The completed sequence diagram.

A Few Words About a Few Tools

In this section, I revisit a few old friends and describe some of their recent developments. As I write this, these tools still comply with UML 1.x (as does the version of Visio I walked you through).

Rational Rose

Still the gold standard in UML modeling tools, Rational Rose is a product of the company where the Three Amigos created UML. Renamed IBM Rose XDE Modeler to reflect IBM's acquisition of Rational, Rose has spawned a variety of tools for modeling in numerous contexts. One is intended for database modeling, another is for working with Microsoft Visual Studio, and still another is aimed at Java. Visit http://www.ibm.com/rational for more information.

Select Component Architect

This tool is the updated and extended version of Select Enterprise, one of the first UML modeling tools I worked with. I described Select Enterprise in editions 1 and 2. Select Component Architect is geared toward development via reusable software components and provides UML extensions for that purpose. It also includes capabilities for database design via entity-relationship diagrams.

As one of the tools in the Select Component Factory, it's part of Select Business Solutions' effort to generally provide and promote component-based development. Their Web site http://www.selectbs.com will tell you all about it.

Visual UML

Now in Version 3.2, Visual UML continues to be a personal favorite. In fact, I used an earlier version of this tool to create many of the diagrams in the first edition. Its opening screen is so easy to use, you'll be diagramming in UML almost as soon as you finish installation. Go to http://www.visualuml.com to learn more about Visual UML and to download a trial copy.

APPENDIX C

A Summary in Pictures

This appendix presents some of the major aspects of each UML diagram.

Activity Diagram

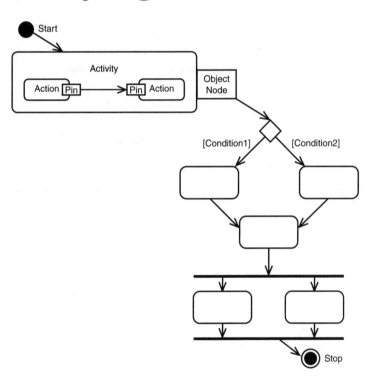

Figure C.1

Figure C.2

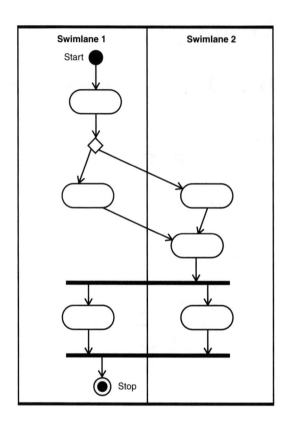

Figure C.3

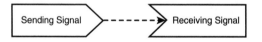

Class Diagram

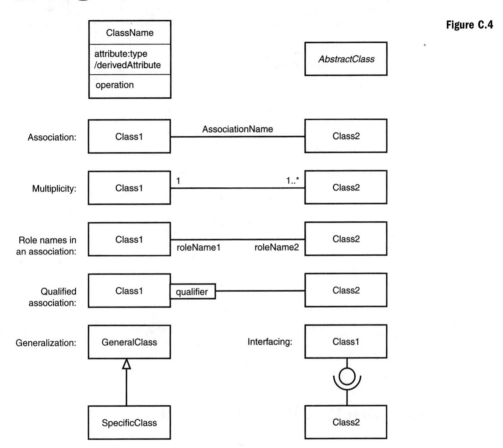

Figure C.4

Figure C.5

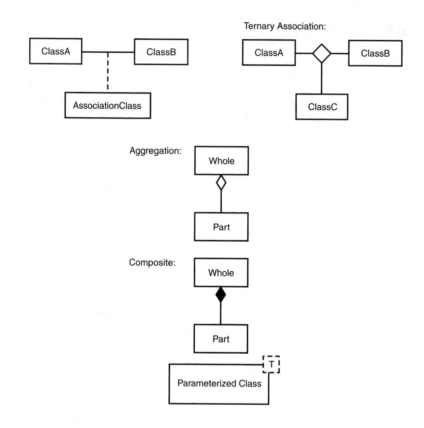

Communication Diagram

Figure C.6

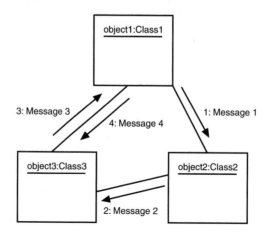

Component Diagram

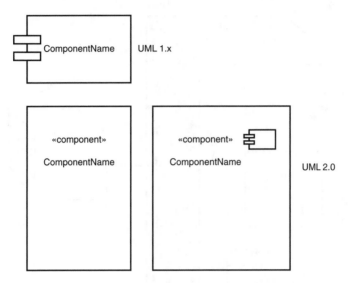

Figure C.7

Composite Structure Diagram

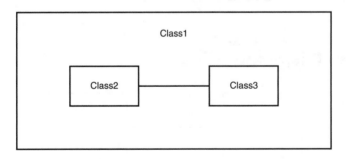

Figure C.8

Deployment Diagram

Figure C.9

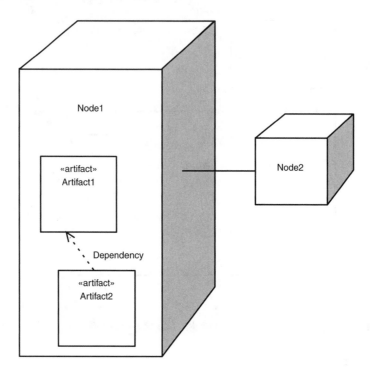

Object Diagram

Figure C.10

Package Diagram

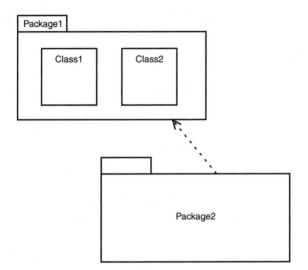

Figure C.11

Parameterized Collaboration

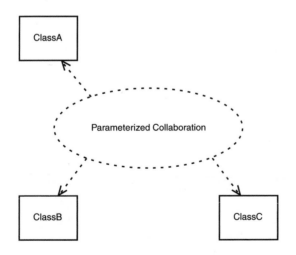

Figure C.12

Sequence Diagram

Figure C.13

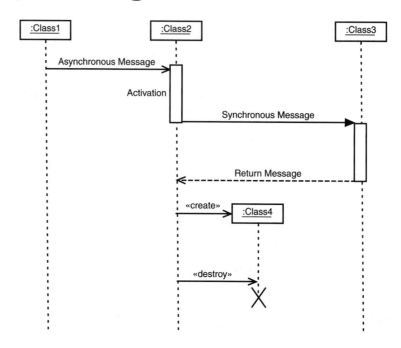

State Diagram

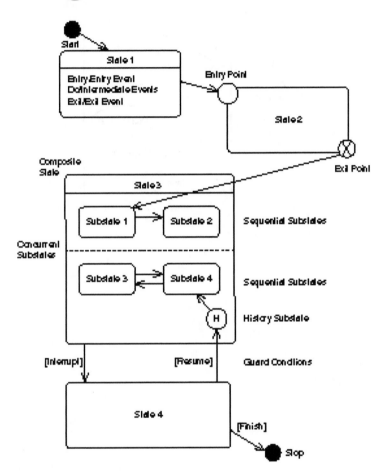

Figure C.14

Timing Diagram

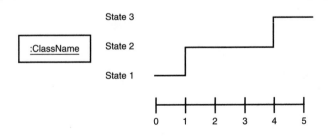

Figure C.15

Use Case Diagram

Figure C.16

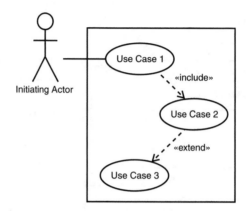

Index

A

abstract classes
definition of, 70
forming groups with,
289-290
UML notation for, 70
abstraction, 34-35
definition of, 34
Abstractions package, 236
**access points for WLANs,
358-359**
actions
definition of, 125
pins on, 184-186
actions in GRAPPLE, 254
**activations in sequence dia-
grams, 344**
active objects
in a communication dia-
gram, 166
activities
decomposed into actions,
184-186
do, 125
with effects on objects,
187
entry, 125
and exceptions, 183-184

exit, 125
inputs and outputs of,
181-183
UML notation for, 124-125
activity diagrams, 16, 255, 259
activities, 174
for case study, 270, 273,
275, 279, 281
concurrent activities, 175
constraint notation in, 187
decision points,
174-175
endpoint, 174
exceptions, 183-184
flow final node, 186
flow of a token in, 193
hourglass symbol, 186
note symbol, 180
object nodes, 181-183
objects and operations in,
180-181
overview of interactions in,
188-191
pictorial summary of,
117-118
sequence diagrams within
an UML notation for,
189
signals, 175

similarity to flowcharts, 173

starting point, 174

swimlanes, 177-180

transitions, 174

UML notation for, 18

actors. *See also* use case

definition of, 13, 92

generalization, 110

initiating versus receiving, 104

UML notation for, 13, 104

aggregation, 41-42

composites, 81

composition, 42

constraints, 80

definition of, 41, 79

UML notation for, 80

alt operator, 151-152

analysis in GRAPPLE, 257-258. *See also* modeling

analysts

clean-up role of, 359

definition of, 7

design documents and, 359

analyzing interactions, 339-350

objective of, 348

annotation, 117

applications

and embedded systems, 134-135

multitasking in, 134-135

tasks within, 134-135

artifacts

definition of, 197

deployment of, 214

assembly connector, 205

association classes, 295

definition of, 63

in embedded systems, 139-140

associations, 40-41

aggregation, 41-42

composition, 42

bi-directional versus unidi-rectional, 40

class, 295

multiplicity, 41, 293

n-ary, 293

ternary, 293

associations (class)

definition of, 61

qualified, 65-67

reflexive, 67

UML notation for, 61-62

asynchronous events, 135

asynchronous messages, 137

attributes (class)

assigning a default value to, 49-50

assigning values to, 49

constraints on, 63

definition of, 48

naming, 48

specifying a data type for, 49-50

UML notation for, 48-50

attributes (object), 32

B

base class. (*See* root class)

base use case

definition of, 107

Basic package, 237

behavioral design patterns, 116

behavioral elements

definition of, 123

state diagram, 123

sequence diagram, 153

binding relationship, 114-115

black box view (of interface), 202

Booch, Grady. *See* Three Amigos

business process diagrams, 308

business-process interview

analyzing the, 286-287

business process modeling. *See* modeling

C

call message, 136

case study, 267-283

activity diagrams, 270, 273, 275, 279, 281

discovering business processes, 268-282

GRAPPLE and, 268-282

swimlane diagrams, 276-277, 280

chain of responsibility pattern

restaurant example, 118-119

structure and purposes of, 117-118

Web browser example, 119-121

child class

definition of, 67-68

child use case, 109

class diagrams, 255-256, 438

definition of, 12

in embedded systems, 139-140

example of, 56, 138-139

and GUI design, 358

pictorial summary of, 119-120

classes

adding a constraint to, 53

adding responsibilities to, 52-53

assigning associations to, 61

assigning links to, 64

associations, 41

attaching notes to, 54

attributes of, 48-50

   data type, 49

   default value, 49

definition of, 11

dependencies, 70-71

eliciting from clients, 54-56

eliding a, 51-52

in embedded systems, 139-140

inheritance, 67-69

modeling internal structure of, 22, 81

multiplicity, 64

naming, 47-48

object, 49

operations of, 50-51

optionality, 65

parameterized, 114

pathname, 48

purposes of, 32-33

qualifier, 66

roles, 62

stereotypes for, 244

types of

   abstract class, 70

   association class, 63

   base class (*see* root class)

   child class, 67-69

   leaf class, 69

   parent class, 68

   root class, 69

   subclass, 35 (*see also* child class)

   superclass, 35 (*see also* parent class)

UML notation for, 11, 47

using client jargon in, 54-56

using keywords in, 52

classifiers, 236

classifier scope

   definition of, 87

   UML notation for, 87

client business logic, 113

client domain

   understanding for system analysis, 111

client jargon, using to create classes, 54-56

client of dependency, 243

clients

   definition of, 7

   and working with development team, 361

clock ticks, 136

collaboration diagrams. *See* **communication diagrams**

communication diagrams, 258

   active objects, 166

   within activity diagrams, 193-194

   as a behavioral element, 168

   changes of state in, 160-162

   compared to sequence diagram, 157-158

   definition of, 16-18

   as an extension of the object diagram, 158

   message sending, 165

   message synchronization in, 166-167

   multiple message receivers, 165

   multiple messages between objects in, 159

   nested-message relationship in a, 161-163

   numbering messages with mutually exclusive guard conditions in, 164

   object creation in, 163

   pictorial summary of, 120

   representing sequential information in a, 158

   semantic equivalence with sequence diagram

      examples of, 160, 162-163

   symbol set for, 158

   syntax for returned result, 165-166

   as a type of interaction diagram, 157

   UML notation for, 17-18

component diagrams, 200-208, 259

   artifacts in, 197

   changes from version 1.x, 19

   components in, 197

   definition of, 18-19

   for a Java application, 203-208

   relationships in

      dependency, 202

      implementation, 201

      realization, 201-202

   role of in the UML, 209

   pictorial summary of, 121

   UML notation for

components, 197-200

   interaction between, 199

   interfaces revealed by use case analysis, 336-337

   replacement and reuse, 199-200

   revealed by use case analysis, 336

   UML notation for, 200-201

composites
    definition of, 81
    UML notation for, 81
composite state
    definition of, 129
composite structure diagrams
    definition of, 22, 81
    pictorial summary of, 121
    UML notation for, 22, 81-82
composition
    definition of, 42
computer hardware
    modeling in the UML,
        19-20
concurrency
    definition of, 166
concurrent substates
    definition of, 128-129
    UML notation for, 129
configuration management, 262
connection points
    definition of, 130
    entry point, 130-131
    exit point, 130-131
    UML notation for,
        130-131
constraints, 245
constraints (aggregation)
    UML notation for, 80
    Or type, 80
constraints (association)
    definition of, 63
    Or type, 63
    UML notation for, 63
constraints (class)
    definition of, 53
    UML notation for, 53
context, 136
context diagramming. See com-
    posite structure diagram

Constructs package, 237
cooperative multitasking
    in kernels, 136-139
Core package, 235
creational design patterns, 116

D

data types, enumerated, 50
decomposing activities, 184-186
delegation connector, 205
dependencies (class)
    definition of, 70
    elided UML notation for, 86
    UML notation for, 70-71, 85
dependencies (component), 202
dependency arrows, decipher-
    ing, 109
dependency relationship, 226-227
    stereotypes for, 243
deployment of embedded
    systems, 144
deployment diagrams, 256
    applied
        to an ARCnet, 218
        to a home system, 216,
            217
        to a ricochet wireless
            network, 219, 221
        to a thin ethernet,
            218-219, 220
        to a token-ring system,
            216-218
    artifacts on node, 214
    connections between
        nodes, 215
    definition of, 19-20
    deployment specifications,
        215

nodes, 213-214, 359, 360
    pictorial summary of, 122
    role within the UML, 221
    UML notation for, 20
deployment in GRAPPLE, 261
deployment relationships, 214
deployment specifications,
    215
design documents, 327. See
    also documentation
    including use cases in, 105
design in GRAPPLE, 259-260.
    See also modeling
design patterns
    categories of, 116
    chain of responsibility
        restaurant example,
            118-119
        structure and purposes
            of, 117-118
        Web browser example,
            119-121
    discovering new, 116,
        120-122
    "Gang of Four," 370
    as parameterized collabora-
        tions in the UML, 116
    represented using the UML,
        116-123
    Series Calculator example,
        121-122
    as solutions of recurring
        problems, 116, 123
«destroy» keyword, 148
developers
    definition of, 7
development in GRAPPLE, 260
development team, client
    relations and, 361

diagrams

need for, 26

types

activity diagram, 16

class diagram, 11-12

communication diagram, 16-18

component diagram, 18-19

composite structure diagram, 22

deployment diagram, 19-20

interaction overview diagram, 23-24

object diagram, 12

package diagram, 25

sequence diagram, 14-16

state diagram, 13-14

timing diagram, 24-25

use case diagram, 13

dictionary, 95-96

do

definition of, 125

documentation, 260. *See also* **design documents**

creation of, 360

document specialists

work of, 360

domain analysis, 285-304

analyzing the interview, 286-287

developing the initial classes, 287-289

forming associations and composites, 290-299

general guidelines for, 297-298, 303-304

refining the classes, 300-303

domain (client)

definition of, 43

duration constraint, 138

E

eliding

definition of, 52

embedded systems

concepts for, 134-139

definition of, 133-134

hard versus soft, 134

interrupts and, 135-136

modeling in the UML, 139-140

multitasking in, 134-135

"smart" devices and, 133-134

tasks and, 134-135

threads and, 134

time and, 134

EMGs (electromyographic signals), 131-132

working with, 132

encapsulation, 37-38, 82, 198

benefits of, 38

definition of, 37

entry

definition of, 125

entry point

definition of, 130

UML notation for, 130-131

enumerated data type

definition of, 50

Ericsson phones

as an interface, 146, 148

event bubbling, 120

event capturing, 120

event handler, 119

exception handler, 184

exceptions, 183-184

exit

definition of, 125

exit point

definition of, 130

UML notation for, 130-131

expert systems, 68-74

explicit binding, 114

extending the UML

mechanisms for, 243-245

extension, 117

extension points

definition of, 107

extension (use case), 97-98, 107-108

definition of, 97-98

F - G

factorials, 121

features (object), 32

Fibonacci numbers, 121

flow final node, 186

«framework», 244

fully qualified names, 226

function, definition of, 51

generalization (actor), UML notation for, 110

generalization (class). *See* **inheritance (class)**

generalization hierarchy (actor), example of, 112

generalization (package), 226-227

generalization (use case), UML notation for, 109

general principles of GUI design, 351-353

general state changes, in embedded systems, 144

generic sequence diagrams, 144-146

definition of, 144

example of, 145

graphic stereotypes, 244-245

graphical user interfaces. *See* GUIs

GRAPPLE (Guidelines for Rapid APPLication Engineering), 253-262. *See also* software development; modeling

case study using, 268-282

structure of

segment 1: requirements gathering, 255-257, 285

segment 2: analysis, 257-258

segment 3: design, 259-260

segment 4: development, 260

segment 5: deployment, 261

use cases, 325-338

grouping, 117

grouping (use case)

UML notation for, 110

guard conditions, 141

definition of, 127

if statement, 145

GUI design

class diagrams and, 358

general principles of, 351-353

state diagrams and, 357

UML diagrams for, 357-358

GUI JAD session, 353-354

objective of, 353

paper mockups and, 354

scheduling, 354

users' participation in, 354

guillemets

definition of, 21

GUIs (graphical user interfaces), 351, 65-67

H - I

hardware modeling

with deployment diagrams (*see* deployment diagrams)

hierarchy for the UML, 230-231, 240. *See also* UML architecture

history states

deep versus shallow, 130

definition of, 129

UML notation for, 129-130

hybrid diagrams, 180-181

in embedded systems, 139

IBM Rose XDE Modeler

Web site, 116, 456

if statement, 145

«implementationClass», 244

implementation relationship, 198

implicit binding, 115

«import» dependency, 243

«include» dependency, 329

inclusion (use case), 96-97, 106-107

definition of, 96-97

UML notation for, 106-107

information hiding. *See* encapsulation

information, movement of, 309-316

Infrastructure Library package, 234, 247

inheritance (class), 67-69

definition of, 35

multiple versus single, 69

UML notation for, 68

versus realization, 85

inheritance (use case), 109

UML notation for, 109

input event, 175

instances

within the layers of the UML, 240

instance scope

definition of, 87

instance sequence diagram

definition of, 144

«instantiate» dependency, 243

interaction diagrams, 14-18, 157

interaction fragments, 151-152

alt operator, 151-152

par operator, 151-152

interaction occurrences, 149-151, 189

interaction overview diagrams, 188-191, 193-194

definition of, 23

interaction occurrences in, 189

UML notation for, 23-24

interactions

analyzing, 339-350

in embedded systems, 141-144

interfaces, 38, 198-199

ball-and-socket notation for, 202-205

and a class, modeling connection between, 86

conforming, 199

definition of, 21, 82

dependency, 85

elided UML notation for, 84

external versus internal views, 202

lollipop diagram for, 84

port, 86

realization, 83

UML notation for, 21, 84, 201-203

internode connections, 199

interrupt latency, 136

interrupt recovery, 136

interrupt response, 136

interrupts

in embedded systems, 135-136

Interrupt Service Routine. *See* ISR

interviewing

tips for, 270, 271, 272, 274, 281-282

ISR (Interrupt Service Routine), 136

J - K - L

Jacobson, Ivar. *See* Three Amigos

JAD (Joint Application Development), 256-257

JAD session, 316-323

GUI, 353-354

objective of, 317

use cases, 325-326

kernels, 136

kernel schedules

nonpreemptive verus preemptive, 136, 138

keywords

definition of, 21

«destroy», 148

UML notation for, 21

using in classes, 52

leaf class

definition of, 69

lifelines, 140

in sequence diagrams, 344

links (association)

definition of, 64

UML notation for, 64

lollipop diagram, 84

lookup

definition of, 65

M

mapping out

system deployment, 358-361

«merge» dependency, 228

merge relationship, 228

messages

asynchronous, 137

call, 136

compartmentalizing and reusing, 189

controlled by active objects, 166

implicit receiver of, 117

with multiple recipients, 165

with mutually exclusive guard conditions, 164

nested, 161-163

ordered, 165

return, 136

in sequence diagrams, 136-137

synchronization among, 166-167

synchronous, 136-137

UML notation for, 159-168

message sending, 38-39

message-signature

definition of, 166

«metaclass», 244

metametamodel layer, 231

foundational concepts of, 232-239

metamodel layer, 231

Meta-Object Facility (MOF), 233

methodologies

GRAPPLE, 253-262

newer, 251

waterfall method, 250-251

model

definition of, 10-11

model dictionary, 303

modeling. *See also* software development

business process diagrams in, 308

with component diagrams (*see* components; component diagrams)

with deployment diagrams (*see* deployment diagrams)

domain analysis in, 285-304

JAD session in, 316-322

movement of information, 309-316

use cases in, 320-323

model layer, 231

modeling tool, UML, 435

«modelLibrary», 244

movement of information, 309-316

multiple inheritance

definition of, 69

multiplicity

definition of, 41

multiplicity (association), 293

definition of, 64

UML notation for, 64-65, 66

multitasking

embedded systems and, 134-135

N

namespace, 226

n-ary associations, 293

nested messages
  UML notation for, 161-162

network modeling
  with deployment diagrams (*see* deployment diagrams)

networks
  WLANs in, 358-359

Nielsen, Jakob
  Web site, 353

nodes
  definition of, 213
  and the deployment diagram, 359, 360

notes
  definition of, 20
  UML notation for, 20

notes (class)
  UML notation for, 54

nouns and verbs in a model, 255, 286-291, 303-304

O

object categorization
  brain research, 43

object creation
  UML notation for, 163

object diagrams, 11, 259, 448
  example, 72-73
  pictorial summary of, 122
  versus class diagrams, 71-73

Object Management Group
  Web site, 54

object nodes, 181-183

object-orientation, 31-45
  abstraction, 34-35
  advantages of, 31
  aggregation, 41-42
    composition, 42
  applying the UML, 47-57
  associations, 40-41
    multiplicity, 41
  encapsulation, 37-38
  inheritance, 35-36
  message sending, 38-39
  and model accuracy, 33
  The Object-Oriented Thought Process, Second Edition, 45
  polymorphism, 36-37

The Object-Oriented Thought Process, Second Edition, 45

objects, 32-34
  abstraction, 34-35
  in activity diagrams, 180-181
  aggregation, 41-42
    composition, 42
  anonymous, 12, 49
  associations, 40-41
    multiplicity, 41
  attributes of, 32
  creating in the sequence, 146-149
  definition of, 12, 32
  encapsulation, 37-38
  features of, 32
  inheritance, 35-36
  interface, 38
  message sending, 38-39
  messages to, 136-137
    asynchronous, 137
    call, 136
    return, 136-137
    synchronous, 136
  naming, 12, 49
  operations of, 32

polymorphism, 36
  in sequence diagrams, 136-137, 344
  structure of, 32
  UML notation for, 12

objects of an activity, 181-183

OCL (Object Constraint Language), 54

operations (class)
  function, 51
  naming, 50
  signature, 51
  UML notation for, 50-51

operations (object), 32

operators
  alt, 151-152
  defined, 149
  par, 151-152

optionality (class)
  definition of, 65

Or constraint (aggregation)
  UML notation for, 80

Or constraint (association)
  UML notation for, 63

output event, 175

ownership, 226

P

package diagrams, 226-229, 256-257
  definition of, 25
  pictorial summary of, 123
  UML notation for, 25

package names
  UML notation for, 226

packages, 226-229
  definition of, 25
  grouping elements in, 226
  merging, 228-229

organizing use cases, 110

relationships between, 226-228

dependency, 226-227

generalization, 226-227

refinement, 227-228

stereotypes for, 244

UML notation for, 47-48

parameterization relationship, 215-216

parameterized class, 114

parameterized collaboration

pictorial summary of, 123

parent class

definition of, 68

parent use case, 109

par operator, 151-152

pathname

definition of, 48

patterns, 244

Petri Nets, 193

pin

definition of, 184

players in GRAPPLE, 254

polymorphism

benefits to modelers, 37

definition of, 36

example, 70

ports

definition of, 86

UML notation for, 86

Primitive Types package, 235

private level (visibility)

definition of, 87

UML notation for, 87

Profiles package, 237

programmers

coding by, 360

testing the work of, 360

protected level (visibility)

definition of, 87

UML notation for, 87

provided interface, 199

public level (visibility)

definition of, 87

UML notation for, 87

Q - R

qualifiers

definition of, 66

UML notation for, 66-67

RAD[3]. *See* **GRAPPLE (Guidelines for Rapid APPLication Engineering), structure of**

Rational Rose. *See* **IBM Rose XDE Modeler**

realization, 199

definition of, 83

UML notation for, 84

versus inheritance, 85

real-time operating system. *See* **RTOS**

«refine» dependency, 243

refinement relationship, 227-228

reflective, 236

reflexive association

definition of, 67

UML notation for, 67

reification, 142

relationships. *See* **associations (class)**

requests

implicit receiver of, 117

required interface, 199

requirements gathering in GRAPPLE, 255-257. *See also* **modeling; software development**

business process diagrams in, 308

discovering business processes, 268-282

domain analysis in, 285-304

JAD session in, 316-323

use cases in, 320-323

responsibilities

definition of, 52

UML notation for, 53

return messages, 136-137

roles (activity), 179-180

roles (class)

definition of, 62

UML notation for, 62

root class

definition of, 69

RTOS (real-time operating system), 136

Rumbaugh, James. *See* **Three Amigos**

run-time instances layer, 231

S

scope

classifier versus instance, 87

of a design pattern, 116

segments in GRAPPLE, 254

Select Business Solutions

Web site, 116

Select Component Architect, 116, 436

Select Component Factory, 116

Select Enterprise. *See Select Component Architect*

sequence diagrams, 258, 451
  activations in, 344
  within activity diagrams
    UML notation for, 189
  in behavioral elements category, 153
  definition of, 14-16, 135-136
  examples of, 138-144
  framing a sequence in, 149-150
  generic, 144-146
  guard conditions
    if statement, 145
  if statement, 145
  instance, 144
  interaction fragment, 151-152
    alt operator, 151-152
    par operator, 151-152
  interaction occurrences, 149-151
  lifelines in, 344
  messages in, 136-137
  for modeling the scenarios of a use case, 141-144
  object creation, 147-148
  object destruction, 148
  objects in, 344
    activation of, 136
    lifeline, 136
    messages to, 136-137
    positioning of, 136
  operators in, 149
  overview of interactions in, 188-191
  pictorial summary of, 124
  preparing, 343-344, 345-346

relation to interaction overview diagram, 188
reusing, 189
semantic equivalence with communication diagram, 157
time in, 137-138
UML notation for, 16, 17
«send» dependency, 243
sequential substates
  definition of, 128
  UML notation for, 128
SGS Partners
  Web site, 132
signature (operation)
  definition of, 51
single inheritance
  definition of, 69
"smart" devices
  and embedded systems, 133-134
software components
  modeling in the UML, 18-19
software development
  challenges of, 251-253
  compartmentalization of effort in, 251
  evolution of understanding of, 251
  feedback across stages of, 252
  GRAPPLE methodology, 253-262
  newer methodology, 251
  team approach to, 252
  time allotted to coding in, 251
  waterfall method of, 250-251
software modeling
  with component diagrams (see components; component diagrams)

stakeholders
  definition of, 26
state
  activities, 124-125
  definition of, 13
  naming conventions, 124
  transition, 124-127
  UML notation for, 13-14
state changes
  UML notation for, 160-162
statechart. *See state diagrams*
state diagrams, 123-132, 258
  definition of, 124
  and GUI design, 357
  history states, 129-130
  importance to system analysis, 131
  pictorial summary of, 125
  substates, 127-129
  UML notation for, 13-14
state machine. *See state diagrams*
stereotypes, 237-239, 243-245. *See also keywords*
  advantages of, 21
  definition of, 20-22
  organizing, 21
  UML notation for, 21
structural design patterns, 116
structure (object), 32
subclass, 35 (*See also child class*)
substates, 127-129
  concurrent, 128-129
  definition of, 128
  sequential, 128
superclass, 35 (*See also parent class*)
supplier of dependency, 243
swimlane diagrams, 276-277, 280

swimlanes, 177-180
   definition of, 179
   example of, 179-180
   UML notation for, 179-180
synchronization of messages, 166-167
   definition of, 166
   UML notation for, 167
synchronous messages, 136
system analysis
   building use case models, 110-111, 113-115
   client business logic, 113
   interviewing users, 111-112
   listing use cases, 113
   modeling change, 123
   state diagrams, 131
   understanding client domain, 111
system boundary, 104
system deployment
   mapping out, 358-361
system development
   challenges of, 7-8
   definition of, 7
   involving users in, 92
   need for the UML, 8-9
systems
   definition of, 7
   documentation for, 360
   and expanding business opportunities, 362-363
   interactions in, 342-350
   listing the working parts of, 339-342
   other applications, 361-362
   reusing, 361
   training materials for, 360
systems modeling
   with deployment diagrams (see deployment diagrams)

T

tag, 245
tagged values, 245
task analysis, 351
tasks
   in embedded systems, 134-135
templates, 244
ternary association, 293
test scripts, 260
time
   represented in sequence diagram, 137-138
timing diagram
   definition of, 24-25
   pictorial summary of, 125
   UML notation for, 25
tips
   for interviewing, 270, 271, 272, 274, 281-282
token
   definition of, 193
training materials
   creation of, 360
transitions, 124-127
   actions, 125
   guard conditions, 127
   trigger events, 125-126
   triggerless transitions, 125-126
triangle numbers, 121
trigger event, 125-126
   definition of, 125
triggerless transition, 125-126
   definition of, 125
«type», 244

U

UML, the
   applied to design patterns, 116-123
   business modeling with, 63-65
   extending (see UML architecture)
   foundational concepts of, 230-231, 240 (see also UML architecture)
   GUI modeling with, 65-67
   importance of, 26-27
   invention of, 9-10
   as a means for communicating ideas to developers, 1
   modeling an embedded system in, 139-140
   modeling expert systems with, 68-74
   modeling Web applications with, 74-76
   need for, 8-9
   structure of (see UML architecture)
   Three Amigos, 9
   WAE, 75
UML architecture
   based on the Meta-Object Facility, 233-234
   customizing a metamodel, 237-239
   defining a metamodel, 235-237
   extending the UML, 243-245
   four layers of, 230-231, 240
   infrastructure of
      Core package, 235-237
      Infrastructure Library package, 234-239, 247

Profiles package, 237-239

reflective metametalanguage for, 236

as a metametamodel, 232-234

as a metamodel, 239-242

superstructure of, 241

AuxiliaryConstructs package, 242

Classes package, 242

CommonBehaviors package, 242

CompositeStructures package, 242

dependencies in, 225

summarized, 241

UseCases package, 242

UML components

interaction between, 14-18

UML diagrams

for GUI design, 357-358

pictorial summary of, 117-126

UML elements

creating new, 21

organizing, 21

UML infrastructure, 234

UML modeling tools

dictionary of, 95-96

features of, 95-96

Select Component Architect, 116

Visio Professional Edition (Microsoft), 96-115, 436

Visual UML, 116

UML notation

conventions of, 32

UML superstructure, 241

UML 2.0 versus 1.x

activity diagram symbols

flow final node, 186

hourglass, 186

collaboration/communication diagram, 18, 158

component diagram, 19

connection points, 130-131

context diagramming/composite structure diagram, 81

dependencies

elided UML notation for, 86

finishing a flow, 186

including versus using a use case, 97

interaction overview diagram, 188-190

marking time, 186

new diagrams, 22-25

ports, 86

sequence diagramming in, 149-150

unbound parameters, 114

use case analysis, 92

as the basis for testing, 360

and components of the system, 336

procedures for, 98

showing system boundary, 104

use case diagrams, 103-117, 258

pictorial summary of, 126

representing use case models, 103-106

showing relationships among use cases, 106-110

and system analysis, 110-111

UML notation for, 13

use case diagrams, high-level

example of, 114

use case models

building, 110-111

example of, 113-115

definition of, 104

UML notation for, 103-104

use cases, 91-99, 258, 320-323, 325-338

actors, 92, 104

analysis

for case study, 326

scenarios and, 326-327

analyzing, 325-327

assumptions and, 328

base use case, 107

case study examples, 326-336

child use case, 109

definition of, 13, 91-92

documenting sequence of steps, 105

in embedded systems, 140-141

examples of, 92-96

extension, 97-98, 107-108

extension points, 107

generalization, 109

grouping, 110, 356

and GUI development, 65

implementing, 354-357

importance of, 92

inclusion, 96-97, 106-107

inheritance, 109

initiation of, 93

modifying, 345-346

organization of, 110

parent use case, 109

postconditions, 93, 331

preconditions, 93, 329-330

relationships among, 106-110

repeating assumptions, 329

sequence diagrams and, 343-344, 345-346

and the system, 327

UML notation for, 13, 104, 107-108

use case analysis, 92

using activity diagram to show sequence of steps, 106

user interface design

Web site, 353

user interfaces

deriving from use cases, 354-357

users

interviewing, 111-112

modeling system for, 91

«utility», 244

V

verbs and nouns in a model, 255, 286-291, 303-304

visibility

definition of, 87

levels of, 87

UML notation for, 87

Visio Professional Edition (Microsoft), 96-115, 436

creating a class diagram, 98-108

creating an object diagram, 108-111

creating a sequence diagram, 111-115

Visual UML, 116, 456

Web site, 116

W - Z

waterfall method, 250-251

WAE (Web Application Extension), 75-76

Web site, 76

Web applications, 74-76

Web sites

IBM Rose XDE Modeler, 116

Nielsen, Jakob, 353

Object Management Group, 54

Select Business Solutions, 116

SGS Partners, 132

user interface design, 353

Visual UML, 116

WAE, 76

WLANs (Wireless LANs), 358-359

work-products in GRAPPLE

management of, 262

Windows Installation Instructions

1. Insert the disc into your CD-ROM drive.

2. From the Windows desktop, double-click the My Computer icon.

3. Double-click the icon representing your CD-ROM drive.

4. Double-click on `start.html`. Follow the instructions to access the CD-ROM information.